Wake Up, Sleeping Beauty

2

MEGUMI
MORINO

Contents

Wake Up,
Sleeping
Beaut

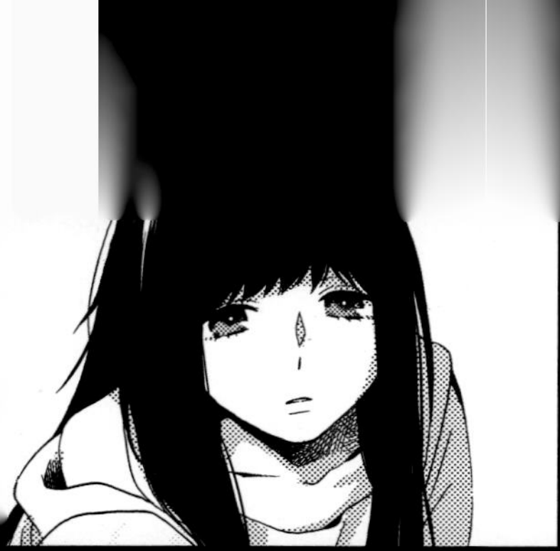

Shizu Karasawa

The only child of Testu's wealthy employers. She is prone to possession by spirits of the dead and has been forbidden from leaving her house.

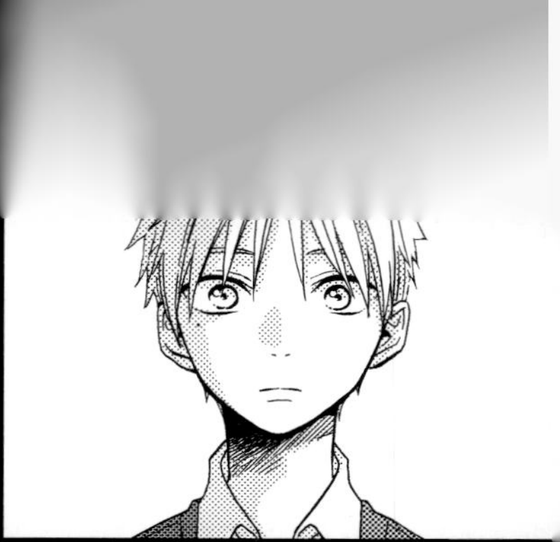

Tetsu Misato

A third-year in high school. Due to personal circumstances, he dove into a part-time job to save up money. He is nimble with his hands and is afraid of ghosts.

Spirits Inside Shizu

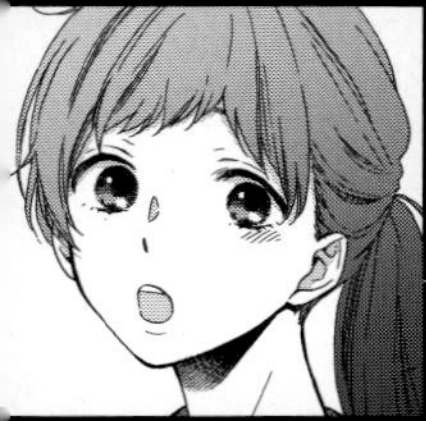

Haru

A caring, athletic man.

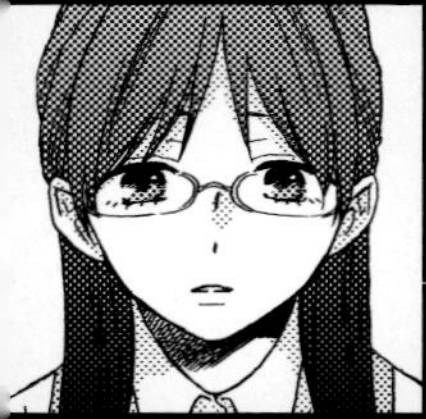

Shinobu

Shizu's great-grandfather. Enjoys gardening.

Tetsu's Family

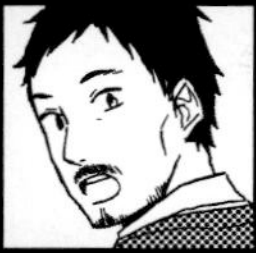

Father

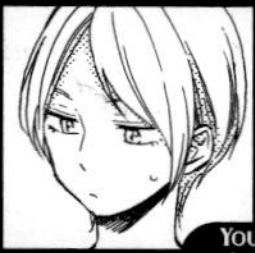

Ryō

Younger Sisters

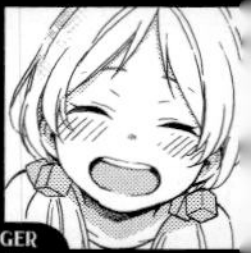

Suzu

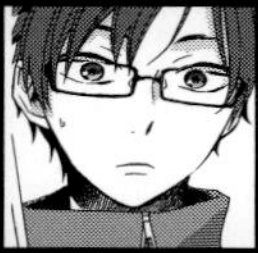

Chihiro Ueno

Tetsu's childhood friend. Soccer Club captain.

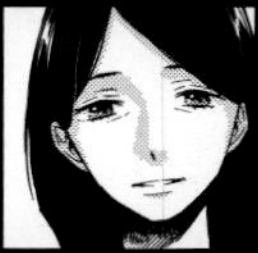

Sanae Karasawa

Shizu's mother.

Story

Tetsu works as a housekeeper at the Karasawa Estate—the rumored "Haunted House on the Hill." One day, he meets Shizu, the mysterious girl who lives alone in the outbuilding. He is drawn to her sad smile, but when he meets her again, she has changed so dramatically it's as if she's a different person. Tetsu initially thinks Shizu has multiple personality disorder and continues to work hard to be her friend. However, after a frightening incident, he learns that she is susceptible to being possessed by spirits. Traumatized, he attempts to wash his hands of the whole ordeal, but Shizu's mother comes to him with a deal and Tetsu ends up continuing to work at

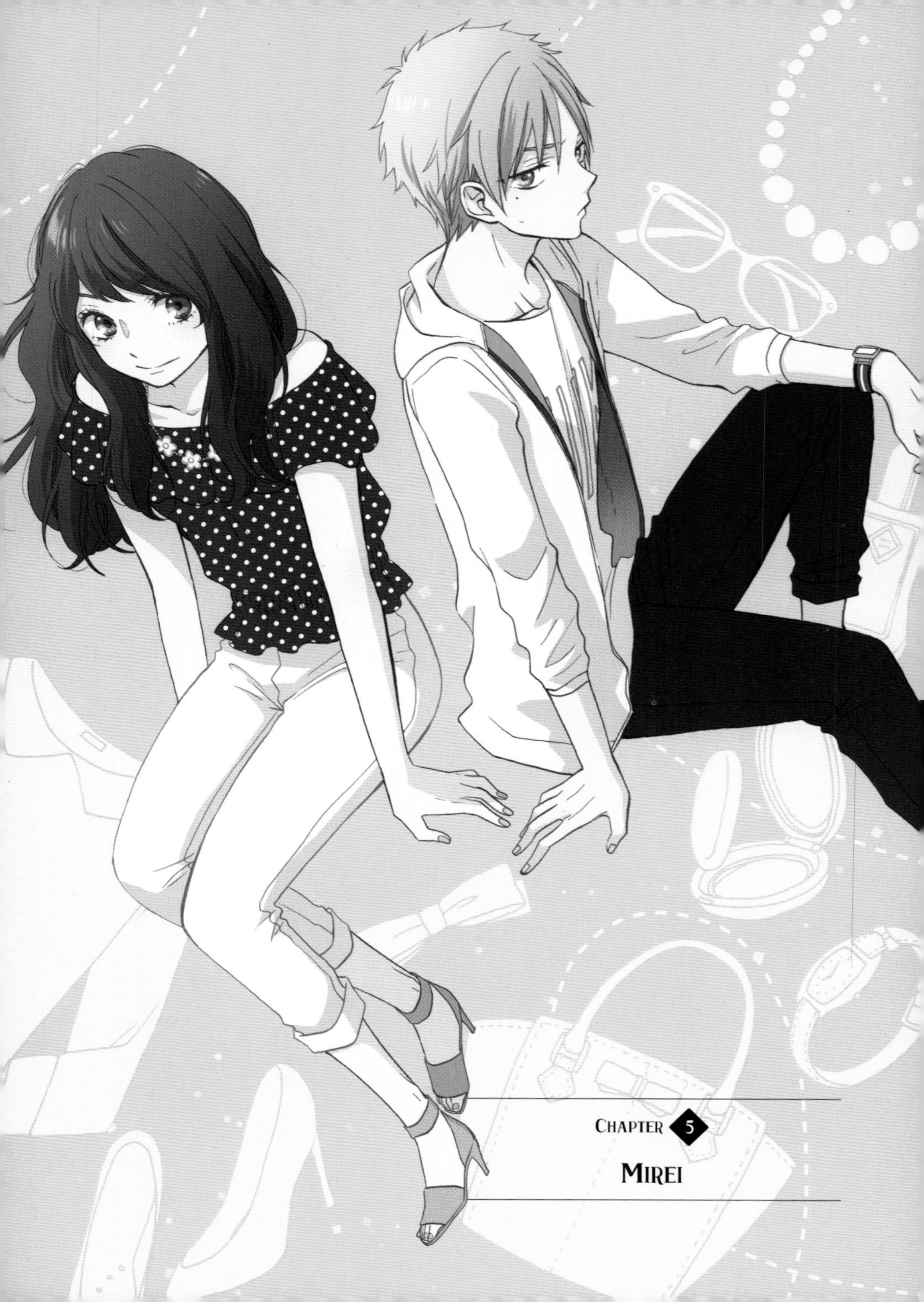

Chapter 5

Mirei

❀ Special Thanks to

My editor Y-san
Ōga-san
Tashiro-san
Kyonko-san
Takematsu-san
Yamamori-san
Kumai-san
Oikawa-san
My family, friends, and
former colleagues who are
always supporting me.

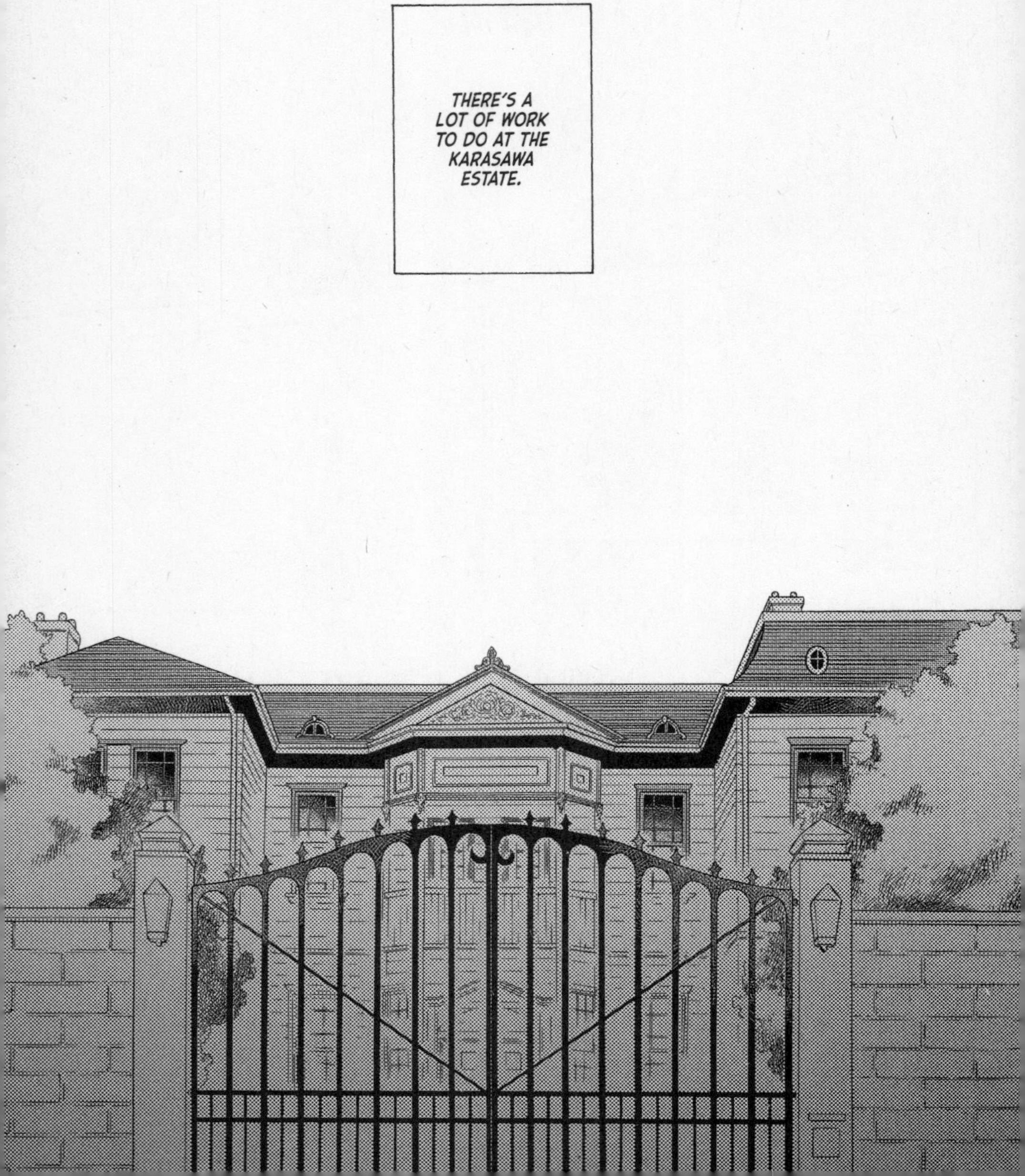
THERE'S A LOT OF WORK TO DO AT THE KARASAWA ESTATE.

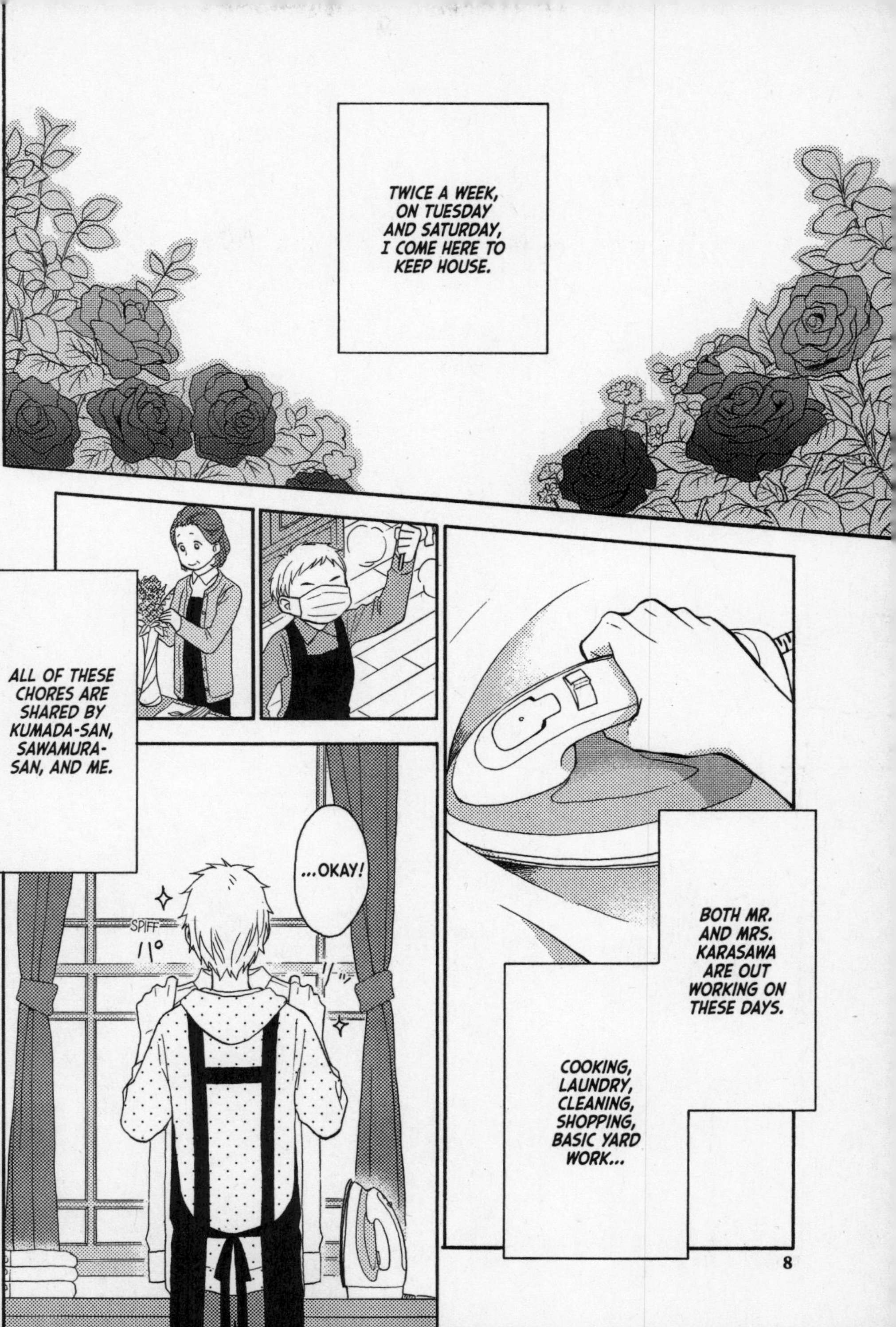
TWICE A WEEK, ON TUESDAY AND SATURDAY, I COME HERE TO KEEP HOUSE.
BOTH MR. AND MRS. KARASAWA ARE OUT WORKING ON THESE DAYS.
COOKING, LAUNDRY, CLEANING, SHOPPING, BASIC YARD WORK...
ALL OF THESE CHORES ARE SHARED BY KUMADA-SAN, SAWAMURA-SAN, AND ME.
...OKAY!
SPIFF

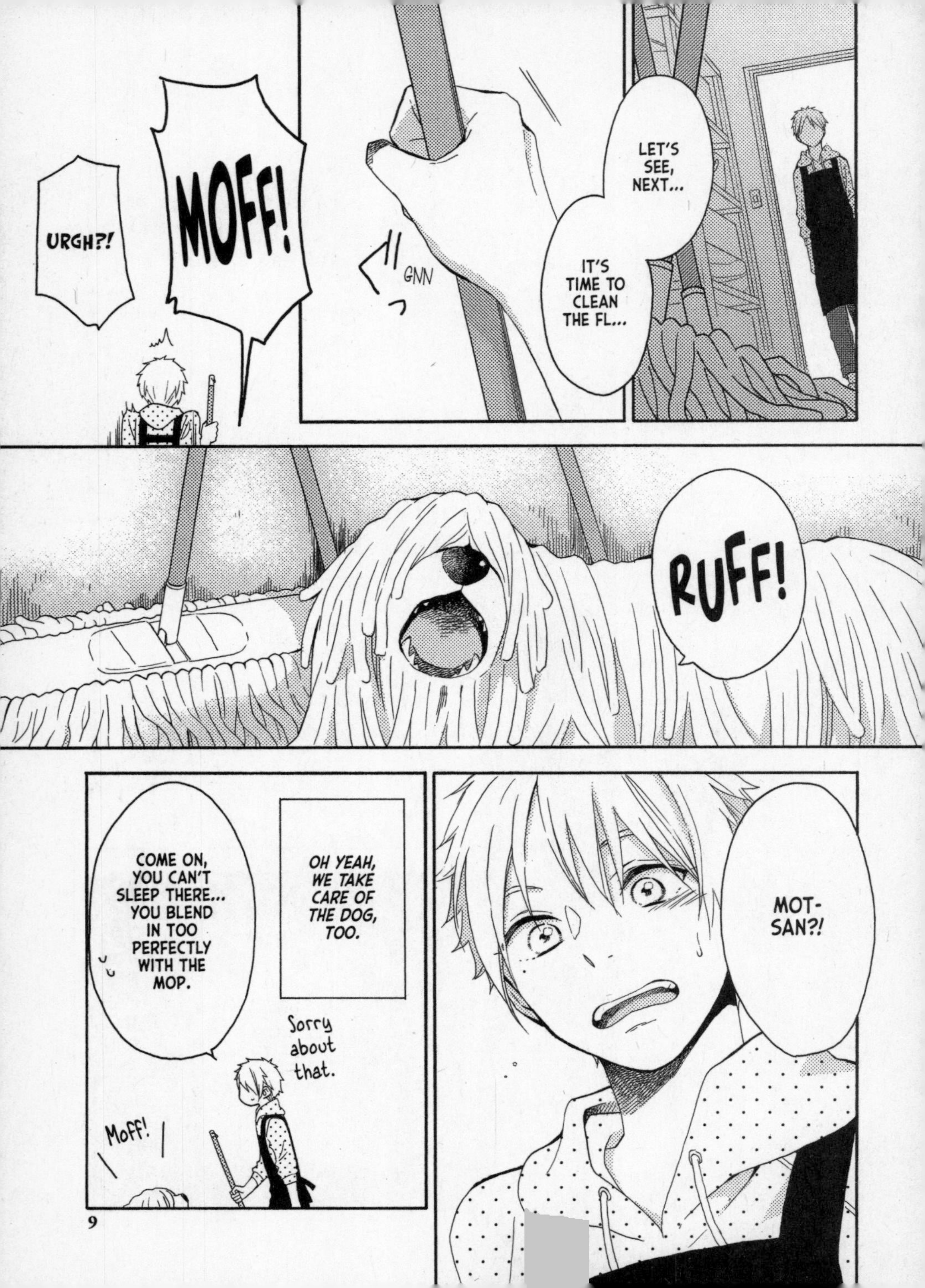
LET'S SEE, NEXT...
IT'S TIME TO CLEAN THE FL...
GNN
MOFF!
URGH?!
RUFF!
MOT-SAN?!
OH YEAH, WE TAKE CARE OF THE DOG, TOO.
COME ON, YOU CAN'T SLEEP THERE... YOU BLEND IN TOO PERFECTLY WITH THE MOP.
Sorry about that.
Moff!

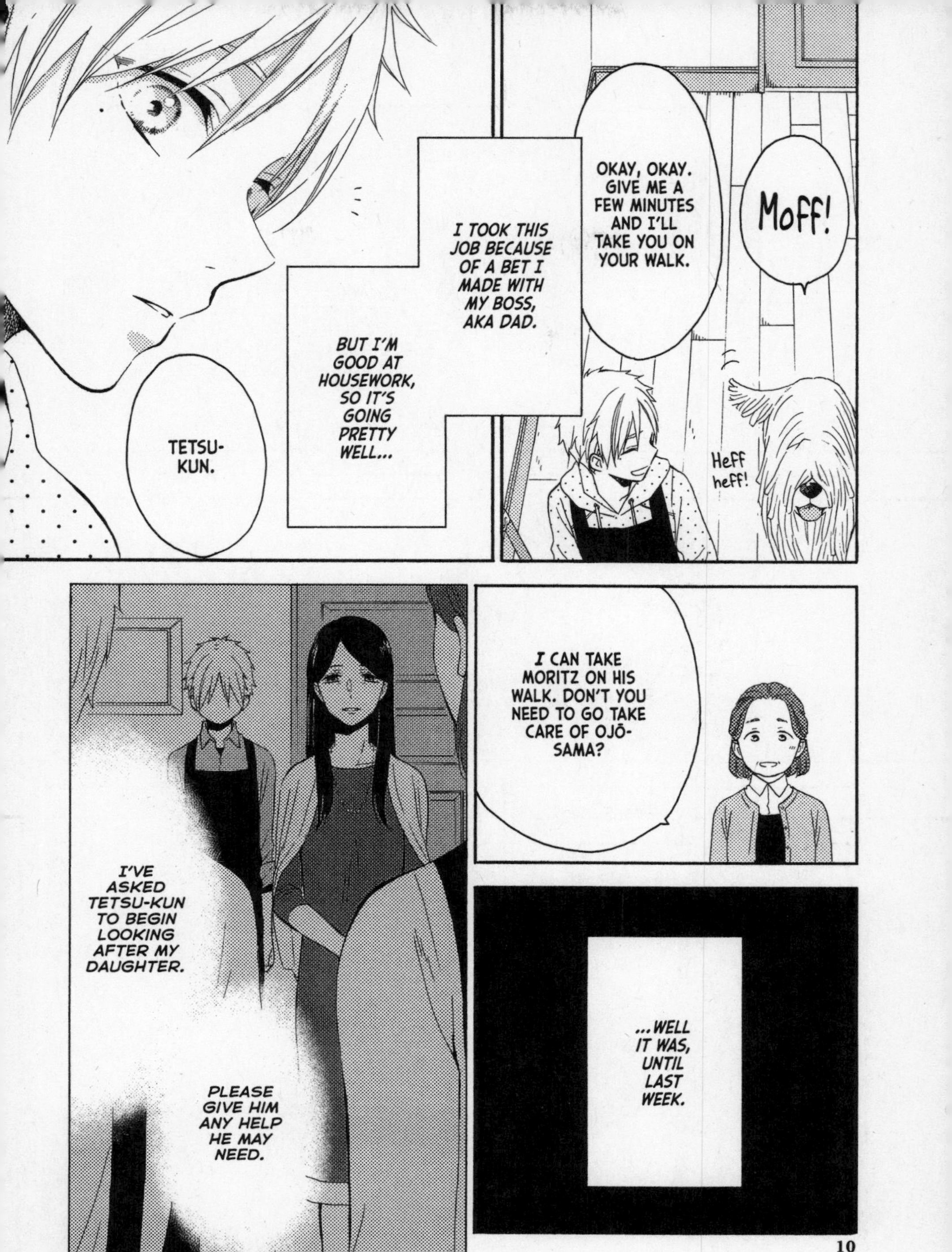
Moff!
OKAY, OKAY. GIVE ME A FEW MINUTES AND I'LL TAKE YOU ON YOUR WALK.
Heff heff!
I TOOK THIS JOB BECAUSE OF A BET I MADE WITH MY BOSS, AKA DAD.
BUT I'M GOOD AT HOUSEWORK, SO IT'S GOING PRETTY WELL...
TETSU-KUN.
I CAN TAKE MORITZ ON HIS WALK. DON'T YOU NEED TO GO TAKE CARE OF OJŌ-SAMA?
...WELL IT WAS, UNTIL LAST WEEK.
I'VE ASKED TETSU-KUN TO BEGIN LOOKING AFTER MY DAUGHTER.
PLEASE GIVE HIM ANY HELP HE MAY NEED.

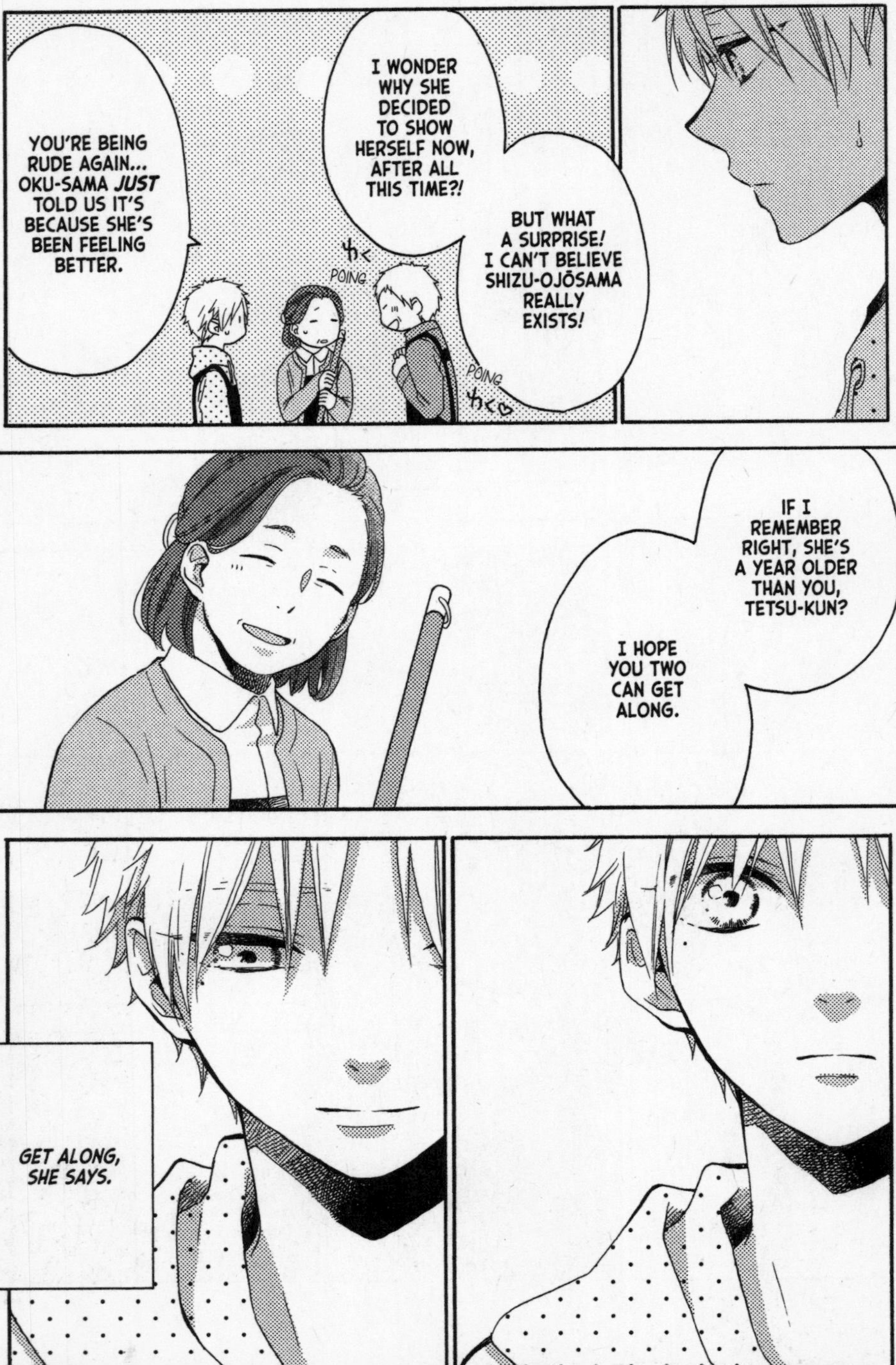
I WONDER WHY SHE DECIDED TO SHOW HERSELF NOW, AFTER ALL THIS TIME?!
BUT WHAT A SURPRISE! I CAN'T BELIEVE SHIZU-OJŌSAMA REALLY EXISTS!
POING
POING
YOU'RE BEING RUDE AGAIN... OKU-SAMA *JUST* TOLD US IT'S BECAUSE SHE'S BEEN FEELING BETTER.
IF I REMEMBER RIGHT, SHE'S A YEAR OLDER THAN YOU, TETSU-KUN?
I HOPE YOU TWO CAN GET ALONG.
GET ALONG, SHE SAYS.

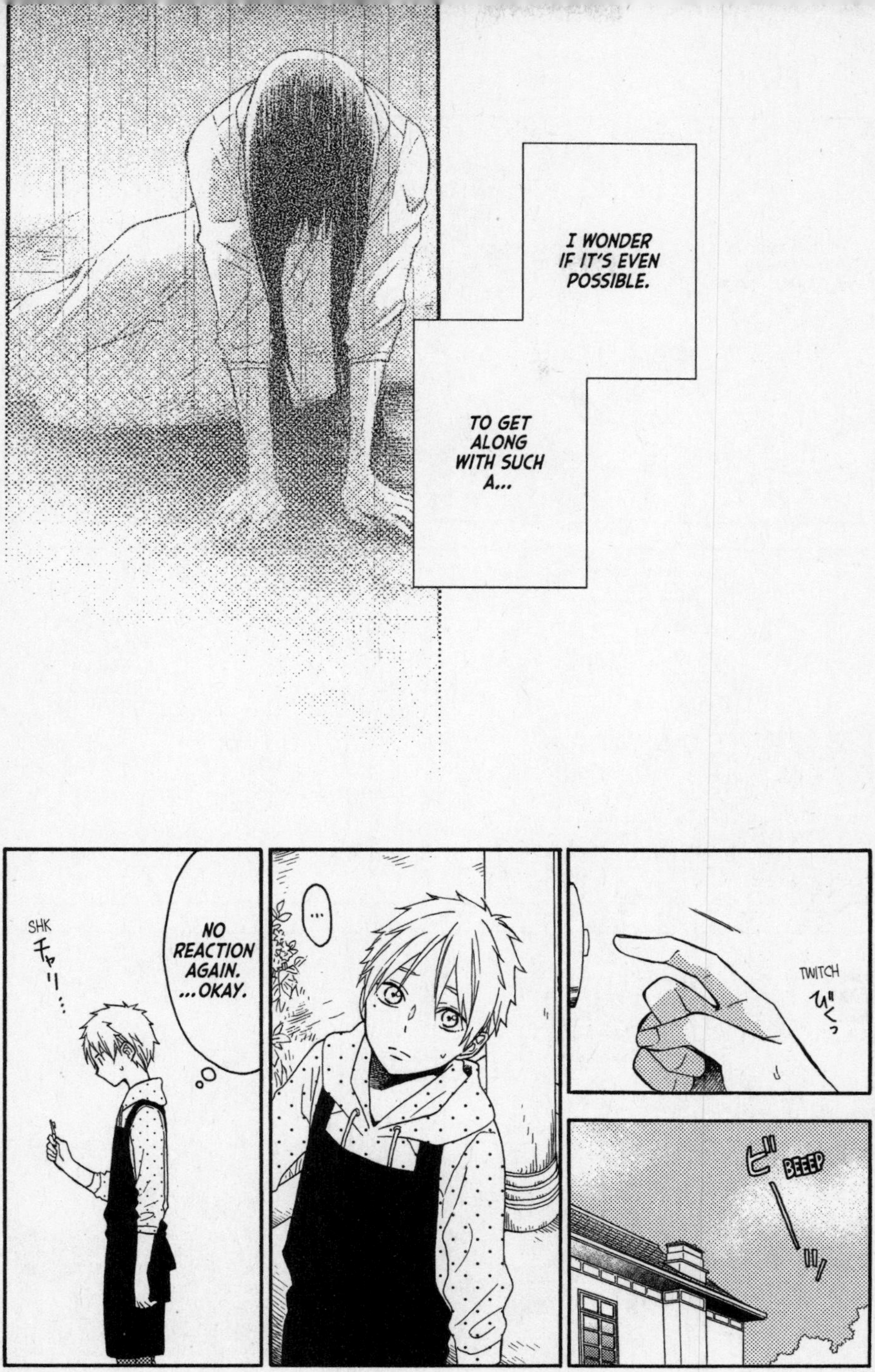
I WONDER IF IT'S EVEN POSSIBLE.
TO GET ALONG WITH SUCH A...
TWITCH
びくっ
ビーーッ
BEEEP
...
NO REACTION AGAIN. ...OKAY.
SHK
チャリ…

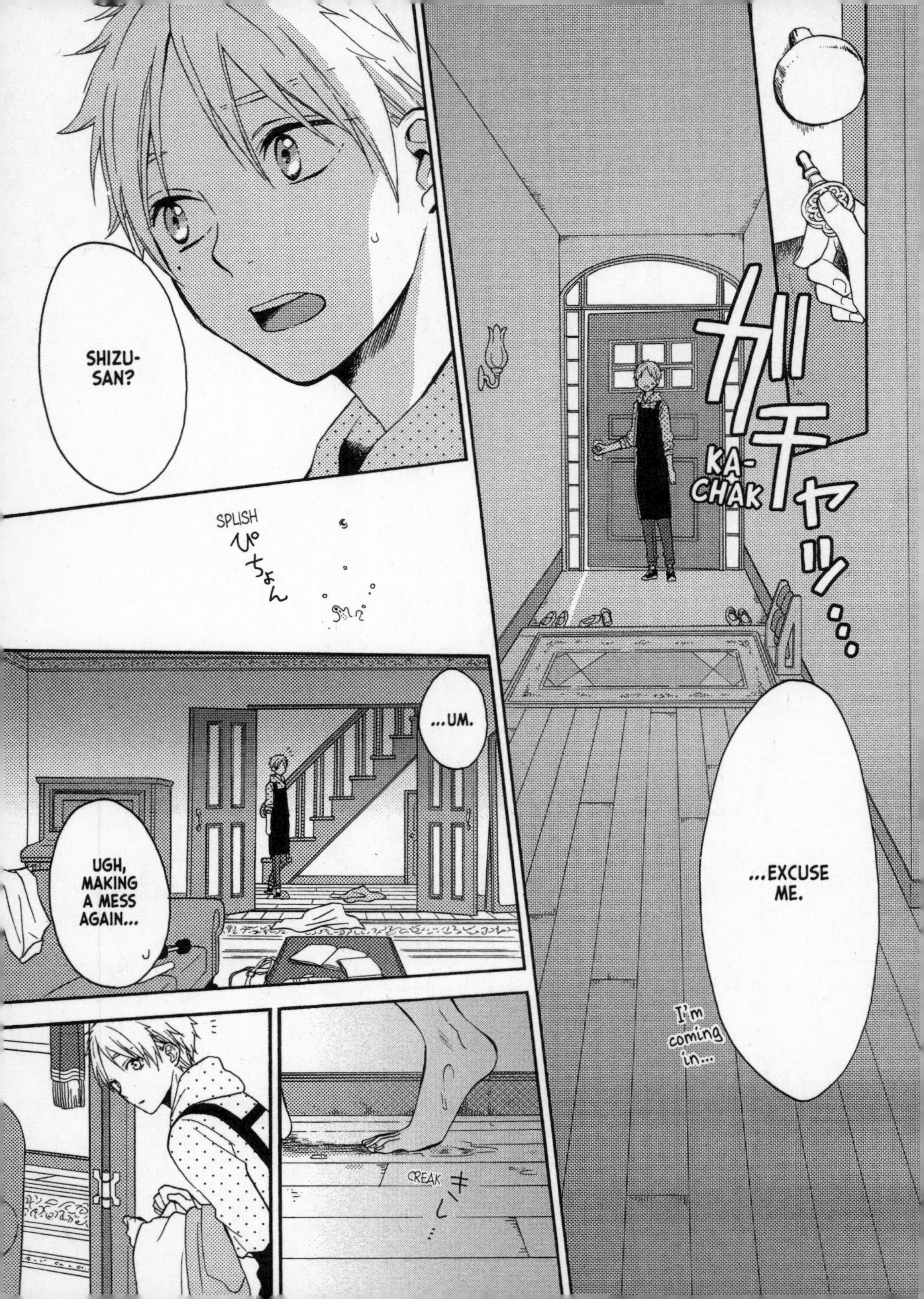
ガチャッ…
KA-CHAK
...EXCUSE ME.
I'm coming in...
SHIZU-SAN?
SPLISH
ぴちょん
...UM.
UGH, MAKING A MESS AGAIN...
CREAK

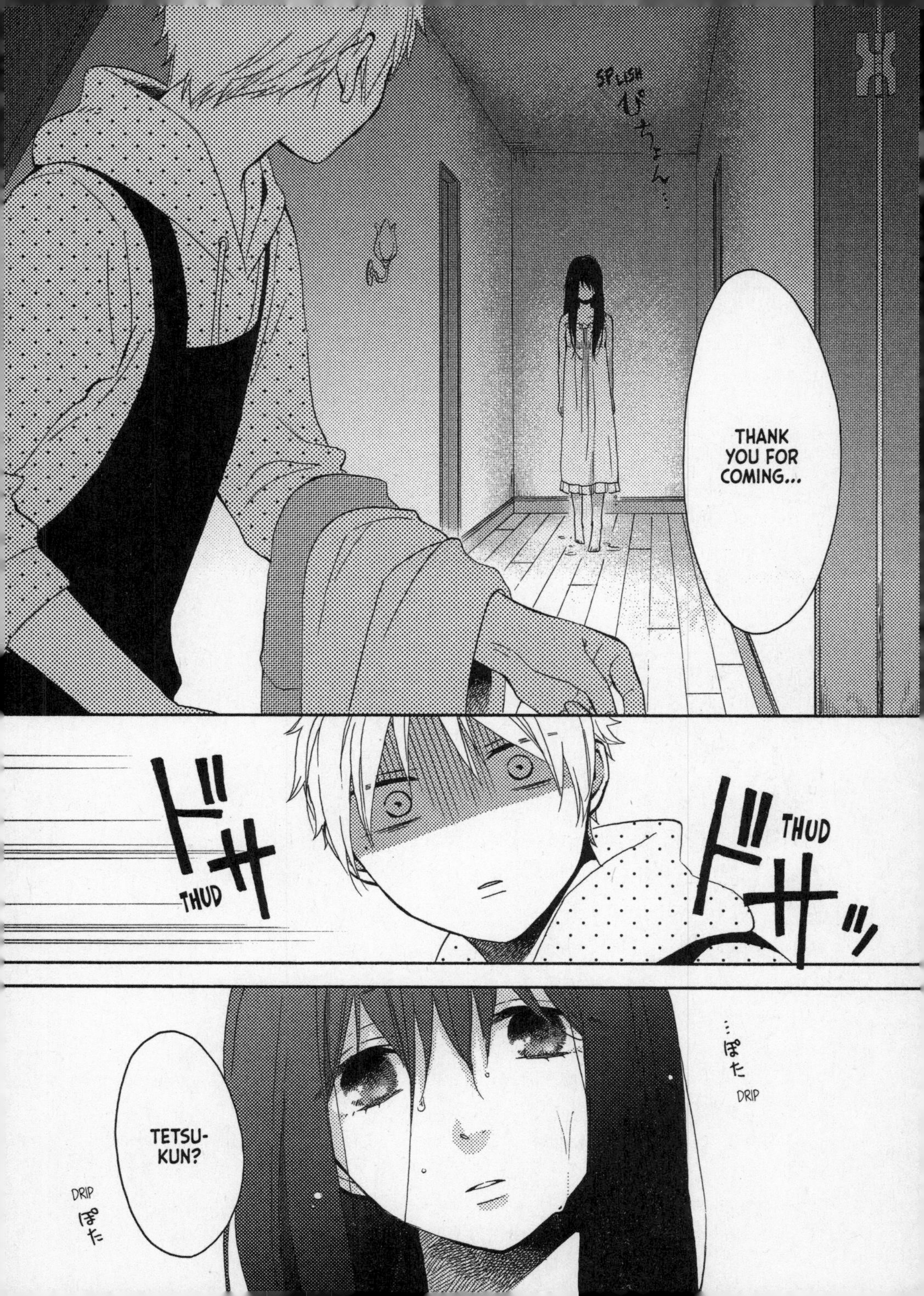
SPLISH
ぴちょん…
THANK YOU FOR COMING...
ドサッ
THUD
ドサ
THUD
…ぽた
DRIP
TETSU-KUN?
DRIP
ぽた

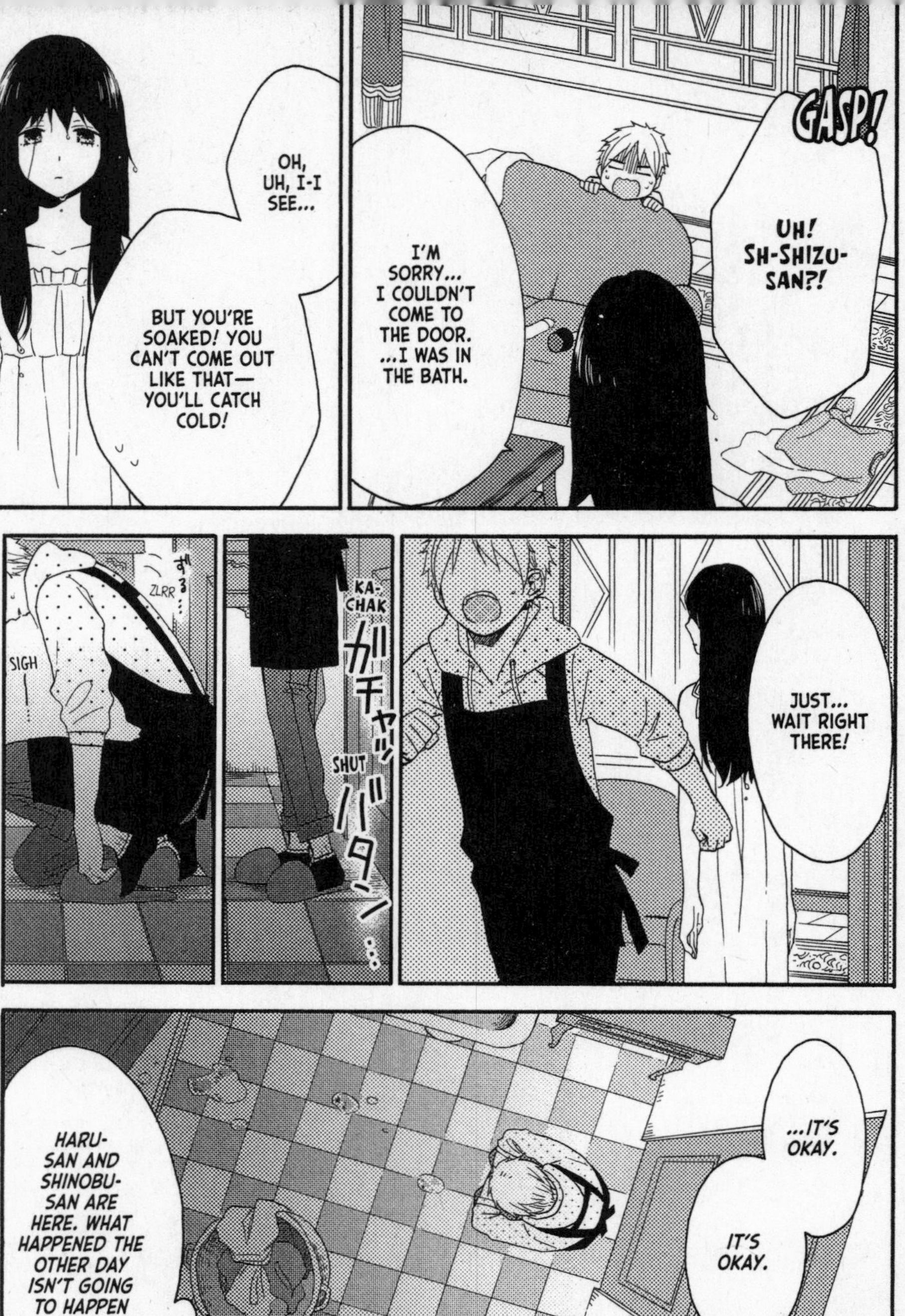
GASP!
UH! SH-SHIZU-SAN?!
I'M SORRY... I COULDN'T COME TO THE DOOR. ...I WAS IN THE BATH.
OH, UH, I-I SEE...
BUT YOU'RE SOAKED! YOU CAN'T COME OUT LIKE THAT—YOU'LL CATCH COLD!
JUST... WAIT RIGHT THERE!
KA-CHAK
ガチャッ
SHUT
バタン
...
ずる
ZLRR
...
SIGH
...
...IT'S OKAY.
IT'S OKAY.
HARU-SAN AND SHINOBU-SAN ARE HERE. WHAT HAPPENED THE OTHER DAY ISN'T GOING TO HAPPEN HERE!

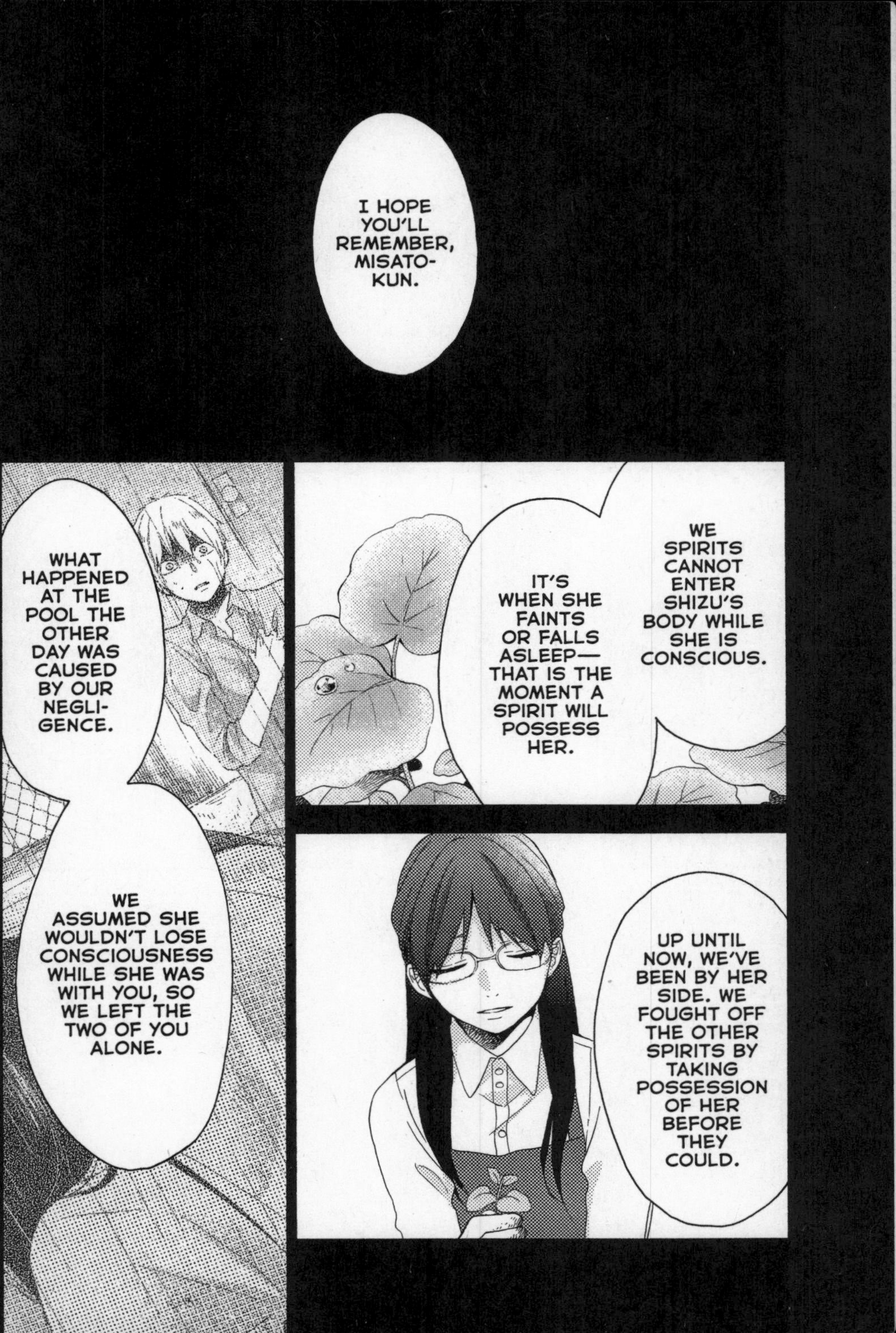
I HOPE YOU'LL REMEMBER, MISATO-KUN.
WE SPIRITS CANNOT ENTER SHIZU'S BODY WHILE SHE IS CONSCIOUS.
IT'S WHEN SHE FAINTS OR FALLS ASLEEP— THAT IS THE MOMENT A SPIRIT WILL POSSESS HER.
UP UNTIL NOW, WE'VE BEEN BY HER SIDE. WE FOUGHT OFF THE OTHER SPIRITS BY TAKING POSSESSION OF HER BEFORE THEY COULD.
WHAT HAPPENED AT THE POOL THE OTHER DAY WAS CAUSED BY OUR NEGLI-GENCE.
WE ASSUMED SHE WOULDN'T LOSE CONSCIOUSNESS WHILE SHE WAS WITH YOU, SO WE LEFT THE TWO OF YOU ALONE.

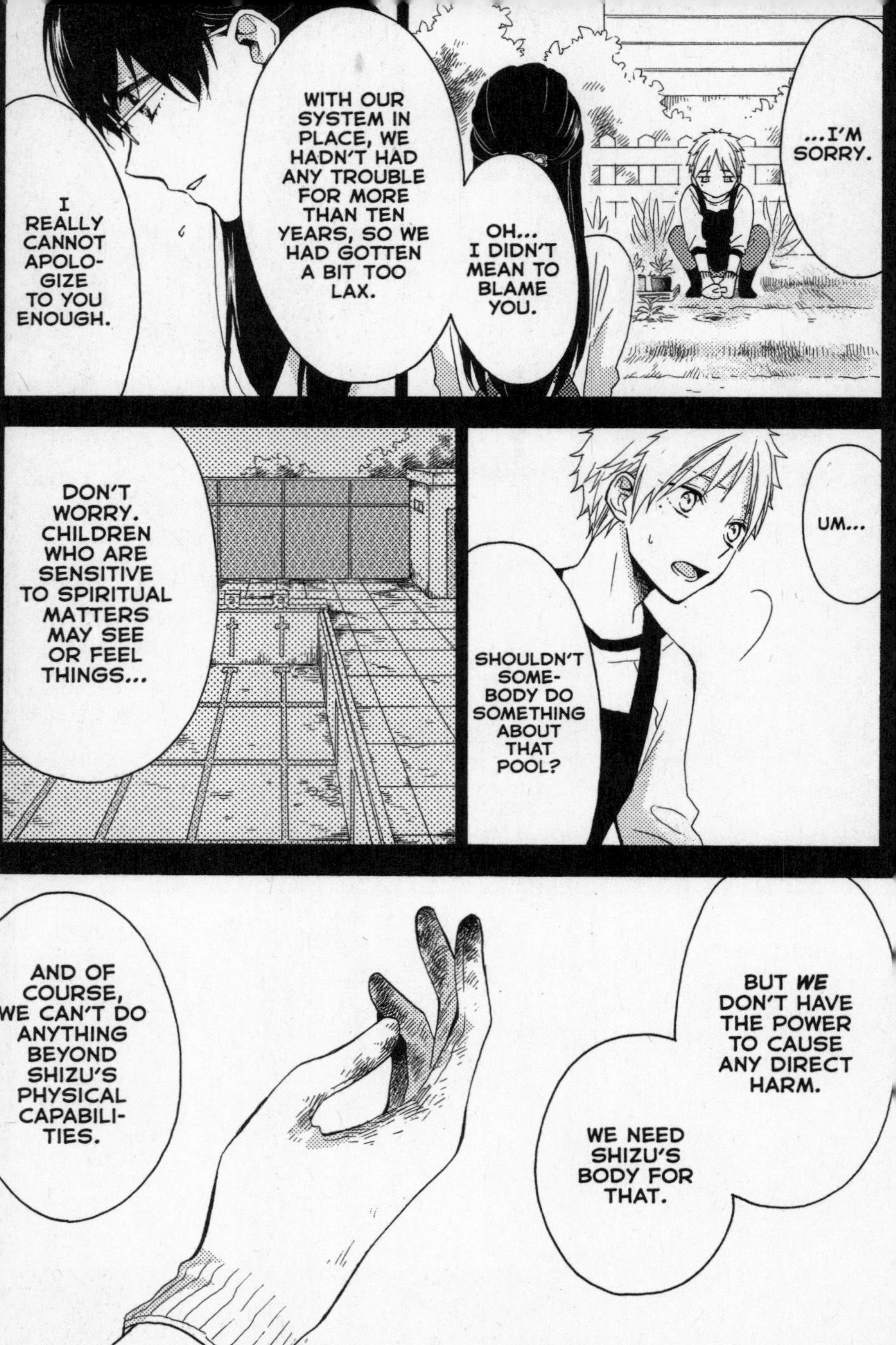
...I'M SORRY.
OH... I DIDN'T MEAN TO BLAME YOU.
WITH OUR SYSTEM IN PLACE, WE HADN'T HAD ANY TROUBLE FOR MORE THAN TEN YEARS, SO WE HAD GOTTEN A BIT TOO LAX.
I REALLY CANNOT APOLOGIZE TO YOU ENOUGH.
UM...
SHOULDN'T SOMEBODY DO SOMETHING ABOUT THAT POOL?
DON'T WORRY. CHILDREN WHO ARE SENSITIVE TO SPIRITUAL MATTERS MAY SEE OR FEEL THINGS...
BUT *WE* DON'T HAVE THE POWER TO CAUSE ANY DIRECT HARM.
WE NEED SHIZU'S BODY FOR THAT.
AND OF COURSE, WE CAN'T DO ANYTHING BEYOND SHIZU'S PHYSICAL CAPABILITIES.

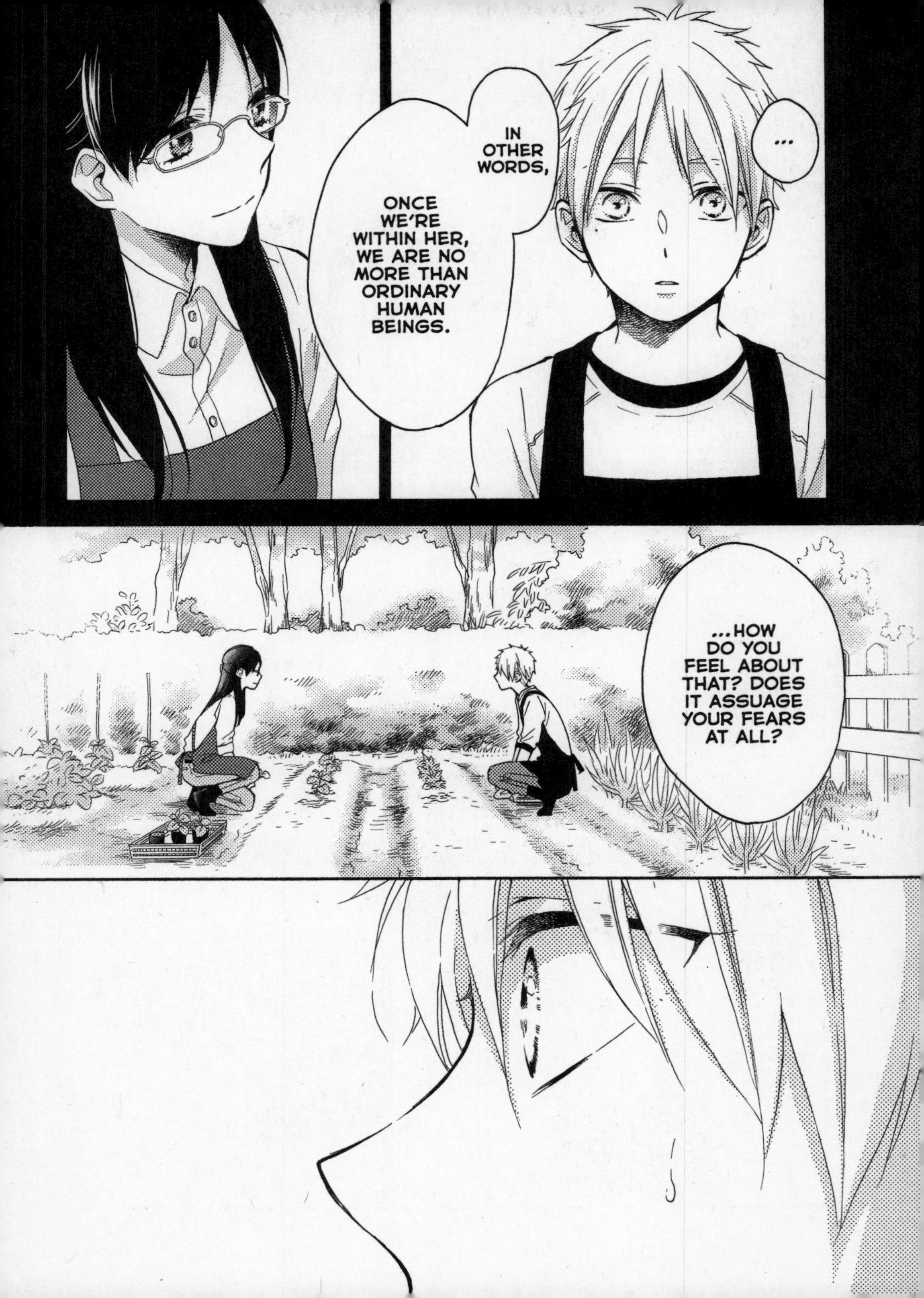
...
IN OTHER WORDS,
ONCE WE'RE WITHIN HER, WE ARE NO MORE THAN ORDINARY HUMAN BEINGS.
...HOW DO YOU FEEL ABOUT THAT? DOES IT ASSUAGE YOUR FEARS AT ALL?

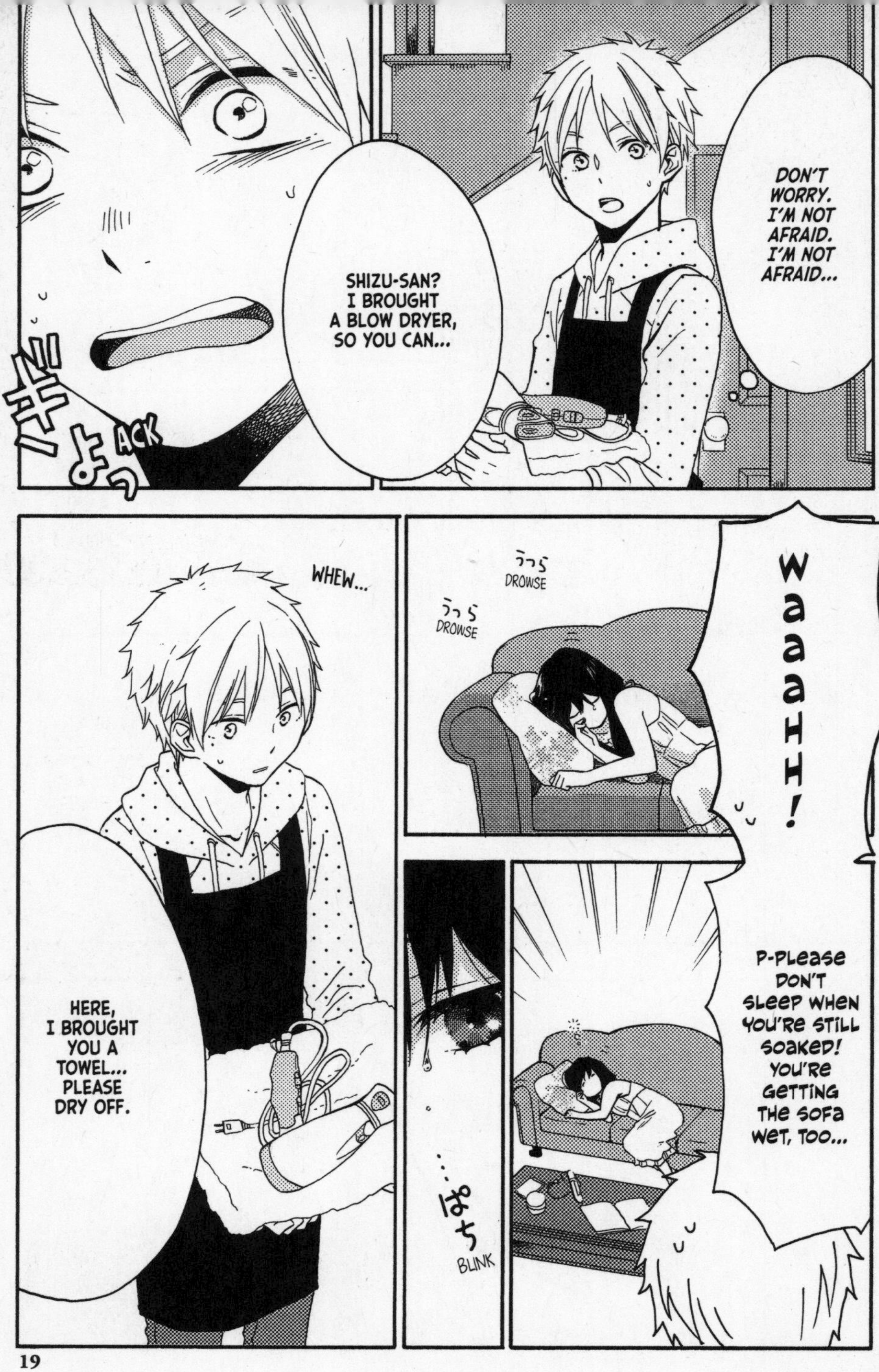
DON'T WORRY. I'M NOT AFRAID. I'M NOT AFRAID...
SHIZU-SAN? I BROUGHT A BLOW DRYER, SO YOU CAN...
ギョッ
ACK
WAAAHH!
うつら
DROWSE
うつら
DROWSE
P-PLEASE DON'T SLEEP WHEN YOU'RE STILL SOAKED! YOU'RE GETTING THE SOFA WET, TOO...
...ぱち
BLINK
WHEW...
HERE, I BROUGHT YOU A TOWEL... PLEASE DRY OFF.

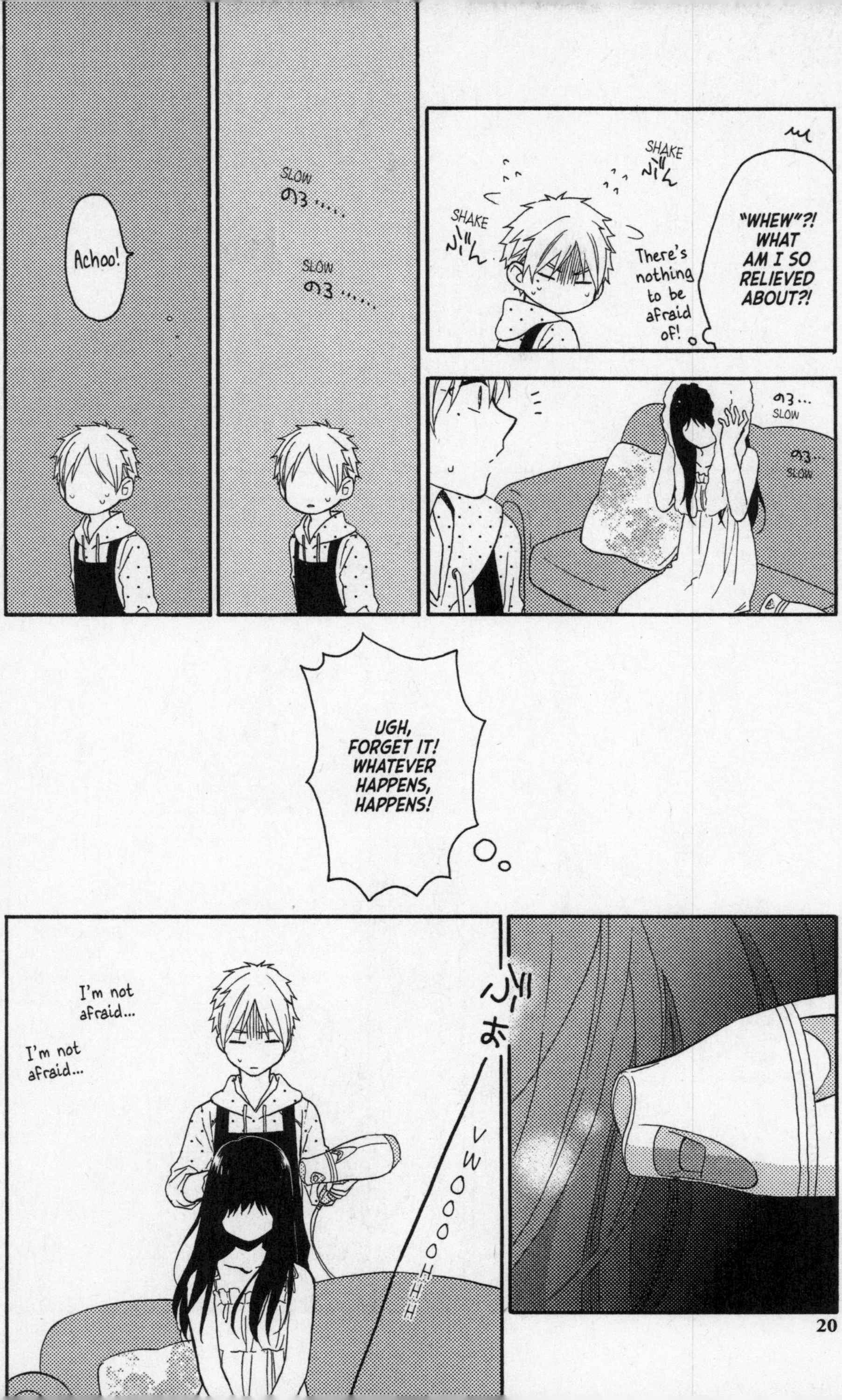
SHAKE
SHAKE
There's nothing to be afraid of!
"WHEW"?! WHAT AM I SO RELIEVED ABOUT?!
SLOW
SLOW
SLOW
SLOW
Achoo!
UGH, FORGET IT! WHATEVER HAPPENS, HAPPENS!
VWOOOOHHHH
I'm not afraid...
I'm not afraid...

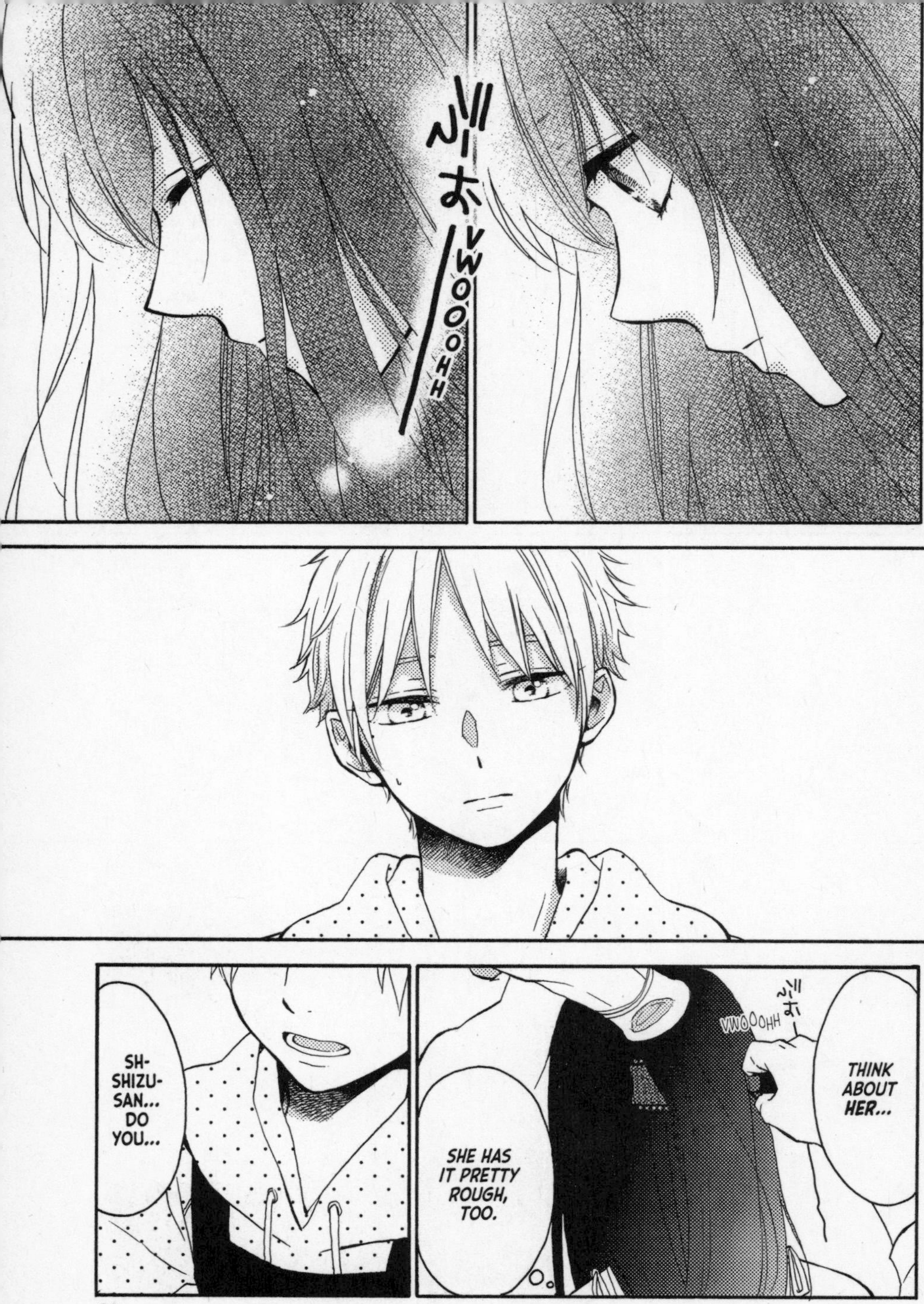
ヴぉ〜
VWOOOOHH
ヴぉ〜
VWOOOHH
THINK ABOUT HER...
SHE HAS IT PRETTY ROUGH, TOO.
SH-SHIZU-SAN... DO YOU...

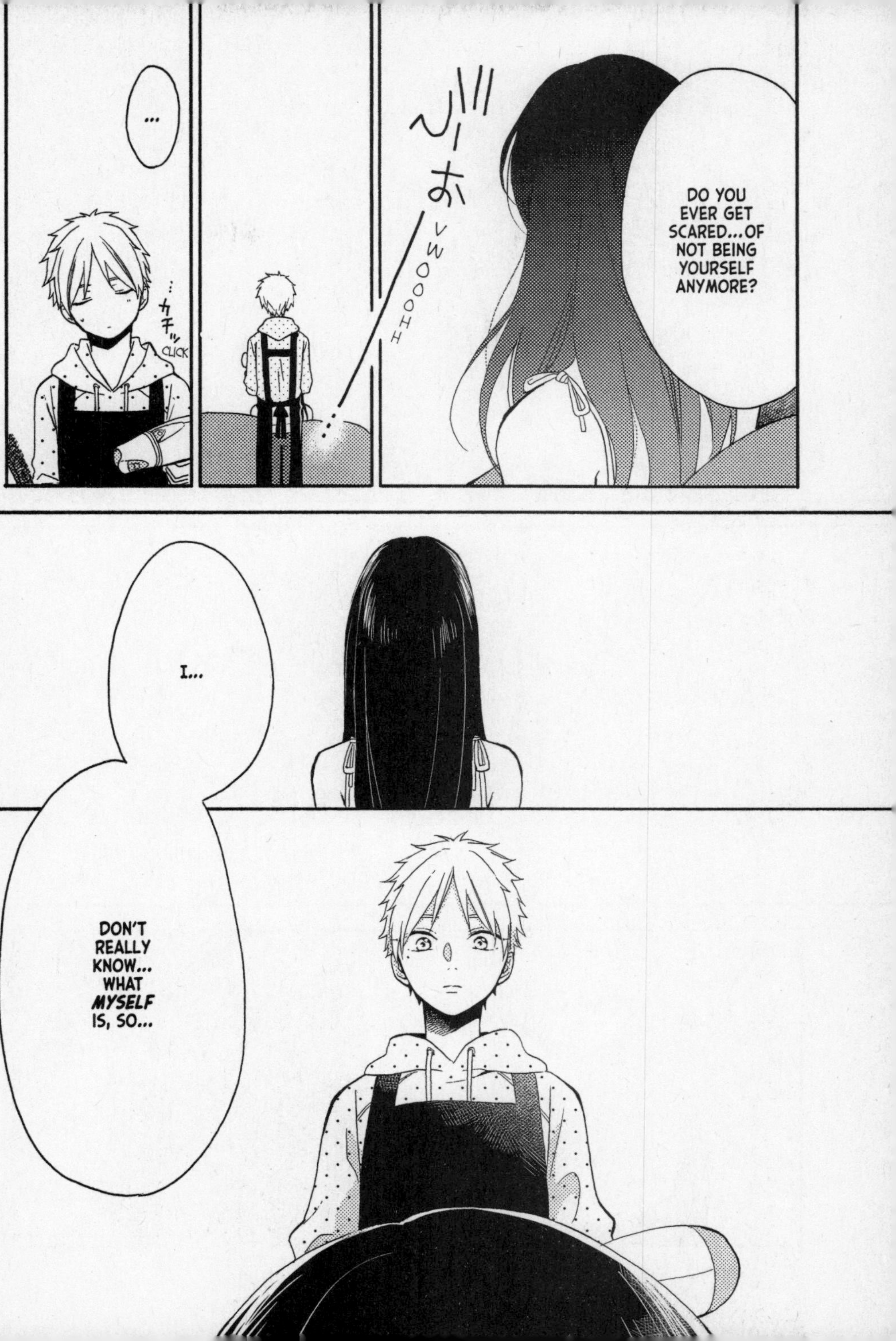

DO YOU EVER GET SCARED...OF NOT BEING YOURSELF ANYMORE?
VWOOOOHH
...
...カチッ
CLICK
I...
DON'T REALLY KNOW... WHAT *MYSELF* IS, SO...

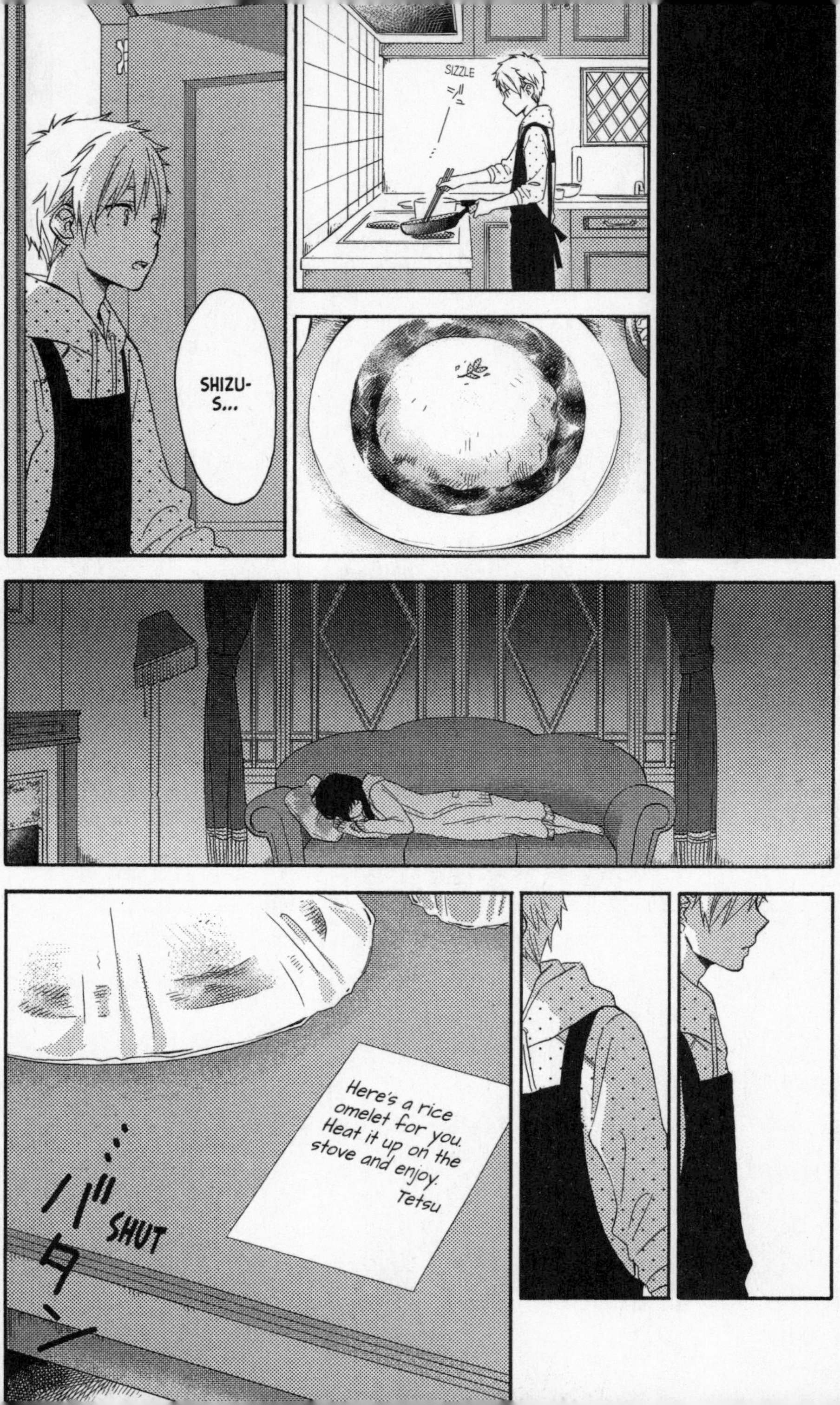
SIZZLE
SHIZU-S...
Here's a rice omelet for you. Heat it up on the stove and enjoy.
Tetsu
SHUT

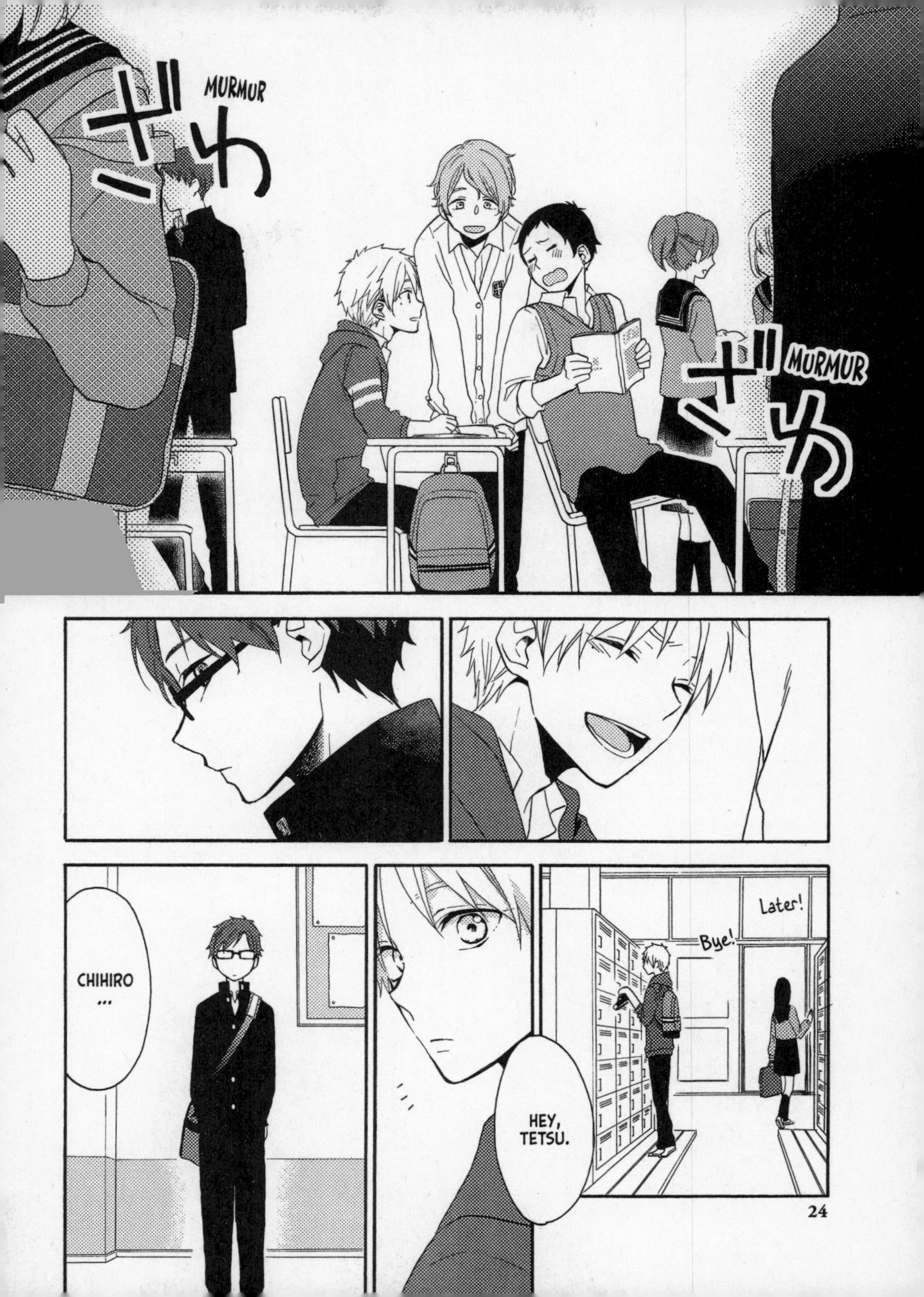
ざわ
MURMUR
ざわ
MURMUR
Later!
Bye!
HEY, TETSU.
CHIHIRO ...

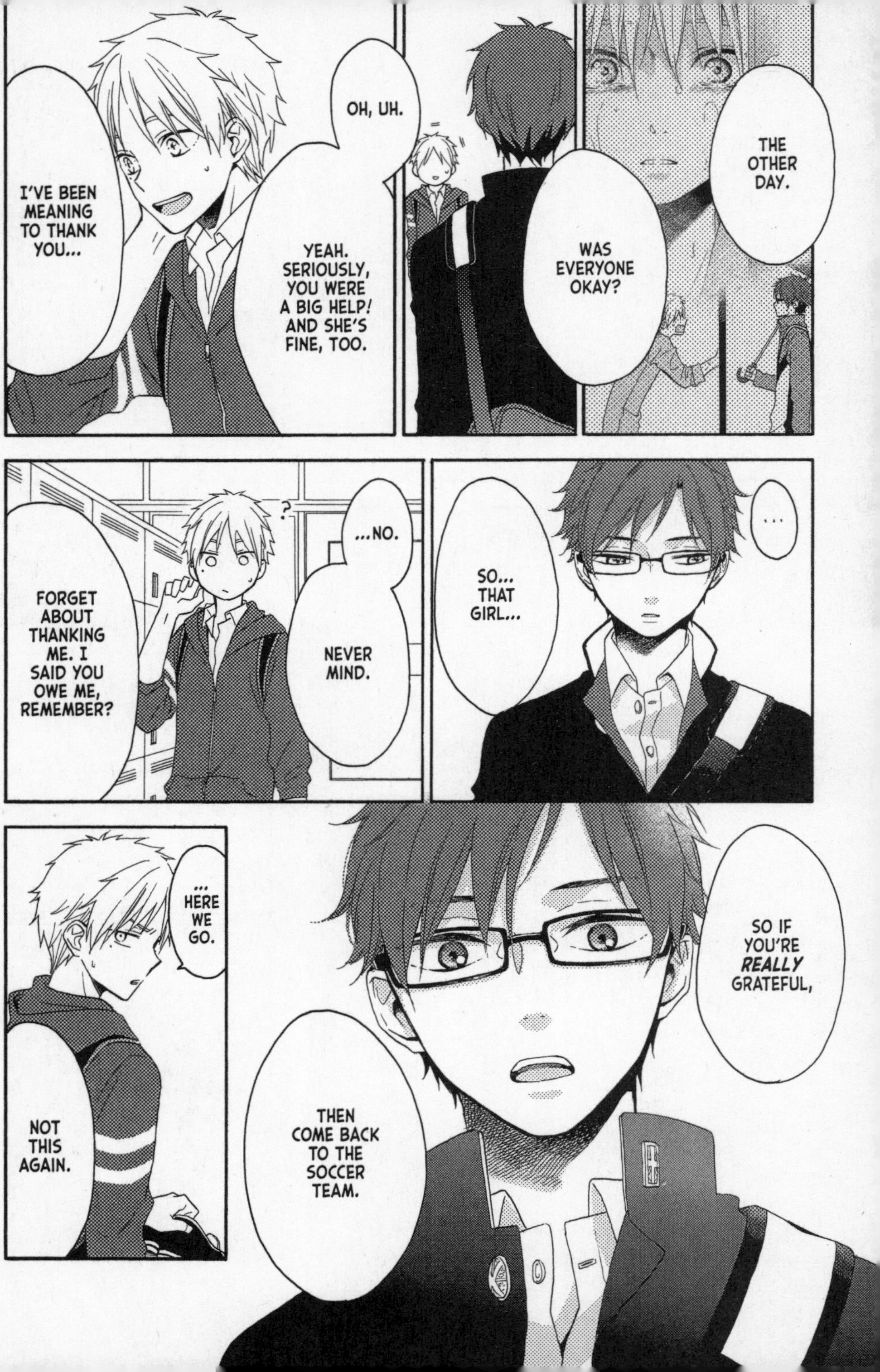
THE OTHER DAY.
WAS EVERYONE OKAY?
OH, UH.
YEAH. SERIOUSLY, YOU WERE A BIG HELP! AND SHE'S FINE, TOO.
I'VE BEEN MEANING TO THANK YOU...
...
SO... THAT GIRL...
...NO.
NEVER MIND.
FORGET ABOUT THANKING ME. I SAID YOU OWE ME, REMEMBER?
SO IF YOU'RE *REALLY* GRATEFUL,
THEN COME BACK TO THE SOCCER TEAM.
...HERE WE GO.
NOT THIS AGAIN.

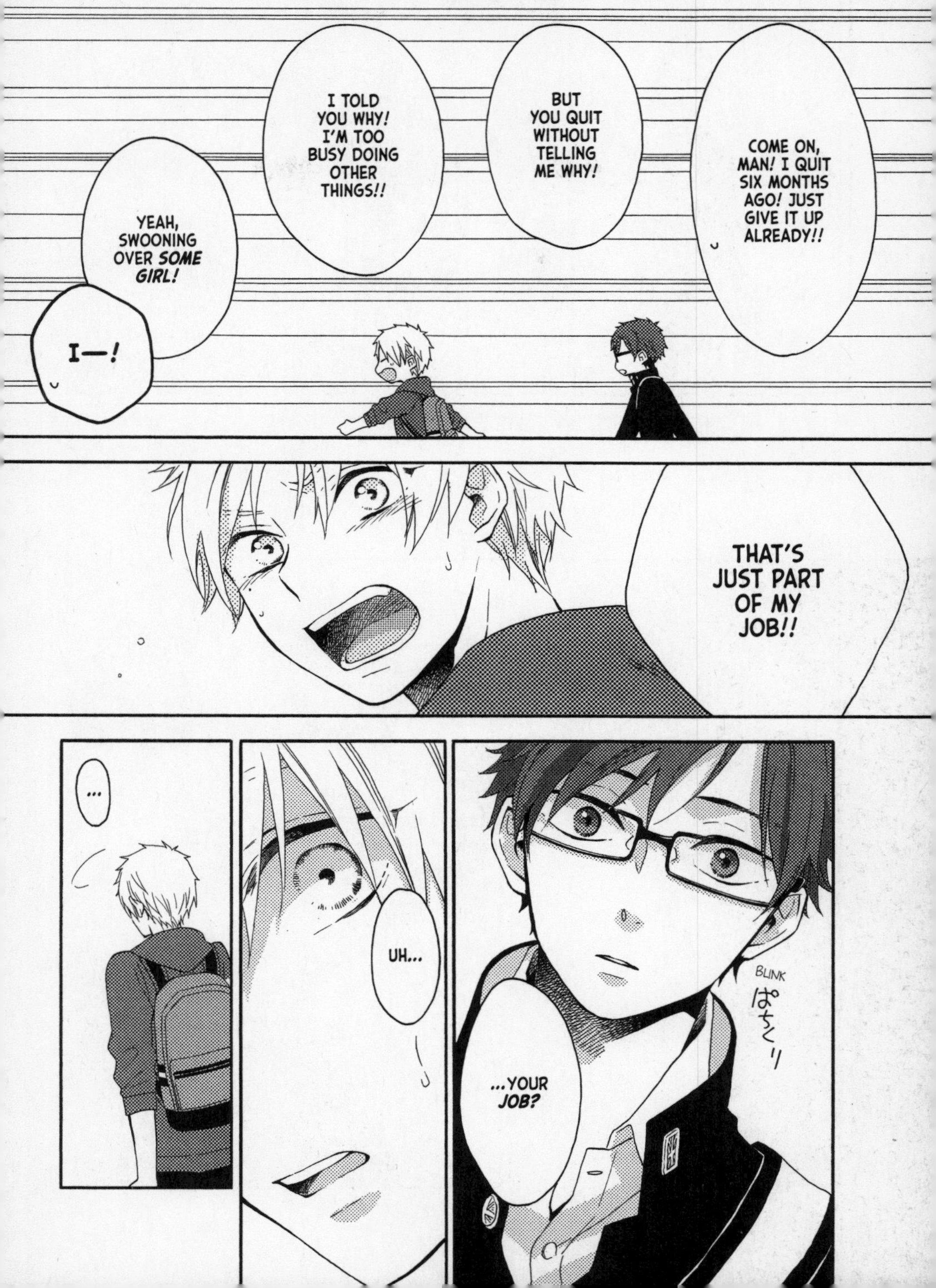
COME ON, MAN! I QUIT SIX MONTHS AGO! JUST GIVE IT UP ALREADY!!
BUT YOU QUIT WITHOUT TELLING ME WHY!
I TOLD YOU WHY! I'M TOO BUSY DOING OTHER THINGS!!
YEAH, SWOONING OVER *SOME GIRL!*
I—!
THAT'S JUST PART OF MY JOB!!
BLINK
ぱちくり
...YOUR *JOB?*
UH...
...

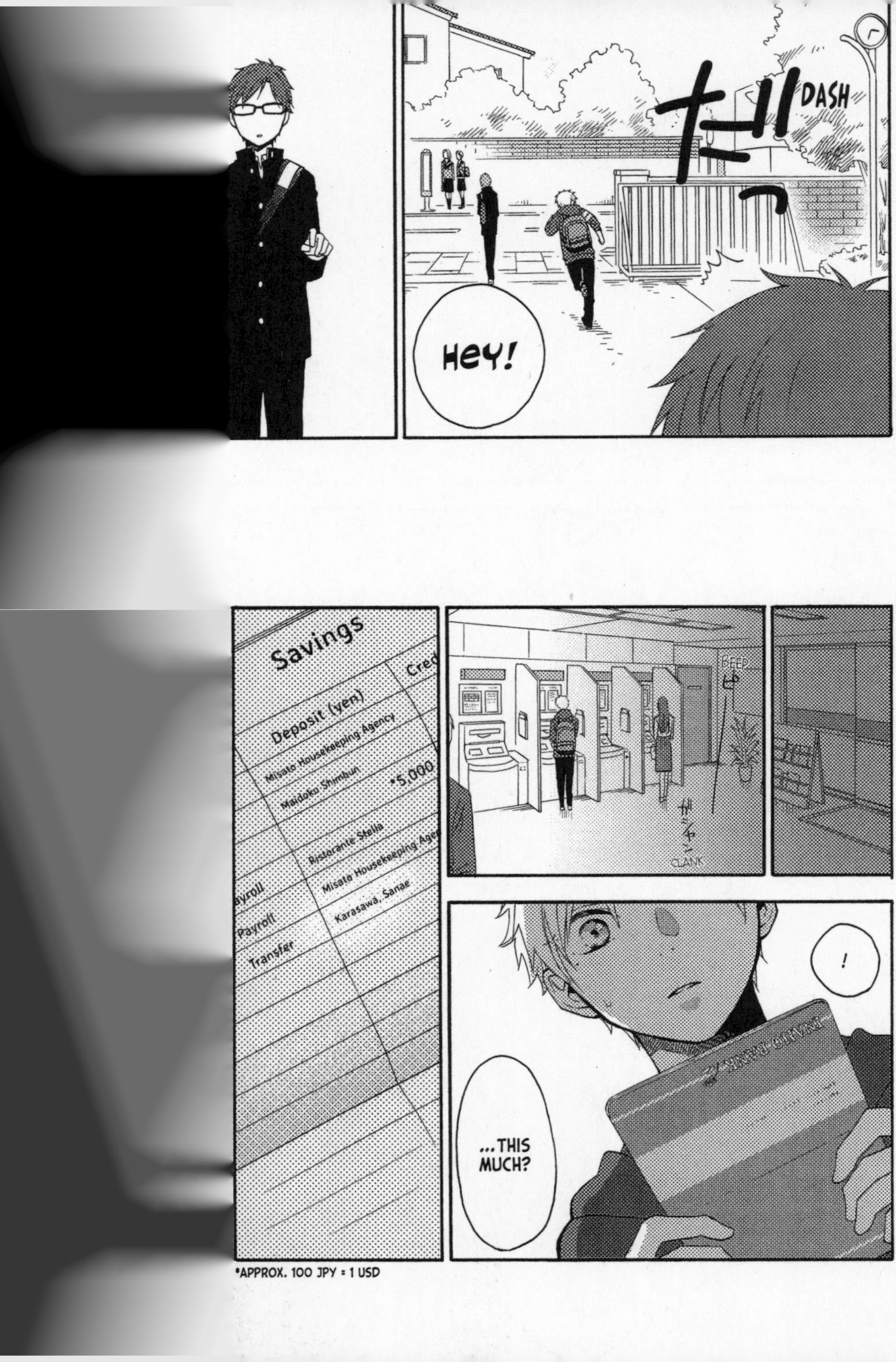
DASH
HEY!
BEEP
CLANK
!
...THIS MUCH?
Savings
Deposit (yen)
Misato Housekeeping Agency
Maidoko Shimbun
*5,000
Ristorante Stella
Payroll
Payroll
Misato Housekeeping Agency
Transfer
Karasawa, Sanae

*APPROX. 100 JPY = 1 USD

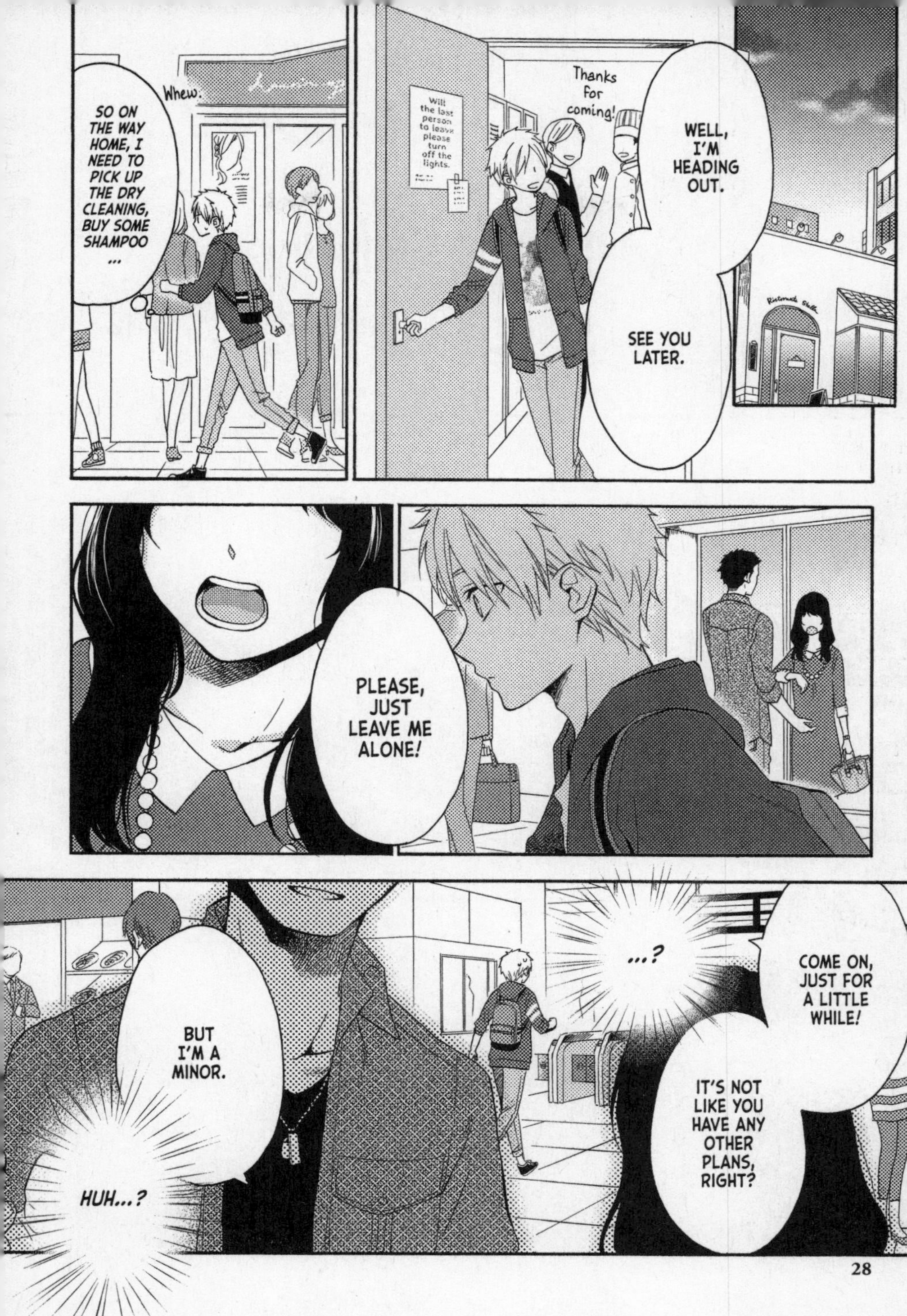
WELL, I'M HEADING OUT.
Thanks for coming!
Will the last person to leave please turn off the lights.
SEE YOU LATER.
Whew.
SO ON THE WAY HOME, I NEED TO PICK UP THE DRY CLEANING, BUY SOME SHAMPOO ...
PLEASE, JUST LEAVE ME ALONE!
COME ON, JUST FOR A LITTLE WHILE!
IT'S NOT LIKE YOU HAVE ANY OTHER PLANS, RIGHT?
...?
BUT I'M A MINOR.
HUH...?

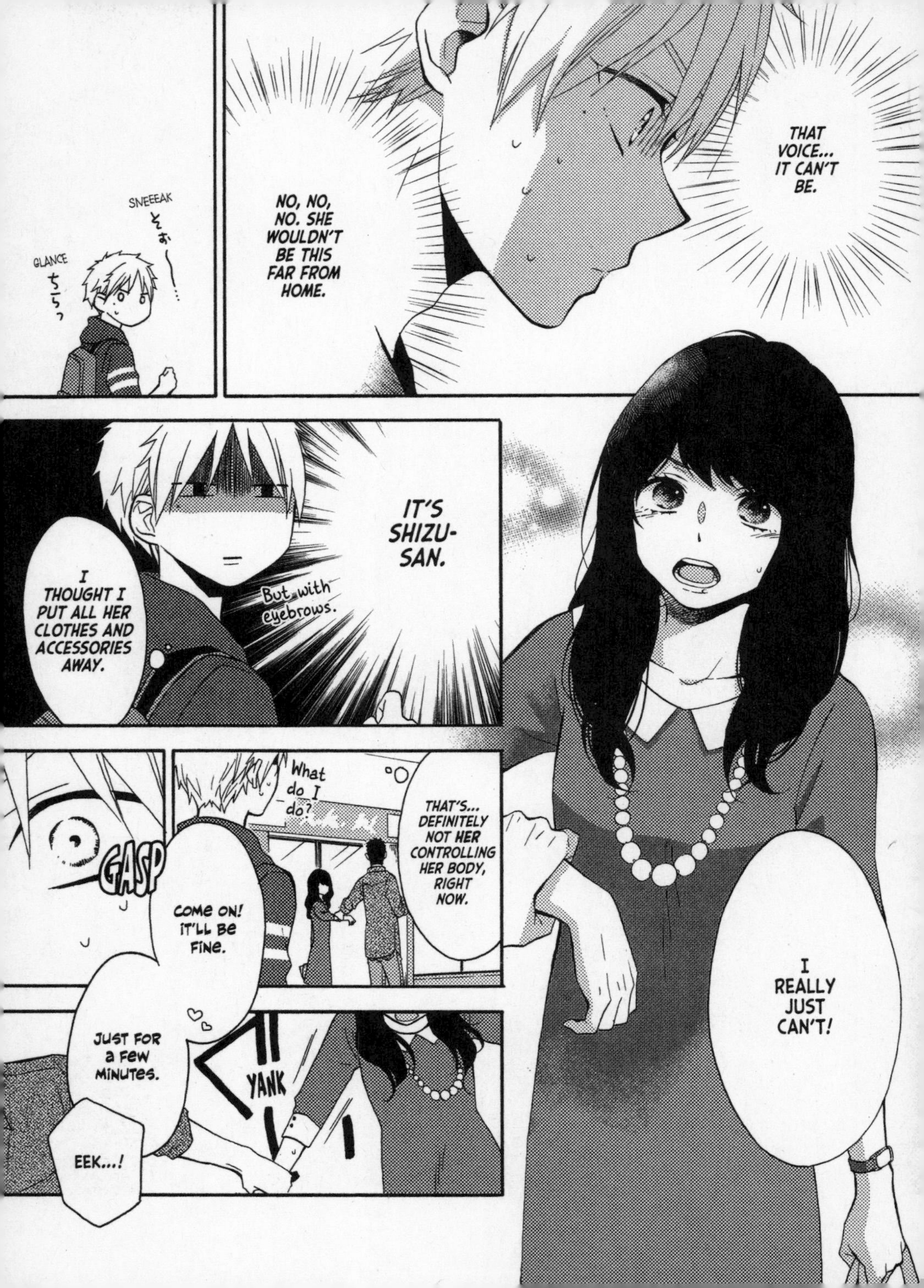
THAT VOICE... IT CAN'T BE.
NO, NO, NO. SHE WOULDN'T BE THIS FAR FROM HOME.
SNEEEAK
そぉ〜…
GLANCE
ちらっ
I REALLY JUST CAN'T!
IT'S SHIZU-SAN.
But with eyebrows.
I THOUGHT I PUT ALL HER CLOTHES AND ACCESSORIES AWAY.
What do I do?
THAT'S... DEFINITELY NOT HER CONTROLLING HER BODY, RIGHT NOW.
COME ON! IT'LL BE FINE.
GASP
JUST FOR A FEW MINUTES.
YANK
EEK...!

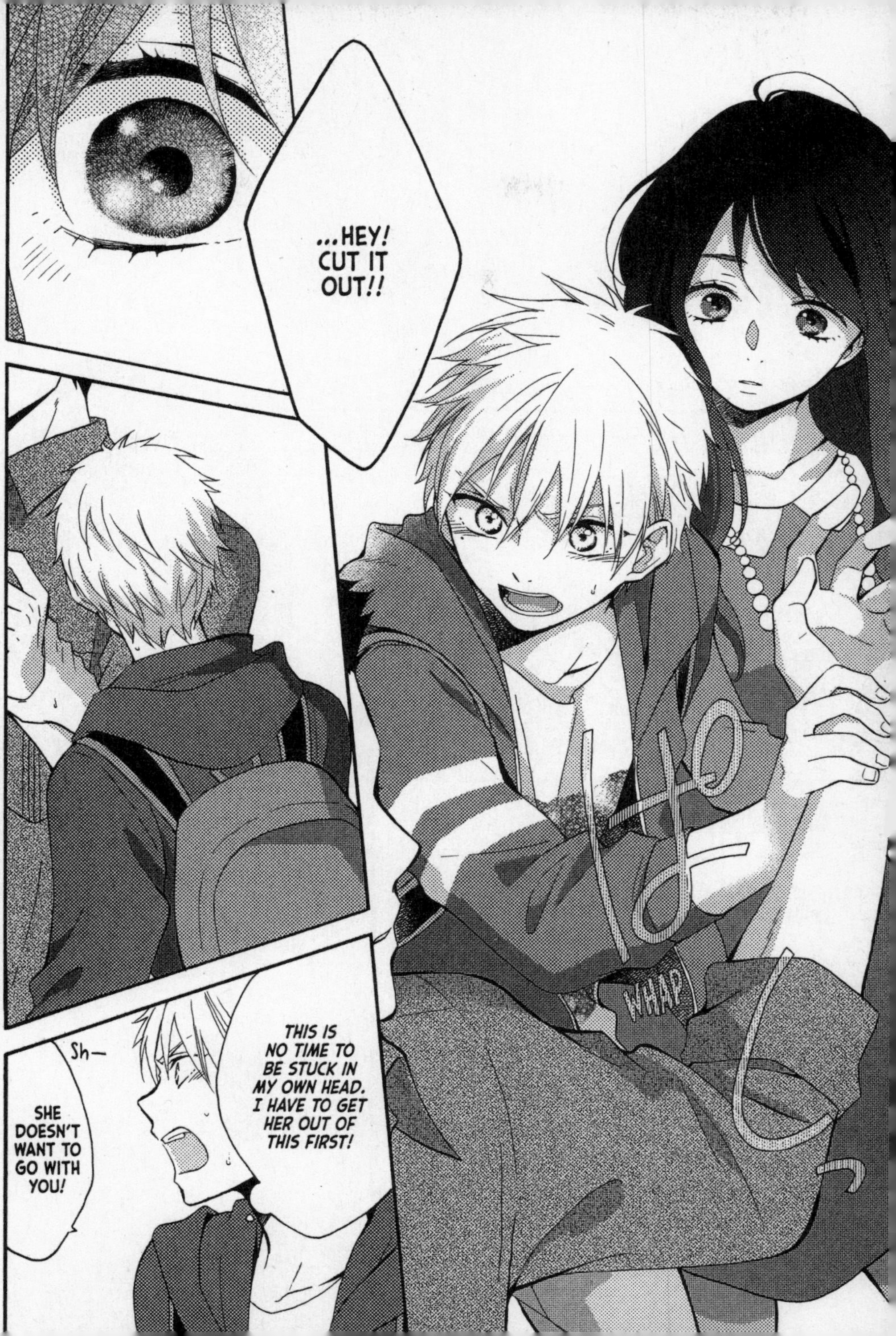

...HEY! CUT IT OUT!!
WHAP
THIS IS NO TIME TO BE STUCK IN MY OWN HEAD. I HAVE TO GET HER OUT OF THIS FIRST!
Sh—
SHE DOESN'T WANT TO GO WITH YOU!

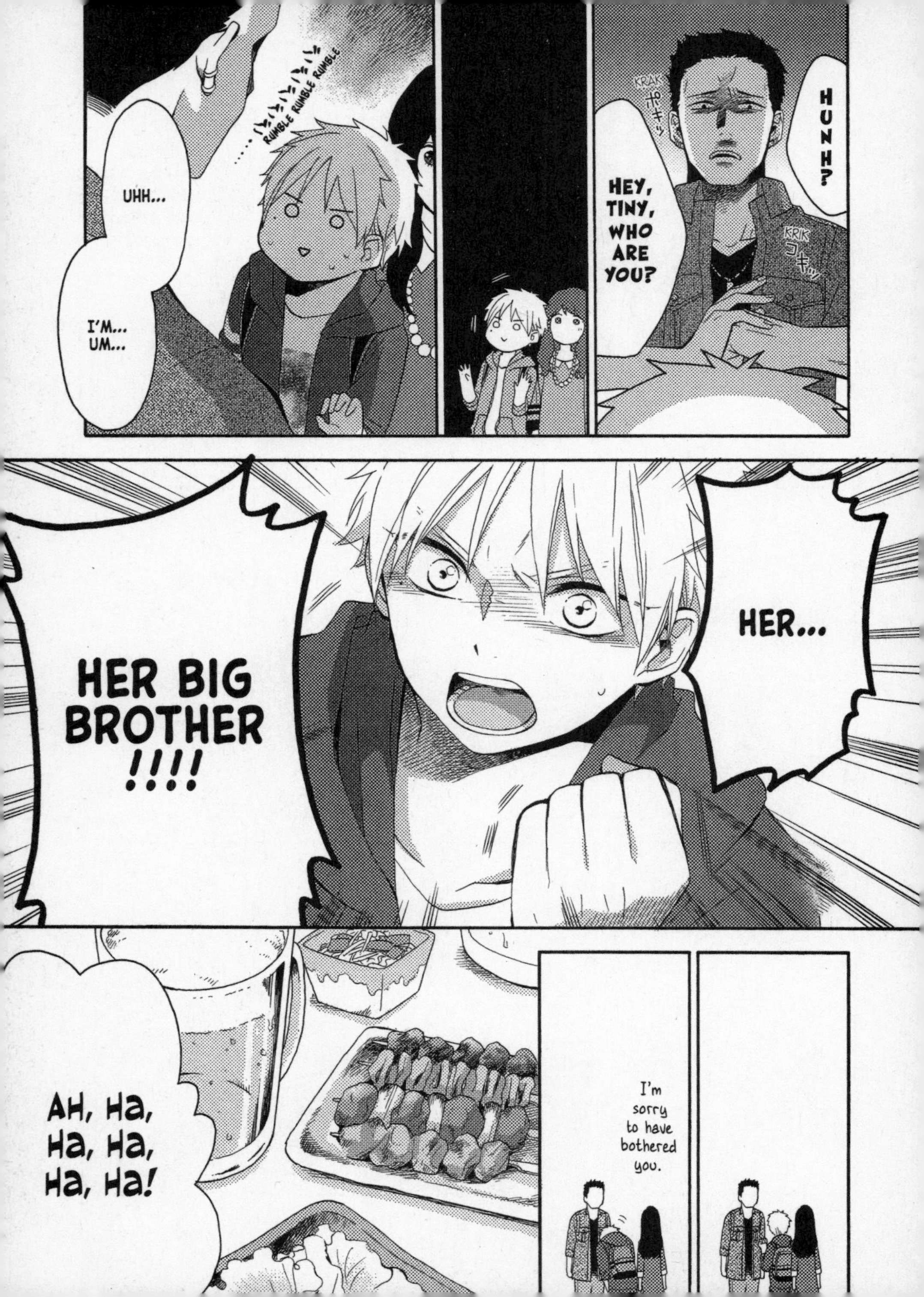
HUNH?
KRAK ポキッ
KRIK コキッ
HEY, TINY, WHO ARE YOU?
......RUMBLE RUMBLE RUMBLE
UHH...
I'M... UM...
HER...
HER BIG BROTHER !!!!
I'm sorry to have bothered you.
AH, HA, HA, HA, HA, HA!

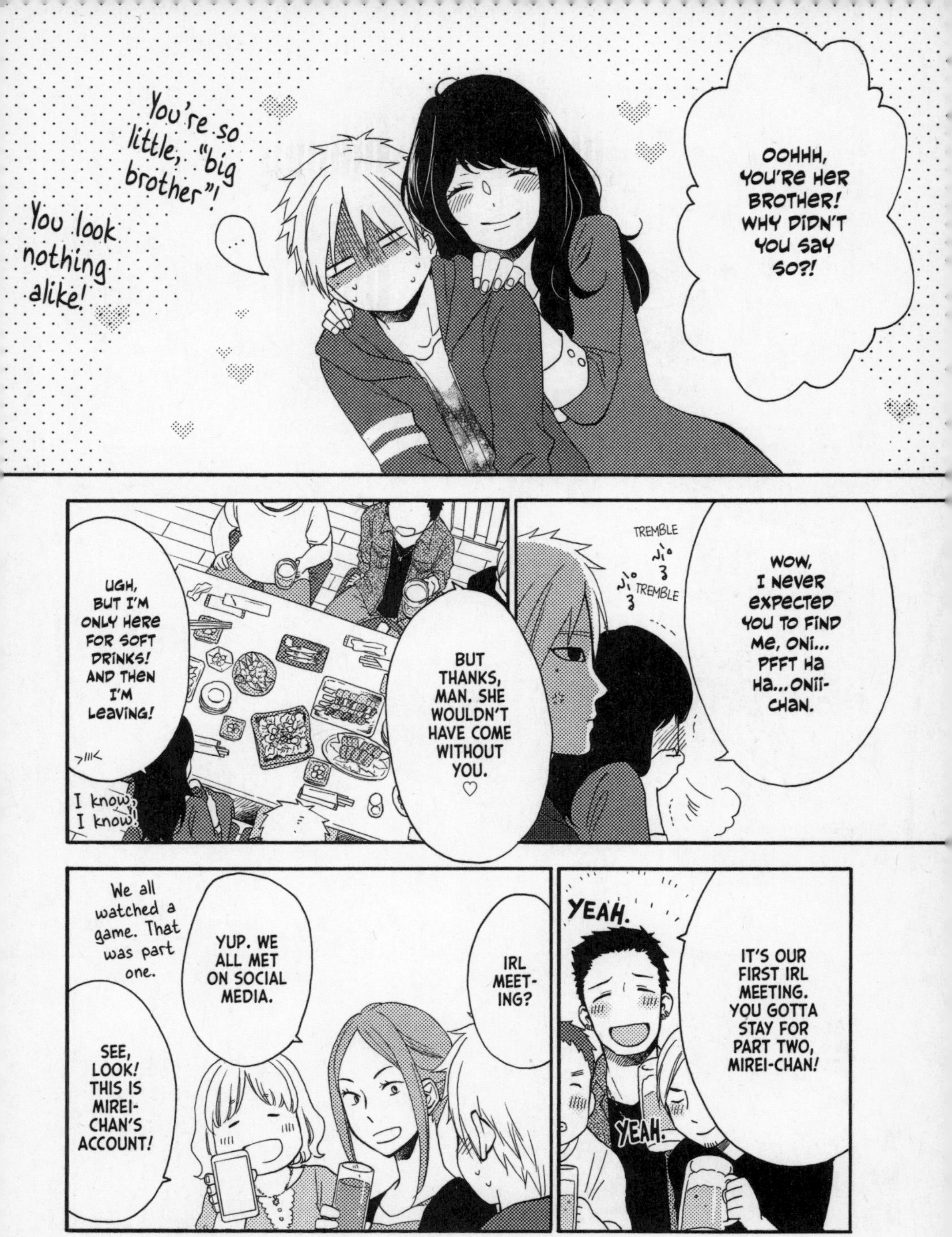
OOHHH, YOU'RE HER BROTHER! WHY DIDN'T YOU SAY SO?!
You're so little, "big brother"!
You look nothing alike!
...
TREMBLE
TREMBLE
WOW, I NEVER EXPECTED YOU TO FIND ME, ONI... PFFT HA HA...ONII-CHAN.
BUT THANKS, MAN. SHE WOULDN'T HAVE COME WITHOUT YOU. ♡
UGH, BUT I'M ONLY HERE FOR SOFT DRINKS! AND THEN I'M LEAVING!
>///<
I know, I know!
YEAH.
IT'S OUR FIRST IRL MEETING. YOU GOTTA STAY FOR PART TWO, MIREI-CHAN!
YEAH.
IRL MEETING?
YUP. WE ALL MET ON SOCIAL MEDIA.
We all watched a game. That was part one.
SEE, LOOK! THIS IS MIREI-CHAN'S ACCOUNT!

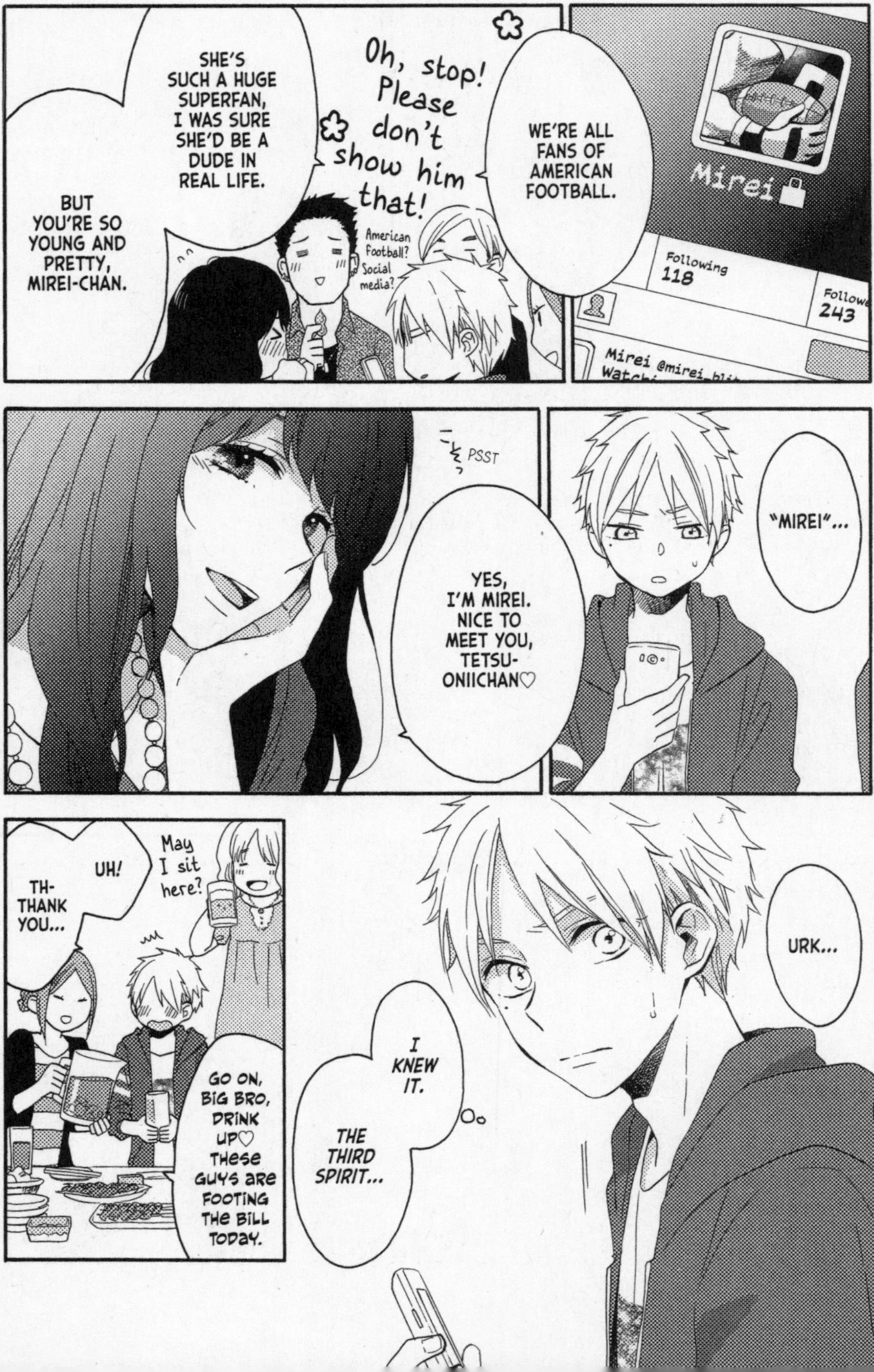
Mirei
Following 118
243
WE'RE ALL FANS OF AMERICAN FOOTBALL.
Oh, stop! Please don't show him that!
American Football? Social media?
SHE'S SUCH A HUGE SUPERFAN, I WAS SURE SHE'D BE A DUDE IN REAL LIFE.
BUT YOU'RE SO YOUNG AND PRETTY, MIREI-CHAN.
"MIREI"...
PSST
YES, I'M MIREI. NICE TO MEET YOU, TETSU-ONIICHAN♡
URK...
I KNEW IT.
THE THIRD SPIRIT...
May I sit here?
UH!
TH-THANK YOU...
GO ON, BIG BRO, DRINK UP♡ These guys are footing the bill today.

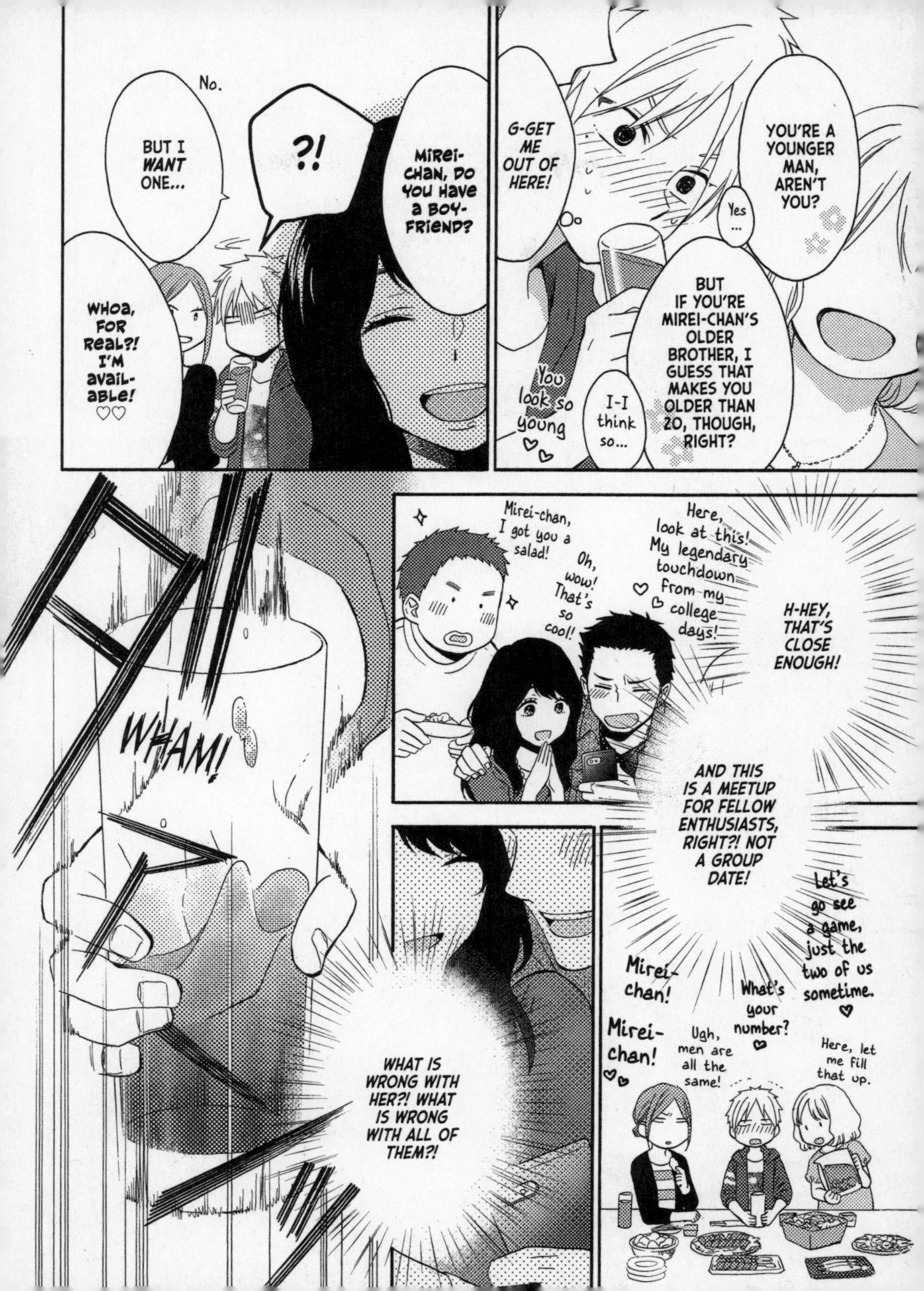

YOU'RE A YOUNGER MAN, AREN'T YOU?
G-GET ME OUT OF HERE!
Yes ...
BUT IF YOU'RE MIREI-CHAN'S OLDER BROTHER, I GUESS THAT MAKES YOU OLDER THAN ZO, THOUGH, RIGHT?
I-I think so...
You look so young ♡♡
Mirei-chan, do you have a boy-friend?
?!
No.
BUT I WANT ONE...
Whoa, for real?! I'm avail-able! ♡♡
H-HEY, THAT'S CLOSE ENOUGH!
Here, look at this! My legendary touchdown from my college days! ♡♡
Oh, wow! That's so cool!
Mirei-chan, I got you a salad!
AND THIS IS A MEETUP FOR FELLOW ENTHUSIASTS, RIGHT?! NOT A GROUP DATE!
Let's go see a game, just the two of us sometime. ♡
Here, let me fill that up.
What's your number? ♡
Ugh, men are all the same!
Mirei-chan!
Mirei-chan! ♡
WHAT IS WRONG WITH HER?! WHAT IS WRONG WITH ALL OF THEM?!
WHAM!

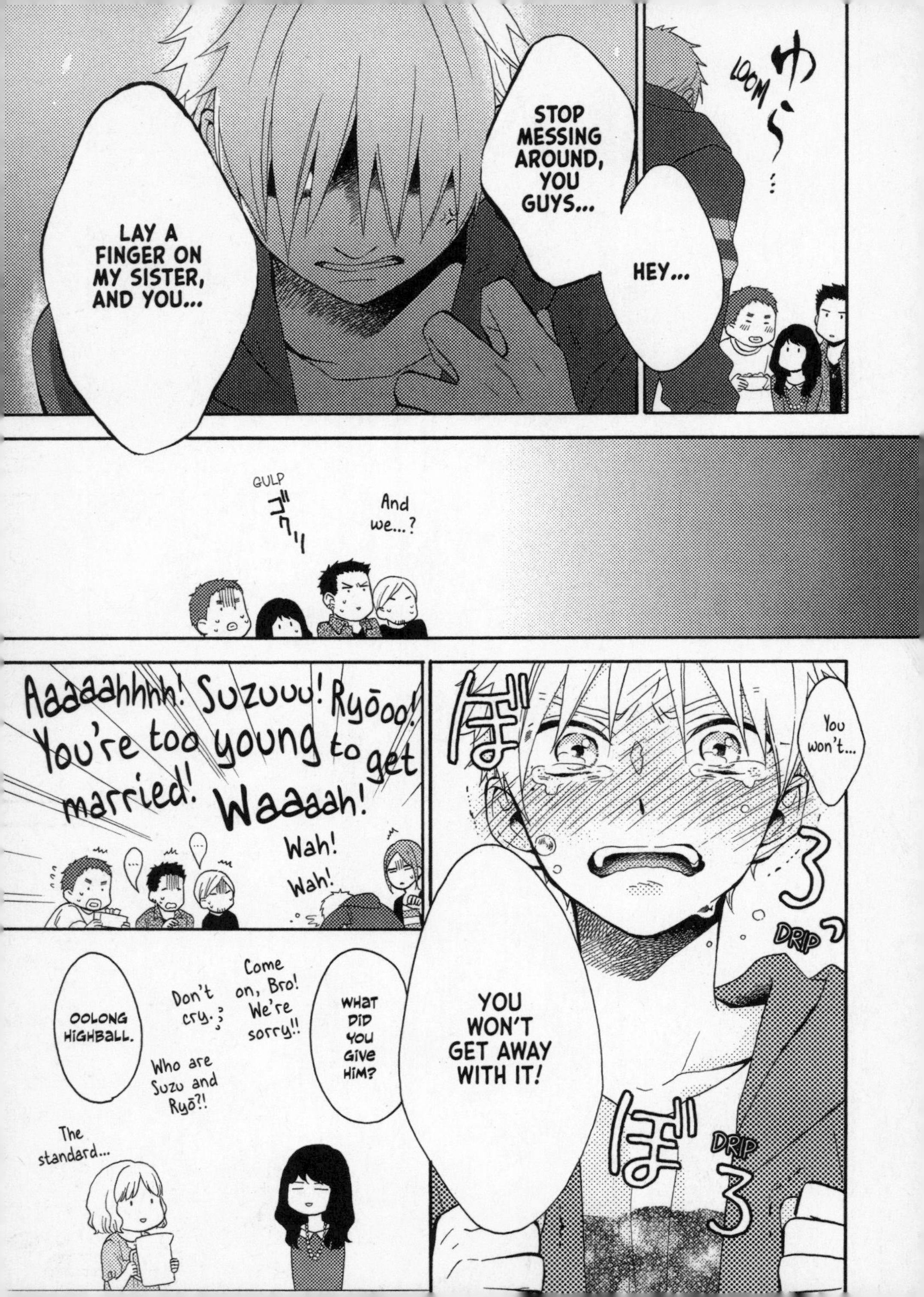

ゆら…
LOOM
HEY...
STOP MESSING AROUND, YOU GUYS...
LAY A FINGER ON MY SISTER, AND YOU...
GULP
ゴクッ
And we...?
ぽろ
You won't...
DRIP
YOU WON'T GET AWAY WITH IT!
ぽろ
DRIP
Aaaaahhhh! Suzuuu! Ryōooo! You're too young to get married! Waaaah!
Wah!
Wah!
...
...
WHAT DID YOU GIVE HIM?
Come on, Bro! We're sorry!!
Don't cry.
OOLONG HIGHBALL.
Who are Suzu and Ryō?!
The standard...

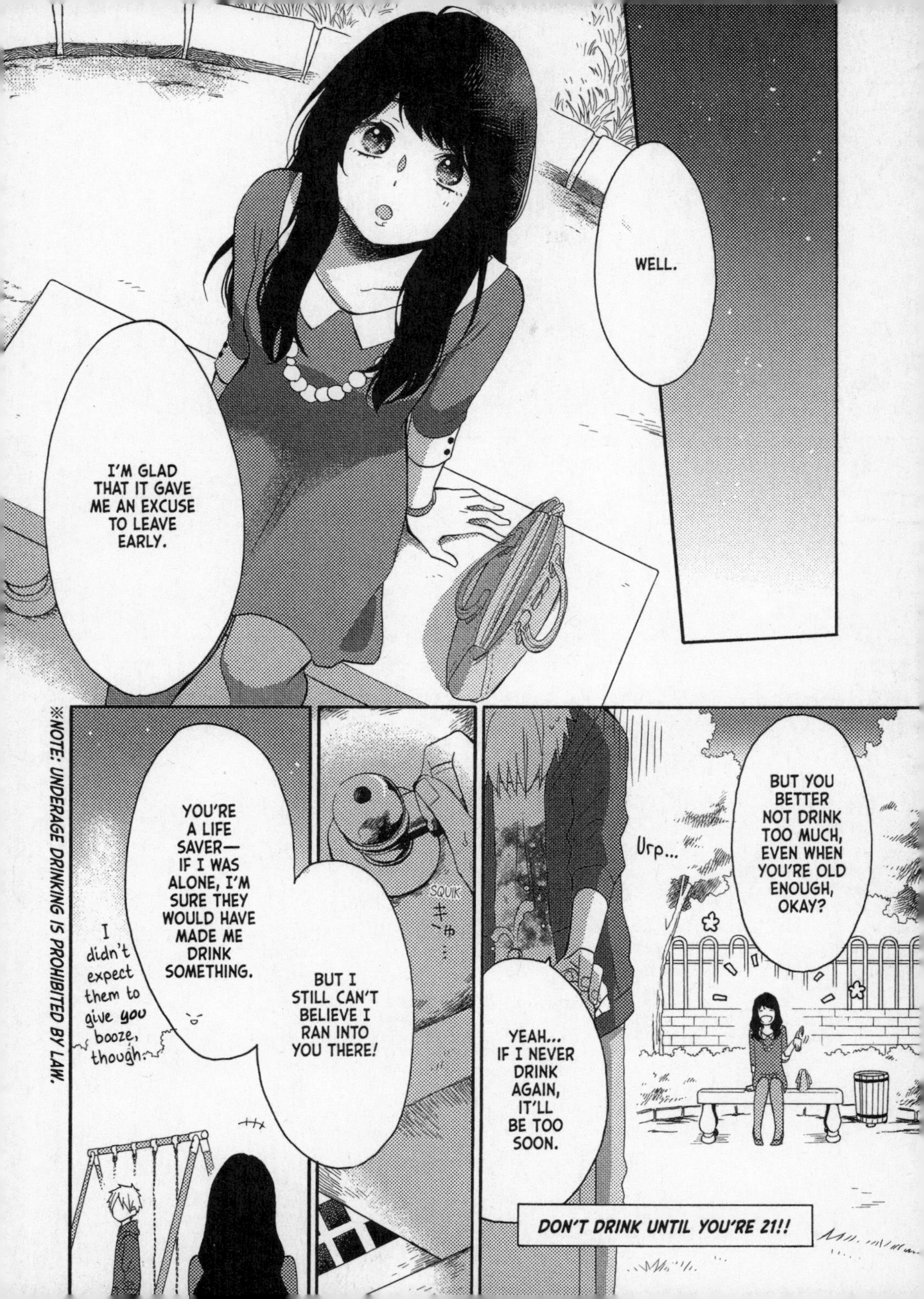
WELL.
I'M GLAD THAT IT GAVE ME AN EXCUSE TO LEAVE EARLY.
BUT YOU BETTER NOT DRINK TOO MUCH, EVEN WHEN YOU'RE OLD ENOUGH, OKAY?
Urp...
YEAH... IF I NEVER DRINK AGAIN, IT'LL BE TOO SOON.
DON'T DRINK UNTIL YOU'RE 21!!
SQUIK
YOU'RE A LIFE SAVER— IF I WAS ALONE, I'M SURE THEY WOULD HAVE MADE ME DRINK SOMETHING.
BUT I STILL CAN'T BELIEVE I RAN INTO YOU THERE!
I didn't expect them to give *you* booze, though.
※NOTE: UNDERAGE DRINKING IS PROHIBITED BY LAW.

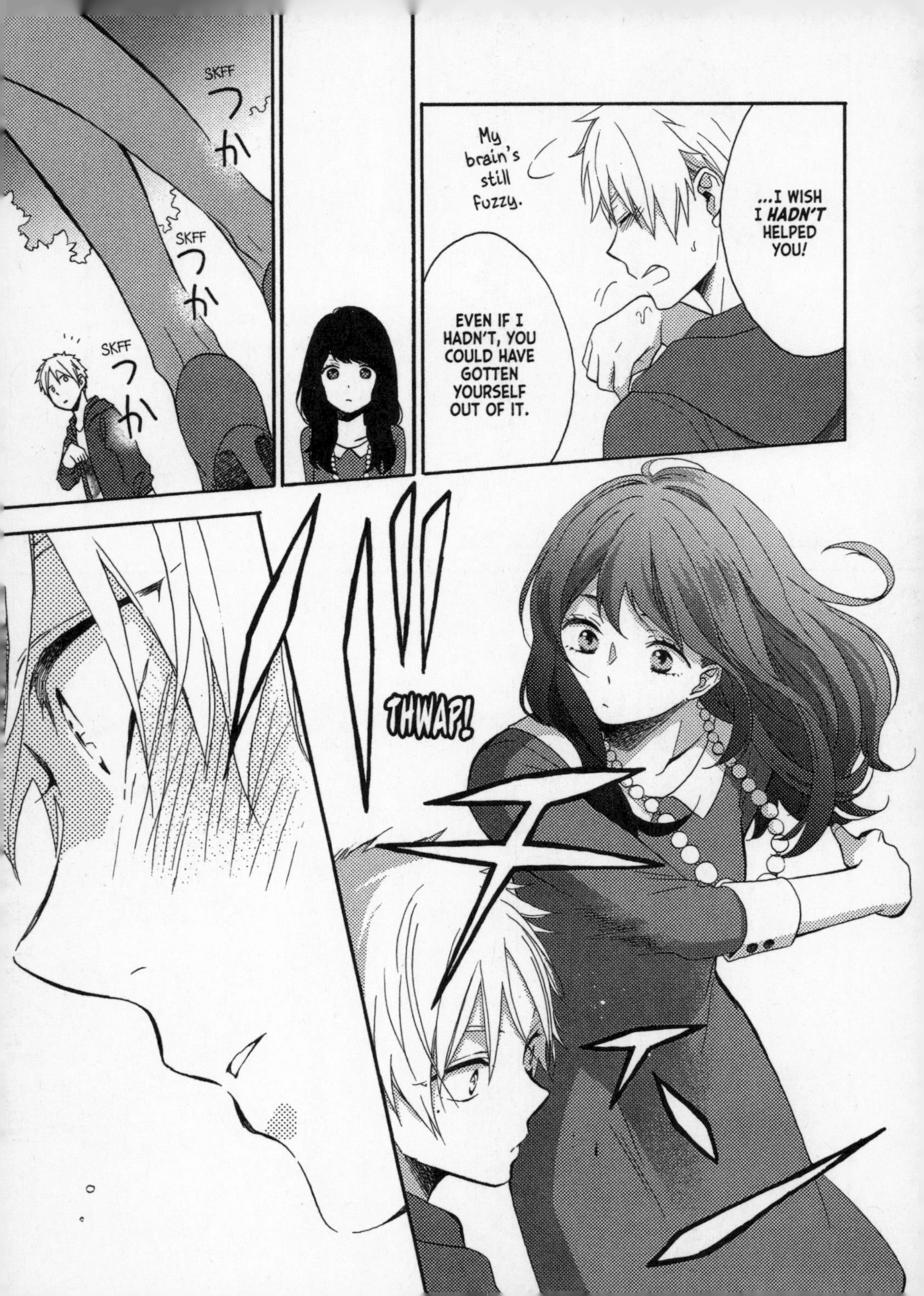
...I WISH I ***HADN'T*** HELPED YOU!
My brain's still fuzzy.
EVEN IF I HADN'T, YOU COULD HAVE GOTTEN YOURSELF OUT OF IT.
SKFF つか
SKFF つか
SKFF つか
THWAP!

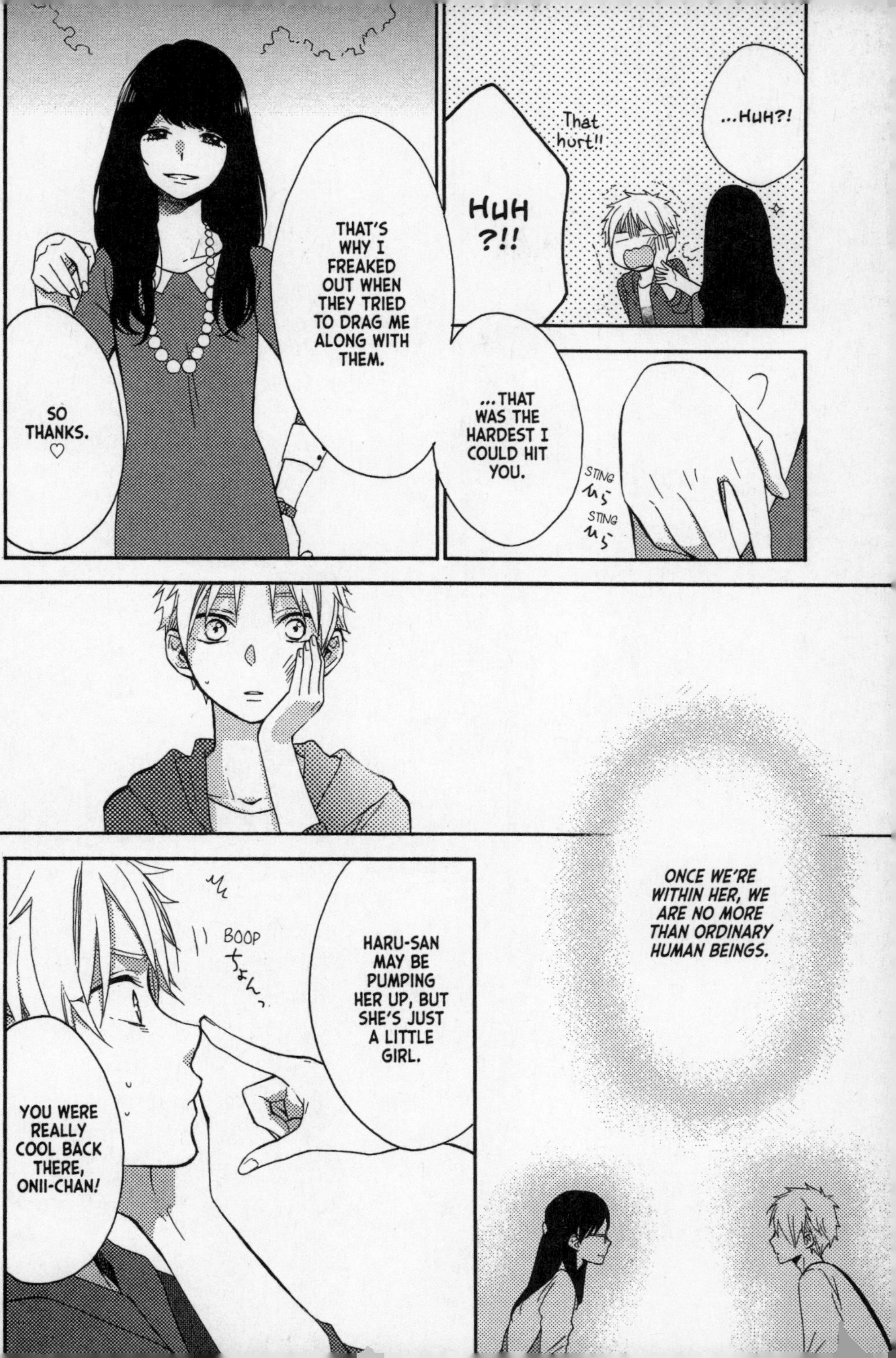

...HUH?!
That hurt!!
HUH ?!!
...THAT WAS THE HARDEST I COULD HIT YOU.
STING
STING
THAT'S WHY I FREAKED OUT WHEN THEY TRIED TO DRAG ME ALONG WITH THEM.
SO THANKS. ♡
ONCE WE'RE WITHIN HER, WE ARE NO MORE THAN ORDINARY HUMAN BEINGS.
HARU-SAN MAY BE PUMPING HER UP, BUT SHE'S JUST A LITTLE GIRL.
BOOP
YOU WERE REALLY COOL BACK THERE, ONII-CHAN!

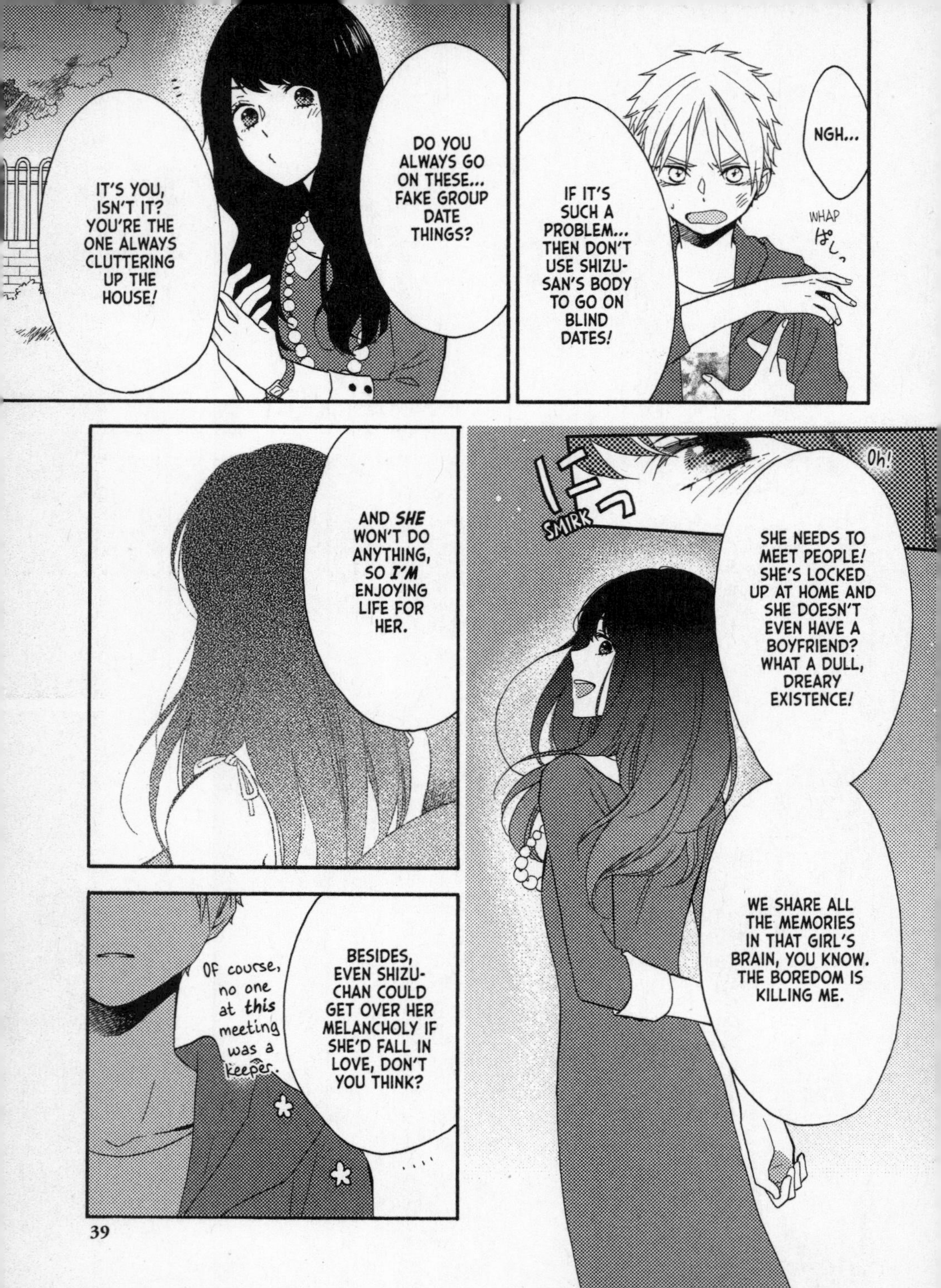
NGH...
IF IT'S SUCH A PROBLEM... THEN DON'T USE SHIZU-SAN'S BODY TO GO ON BLIND DATES!
WHAP
DO YOU ALWAYS GO ON THESE... FAKE GROUP DATE THINGS?
IT'S YOU, ISN'T IT? YOU'RE THE ONE ALWAYS CLUTTERING UP THE HOUSE!
Oh!
SMIRK
SHE NEEDS TO MEET PEOPLE! SHE'S LOCKED UP AT HOME AND SHE DOESN'T EVEN HAVE A BOYFRIEND? WHAT A DULL, DREARY EXISTENCE!
WE SHARE ALL THE MEMORIES IN THAT GIRL'S BRAIN, YOU KNOW. THE BOREDOM IS KILLING ME.
AND SHE WON'T DO ANYTHING, SO I'M ENJOYING LIFE FOR HER.
BESIDES, EVEN SHIZU-CHAN COULD GET OVER HER MELANCHOLY IF SHE'D FALL IN LOVE, DON'T YOU THINK?
Of course, no one at this meeting was a keeper.
....

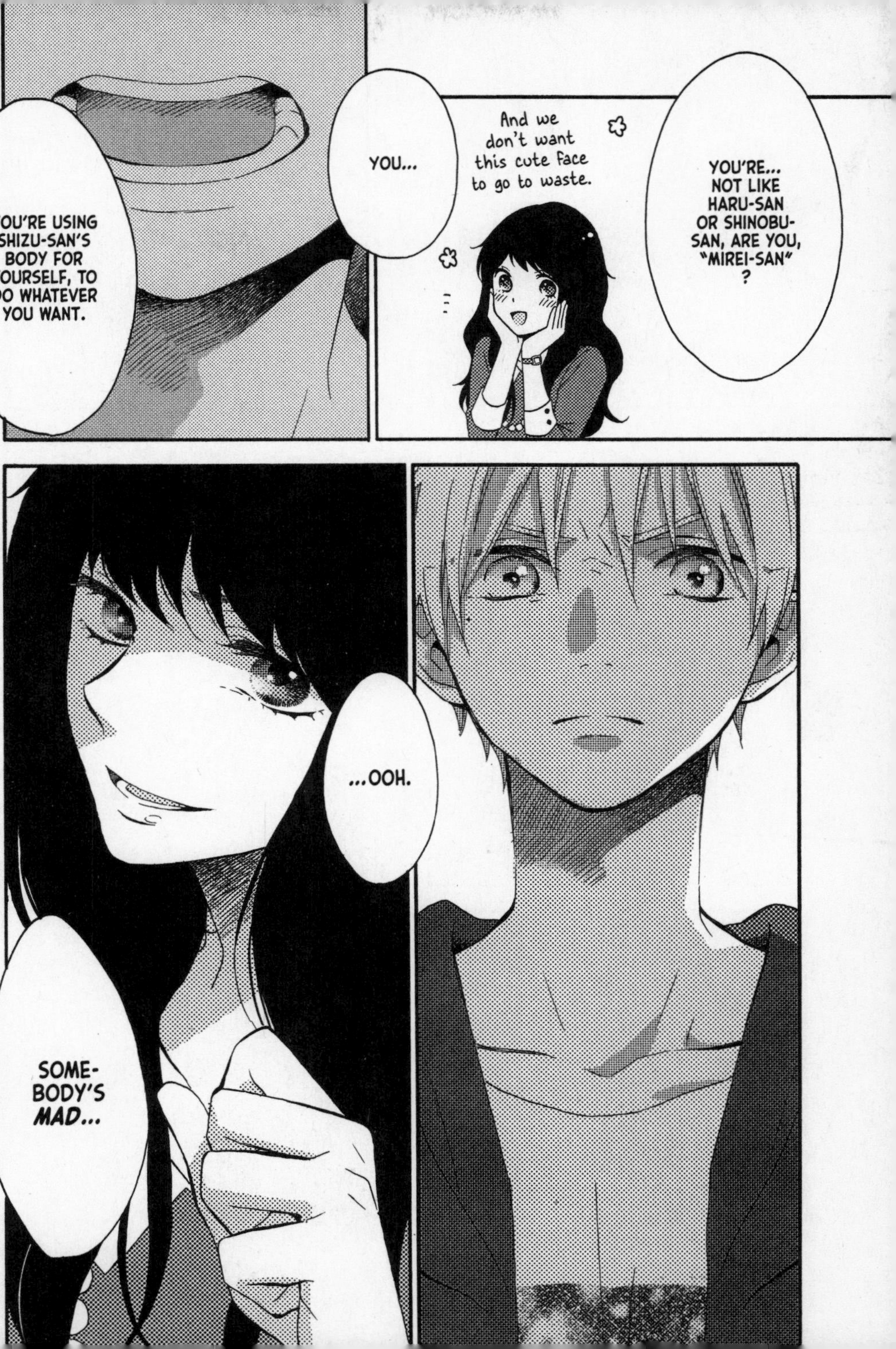
YOU'RE... NOT LIKE HARU-SAN OR SHINOBU-SAN, ARE YOU, "MIREI-SAN"?
And we don't want this cute face to go to waste.
YOU...
YOU'RE USING SHIZU-SAN'S BODY FOR YOURSELF, TO DO WHATEVER YOU WANT.
...OOH.
SOME-BODY'S *MAD*...

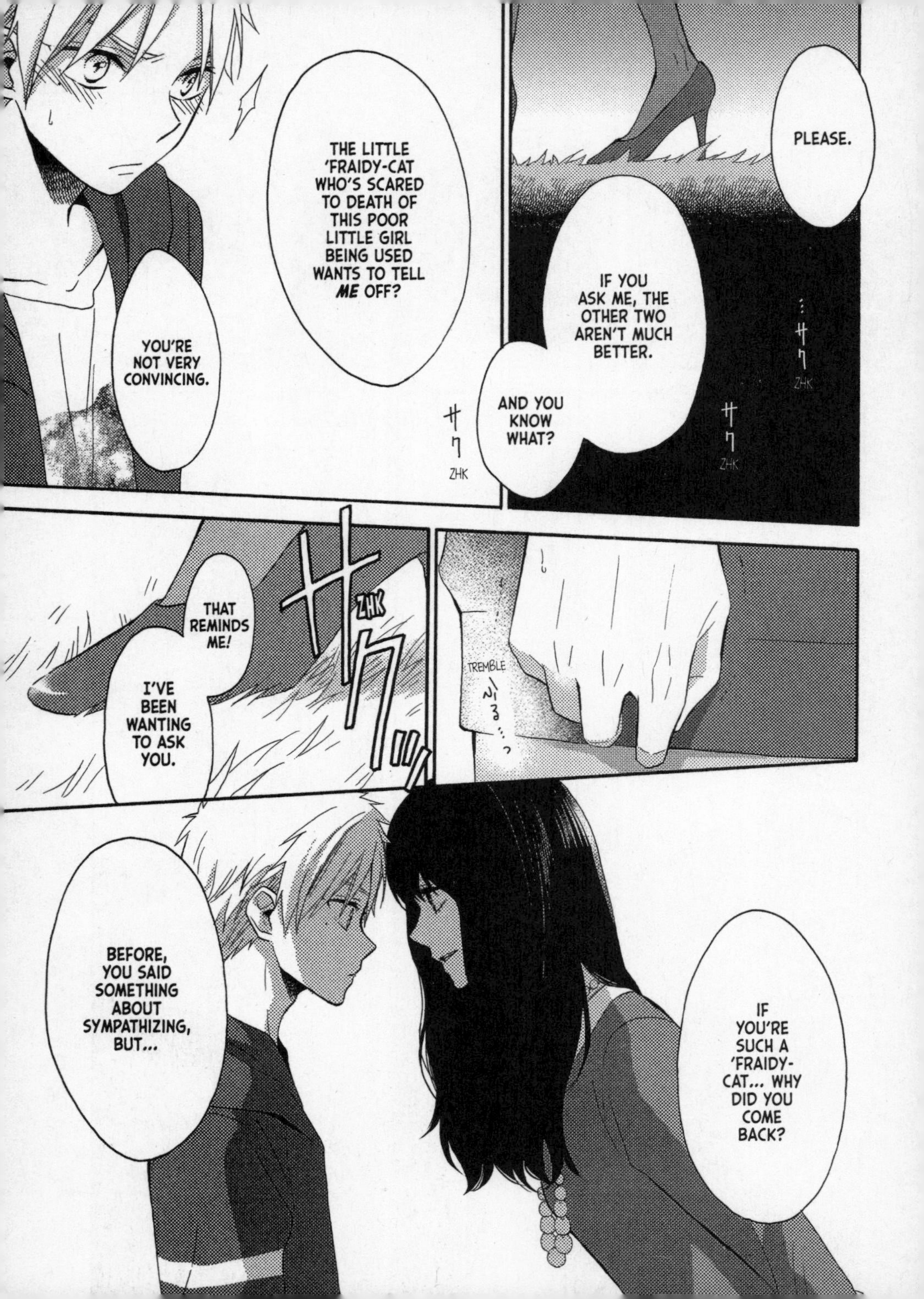
PLEASE.
IF YOU ASK ME, THE OTHER TWO AREN'T MUCH BETTER.
ZHK
ZHK
AND YOU KNOW WHAT?
ZHK
THE LITTLE 'FRAIDY-CAT WHO'S SCARED TO DEATH OF THIS POOR LITTLE GIRL BEING USED WANTS TO TELL *ME* OFF?
YOU'RE NOT VERY CONVINCING.
TREMBLE
ZHK
THAT REMINDS ME!
I'VE BEEN WANTING TO ASK YOU.
BEFORE, YOU SAID SOMETHING ABOUT SYMPATHIZING, BUT...
IF YOU'RE SUCH A 'FRAIDY-CAT... WHY DID YOU COME BACK?

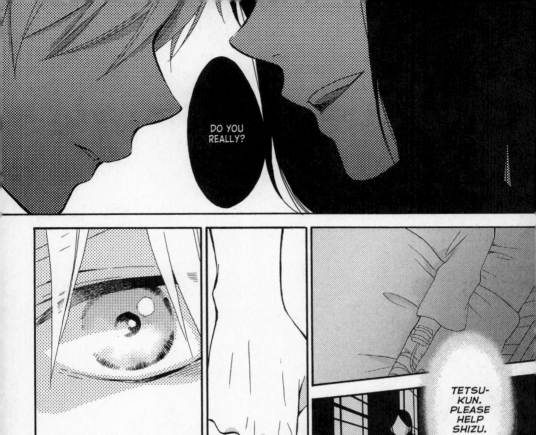

DO YOU REALLY?

CLENCH

...YES.

TETSU-KUN. PLEASE HELP SHIZU.

I KNOW IT'S NOT FAIR OF ME TO ASSUME, BUT I FEEL LIKE

IF ANYONE CAN HELP HER, IT'S YOU.

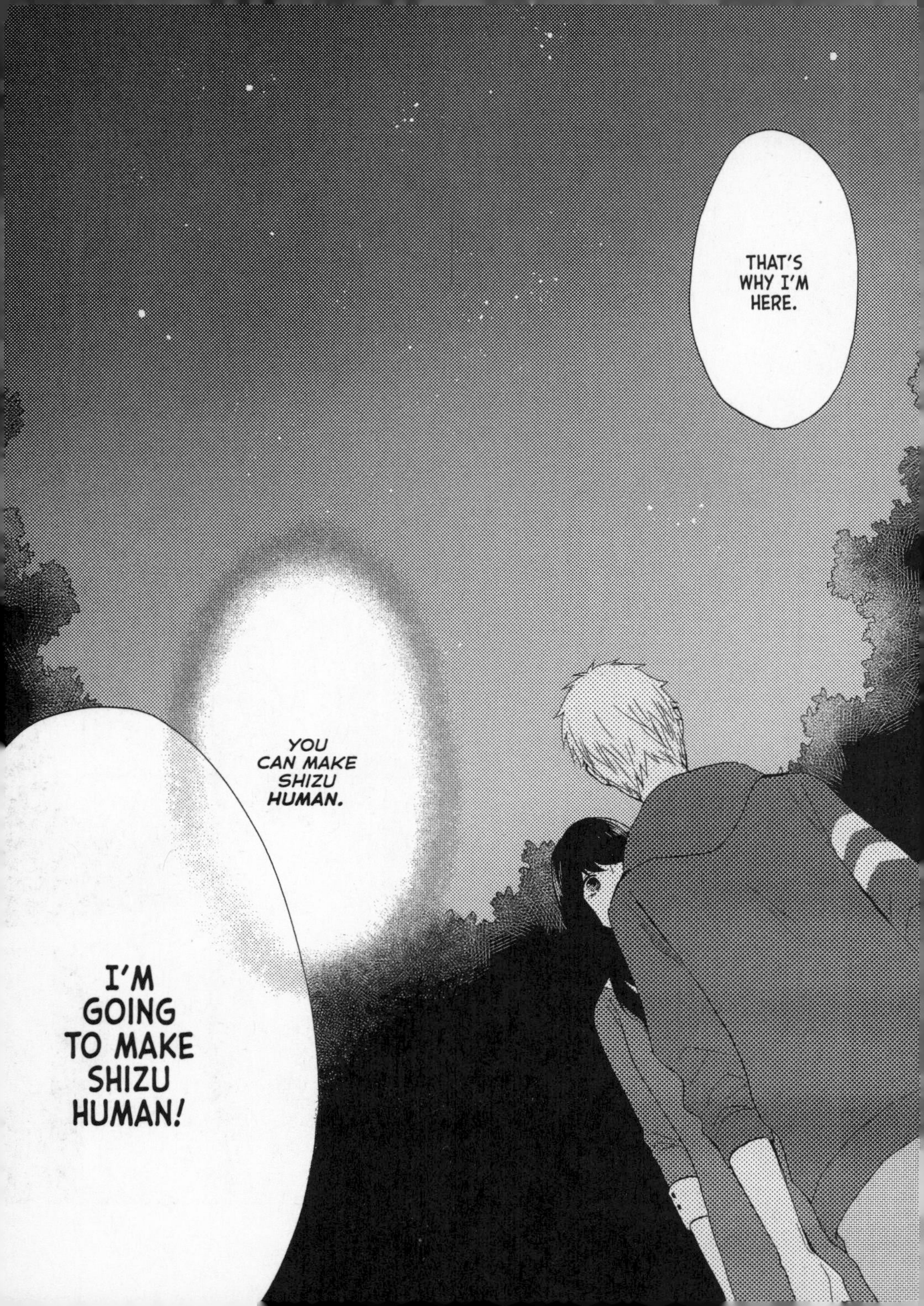
THAT'S WHY I'M HERE.
YOU CAN MAKE SHIZU HUMAN.
I'M GOING TO MAKE SHIZU HUMAN!

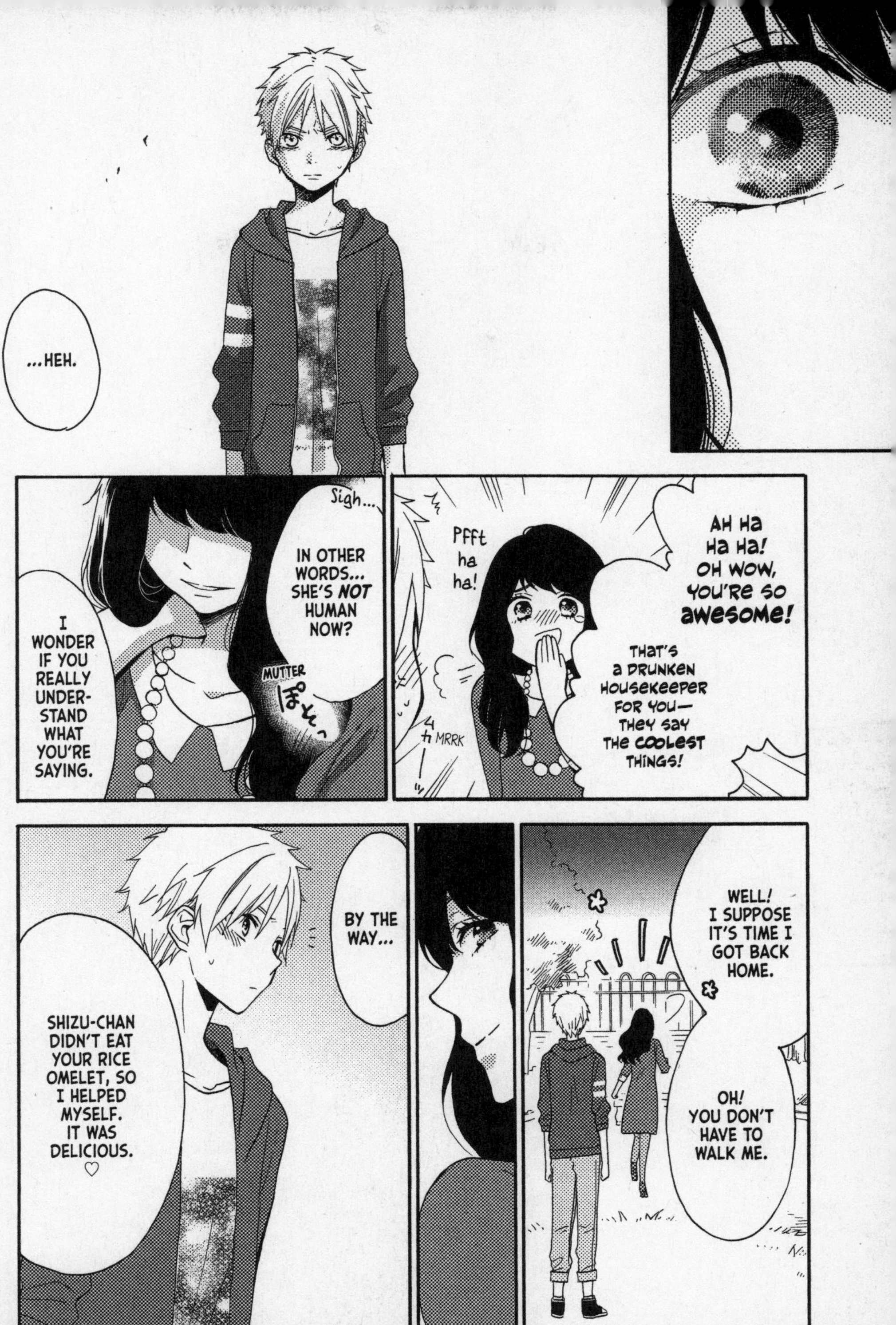
...HEH.
AH HA HA HA! OH WOW, YOU'RE SO AWESOME!
Pfft ha ha!
THAT'S A DRUNKEN HOUSEKEEPER FOR YOU— THEY SAY THE COOLEST THINGS!
MRRK
Sigh...
IN OTHER WORDS... SHE'S NOT HUMAN NOW?
MUTTER ぽそっ
I WONDER IF YOU REALLY UNDERSTAND WHAT YOU'RE SAYING.
WELL! I SUPPOSE IT'S TIME I GOT BACK HOME.
OH! YOU DON'T HAVE TO WALK ME.
BY THE WAY...
SHIZU-CHAN DIDN'T EAT YOUR RICE OMELET, SO I HELPED MYSELF. IT WAS DELICIOUS. ♡

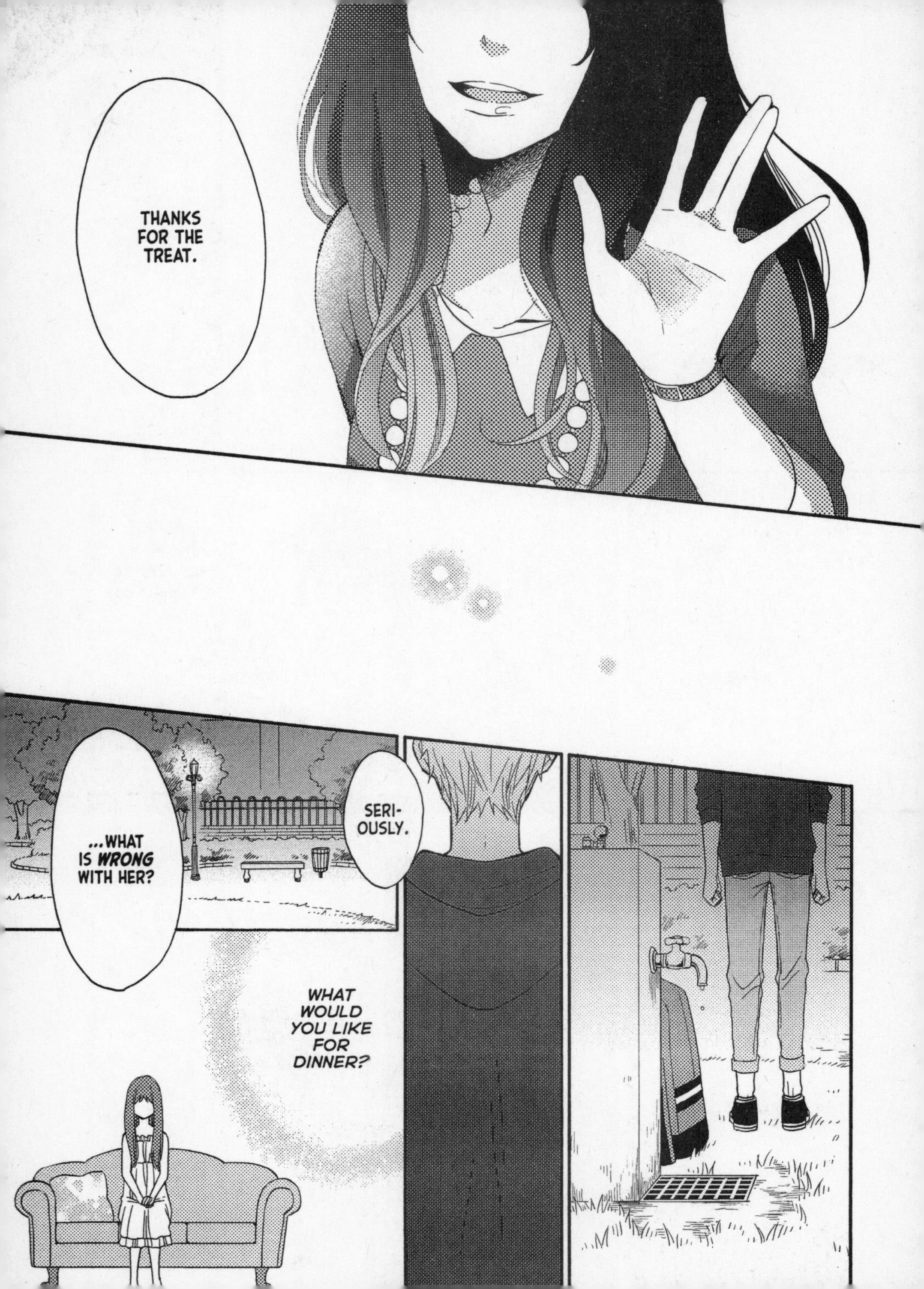
THANKS FOR THE TREAT.
SERI-OUSLY.
...WHAT IS *WRONG* WITH HER?
WHAT WOULD YOU LIKE FOR DINNER?

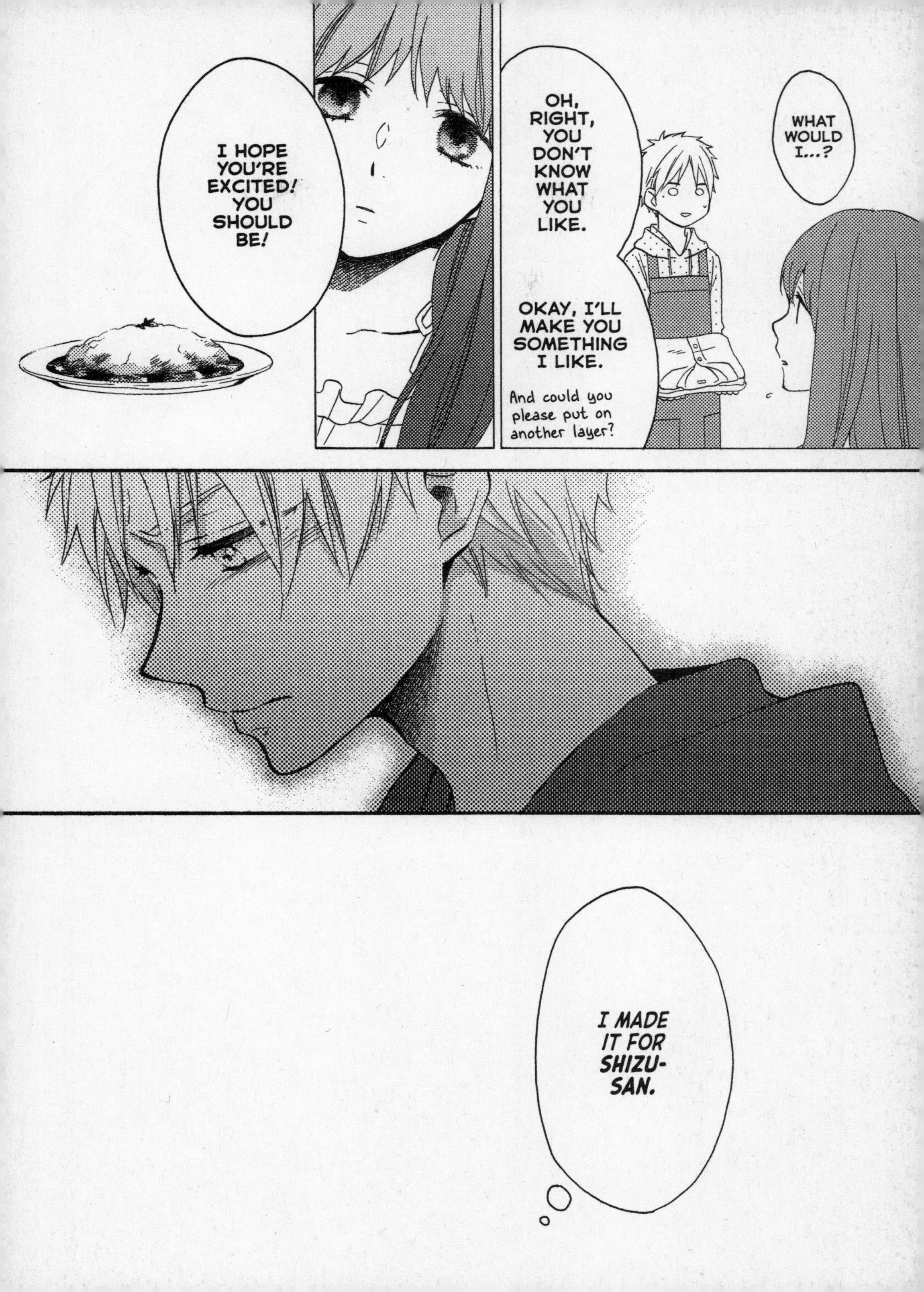
WHAT WOULD I...?
OH, RIGHT, YOU DON'T KNOW WHAT YOU LIKE.
OKAY, I'LL MAKE YOU SOMETHING I LIKE.
And could you please put on another layer?
I HOPE YOU'RE EXCITED! YOU SHOULD BE!
I MADE IT FOR SHIZU-SAN.

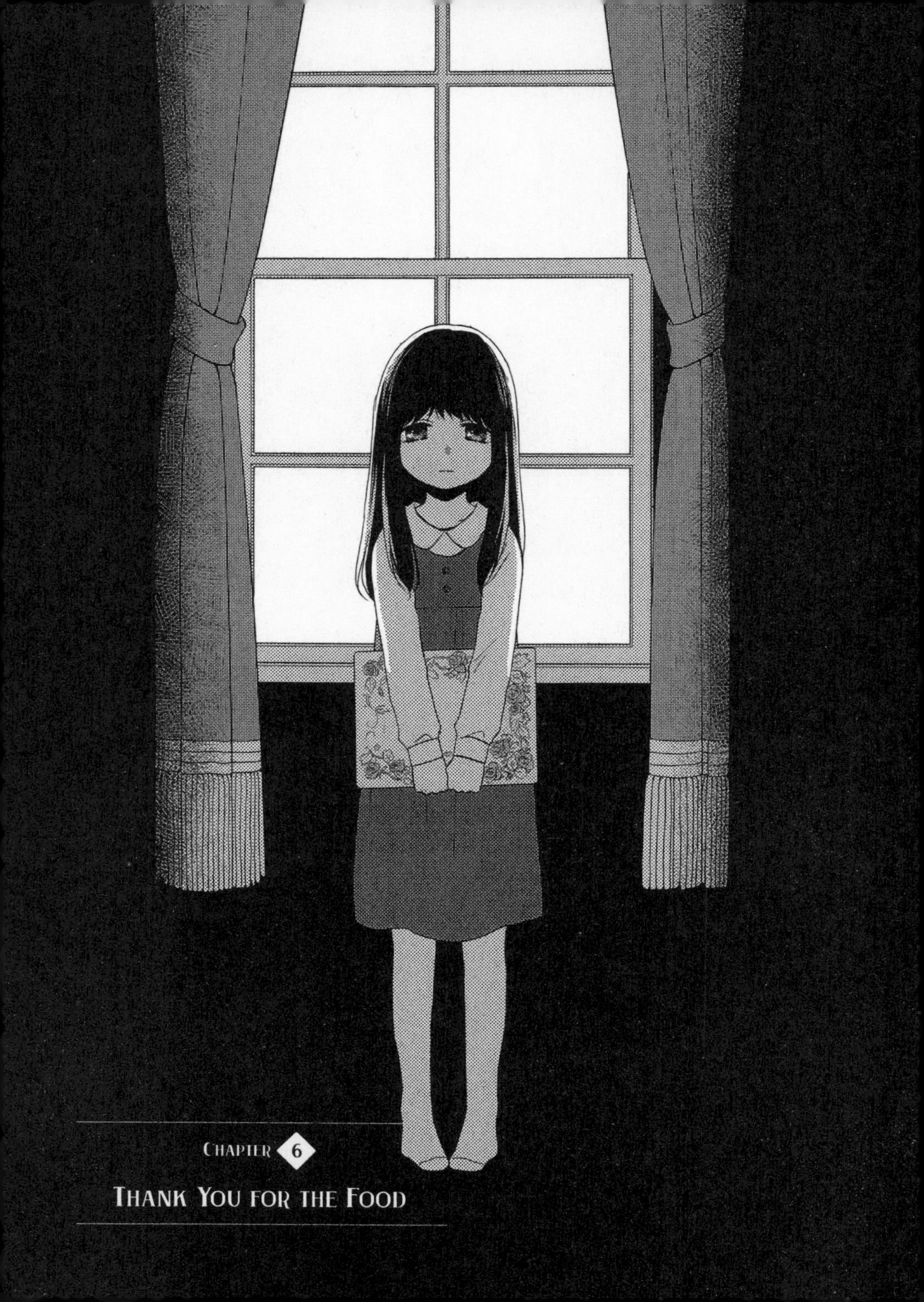

Chapter 6

Thank You for the Food

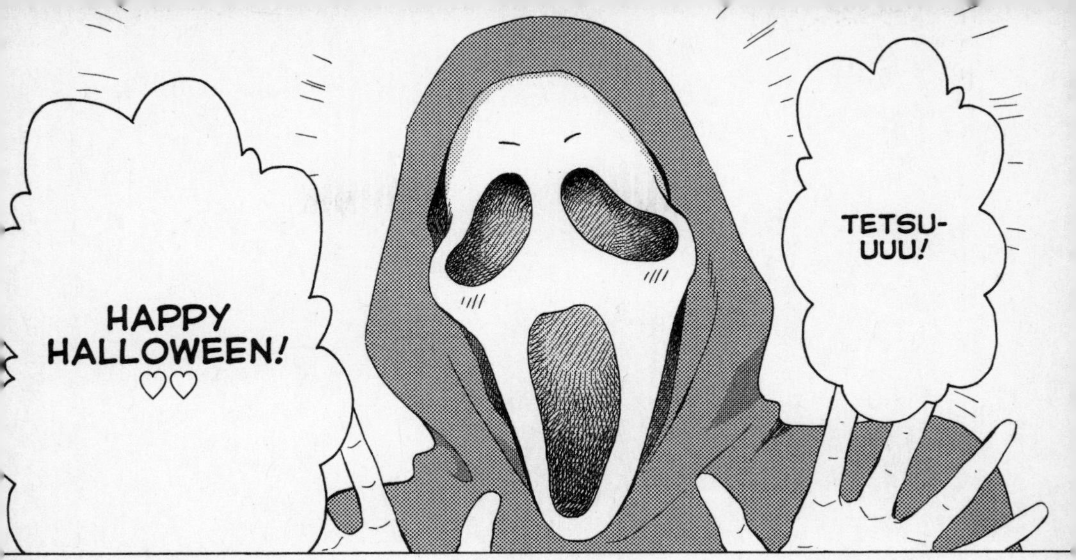
TETSU-UUU!
HAPPY HALLOWEEN! ♡♡

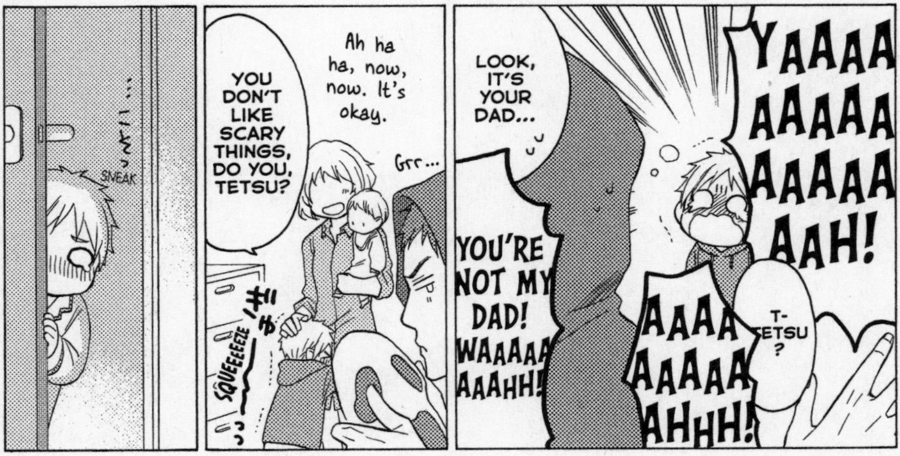
YAAAA AAAAA AAAAA AAH!
T-TETSU?
AAAA AAAAA AHHHH!
LOOK, IT'S YOUR DAD...
YOU'RE NOT MY DAD! WAAAAAAAAHH!
Ah ha ha, now, now. It's okay.
YOU DON'T LIKE SCARY THINGS, DO YOU, TETSU?
Grr...
SQUEEEEEZE
SNEAK

Wake Up, Sleeping Beauty

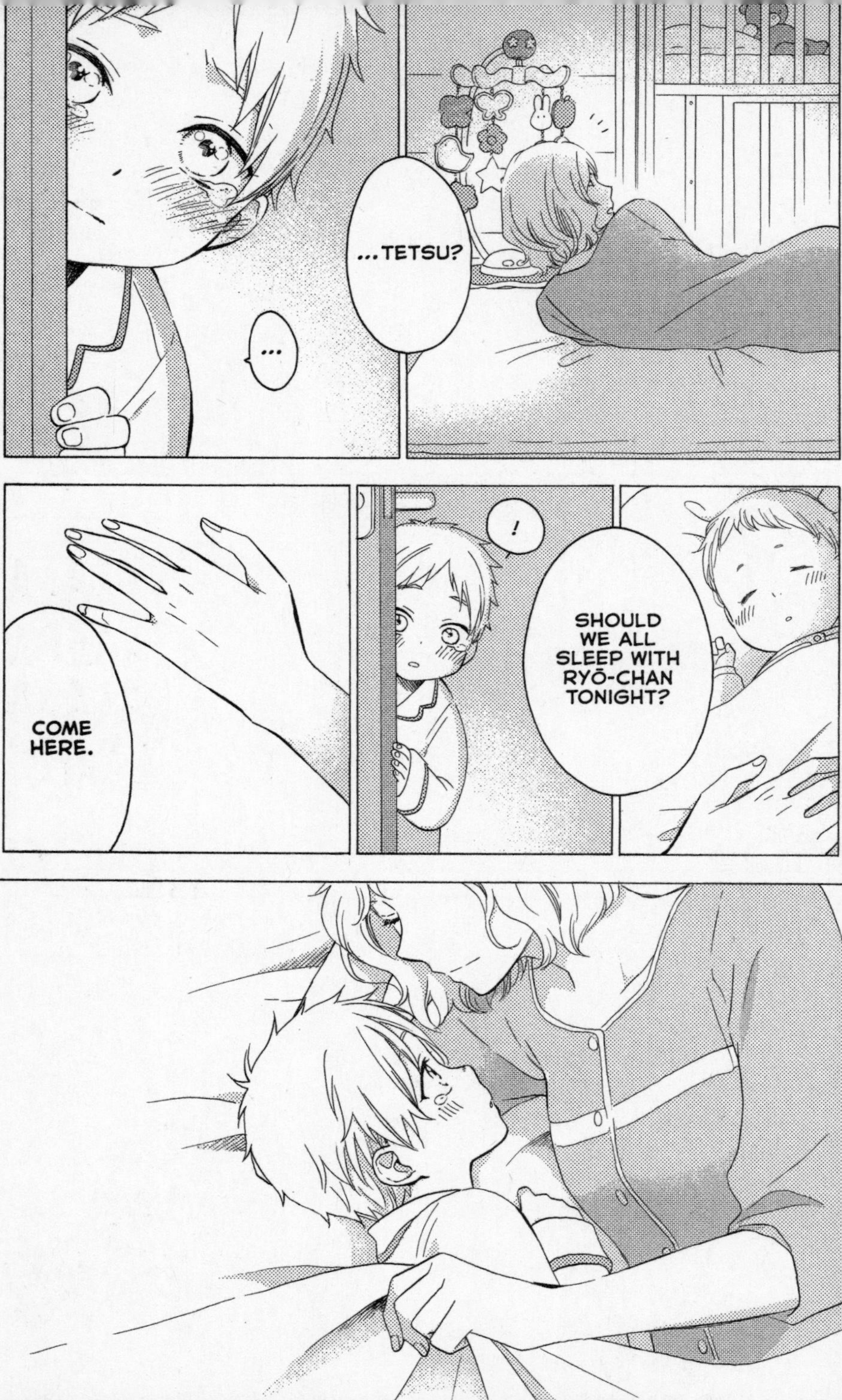
...TETSU?
...
SHOULD WE ALL SLEEP WITH RYŌ-CHAN TONIGHT?
!
COME HERE.

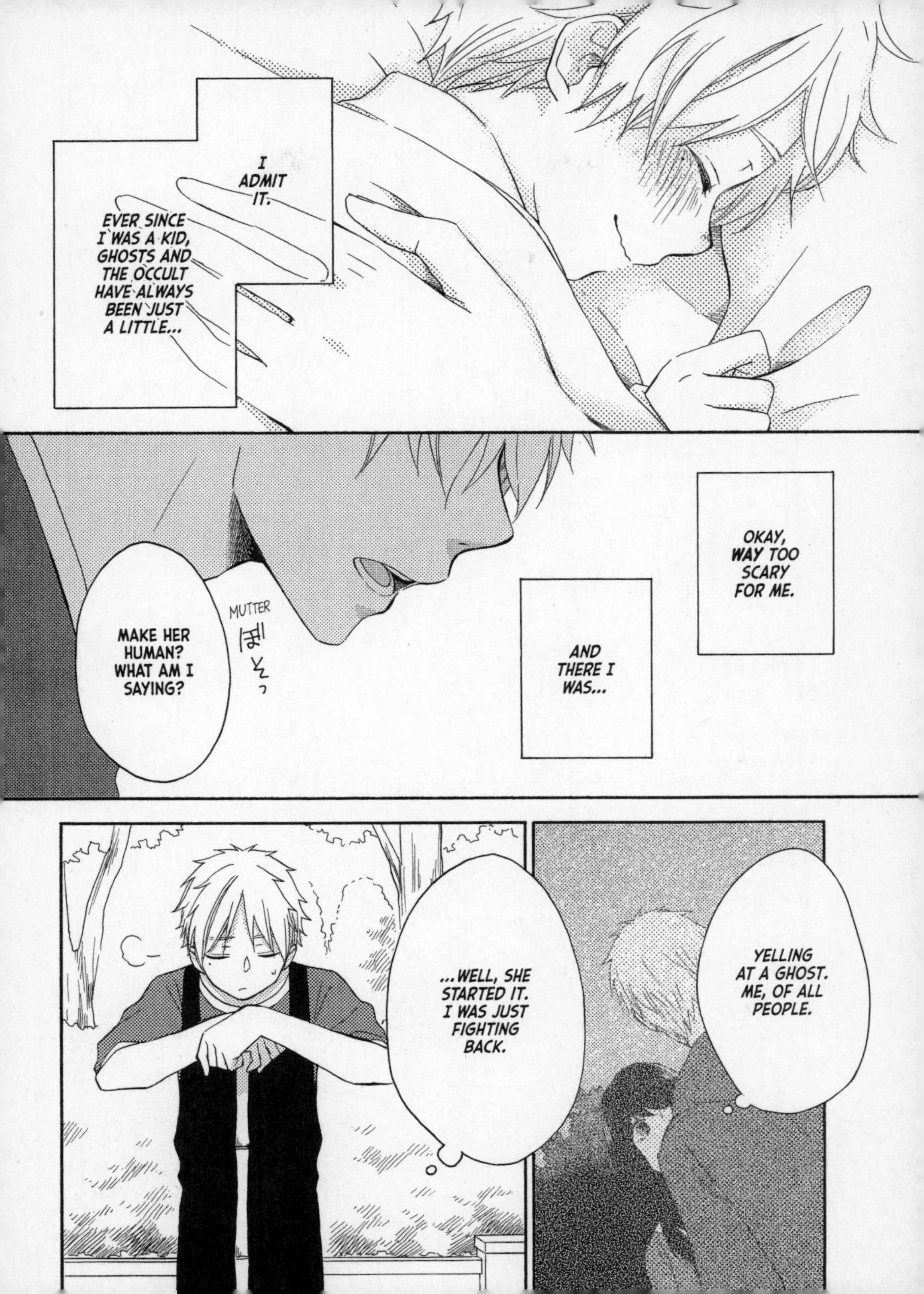
I ADMIT IT.
EVER SINCE I WAS A KID, GHOSTS AND THE OCCULT HAVE ALWAYS BEEN JUST A LITTLE...
OKAY, WAY TOO SCARY FOR ME.
AND THERE I WAS...
MUTTER
ぼそっ
MAKE HER HUMAN? WHAT AM I SAYING?
YELLING AT A GHOST. ME, OF ALL PEOPLE.
...WELL, SHE STARTED IT. I WAS JUST FIGHTING BACK.

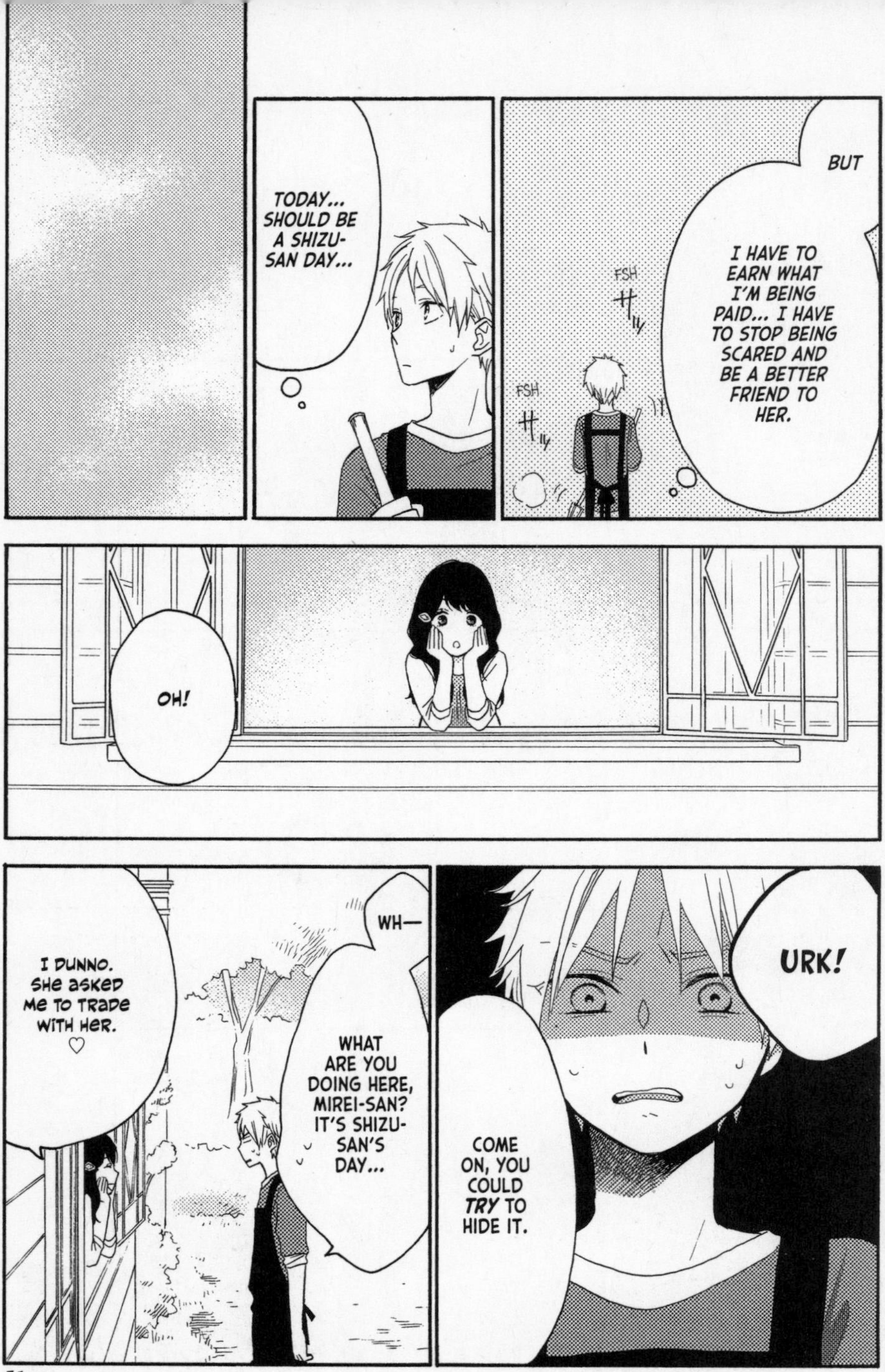
BUT
I HAVE TO EARN WHAT I'M BEING PAID... I HAVE TO STOP BEING SCARED AND BE A BETTER FRIEND TO HER.
FSH
FSH
TODAY... SHOULD BE A SHIZU-SAN DAY...
OH!
URK!
COME ON, YOU COULD *TRY* TO HIDE IT.
WH—
WHAT ARE YOU DOING HERE, MIREI-SAN? IT'S SHIZU-SAN'S DAY...
I DUNNO. SHE ASKED ME TO TRADE WITH HER. ♡

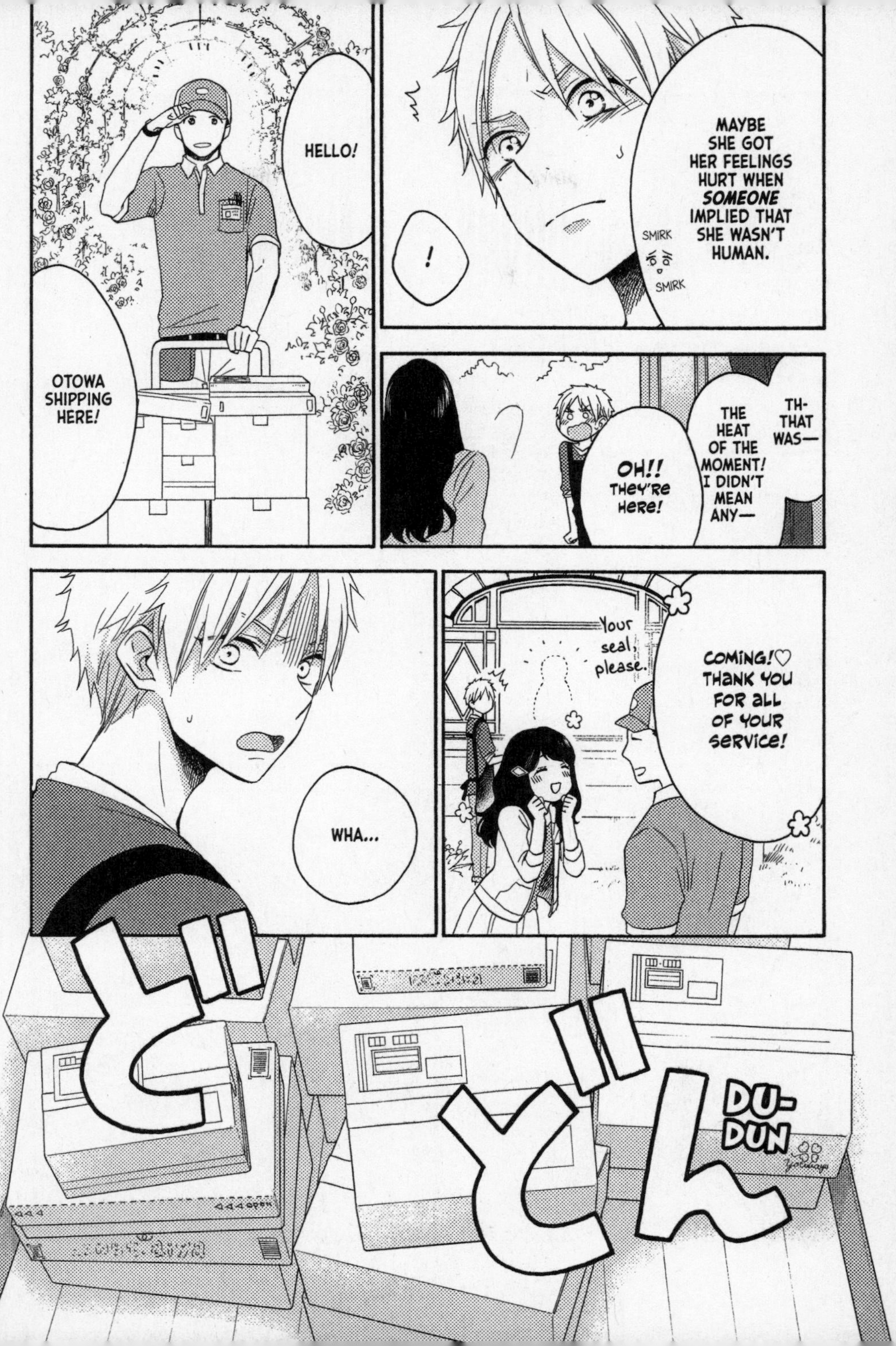

MAYBE SHE GOT HER FEELINGS HURT WHEN *SOMEONE* IMPLIED THAT SHE WASN'T HUMAN.
SMIRK SMIRK
!
TH-THAT WAS—
THE HEAT OF THE MOMENT! I DIDN'T MEAN ANY—
OH!! They're here!
HELLO!
OTOWA SHIPPING HERE!
Your seal, please.
COMING!♡ THANK YOU FOR ALL OF YOUR SERVICE!
WHA...
DU-DUN

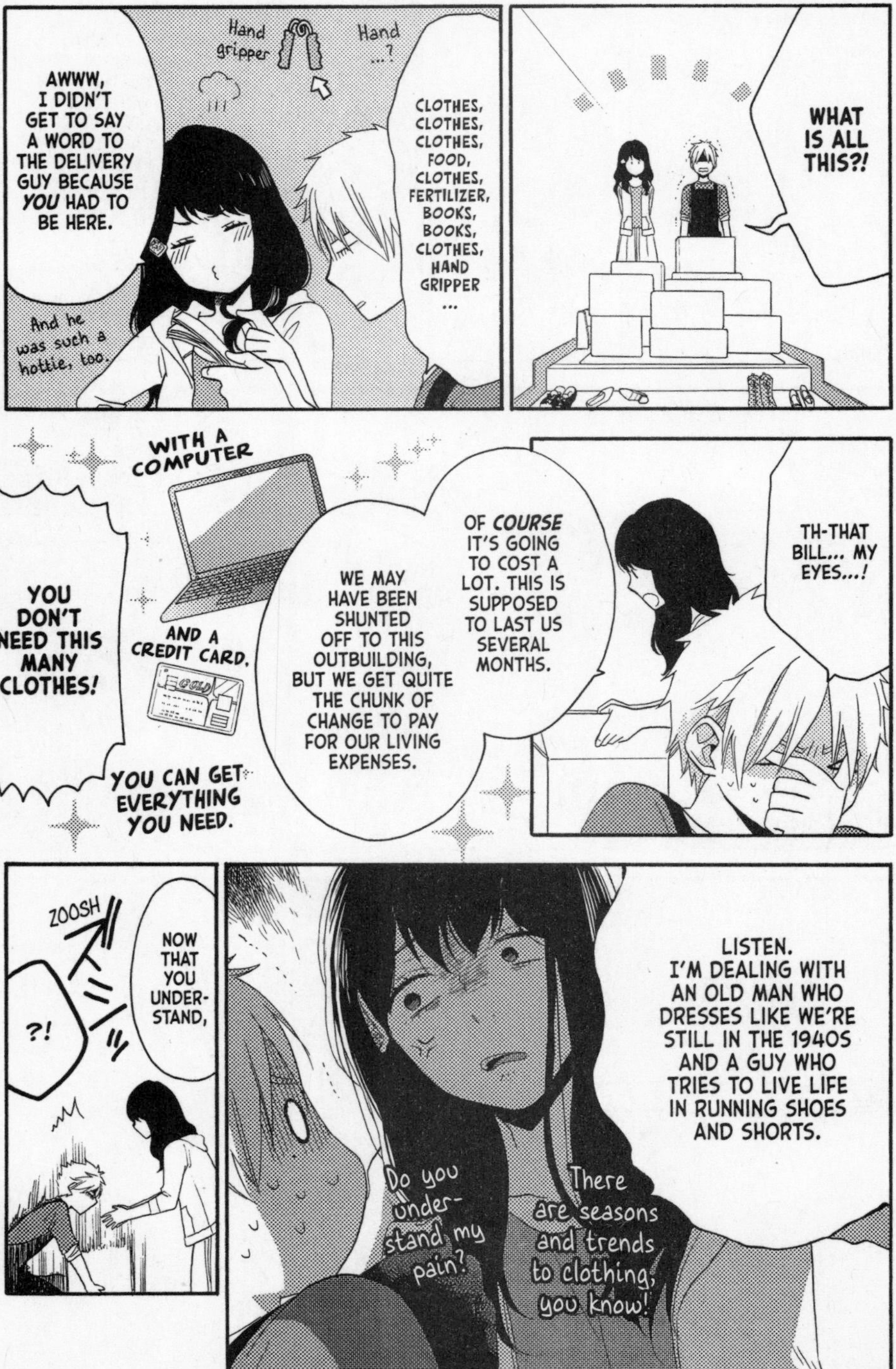
WHAT IS ALL THIS?!
Hand ...?
Hand gripper
CLOTHES, CLOTHES, CLOTHES, FOOD, CLOTHES, FERTILIZER, BOOKS, BOOKS, CLOTHES, HAND GRIPPER ...
AWWW, I DIDN'T GET TO SAY A WORD TO THE DELIVERY GUY BECAUSE *YOU* HAD TO BE HERE.
And he was such a hottie, too.
TH-THAT BILL... MY EYES...!
OF *COURSE* IT'S GOING TO COST A LOT. THIS IS SUPPOSED TO LAST US SEVERAL MONTHS.
WE MAY HAVE BEEN SHUNTED OFF TO THIS OUTBUILDING, BUT WE GET QUITE THE CHUNK OF CHANGE TO PAY FOR OUR LIVING EXPENSES.
WITH A COMPUTER
AND A CREDIT CARD.
GOLD
YOU CAN GET EVERYTHING YOU NEED.
YOU DON'T NEED THIS MANY CLOTHES!
LISTEN. I'M DEALING WITH AN OLD MAN WHO DRESSES LIKE WE'RE STILL IN THE 1940S AND A GUY WHO TRIES TO LIVE LIFE IN RUNNING SHOES AND SHORTS.
There are seasons and trends to clothing, you know!
Do you under-stand my pain?
NOW THAT YOU UNDER-STAND,
ZOOSH
?!

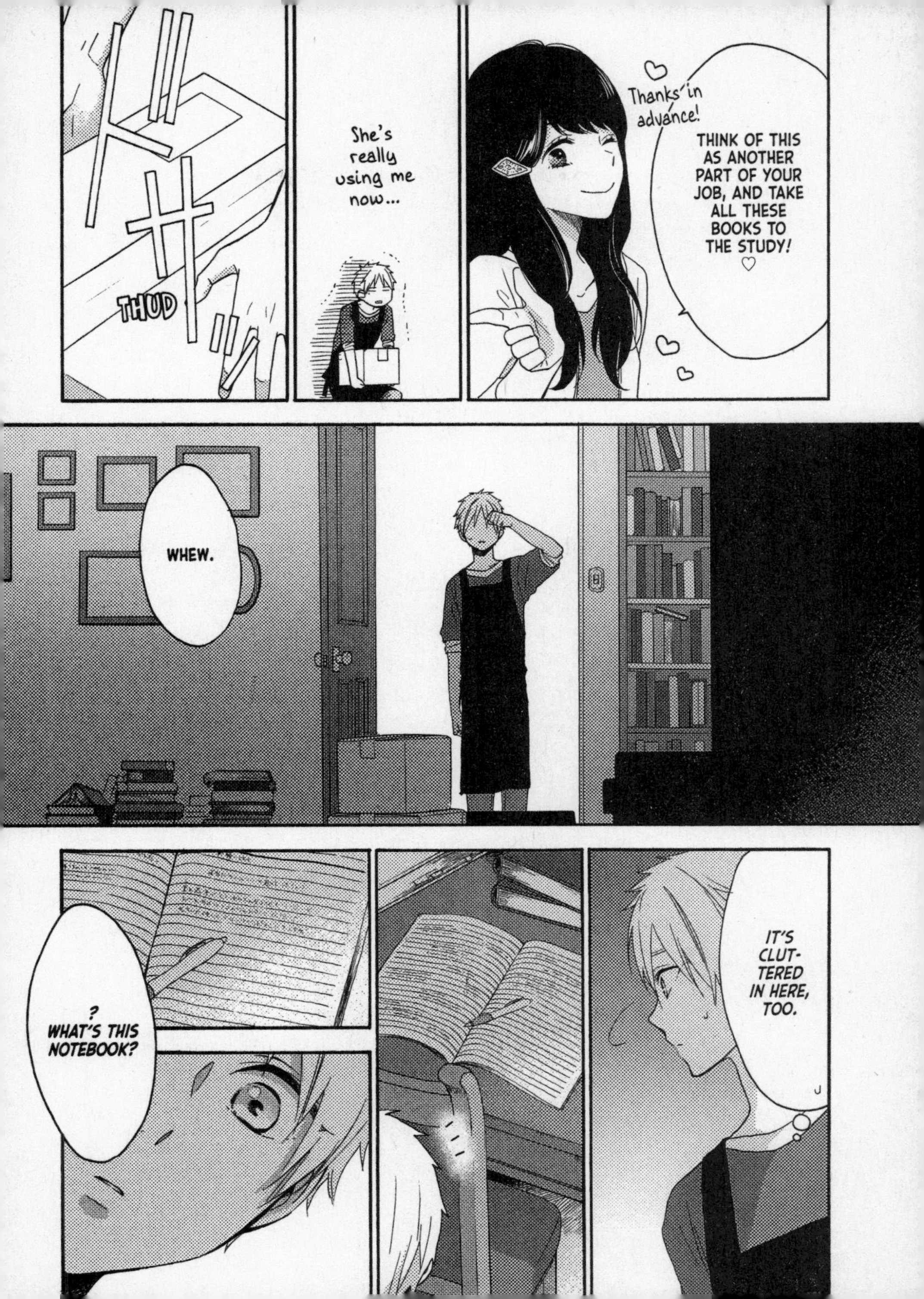
Thanks in advance!
THINK OF THIS AS ANOTHER PART OF YOUR JOB, AND TAKE ALL THESE BOOKS TO THE STUDY! ♡
She's really using me now...
THUD
WHEW.
IT'S CLUT-TERED IN HERE, TOO.
? WHAT'S THIS NOTEBOOK?

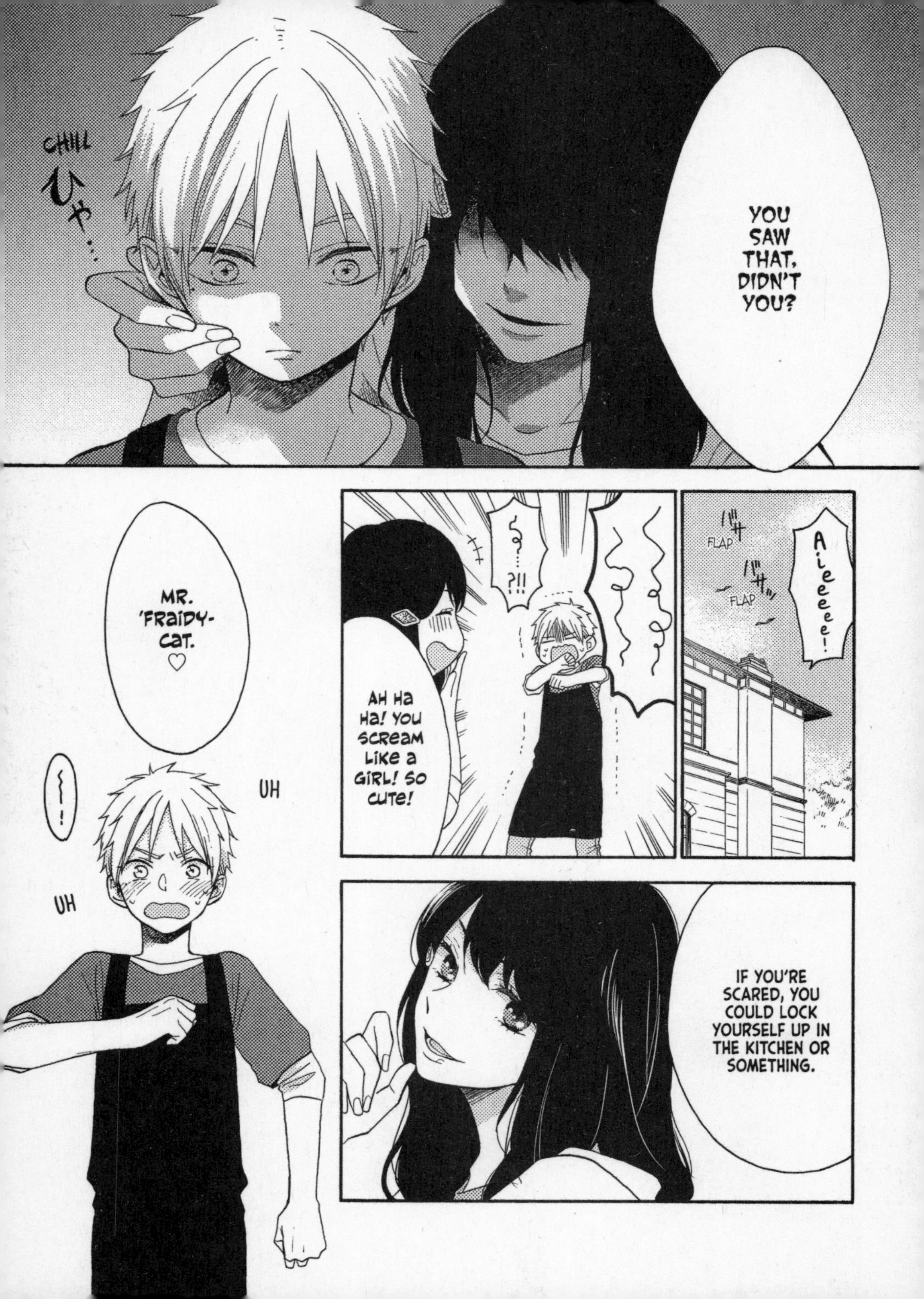
YOU SAW THAT, DIDN'T YOU?
CHILL
ひや…
FLAP
A-ieeeee!
FLAP
?!!
AH HA HA! YOU SCREAM LIKE A GIRL! SO CUTE!
IF YOU'RE SCARED, YOU COULD LOCK YOURSELF UP IN THE KITCHEN OR SOMETHING.
MR. 'FRAIDY-CAT. ♡
UH
UH

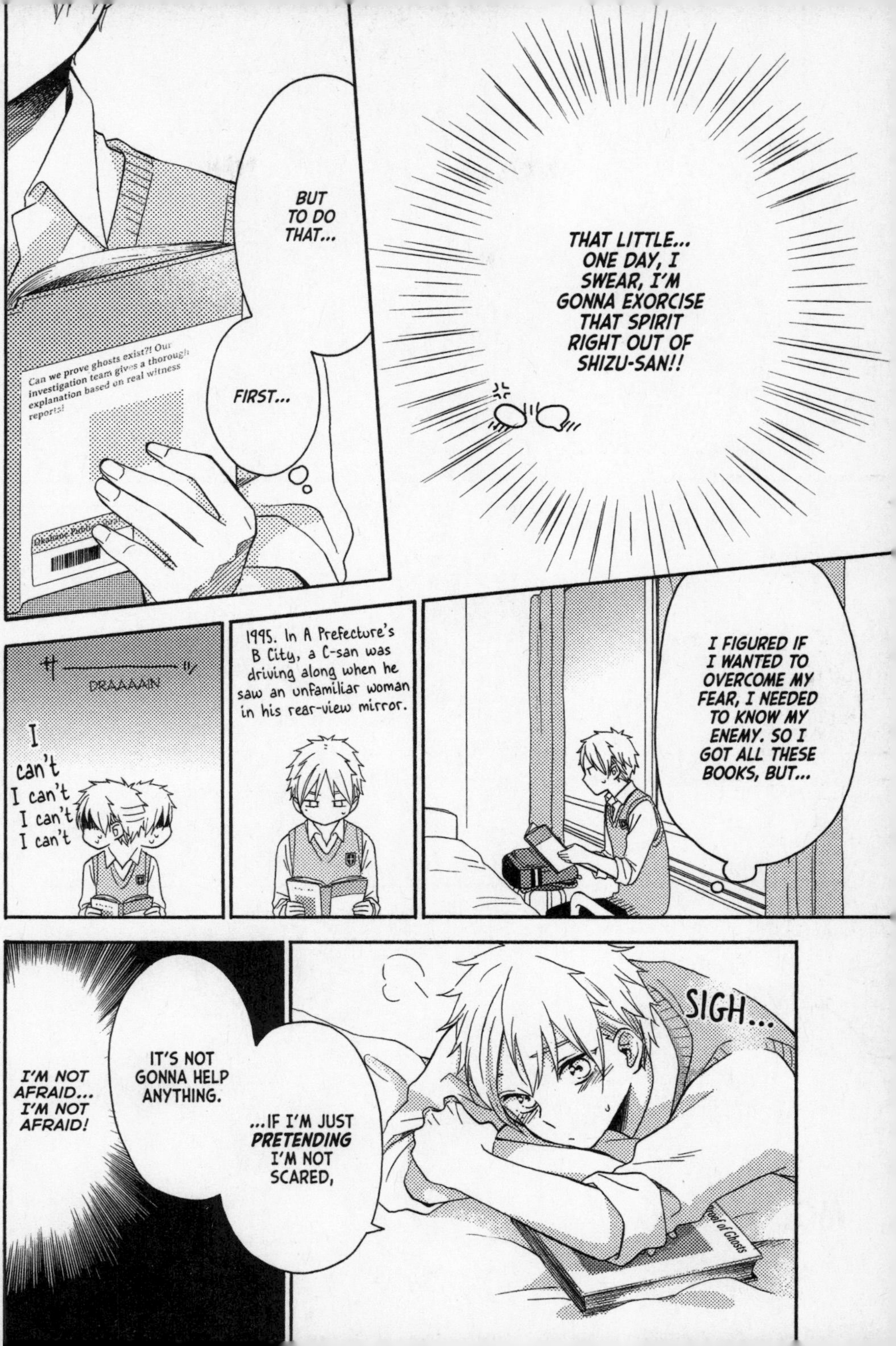
THAT LITTLE... ONE DAY, I SWEAR, I'M GONNA EXORCISE THAT SPIRIT RIGHT OUT OF SHIZU-SAN!!
BUT TO DO THAT...
FIRST...
Can we prove ghosts exist?! Our investigation team gives a thorough explanation based on real witness reports!
I FIGURED IF I WANTED TO OVERCOME MY FEAR, I NEEDED TO KNOW MY ENEMY. SO I GOT ALL THESE BOOKS, BUT...
1995. In A Prefecture's B City, a C-san was driving along when he saw an unfamiliar woman in his rear-view mirror.
DRAAAAIN
I can't I can't I can't I can't
SIGH...
...IF I'M JUST PRETENDING I'M NOT SCARED,
IT'S NOT GONNA HELP ANYTHING.
I'M NOT AFRAID... I'M NOT AFRAID!

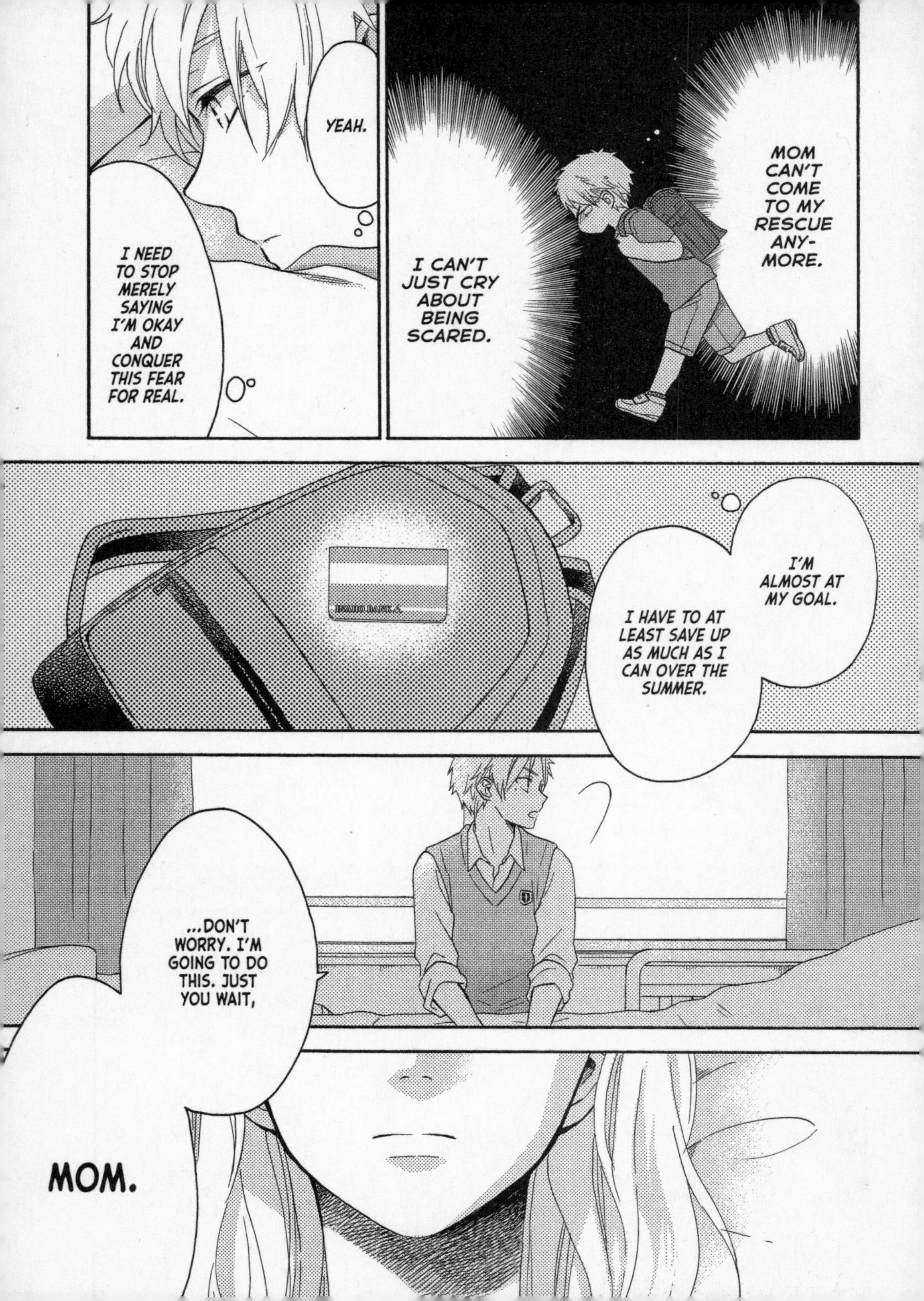
MOM CAN'T COME TO MY RESCUE ANYMORE.
I CAN'T JUST CRY ABOUT BEING SCARED.
YEAH.
I NEED TO STOP MERELY SAYING I'M OKAY AND CONQUER THIS FEAR FOR REAL.
I'M ALMOST AT MY GOAL.
I HAVE TO AT LEAST SAVE UP AS MUCH AS I CAN OVER THE SUMMER.
...DON'T WORRY. I'M GOING TO DO THIS. JUST YOU WAIT,
MOM.

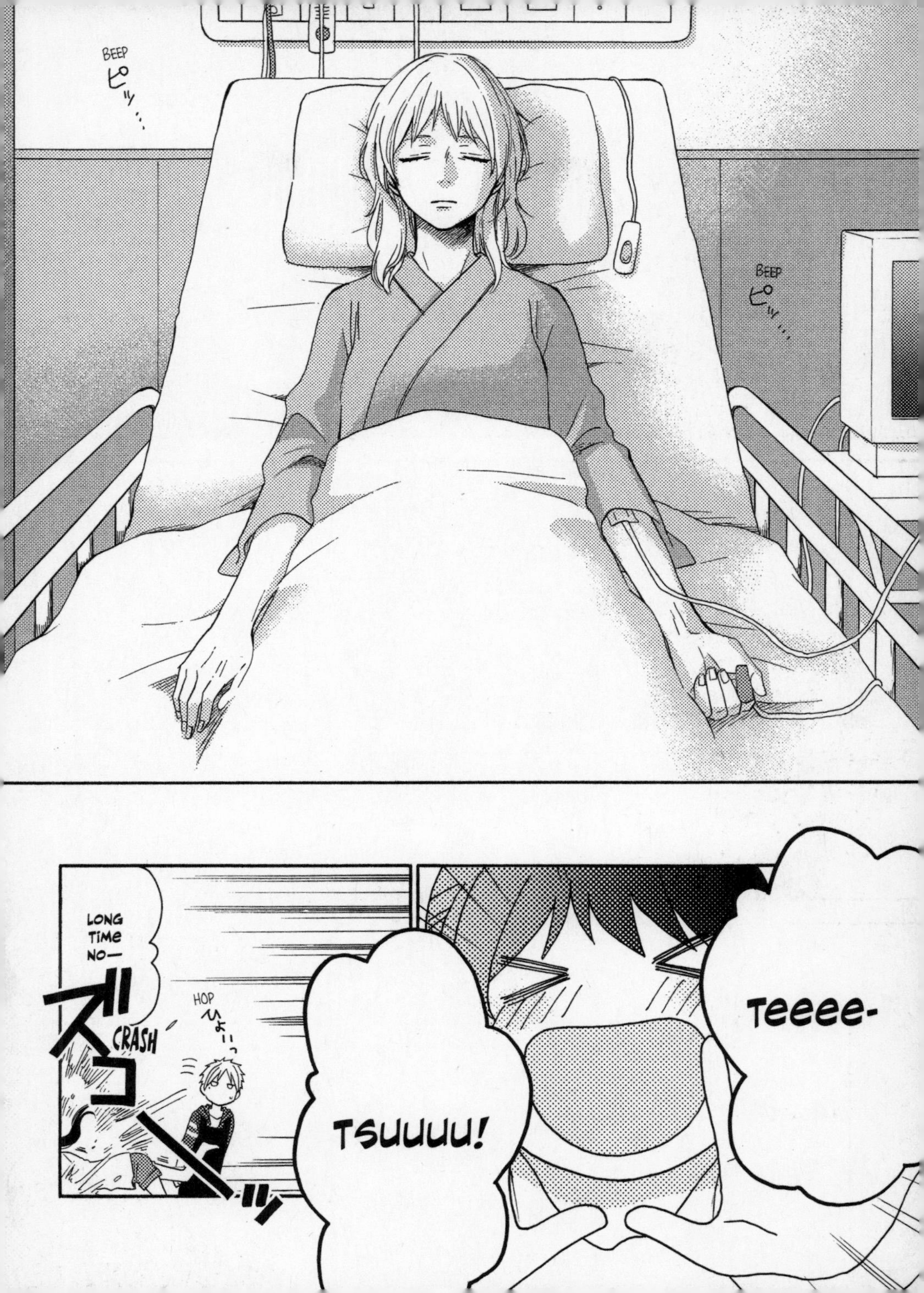
BEEP
ピッ…
BEEP
ピッ…
Teeee-
Tsuuuu!
LONG TIME NO—
HOP
ひょこっ
CRASH
ズコーッ

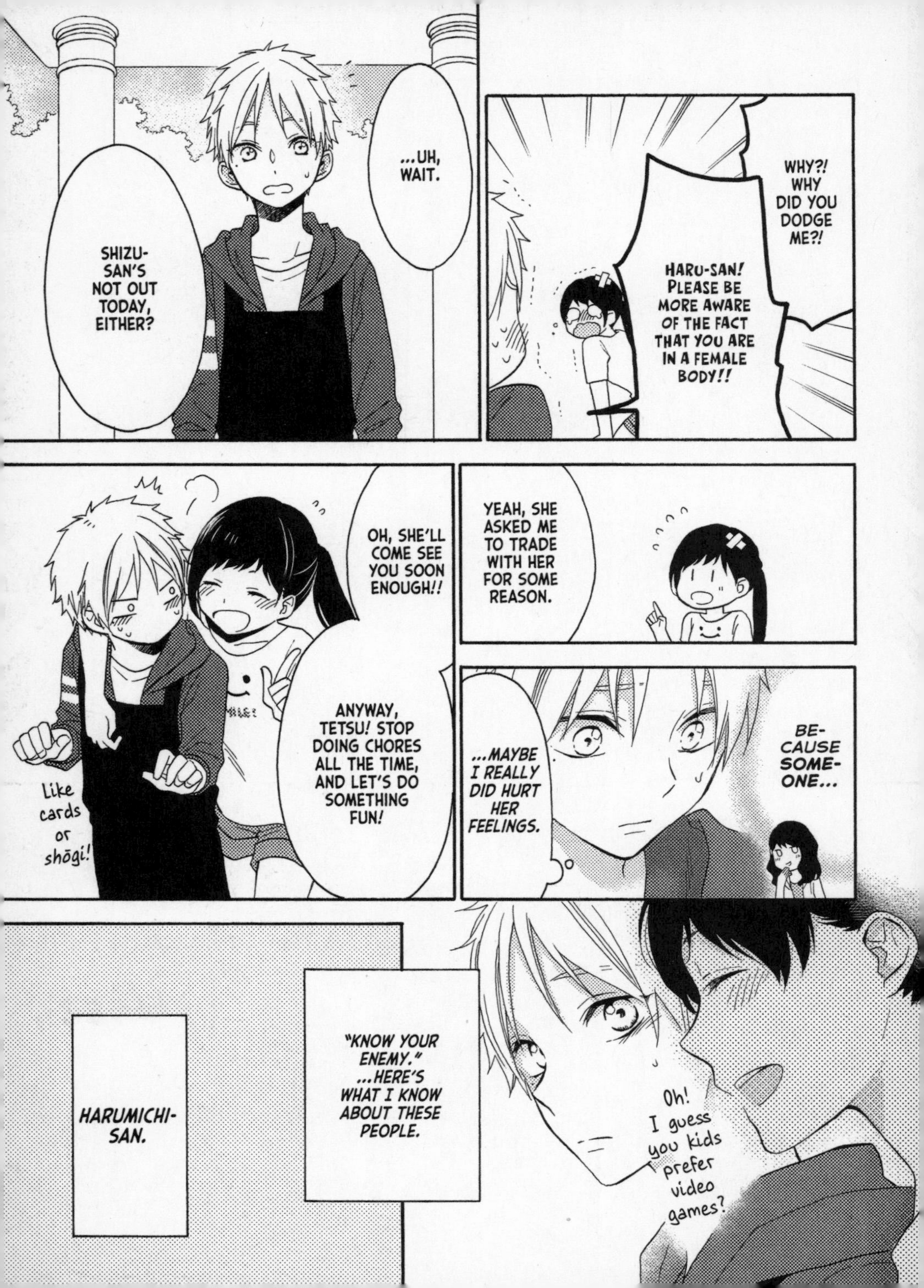
WHY?! WHY DID YOU DODGE ME?!
HARU-SAN! PLEASE BE MORE AWARE OF THE FACT THAT YOU ARE IN A FEMALE BODY!!
...UH, WAIT.
SHIZU-SAN'S NOT OUT TODAY, EITHER?
YEAH, SHE ASKED ME TO TRADE WITH HER FOR SOME REASON.
BE-CAUSE SOME-ONE...
...MAYBE I REALLY DID HURT HER FEELINGS.
OH, SHE'LL COME SEE YOU SOON ENOUGH!!
ANYWAY, TETSU! STOP DOING CHORES ALL THE TIME, AND LET'S DO SOMETHING FUN!
Like cards or shōgi!
Oh! I guess you kids prefer video games?
"KNOW YOUR ENEMY." ...HERE'S WHAT I KNOW ABOUT THESE PEOPLE.
HARUMICHI-SAN.

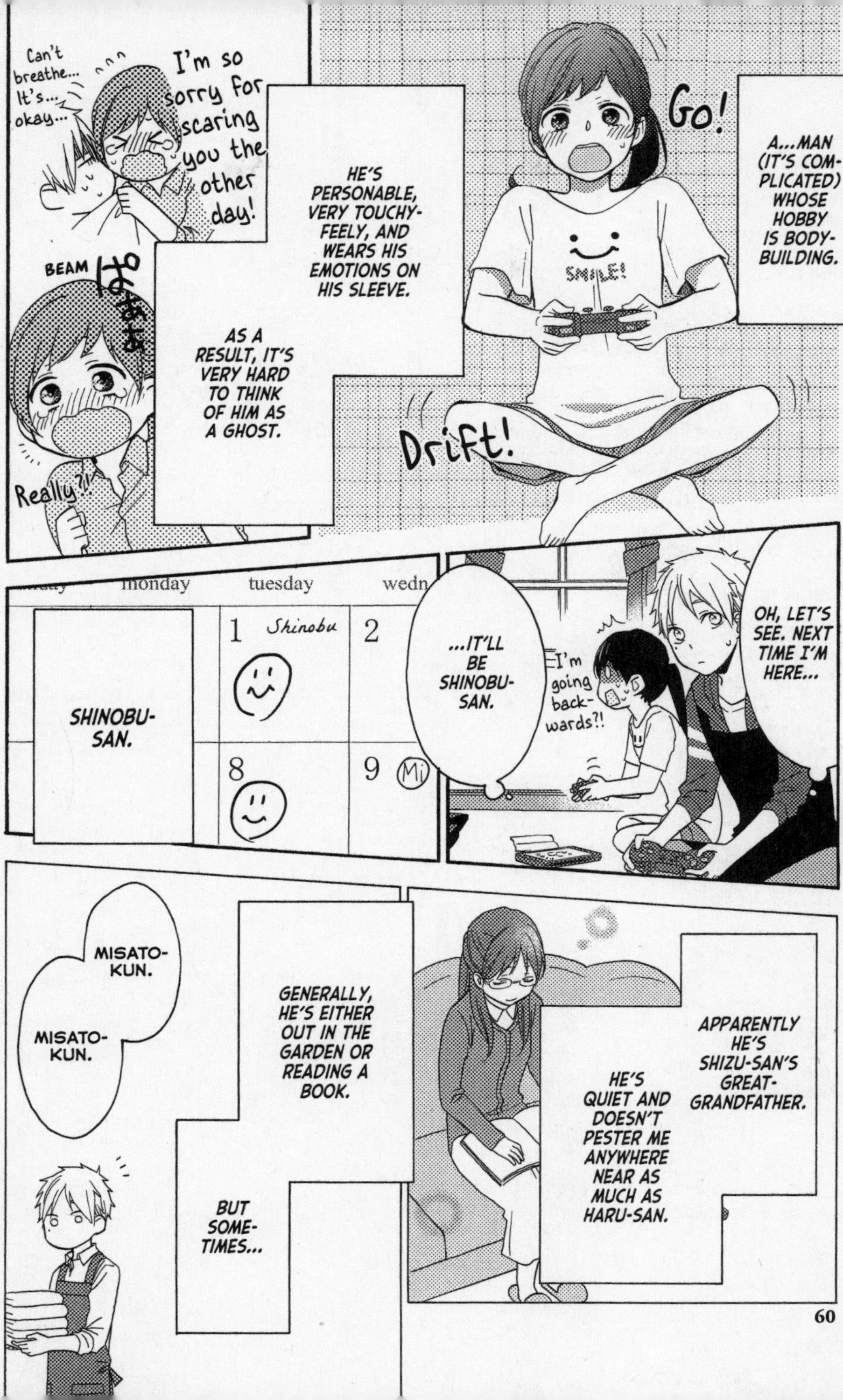
A...MAN (IT'S COMPLICATED) WHOSE HOBBY IS BODY-BUILDING.
Go!
Drift!
HE'S PERSONABLE, VERY TOUCHY-FEELY, AND WEARS HIS EMOTIONS ON HIS SLEEVE.
AS A RESULT, IT'S VERY HARD TO THINK OF HIM AS A GHOST.
I'm so sorry for scaring you the other day!
Can't breathe... It's... okay...
BEAM
Really?!
OH, LET'S SEE. NEXT TIME I'M HERE...
I'm going backwards?!
...IT'LL BE SHINOBU-SAN.
monday
tuesday
wedn
1
Shinobu
2
8
9
Mi
SHINOBU-SAN.
APPARENTLY HE'S SHIZU-SAN'S GREAT-GRANDFATHER.
HE'S QUIET AND DOESN'T PESTER ME ANYWHERE NEAR AS MUCH AS HARU-SAN.
GENERALLY, HE'S EITHER OUT IN THE GARDEN OR READING A BOOK.
BUT SOME-TIMES...
MISATO-KUN.
MISATO-KUN.

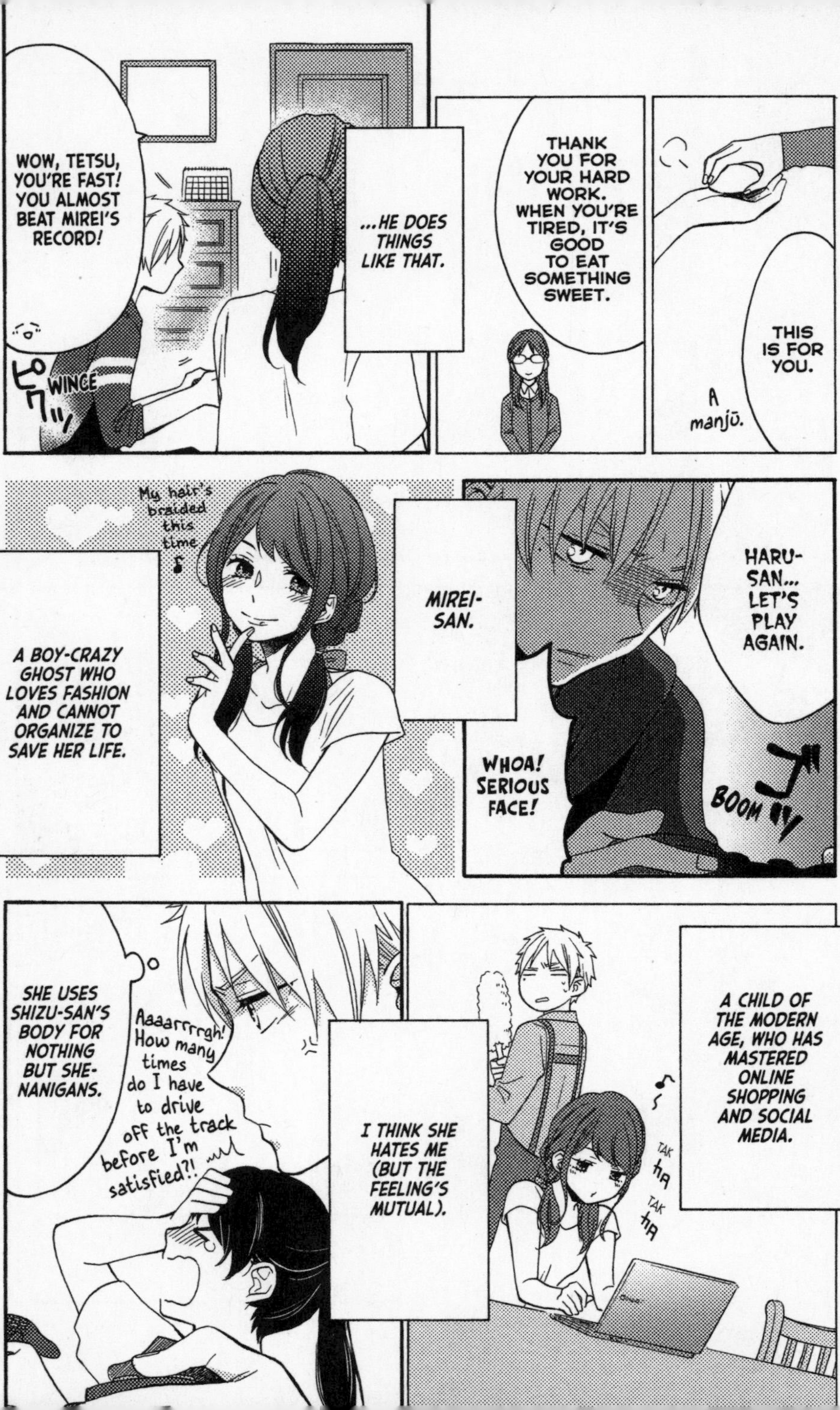

THIS IS FOR YOU.
A manjū.
THANK YOU FOR YOUR HARD WORK. WHEN YOU'RE TIRED, IT'S GOOD TO EAT SOMETHING SWEET.
...HE DOES THINGS LIKE THAT.
WOW, TETSU, YOU'RE FAST! YOU ALMOST BEAT MIREI'S RECORD!
WINCE
HARU-SAN... LET'S PLAY AGAIN.
MIREI-SAN.
BOOM
WHOA! SERIOUS FACE!
My hair's braided this time
A BOY-CRAZY GHOST WHO LOVES FASHION AND CANNOT ORGANIZE TO SAVE HER LIFE.
A CHILD OF THE MODERN AGE, WHO HAS MASTERED ONLINE SHOPPING AND SOCIAL MEDIA.
TAK
TAK
I THINK SHE HATES ME (BUT THE FEELING'S MUTUAL).
Aaaarrrrgh! How many times do I have to drive off the track before I'm satisfied?!
SHE USES SHIZU-SAN'S BODY FOR NOTHING BUT SHE-NANIGANS.

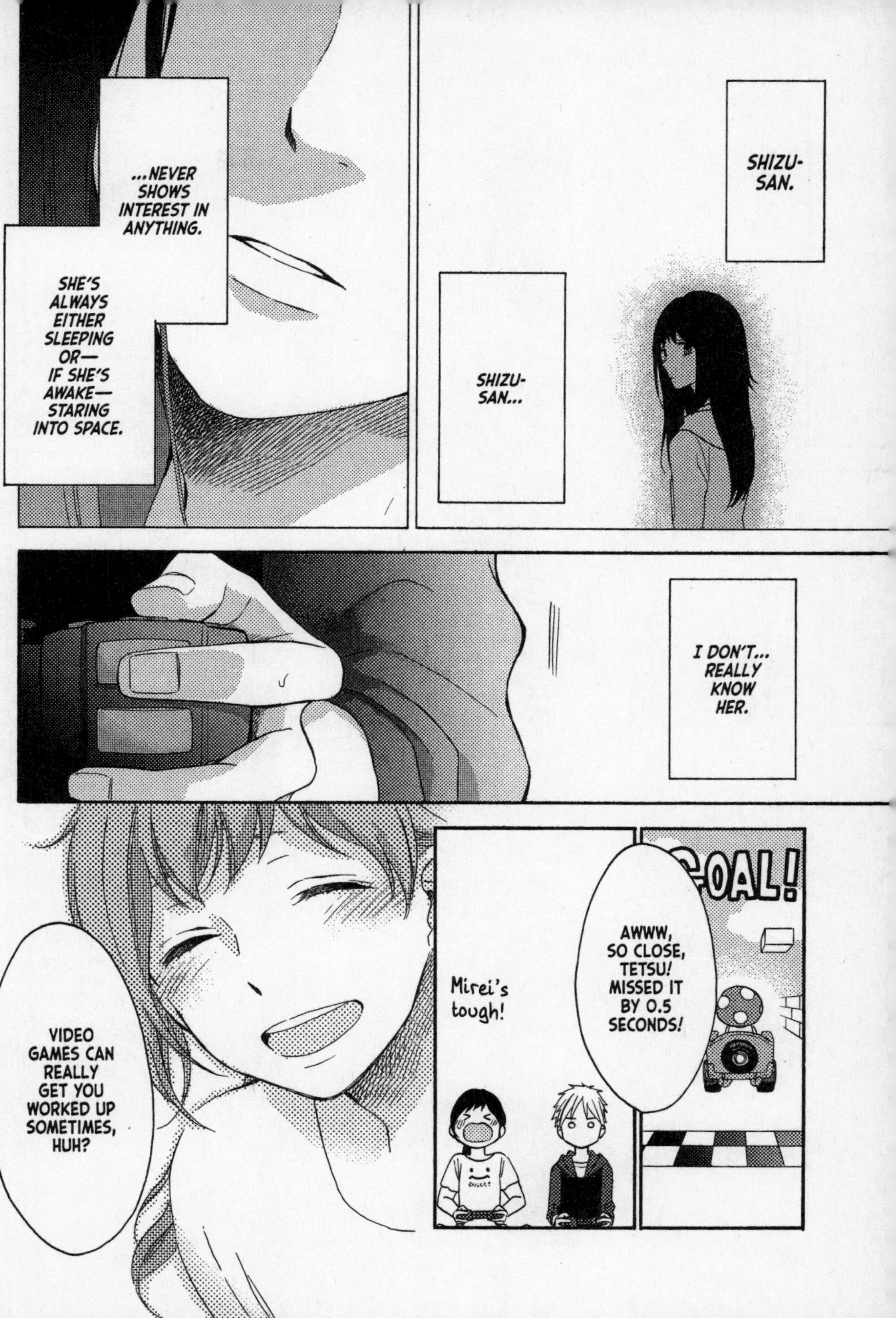
SHIZU-SAN.
SHIZU-SAN...
...NEVER SHOWS INTEREST IN ANYTHING.
SHE'S ALWAYS EITHER SLEEPING OR— IF SHE'S AWAKE— STARING INTO SPACE.
I DON'T... REALLY KNOW HER.
GOAL!
AWWW, SO CLOSE, TETSU! MISSED IT BY 0.5 SECONDS!
Mirei's tough!
VIDEO GAMES CAN REALLY GET YOU WORKED UP SOMETIMES, HUH?

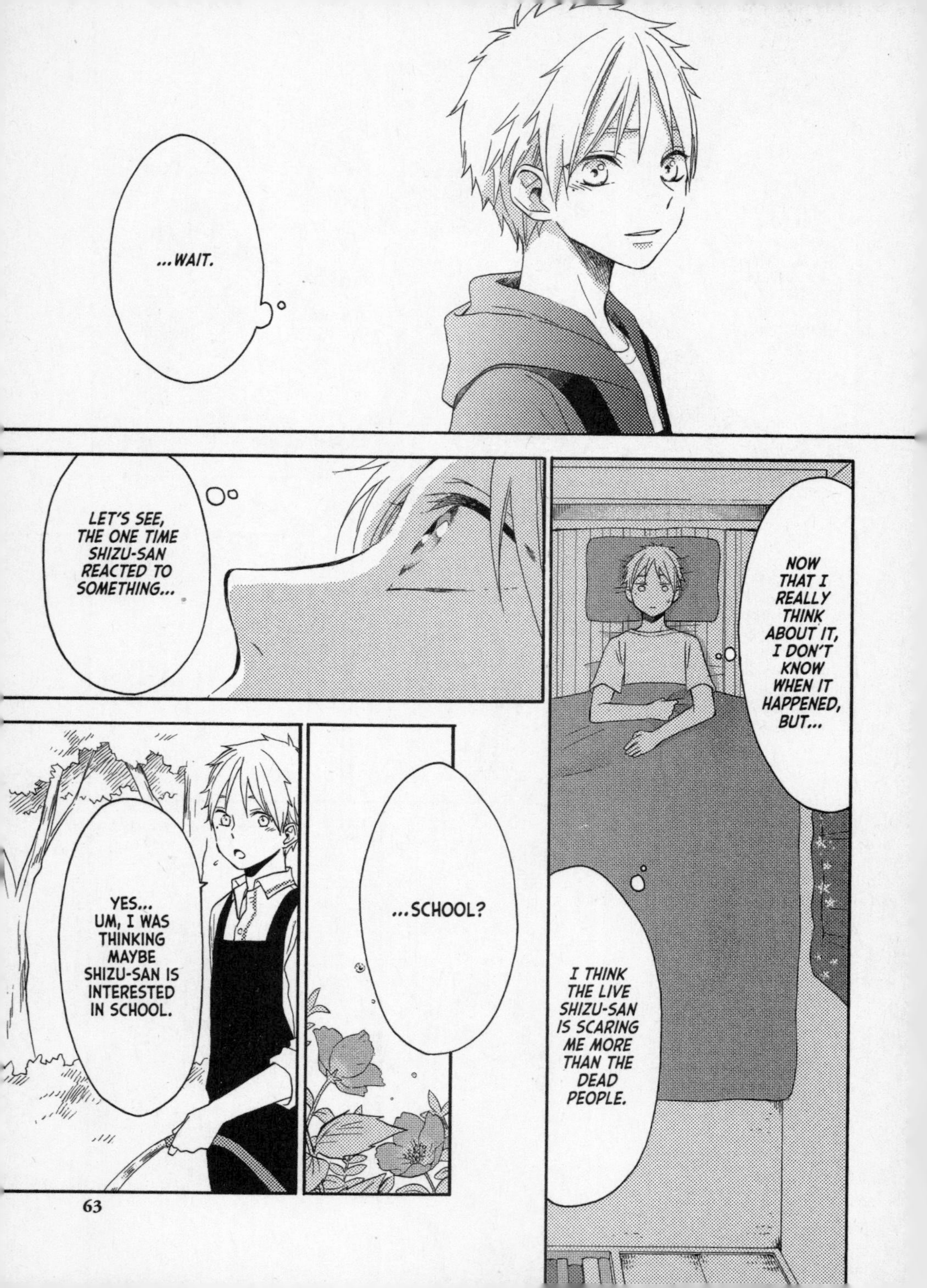
...WAIT.
NOW THAT I REALLY THINK ABOUT IT, I DON'T KNOW WHEN IT HAPPENED, BUT...
I THINK THE LIVE SHIZU-SAN IS SCARING ME MORE THAN THE DEAD PEOPLE.
LET'S SEE, THE ONE TIME SHIZU-SAN REACTED TO SOMETHING...
...SCHOOL?
YES... UM, I WAS THINKING MAYBE SHIZU-SAN IS INTERESTED IN SCHOOL.

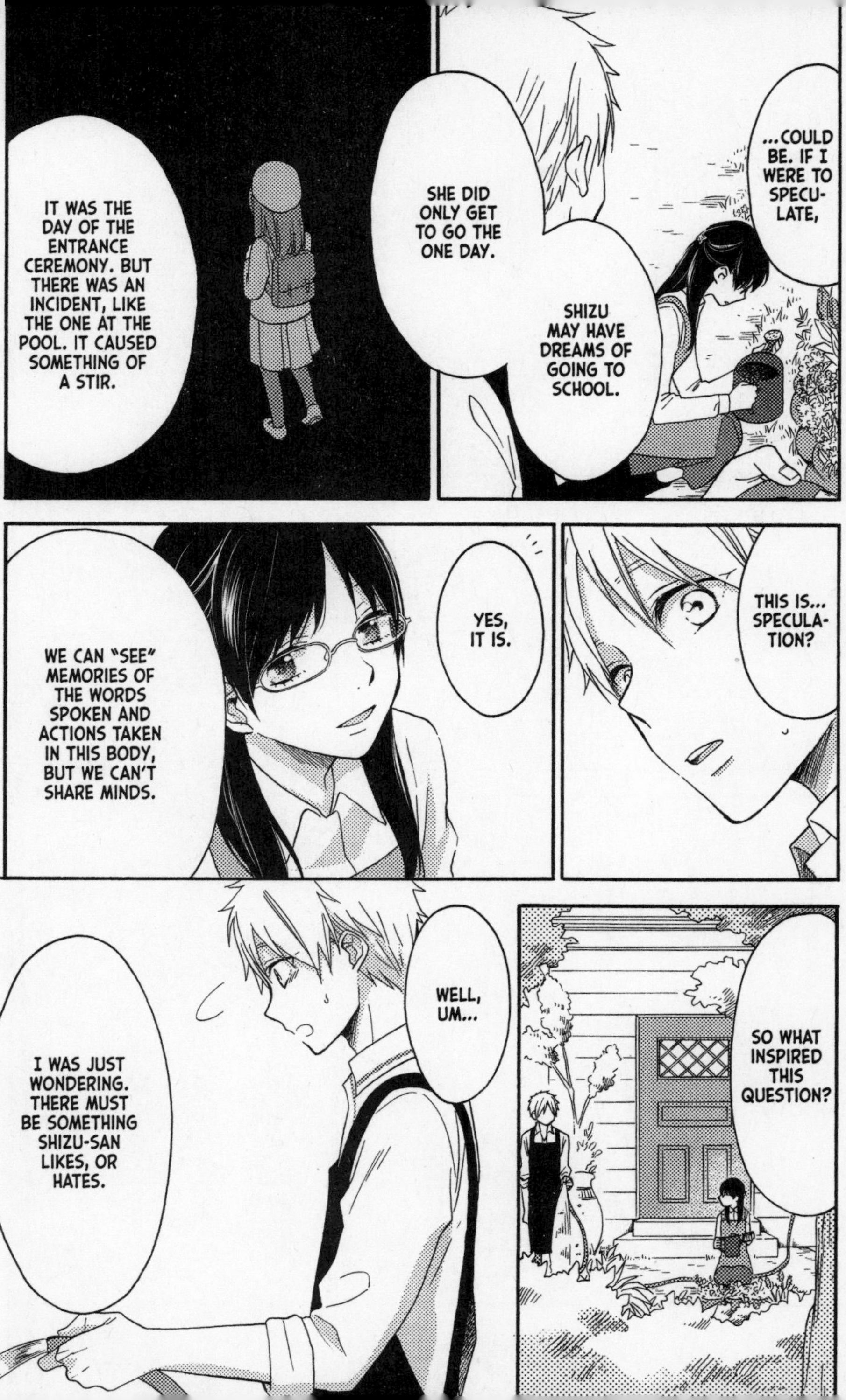
...COULD BE. IF I WERE TO SPECULATE,
SHIZU MAY HAVE DREAMS OF GOING TO SCHOOL.
SHE DID ONLY GET TO GO THE ONE DAY.
IT WAS THE DAY OF THE ENTRANCE CEREMONY. BUT THERE WAS AN INCIDENT, LIKE THE ONE AT THE POOL. IT CAUSED SOMETHING OF A STIR.
THIS IS... SPECULATION?
YES, IT IS.
WE CAN "SEE" MEMORIES OF THE WORDS SPOKEN AND ACTIONS TAKEN IN THIS BODY, BUT WE CAN'T SHARE MINDS.
SO WHAT INSPIRED THIS QUESTION?
WELL, UM...
I WAS JUST WONDERING. THERE MUST BE SOMETHING SHIZU-SAN LIKES, OR HATES.

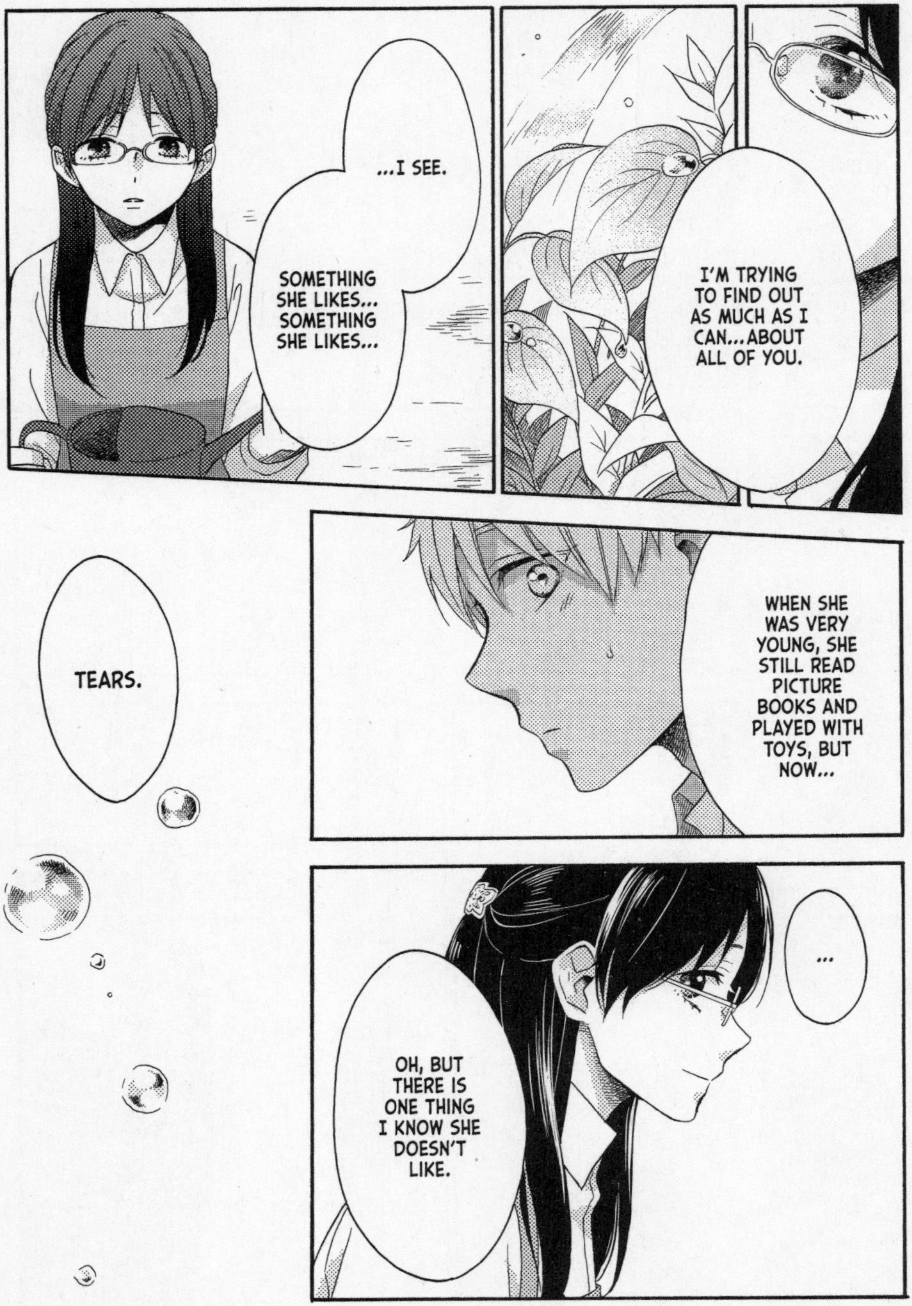
I'M TRYING TO FIND OUT AS MUCH AS I CAN...ABOUT ALL OF YOU.
...I SEE.
SOMETHING SHE LIKES... SOMETHING SHE LIKES...
WHEN SHE WAS VERY YOUNG, SHE STILL READ PICTURE BOOKS AND PLAYED WITH TOYS, BUT NOW...
...
OH, BUT THERE IS ONE THING I KNOW SHE DOESN'T LIKE.
TEARS.

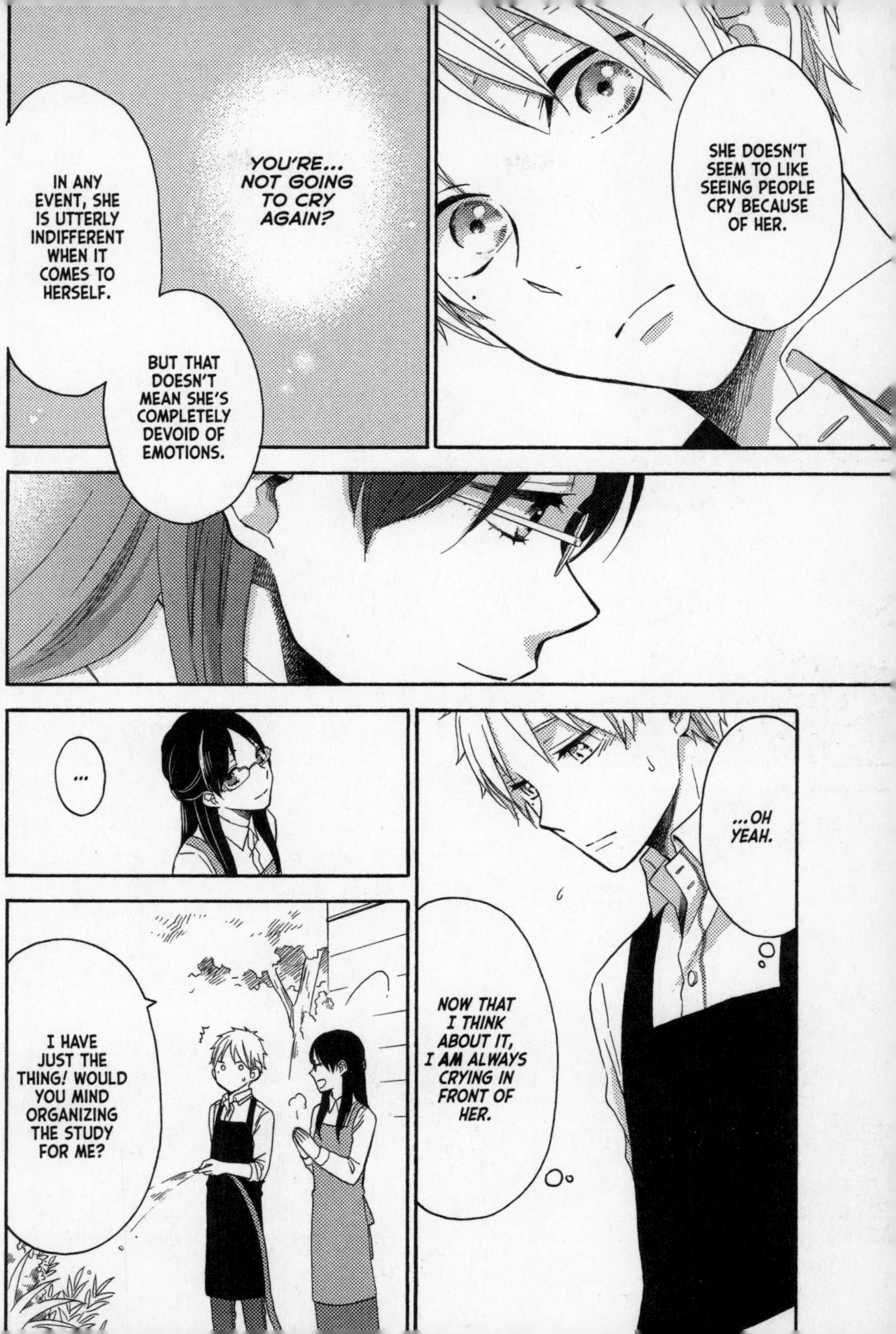
SHE DOESN'T SEEM TO LIKE SEEING PEOPLE CRY BECAUSE OF HER.
YOU'RE... NOT GOING TO CRY AGAIN?
IN ANY EVENT, SHE IS UTTERLY INDIFFERENT WHEN IT COMES TO HERSELF.
BUT THAT DOESN'T MEAN SHE'S COMPLETELY DEVOID OF EMOTIONS.
...OH YEAH.
...
NOW THAT I THINK ABOUT IT, I AM ALWAYS CRYING IN FRONT OF HER.
I HAVE JUST THE THING! WOULD YOU MIND ORGANIZING THE STUDY FOR ME?

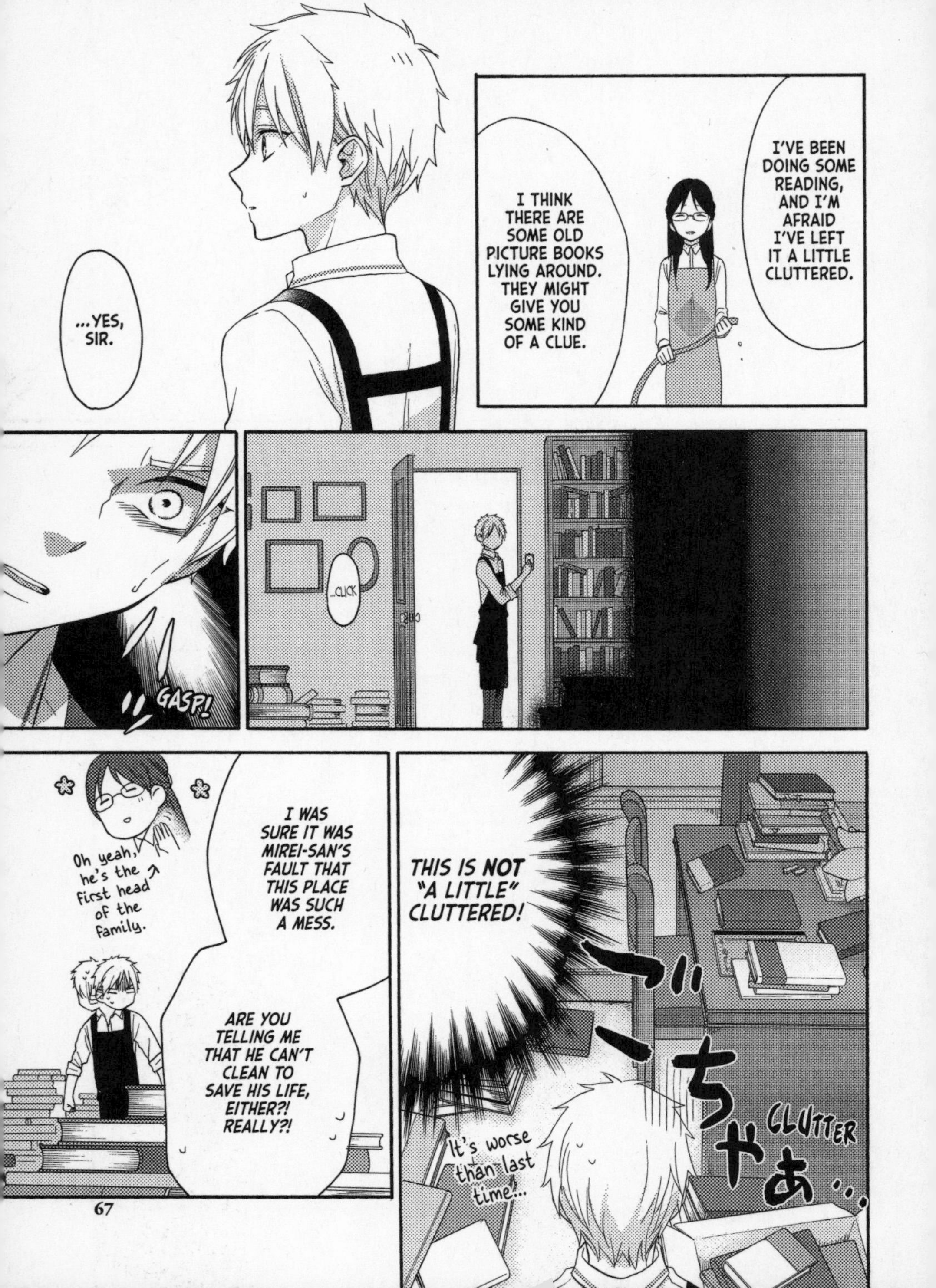
I'VE BEEN DOING SOME READING, AND I'M AFRAID I'VE LEFT IT A LITTLE CLUTTERED.
I THINK THERE ARE SOME OLD PICTURE BOOKS LYING AROUND. THEY MIGHT GIVE YOU SOME KIND OF A CLUE.
...YES, SIR.
...CLICK
GASP!
THIS IS NOT "A LITTLE" CLUTTERED!
ごちゃあ..
CLUTTER
It's worse than last time...
I WAS SURE IT WAS MIREI-SAN'S FAULT THAT THIS PLACE WAS SUCH A MESS.
ARE YOU TELLING ME THAT HE CAN'T CLEAN TO SAVE HIS LIFE, EITHER?! REALLY?!
Oh yeah, he's the first head of the family.

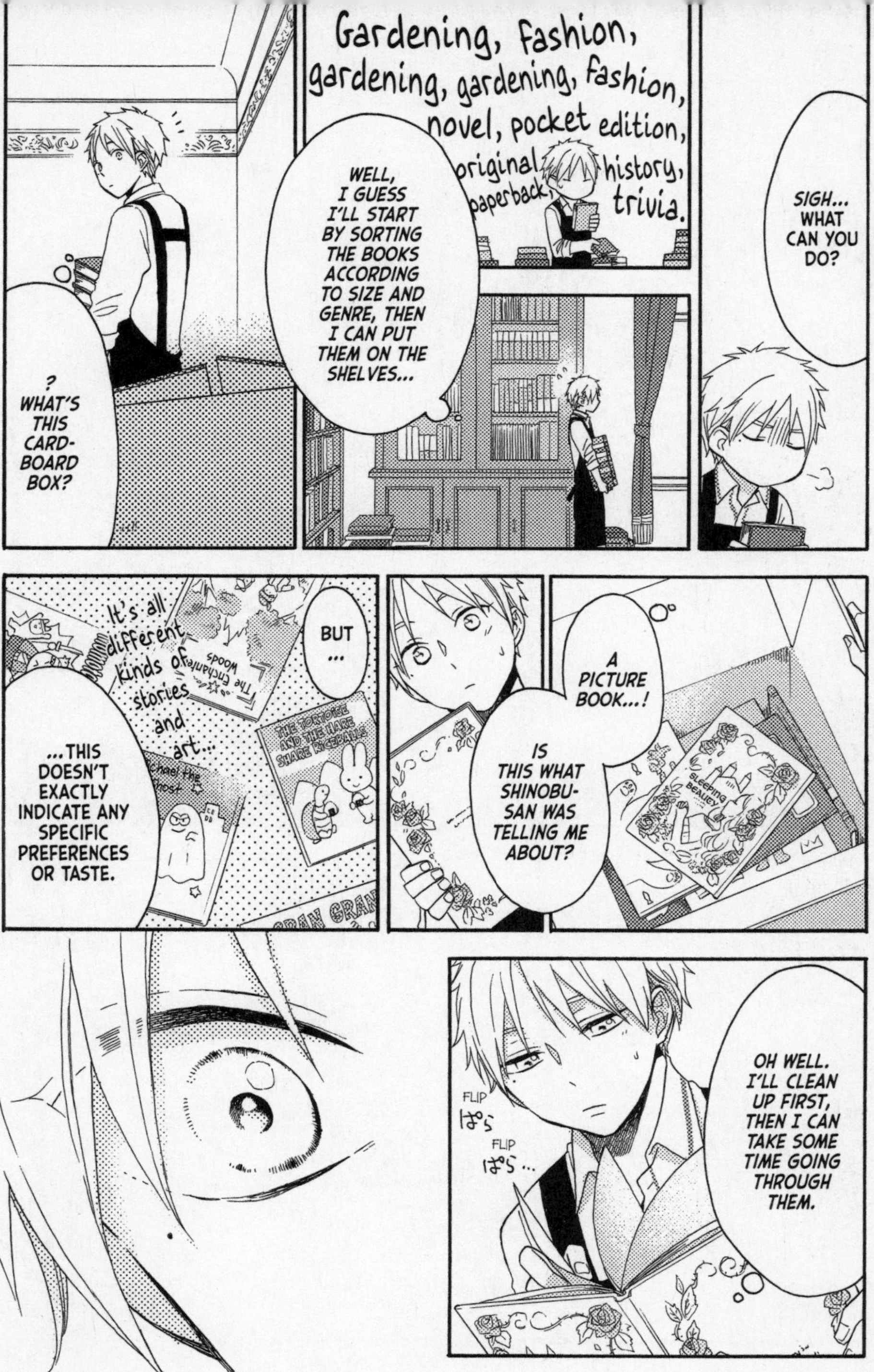
SIGH... WHAT CAN YOU DO?
Gardening, fashion, gardening, gardening, fashion, novel, pocket edition, original paperback, history, trivia.
WELL, I GUESS I'LL START BY SORTING THE BOOKS ACCORDING TO SIZE AND GENRE, THEN I CAN PUT THEM ON THE SHELVES...
? WHAT'S THIS CARDBOARD BOX?
A PICTURE BOOK...!
SLEEPING BEAUTY
IS THIS WHAT SHINOBU-SAN WAS TELLING ME ABOUT?
BUT ...
It's all different kinds of stories and art...
The Enchanted Woods
THE TORTOISE AND THE HARE SHARE RICEBALLS
...THIS DOESN'T EXACTLY INDICATE ANY SPECIFIC PREFERENCES OR TASTE.
FLIP
ぱら
FLIP
ぱら…
OH WELL. I'LL CLEAN UP FIRST, THEN I CAN TAKE SOME TIME GOING THROUGH THEM.

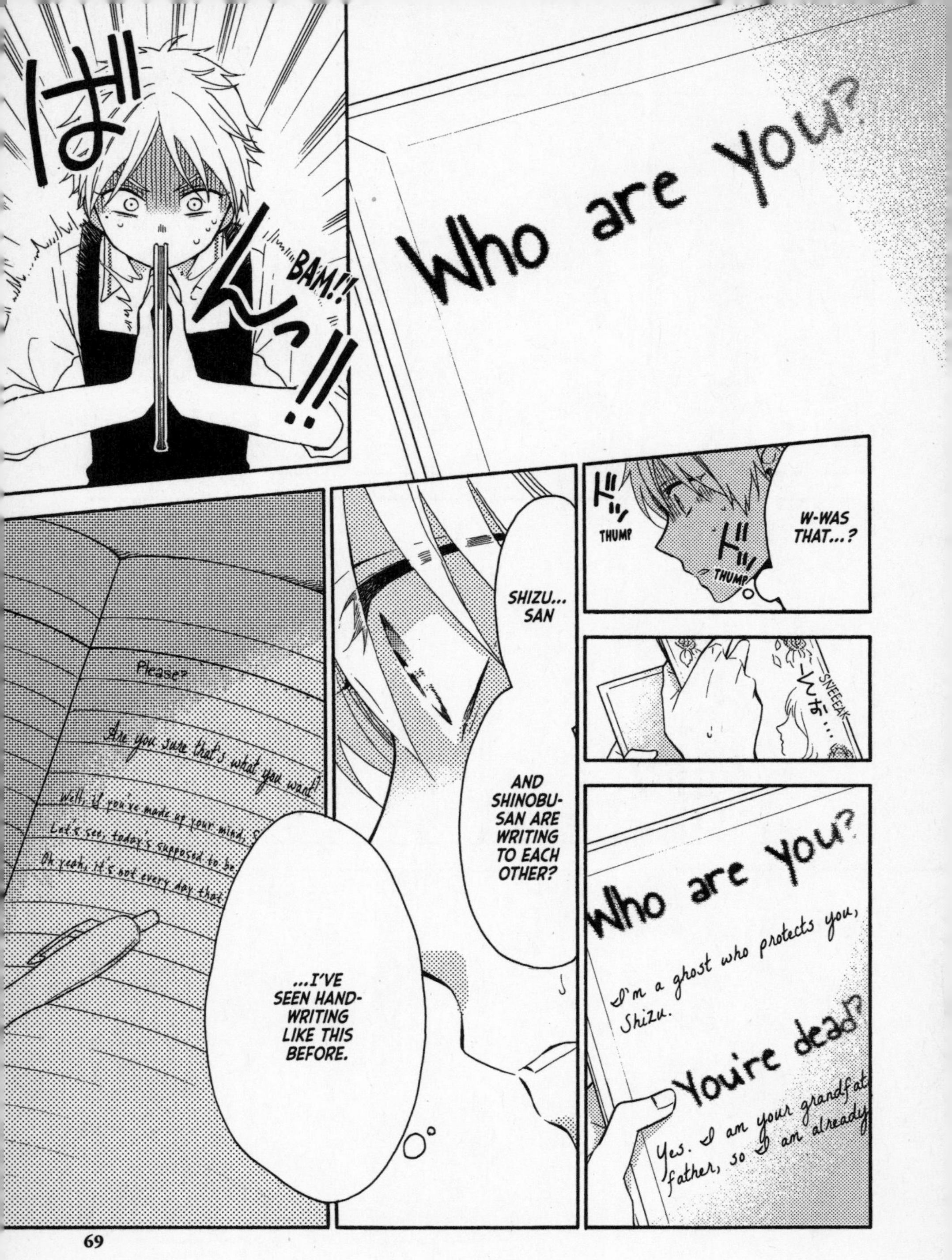
Who are you?
BAM!!
W-WAS THAT...?
THUMP
THUMP
SNEEEAK
Who are you?
I'm a ghost who protects you, Shizu.
You're dead?
Yes. I am your grandfat
father, so I am already
SHIZU... SAN
AND SHINOBU-SAN ARE WRITING TO EACH OTHER?
Please?
Are you sure that's what you want?
Well, if you've made up your mind,
Let's see, today's supposed to be
Oh yeah, it's not every day that
...I'VE SEEN HAND-WRITING LIKE THIS BEFORE.

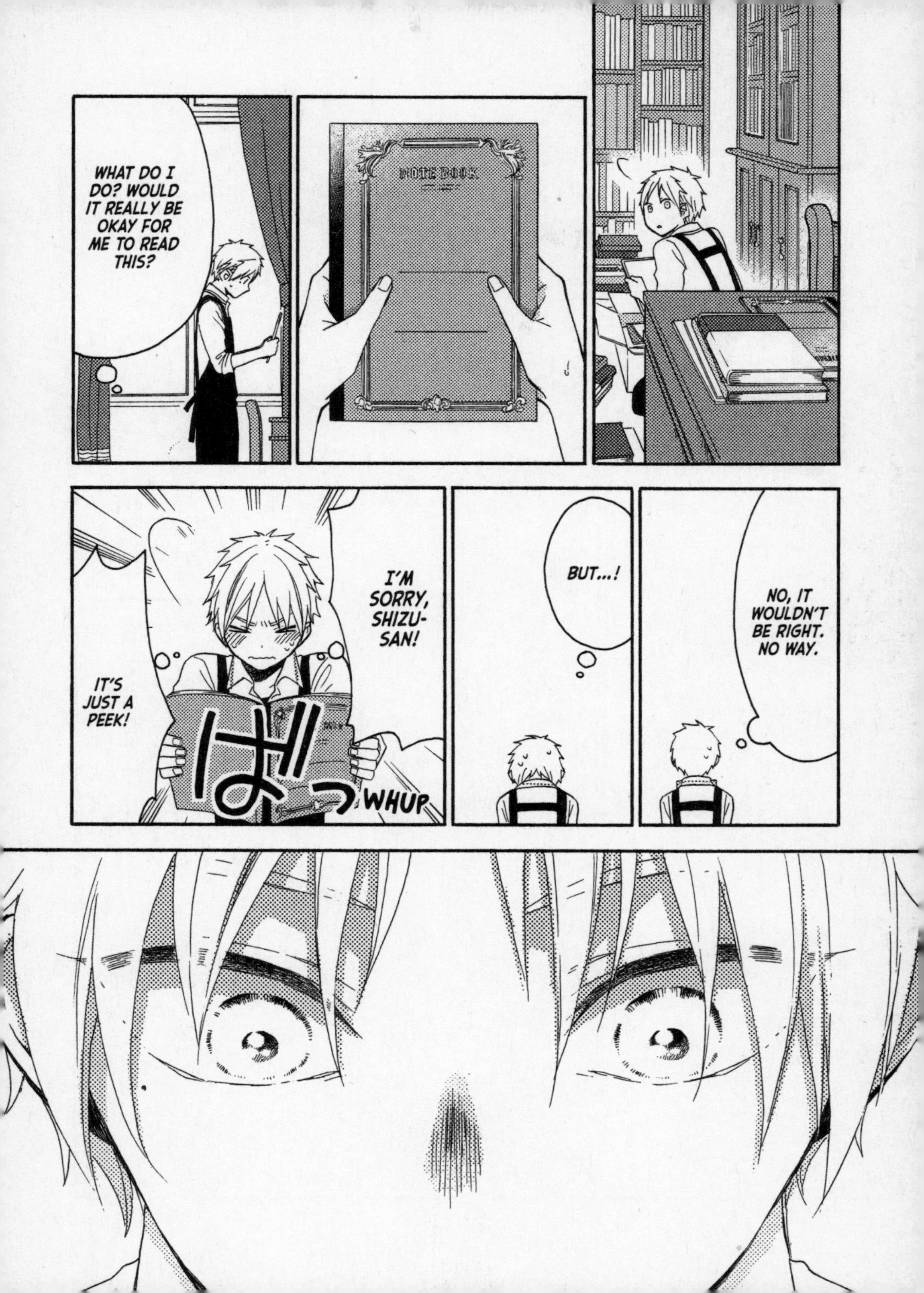
NOTE BOOK
WHAT DO I DO? WOULD IT REALLY BE OKAY FOR ME TO READ THIS?
NO, IT WOULDN'T BE RIGHT. NO WAY.
BUT...!
I'M SORRY, SHIZU-SAN!
IT'S JUST A PEEK!
ぱっ
WHUP

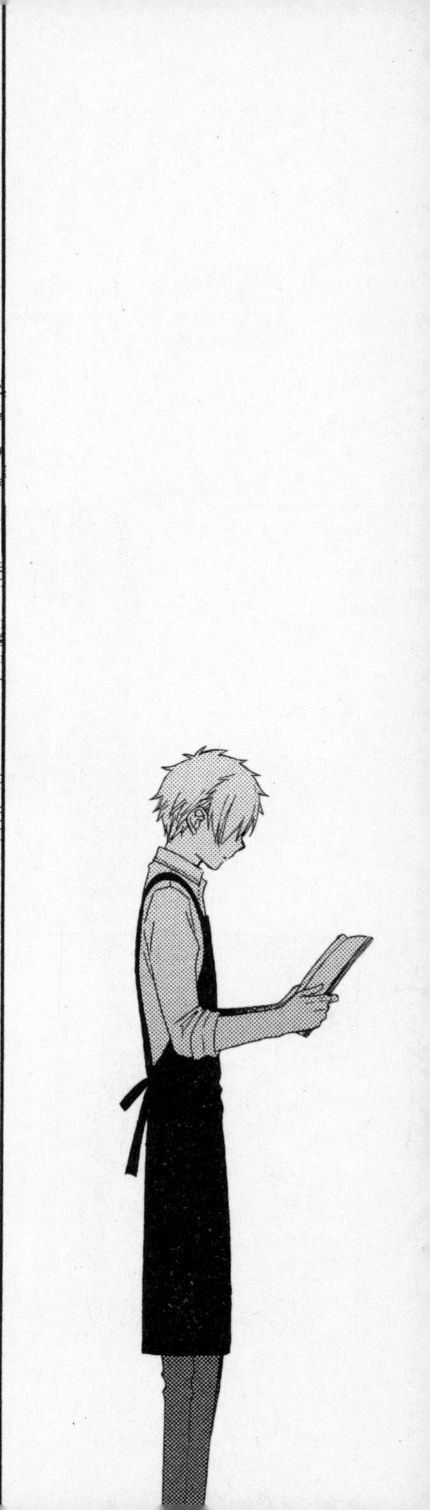

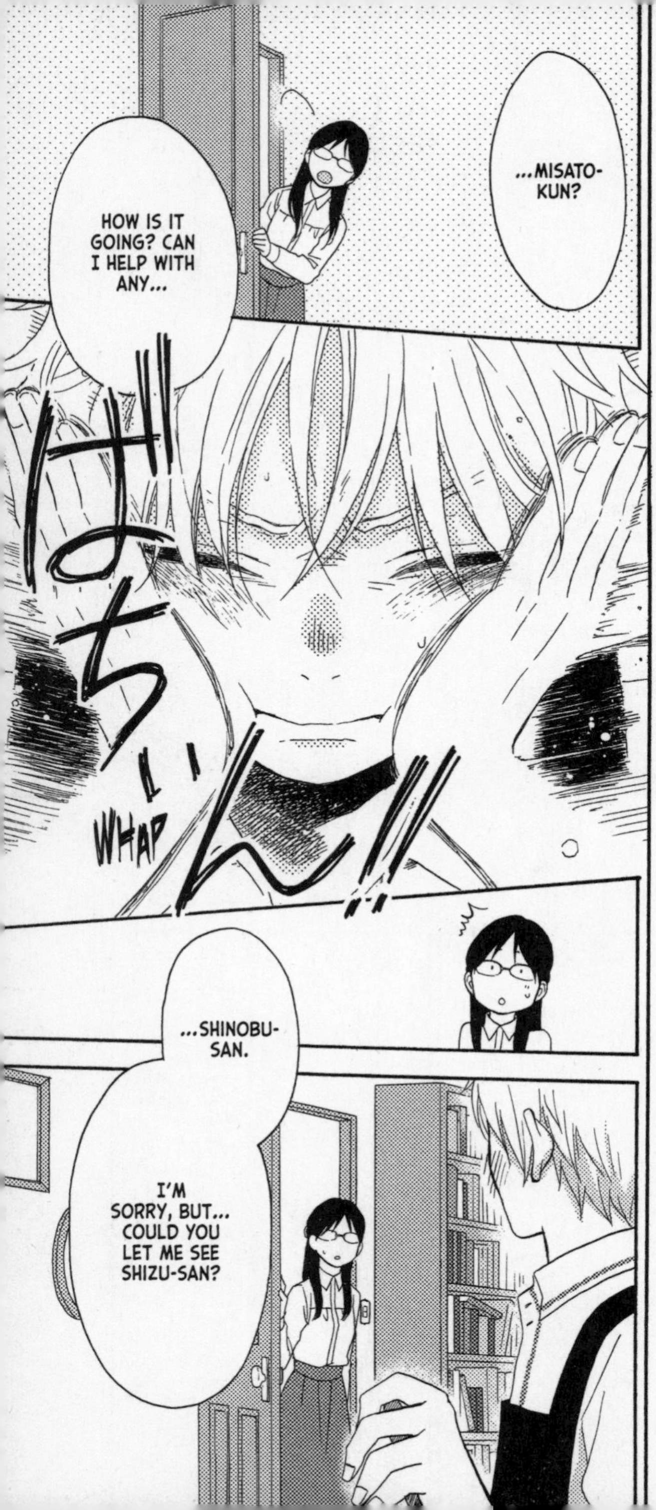
...MISATO-KUN?
HOW IS IT GOING? CAN I HELP WITH ANY...
WHAP
...SHINOBU-SAN.
I'M SORRY, BUT... COULD YOU LET ME SEE SHIZU-SAN?

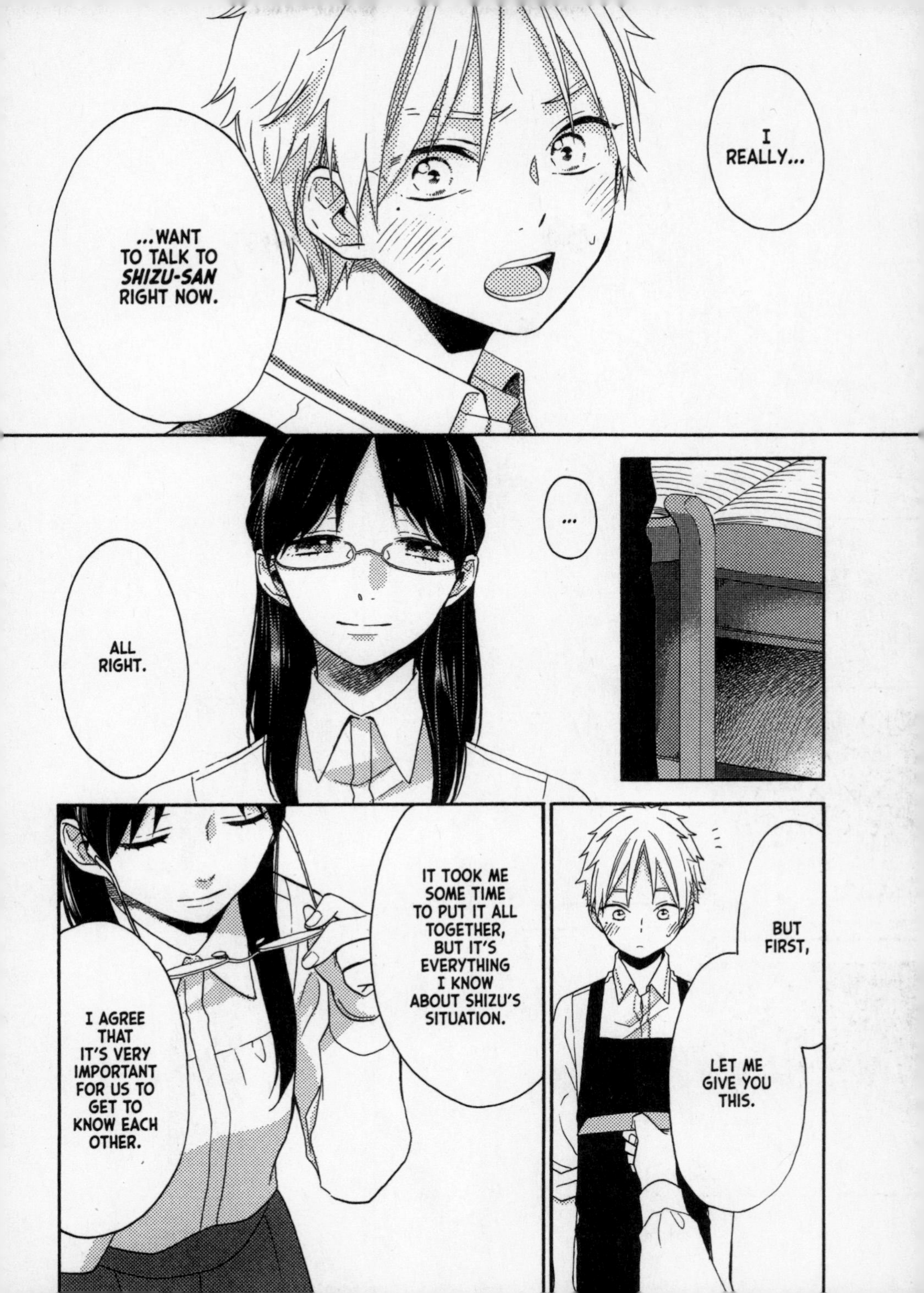
I REALLY...
...WANT TO TALK TO *SHIZU-SAN* RIGHT NOW.
...
ALL RIGHT.
BUT FIRST,
LET ME GIVE YOU THIS.
IT TOOK ME SOME TIME TO PUT IT ALL TOGETHER, BUT IT'S EVERYTHING I KNOW ABOUT SHIZU'S SITUATION.
I AGREE THAT IT'S VERY IMPORTANT FOR US TO GET TO KNOW EACH OTHER.

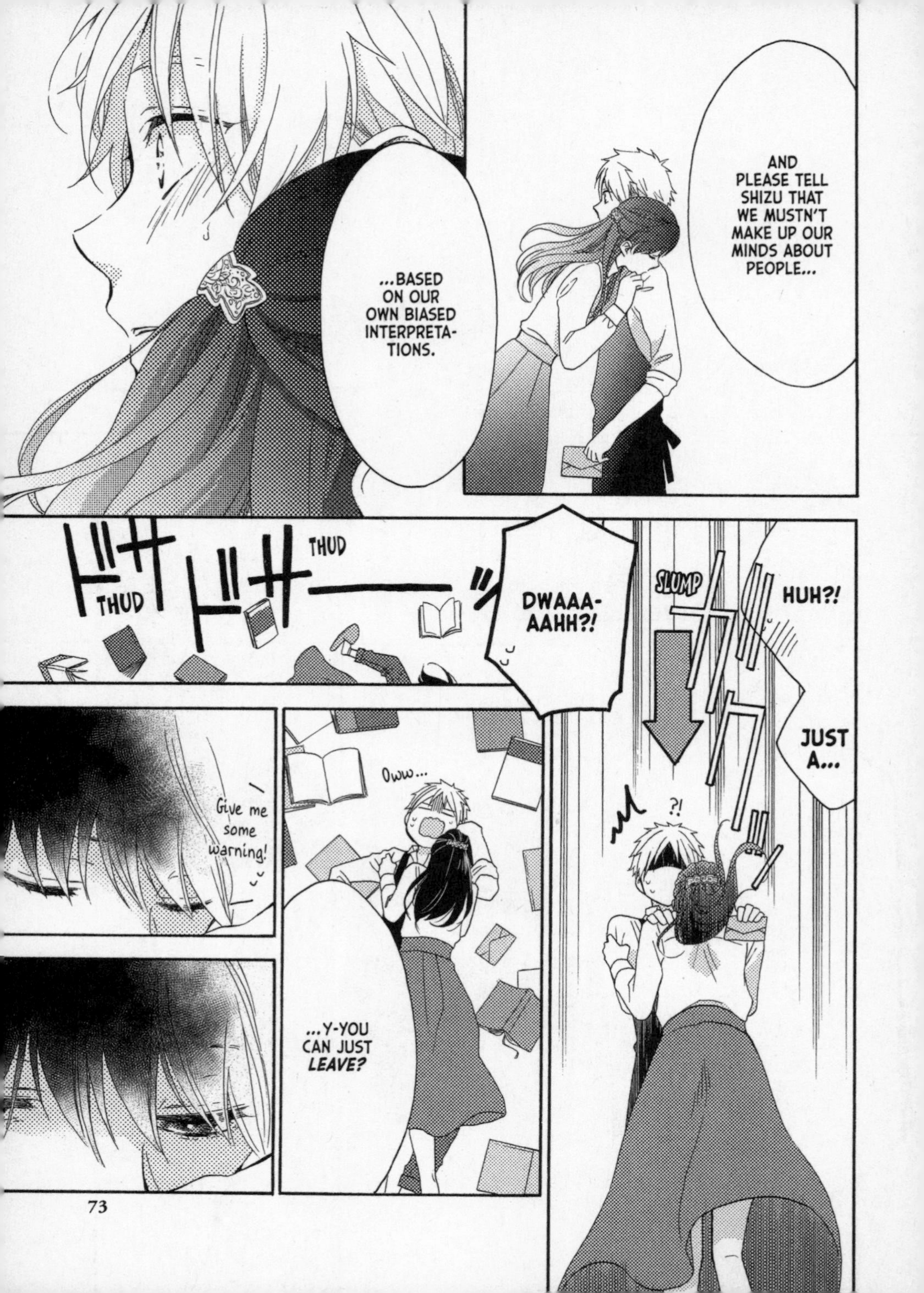
AND PLEASE TELL SHIZU THAT WE MUSTN'T MAKE UP OUR MINDS ABOUT PEOPLE...
...BASED ON OUR OWN BIASED INTERPRETA-TIONS.
HUH?!
SLUMP
JUST A...
?!
DWAAA-AAHH?!
THUD
THUD
Oww...
...Y-YOU CAN JUST *LEAVE?*
Give me some warning!

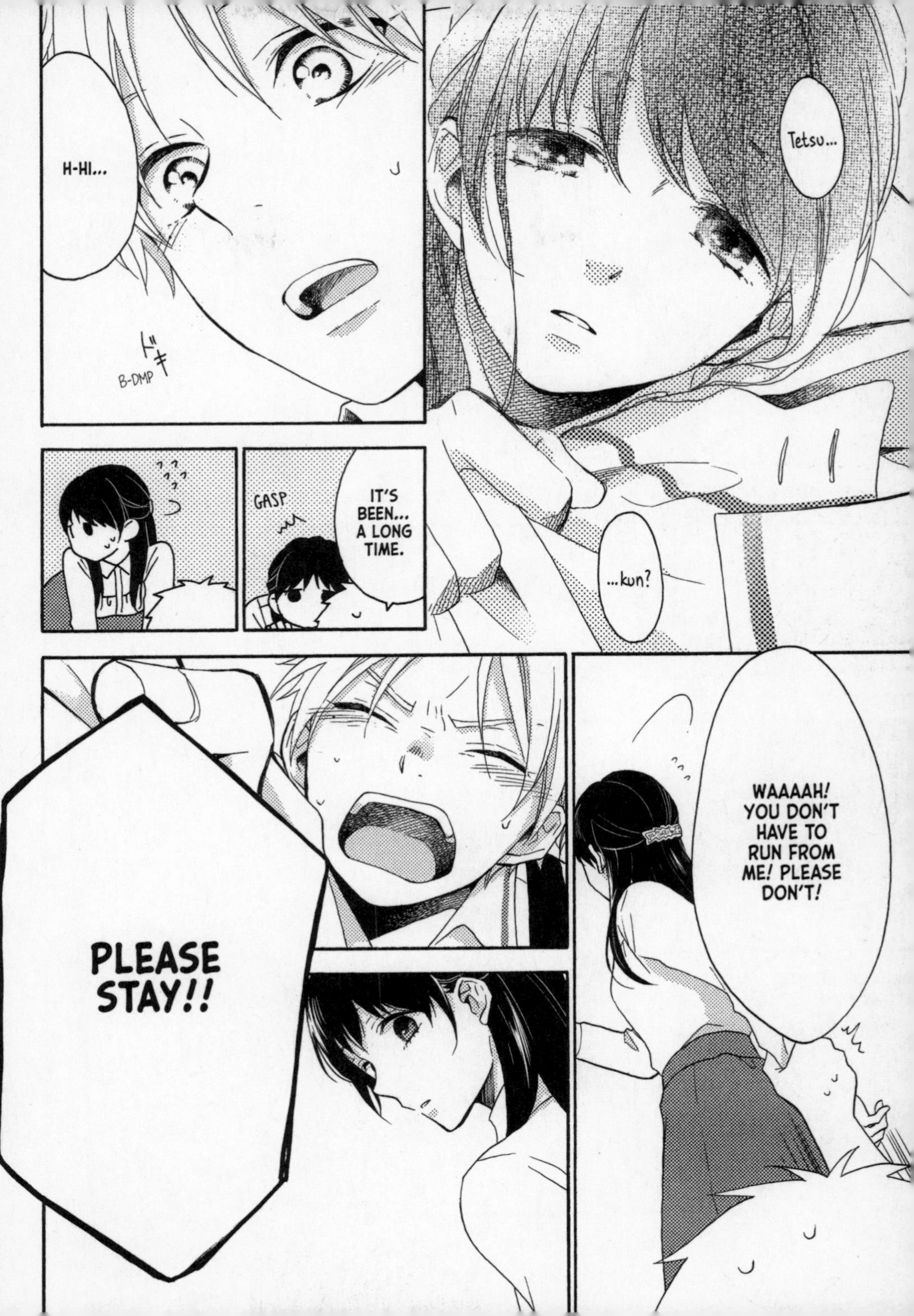

Tetsu...
...kun?
H-HI...
ドキ
B-DMP
IT'S BEEN... A LONG TIME.
GASP
WAAAAH! YOU DON'T HAVE TO RUN FROM ME! PLEASE DON'T!
PLEASE STAY!!

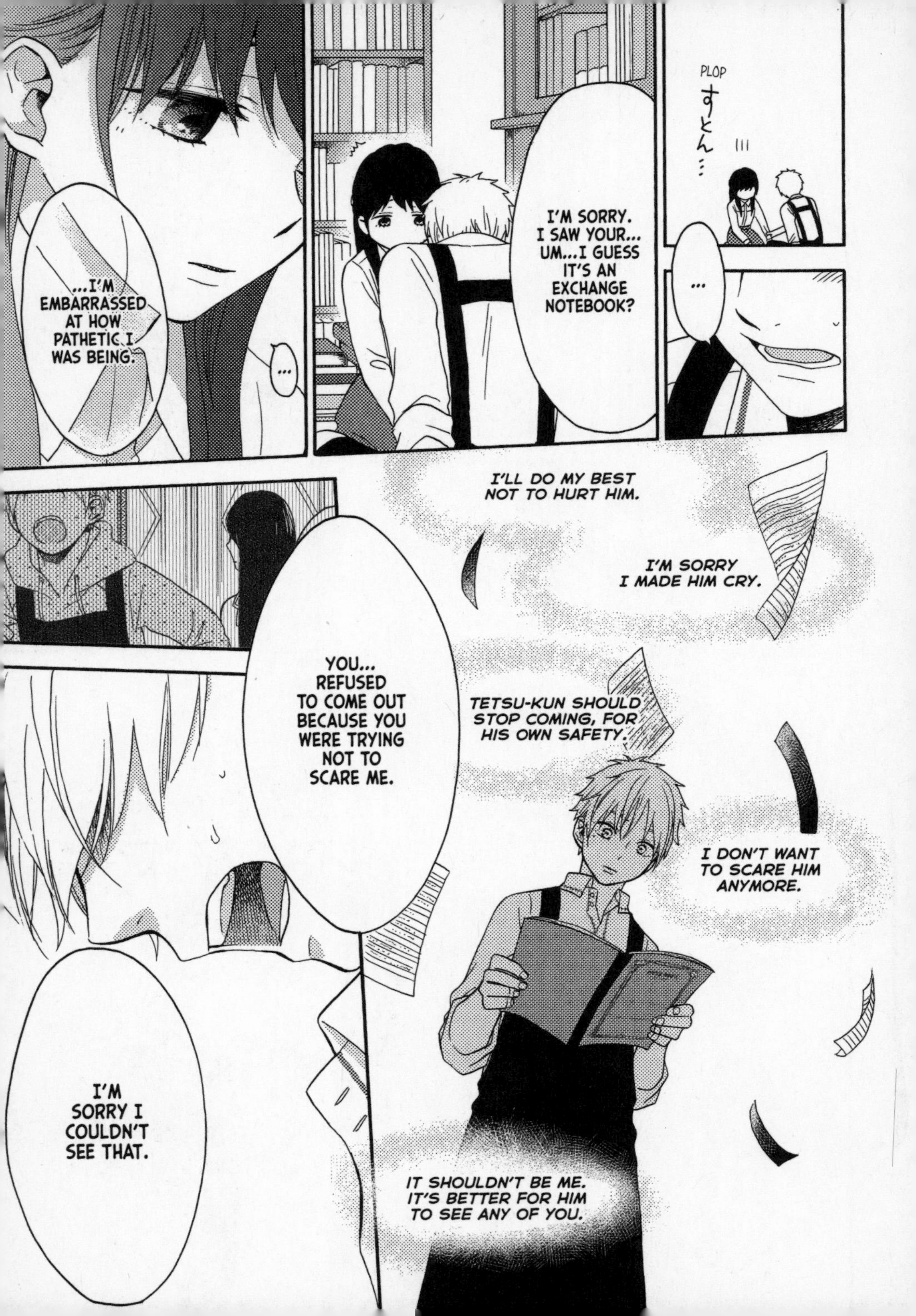

PLOP
すとん…
…
I'M SORRY. I SAW YOUR... UM...I GUESS IT'S AN EXCHANGE NOTEBOOK?
...I'M EMBARRASSED AT HOW PATHETIC I WAS BEING.
...
I'LL DO MY BEST NOT TO HURT HIM.
I'M SORRY I MADE HIM CRY.
TETSU-KUN SHOULD STOP COMING, FOR HIS OWN SAFETY.
I DON'T WANT TO SCARE HIM ANYMORE.
IT SHOULDN'T BE ME. IT'S BETTER FOR HIM TO SEE ANY OF YOU.
YOU... REFUSED TO COME OUT BECAUSE YOU WERE TRYING NOT TO SCARE ME.
I'M SORRY I COULDN'T SEE THAT.

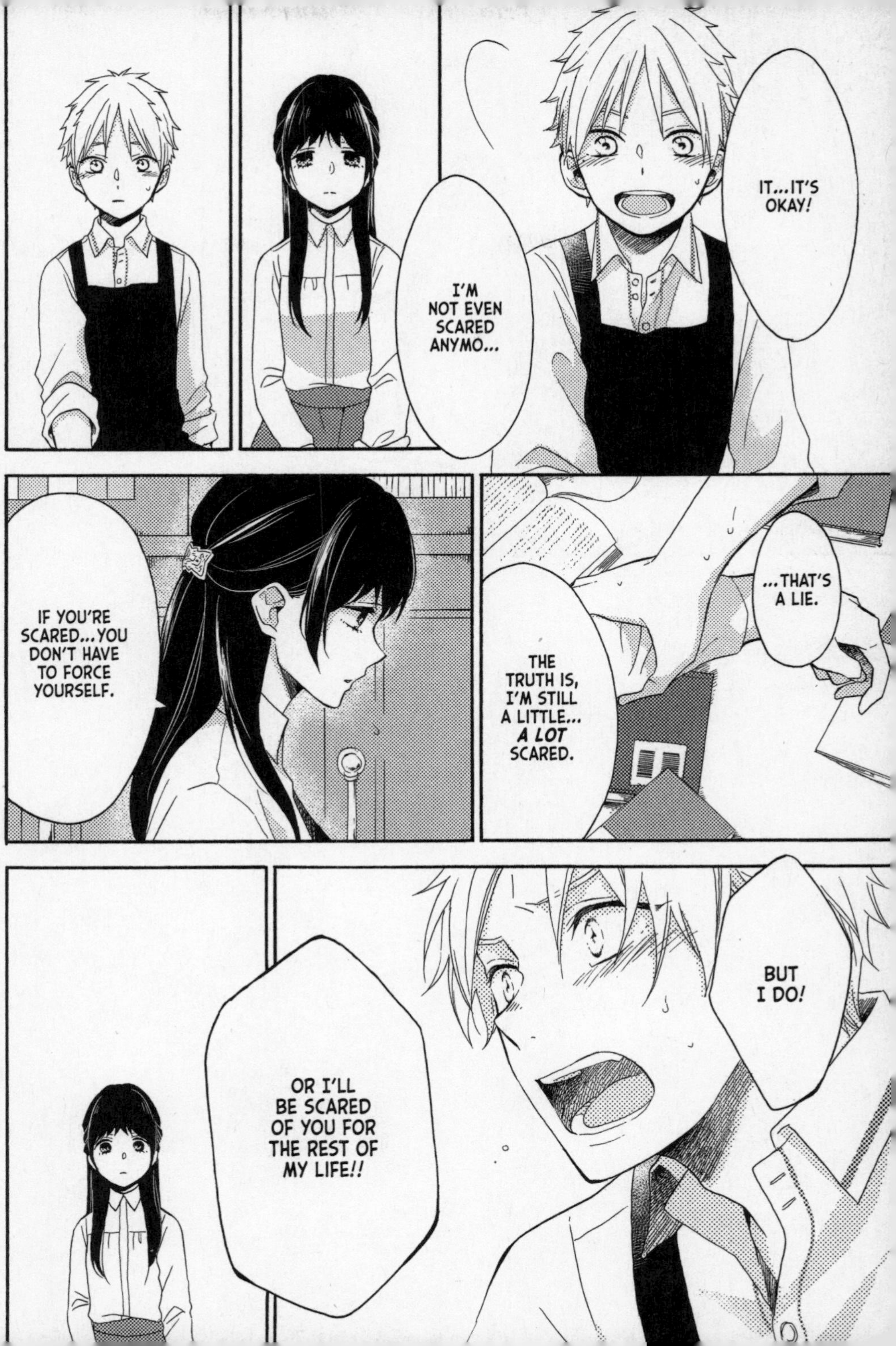
IT...IT'S OKAY!
I'M NOT EVEN SCARED ANYMO...
...THAT'S A LIE.
THE TRUTH IS, I'M STILL A LITTLE... *A LOT* SCARED.
IF YOU'RE SCARED...YOU DON'T HAVE TO FORCE YOURSELF.
BUT I DO!
OR I'LL BE SCARED OF YOU FOR THE REST OF MY LIFE!!

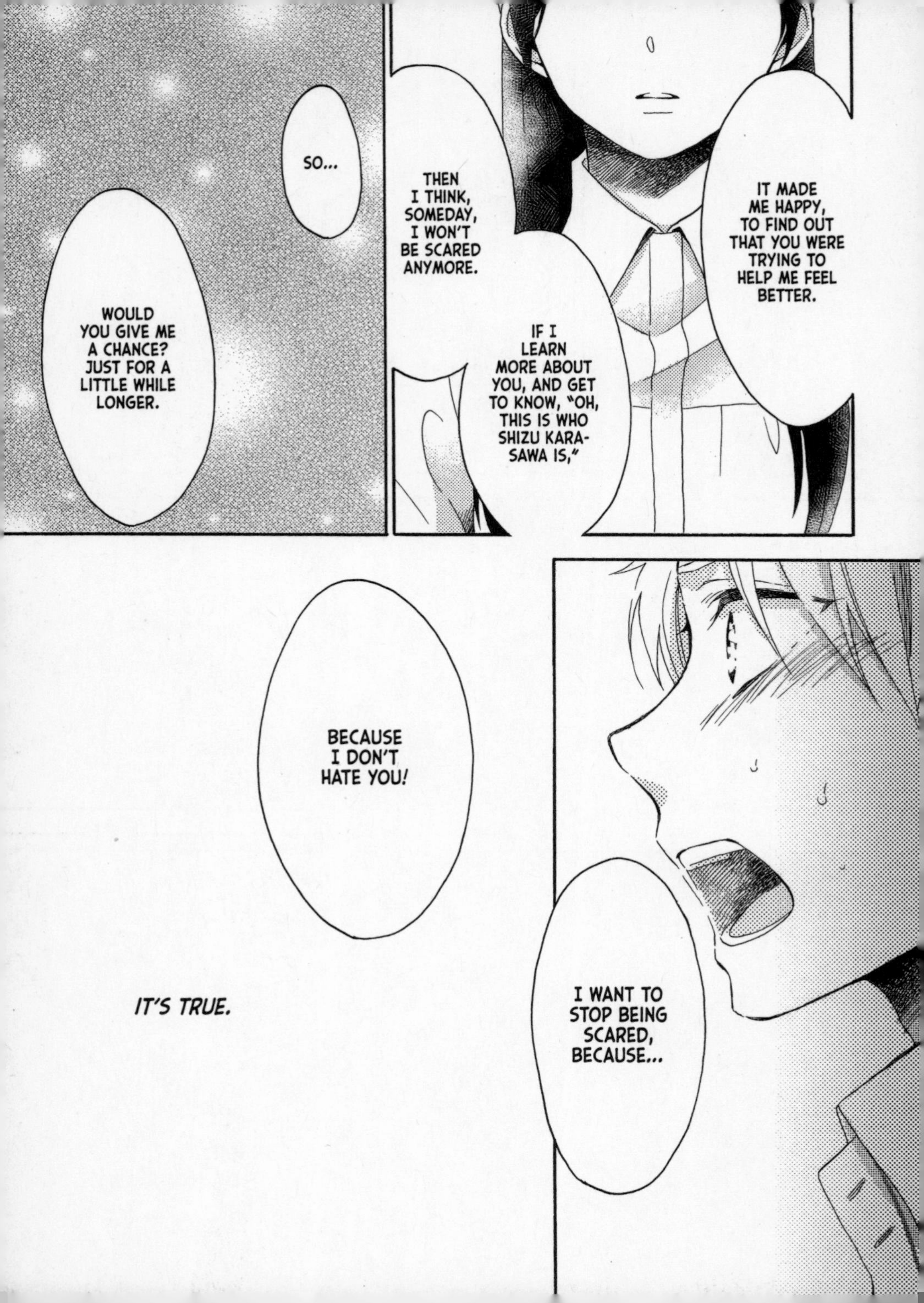
IT MADE ME HAPPY, TO FIND OUT THAT YOU WERE TRYING TO HELP ME FEEL BETTER.
IF I LEARN MORE ABOUT YOU, AND GET TO KNOW, "OH, THIS IS WHO SHIZU KARA-SAWA IS,"
THEN I THINK, SOMEDAY, I WON'T BE SCARED ANYMORE.
SO...
WOULD YOU GIVE ME A CHANCE? JUST FOR A LITTLE WHILE LONGER.
I WANT TO STOP BEING SCARED, BECAUSE...
BECAUSE I DON'T HATE YOU!
IT'S TRUE.

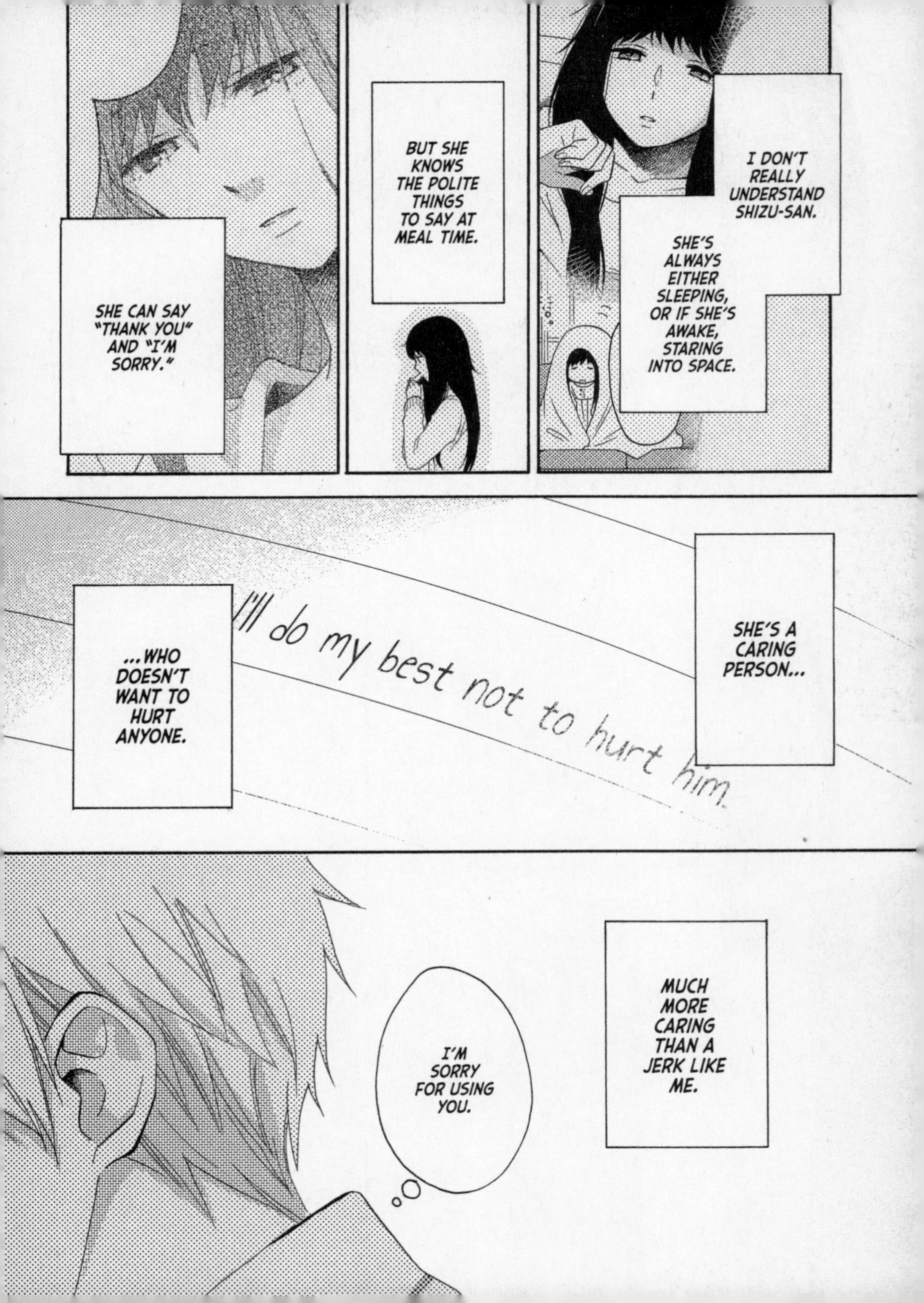
I DON'T REALLY UNDERSTAND SHIZU-SAN.
SHE'S ALWAYS EITHER SLEEPING, OR IF SHE'S AWAKE, STARING INTO SPACE.
BUT SHE KNOWS THE POLITE THINGS TO SAY AT MEAL TIME.
SHE CAN SAY "THANK YOU" AND "I'M SORRY."
SHE'S A CARING PERSON...
I'll do my best not to hurt him.
...WHO DOESN'T WANT TO HURT ANYONE.
MUCH MORE CARING THAN A JERK LIKE ME.
I'M SORRY FOR USING YOU.

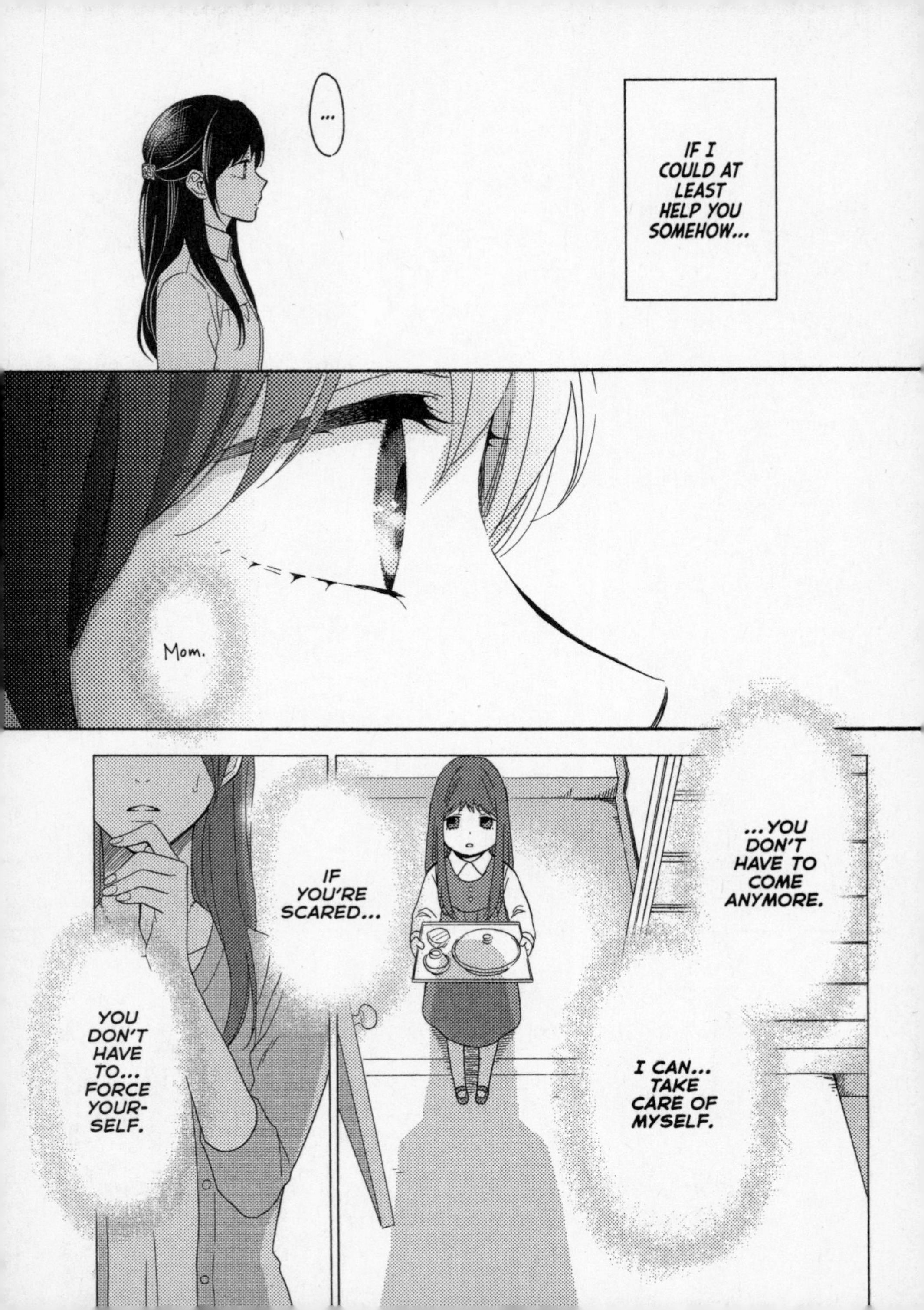
IF I COULD AT LEAST HELP YOU SOMEHOW...
...
Mom.
IF YOU'RE SCARED...
...YOU DON'T HAVE TO COME ANYMORE.
I CAN... TAKE CARE OF MYSELF.
YOU DON'T HAVE TO... FORCE YOUR-SELF.

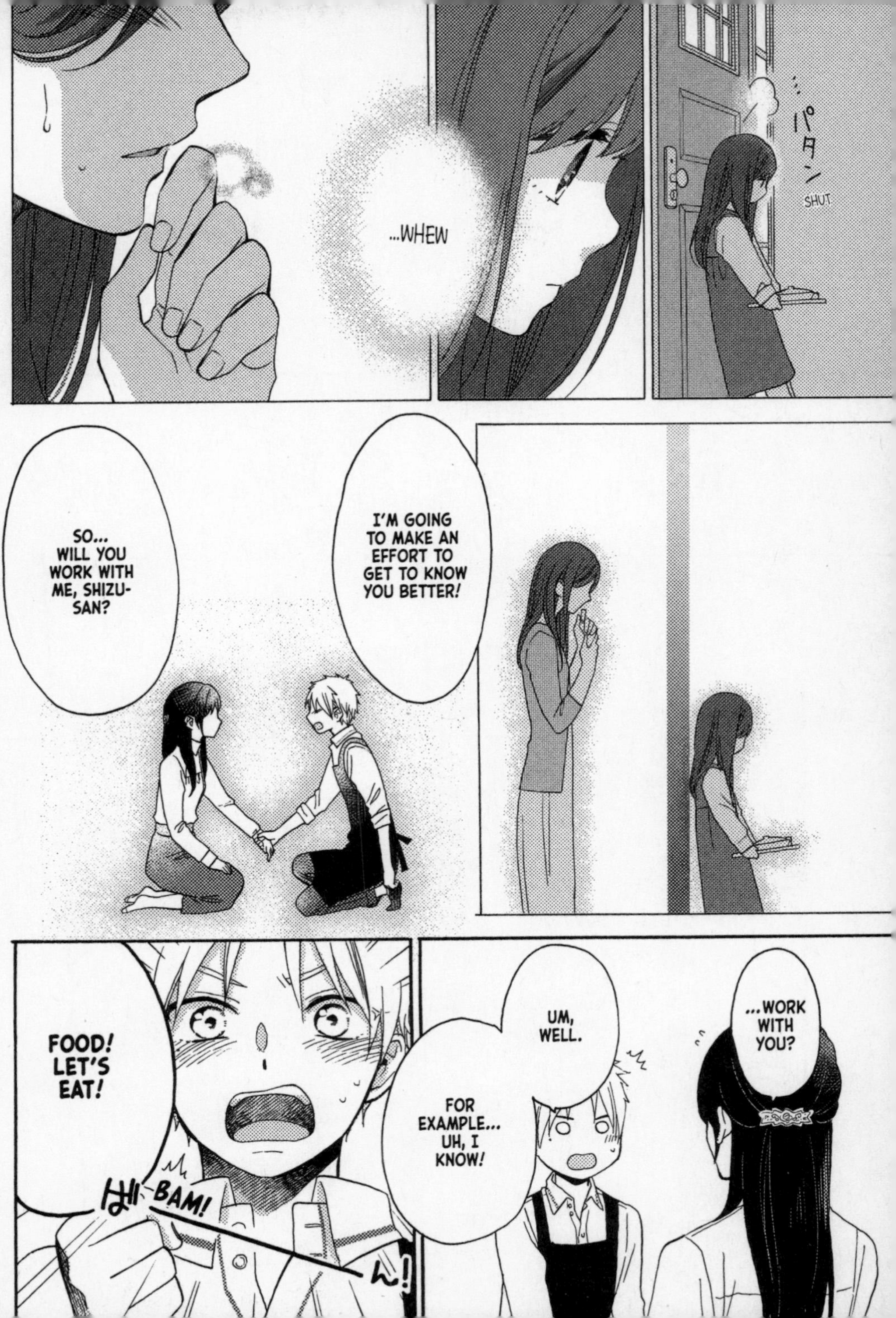
パタン
SHUT
...WHEW
I'M GOING TO MAKE AN EFFORT TO GET TO KNOW YOU BETTER!
SO... WILL YOU WORK WITH ME, SHIZU-SAN?
...WORK WITH YOU?
UM, WELL.
FOR EXAMPLE... UH, I KNOW!
FOOD! LET'S EAT!
BAM!

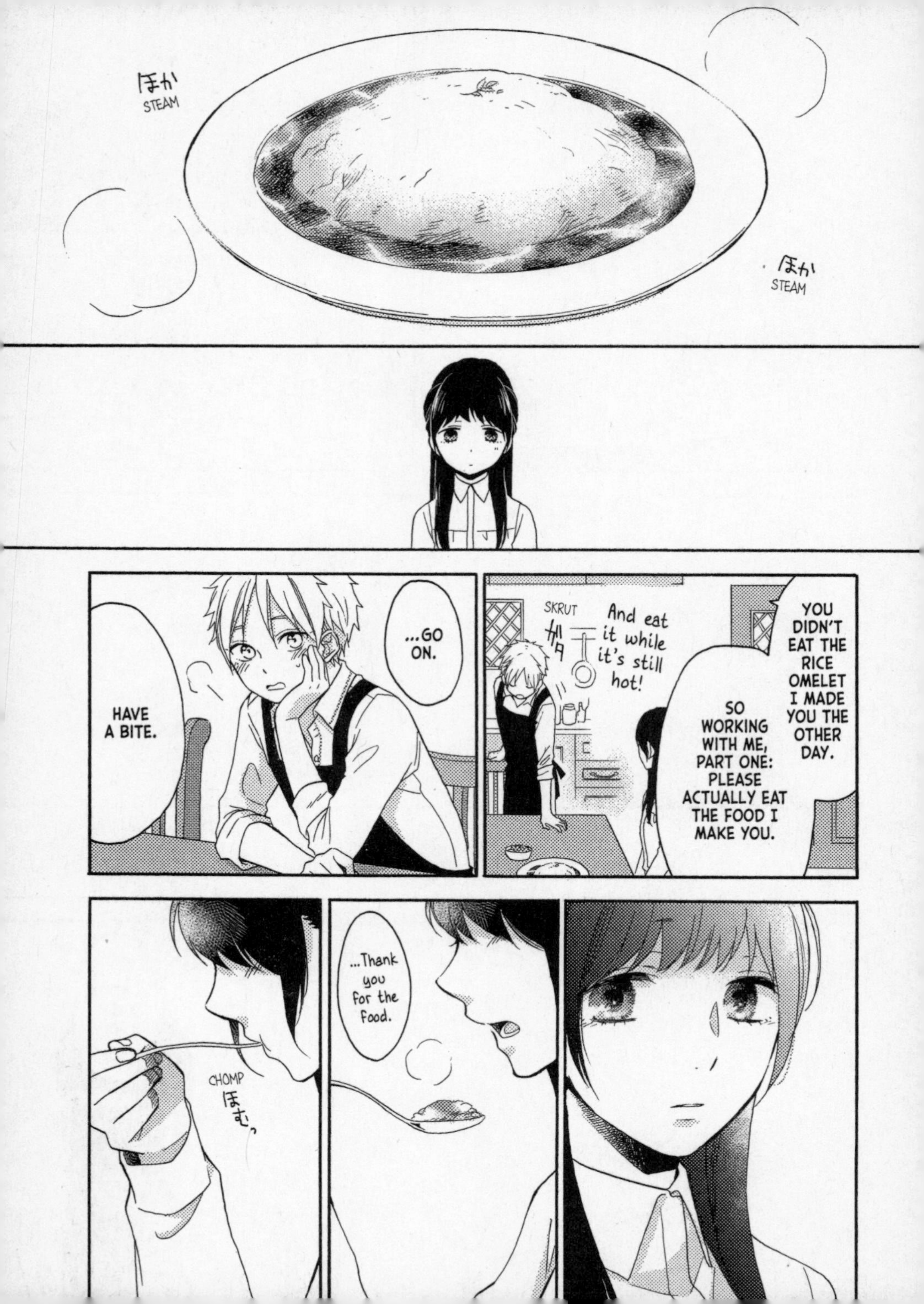
ほか
STEAM
ほか
STEAM
YOU DIDN'T EAT THE RICE OMELET I MADE YOU THE OTHER DAY.
SO WORKING WITH ME, PART ONE: PLEASE ACTUALLY EAT THE FOOD I MAKE YOU.
And eat it while it's still hot!
SKRUT
ガタ
...GO ON.
HAVE A BITE.
...Thank you for the food.
CHOMP
ほむっ

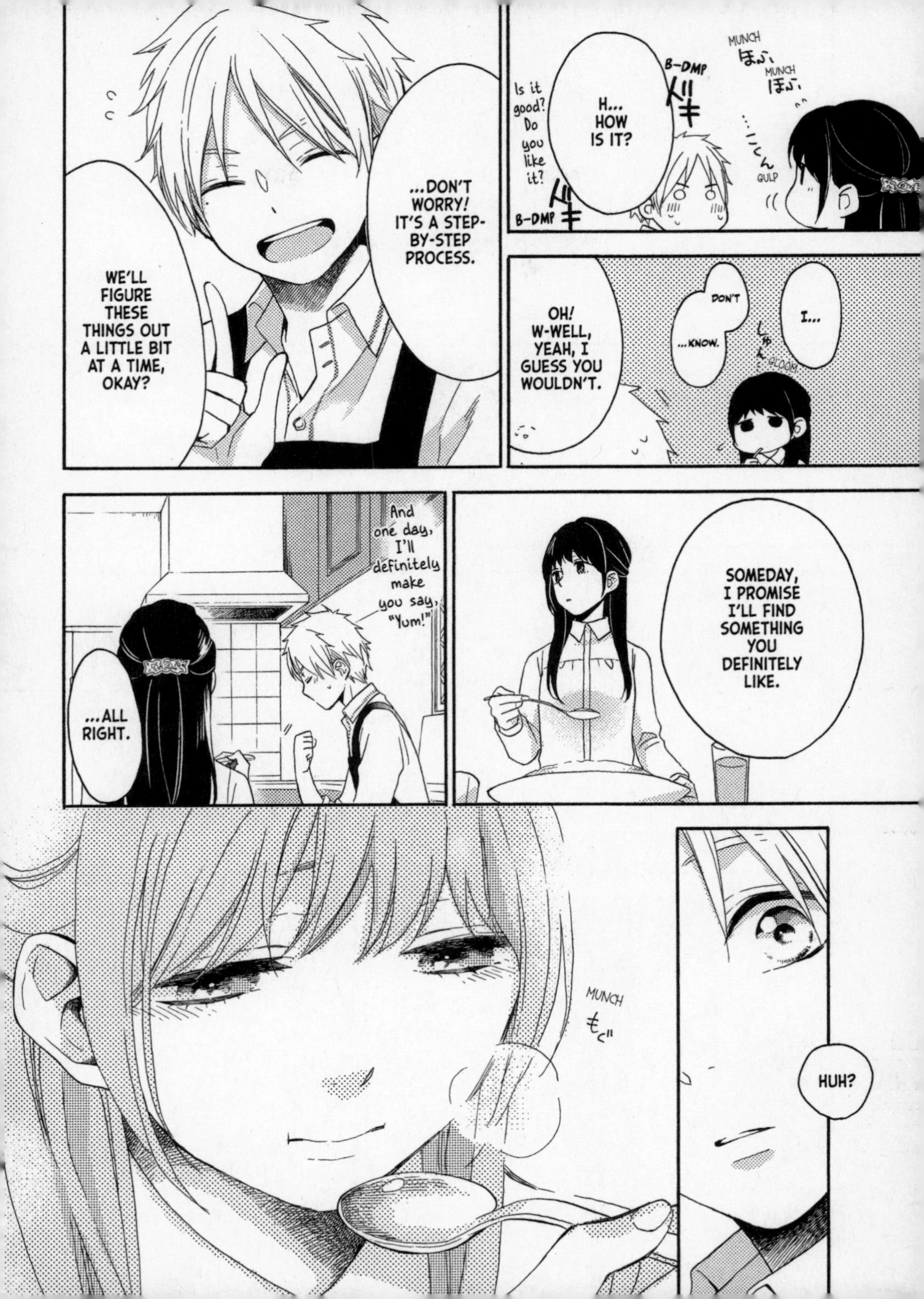
MUNCH
ほふ
MUNCH
ほふ
GULP
H... HOW IS IT?
B-DMP
Is it good? Do you like it?
B-DMP
I...
DON'T ...KNOW.
GLOOM
OH! W-WELL, YEAH, I GUESS YOU WOULDN'T.
...DON'T WORRY! IT'S A STEP-BY-STEP PROCESS.
WE'LL FIGURE THESE THINGS OUT A LITTLE BIT AT A TIME, OKAY?
SOMEDAY, I PROMISE I'LL FIND SOMETHING YOU DEFINITELY LIKE.
And one day, I'll definitely make you say, "Yum!"
...ALL RIGHT.
HUH?
MUNCH

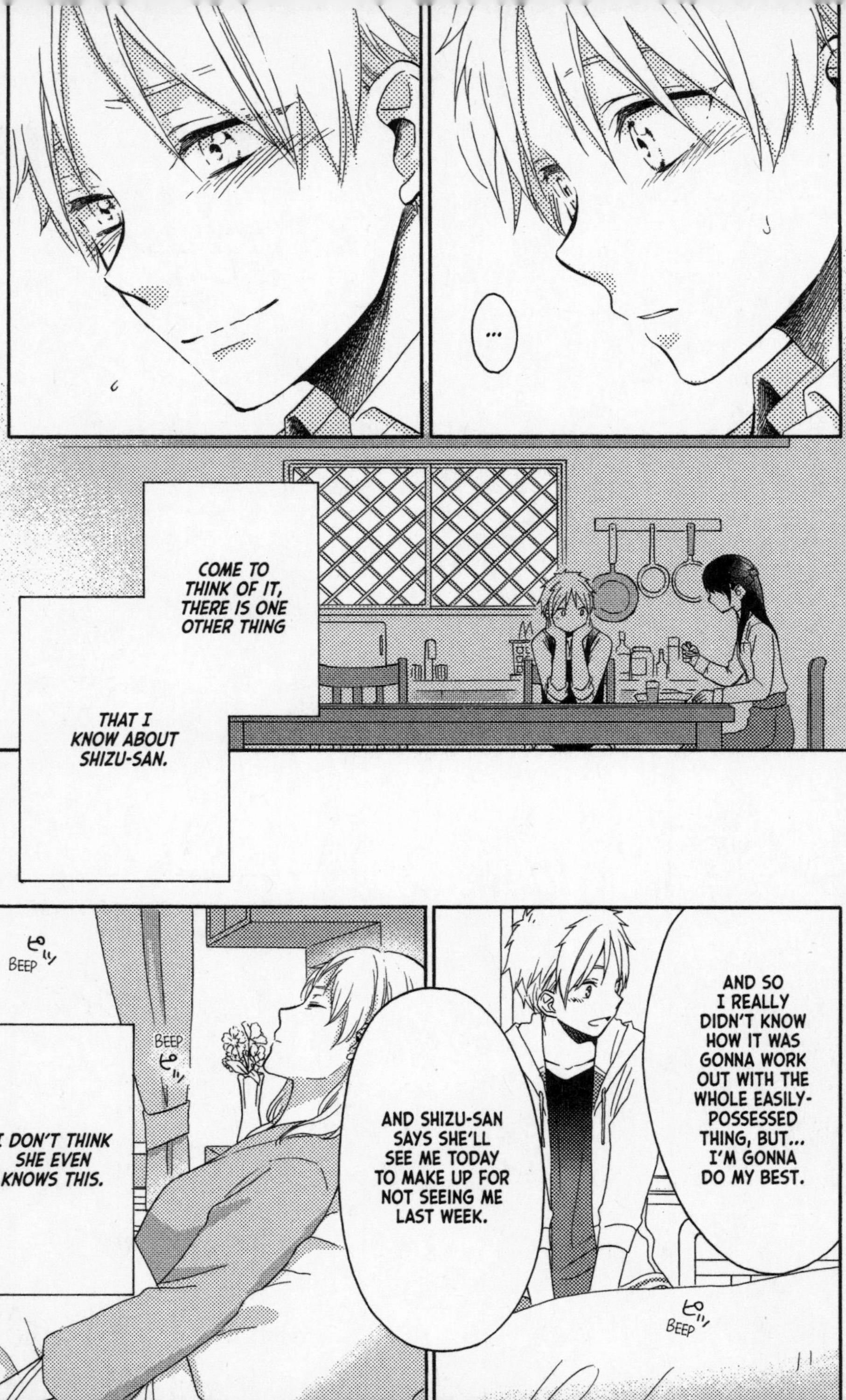
...
COME TO THINK OF IT, THERE IS ONE OTHER THING
THAT I KNOW ABOUT SHIZU-SAN.
AND SO I REALLY DIDN'T KNOW HOW IT WAS GONNA WORK OUT WITH THE WHOLE EASILY-POSSESSED THING, BUT... I'M GONNA DO MY BEST.
AND SHIZU-SAN SAYS SHE'LL SEE ME TODAY TO MAKE UP FOR NOT SEEING ME LAST WEEK.
ピッ
BEEP
ピッ
BEEP
BEEP
ピッ
I DON'T THINK SHE EVEN KNOWS THIS.

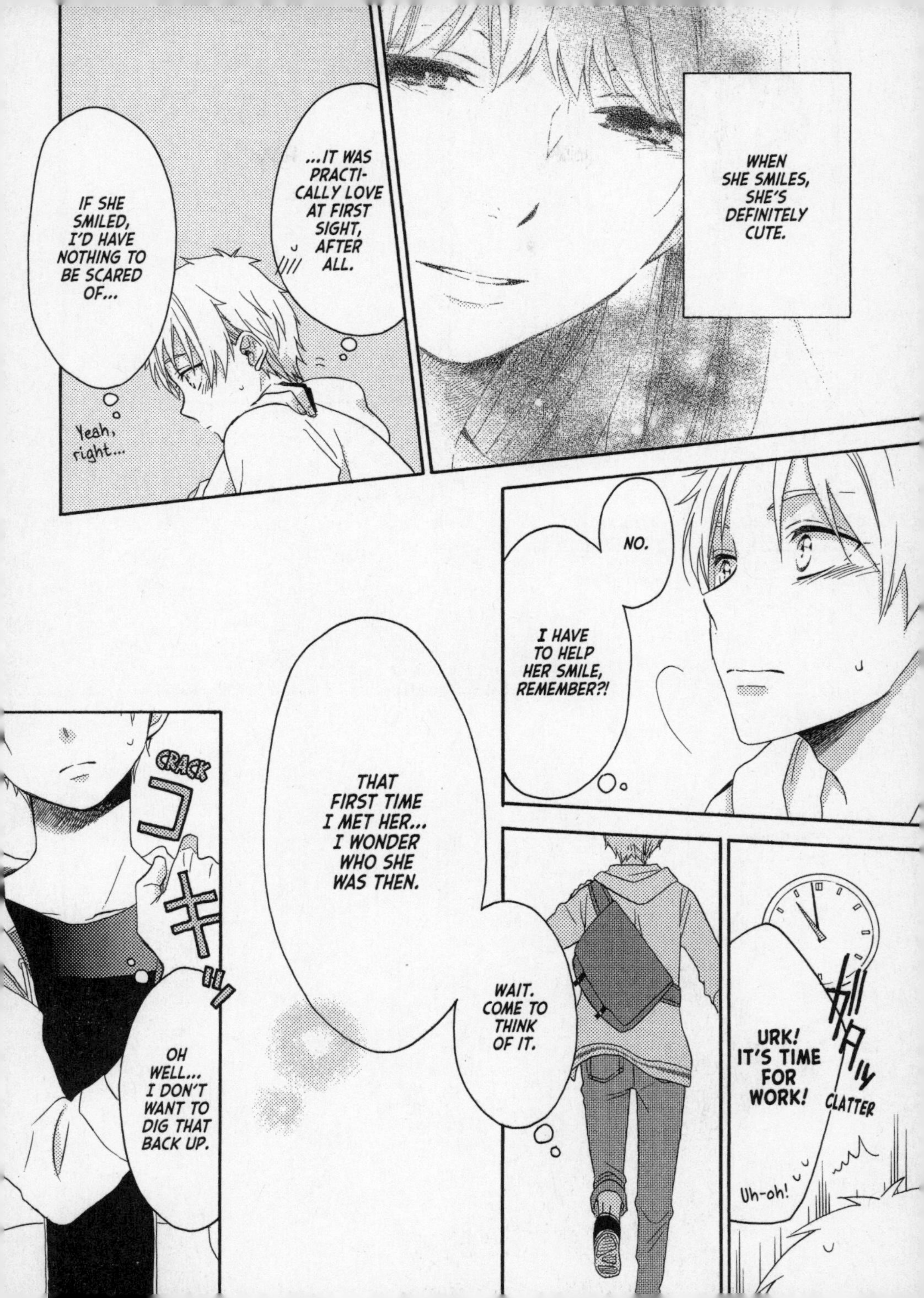
WHEN SHE SMILES, SHE'S DEFINITELY CUTE.
...IT WAS PRACTICALLY LOVE AT FIRST SIGHT, AFTER ALL.
IF SHE SMILED, I'D HAVE NOTHING TO BE SCARED OF...
Yeah, right...
NO.
I HAVE TO HELP HER SMILE, REMEMBER?!
URK! IT'S TIME FOR WORK!
CLATTER
Uh-oh!
WAIT. COME TO THINK OF IT.
THAT FIRST TIME I MET HER... I WONDER WHO SHE WAS THEN.
CRACK
OH WELL... I DON'T WANT TO DIG THAT BACK UP.

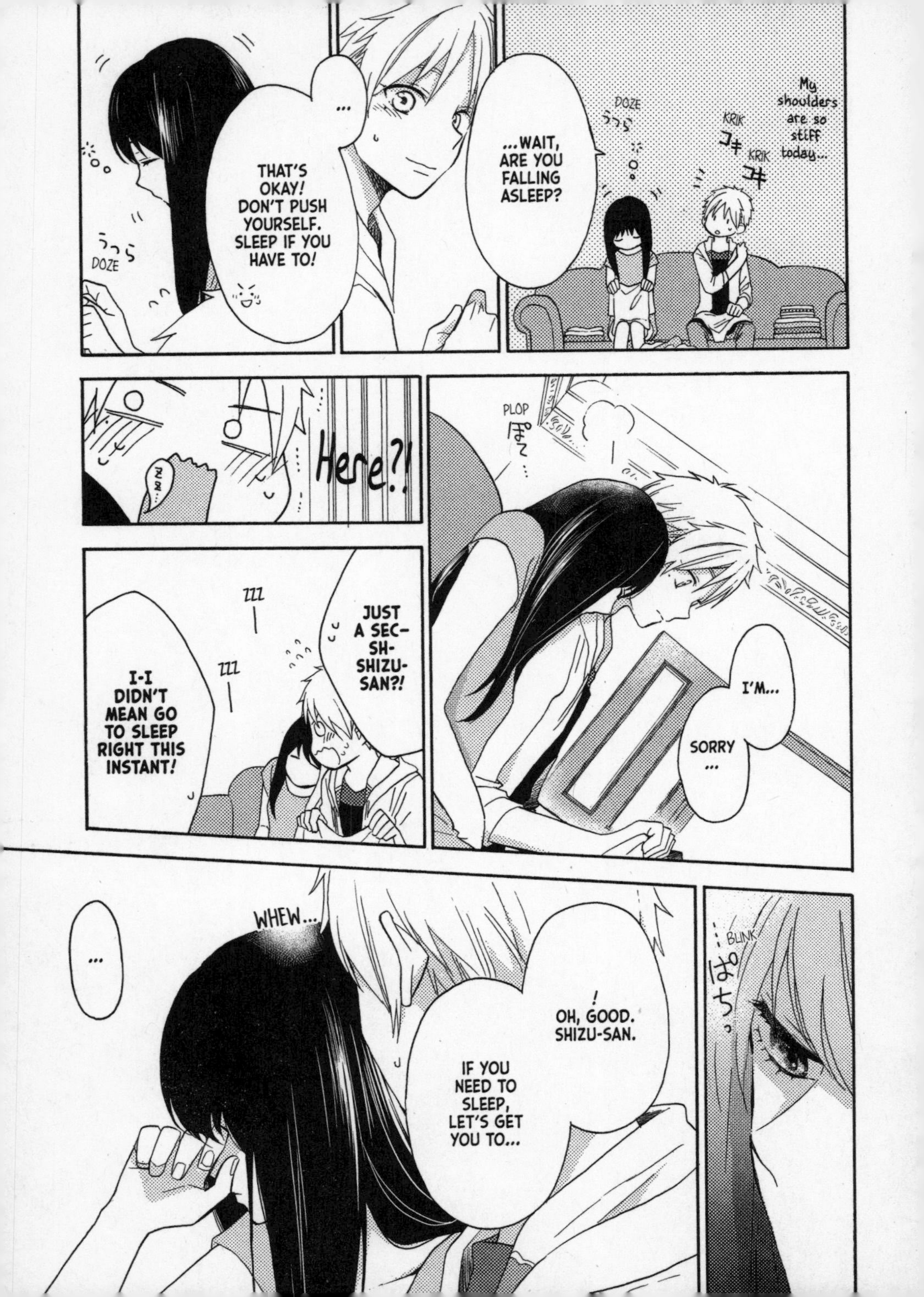
My shoulders are so stiff today...
KRIK
コキ
KRIK
コキ
DOZE
うつら
...WAIT, ARE YOU FALLING ASLEEP?
...
THAT'S OKAY! DON'T PUSH YOURSELF. SLEEP IF YOU HAVE TO!
うつら
DOZE
PLOP
ぽて
I'M...
SORRY...
Here?!
JUST A SEC- SH-SHIZU-SAN?!
ZZZ
ZZZ
I-I DIDN'T MEAN GO TO SLEEP RIGHT THIS INSTANT!
BLINK
ぱち
WHEW...
!
OH, GOOD. SHIZU-SAN.
IF YOU NEED TO SLEEP, LET'S GET YOU TO...
...

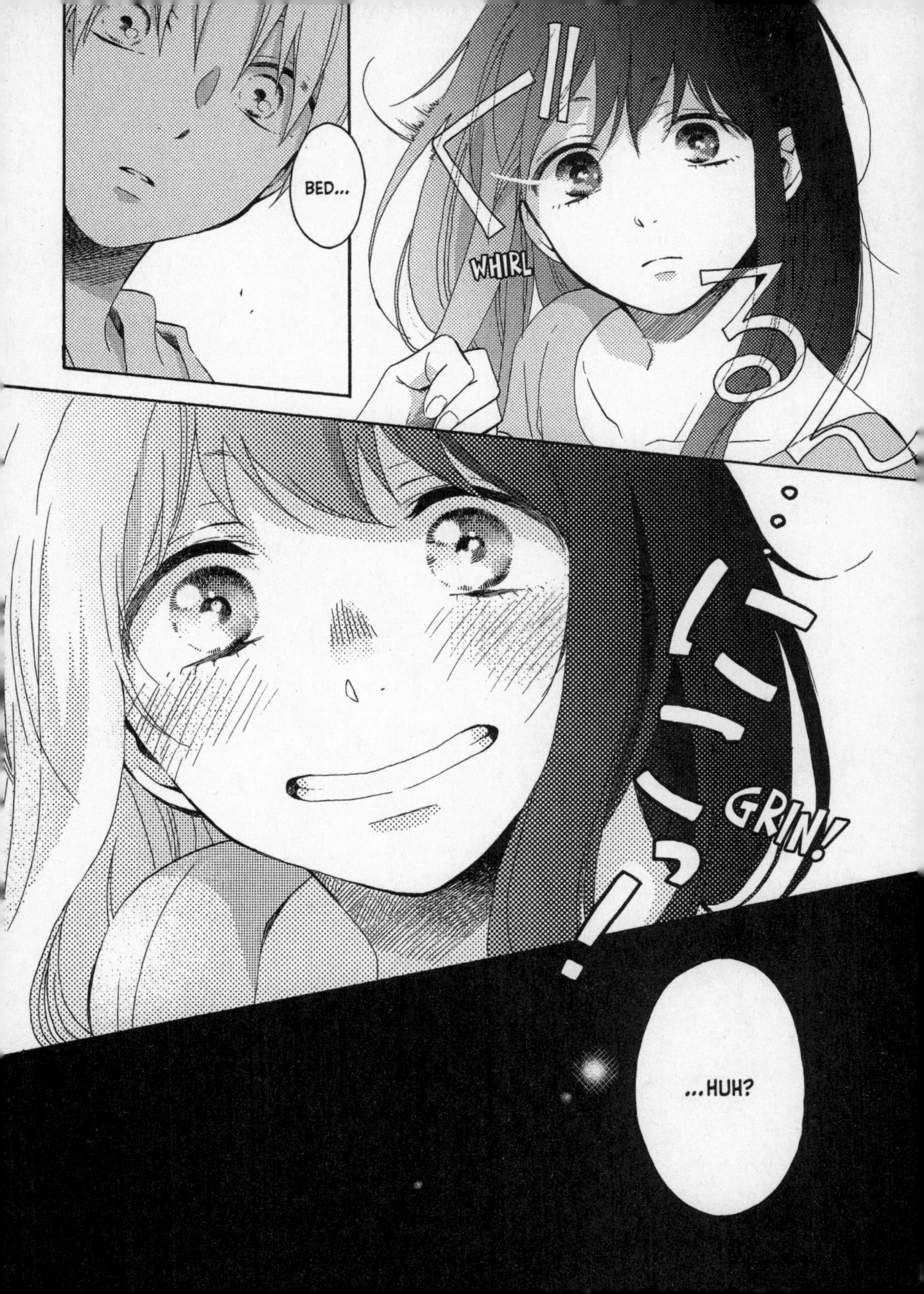
BED...
WHIRL
GRIN!
...HUH?

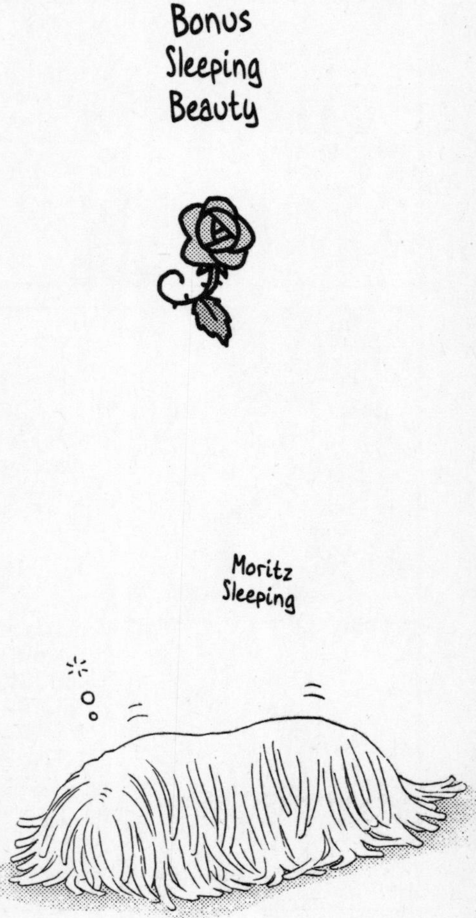
Bonus
Sleeping
Beauty
Moritz
Sleeping

STAFF SUPERVISOR

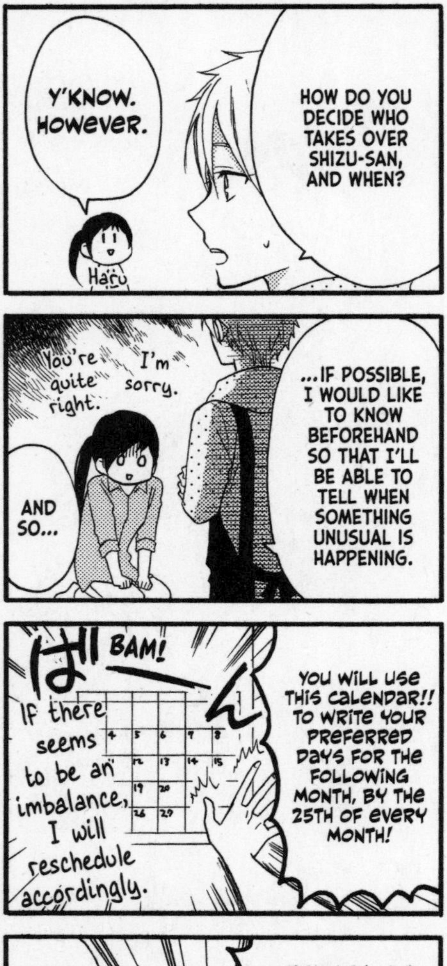
HOW DO YOU DECIDE WHO TAKES OVER SHIZU-SAN, AND WHEN?
Y'KNOW. HOWEVER.
Haru
...IF POSSIBLE, I WOULD LIKE TO KNOW BEFOREHAND SO THAT I'LL BE ABLE TO TELL WHEN SOMETHING UNUSUAL IS HAPPENING.
I'm sorry.
You're quite right.
AND SO...
BAM!
YOU WILL USE THIS CALENDAR!! TO WRITE YOUR PREFERRED DAYS FOR THE FOLLOWING MONTH, BY THE 25TH OF EVERY MONTH!
If there seems to be an imbalance, I will reschedule accordingly.
IF YOU SHOULD DESIRE A LAST-MINUTE CHANGE, YOU WILL FIND SOMEONE TO TAKE YOUR SHIFT AND NOTIFY ME AS SOON AS POSSIBLE! IS THAT OKAY WITH YOU?!
IT'S KIND OF LIKE A PART-TIME JOB.

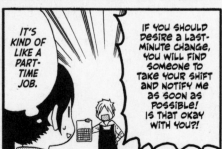

NAMING PART 1

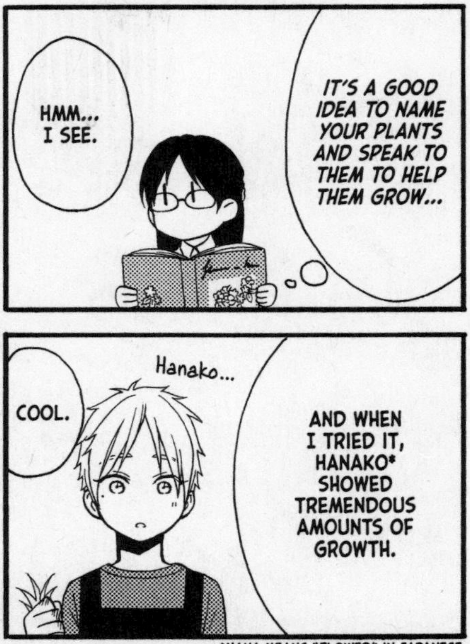
IT'S A GOOD IDEA TO NAME YOUR PLANTS AND SPEAK TO THEM TO HELP THEM GROW...
HMM... I SEE.
AND WHEN I TRIED IT, HANAKO* SHOWED TREMENDOUS AMOUNTS OF GROWTH.
Hanako...
COOL.

*HANA MEANS "FLOWER" IN JAPANESE.

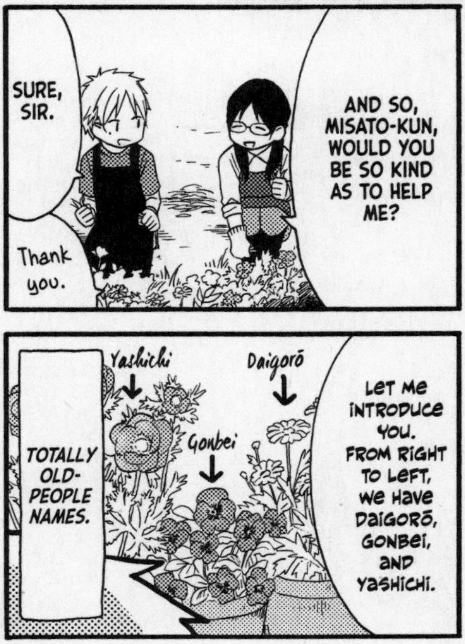
AND SO, MISATO-KUN, WOULD YOU BE SO KIND AS TO HELP ME?
SURE, SIR.
Thank you.
LET ME INTRODUCE YOU. FROM RIGHT TO LEFT, WE HAVE DAIGORŌ, GONBEI, AND YASHICHI.
Daigorō
Gonbei
Yashichi
TOTALLY OLD-PEOPLE NAMES.

NAMING PART 2

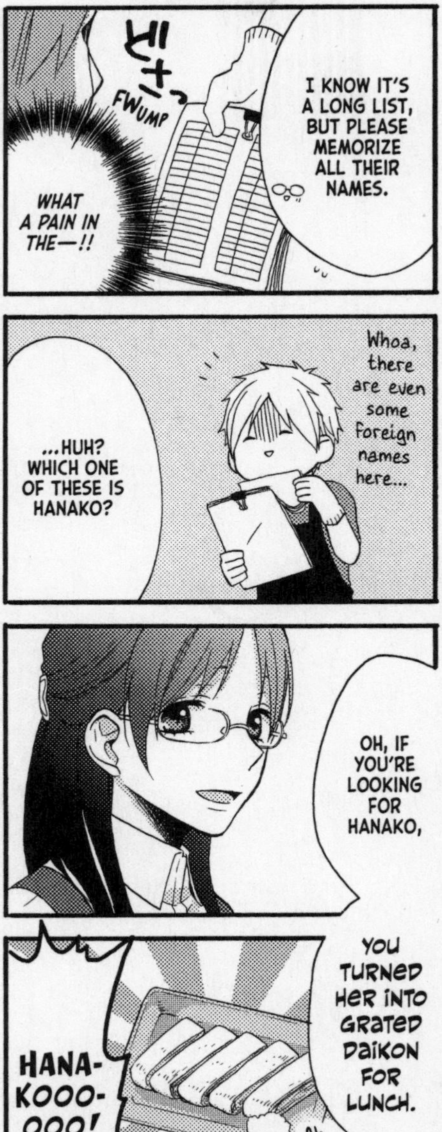
I KNOW IT'S A LONG LIST, BUT PLEASE MEMORIZE ALL THEIR NAMES.
どさっ
FWUMP
WHAT A PAIN IN THE—!!
Whoa, there are even some foreign names here...
...HUH? WHICH ONE OF THESE IS HANAKO?
OH, IF YOU'RE LOOKING FOR HANAKO,
YOU TURNED HER INTO GRATED DAIKON FOR LUNCH.
Ah, she was delicious.
HANA-KOOO-OOO!
Hanako

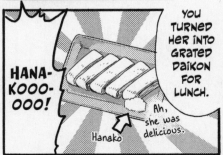

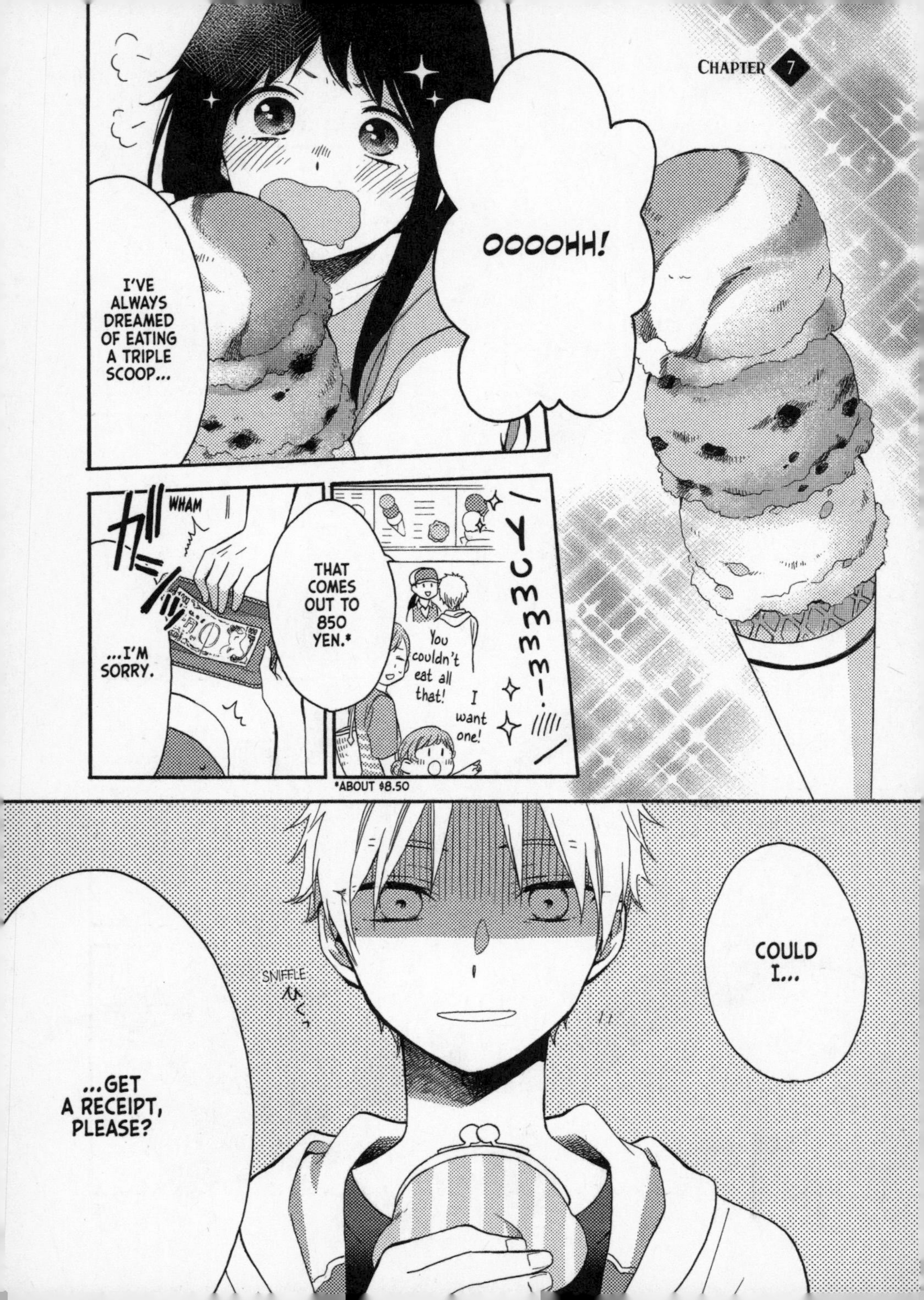
OOOOHH!
I'VE ALWAYS DREAMED OF EATING A TRIPLE SCOOP...
YUMMMM!
THAT COMES OUT TO 850 YEN.*
You couldn't eat all that!
I want one!
WHAM
...I'M SORRY.
*ABOUT $8.50
COULD I...
SNIFFLE
...GET A RECEIPT, PLEASE?

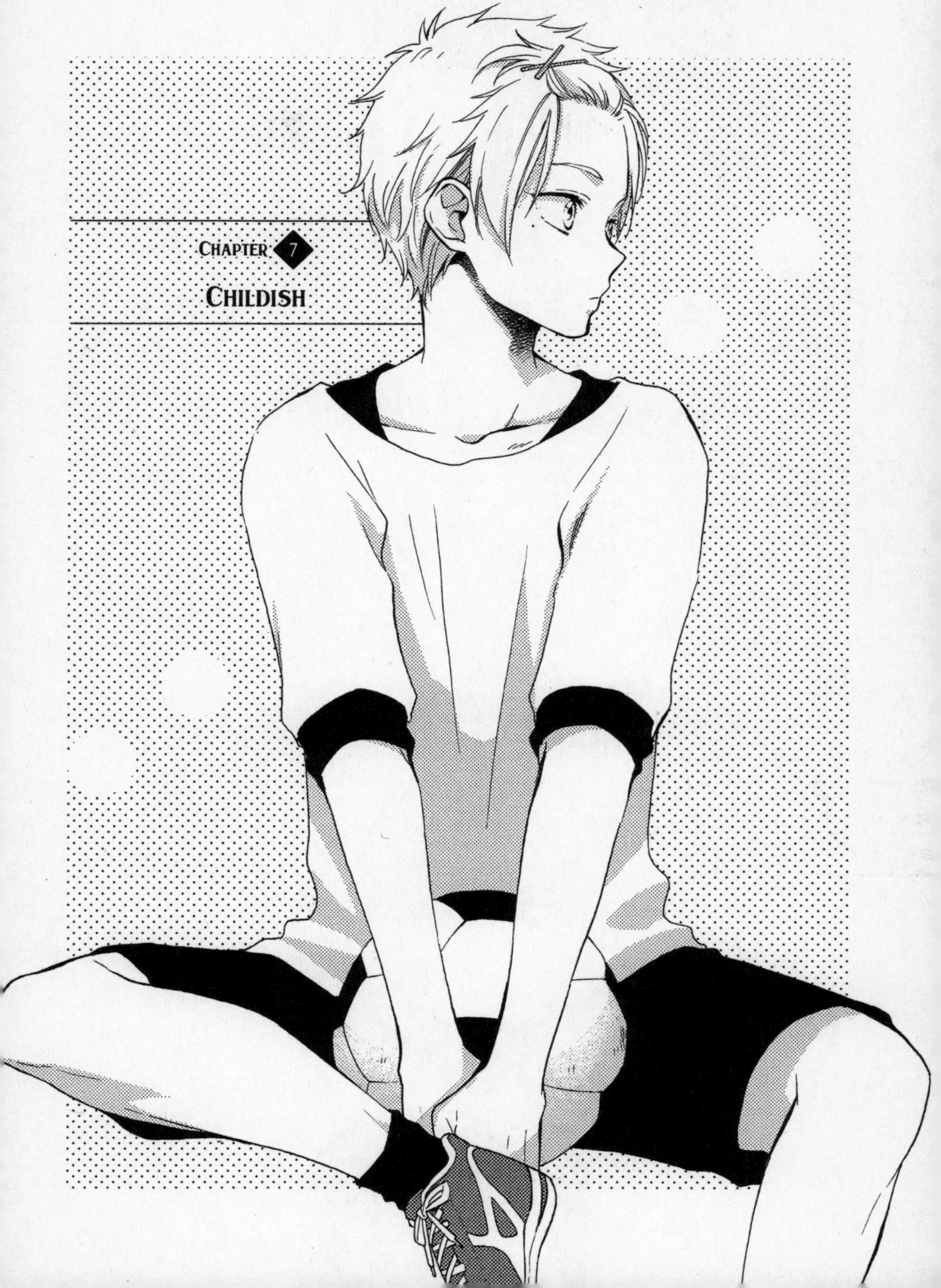
CHAPTER 7
CHILDISH

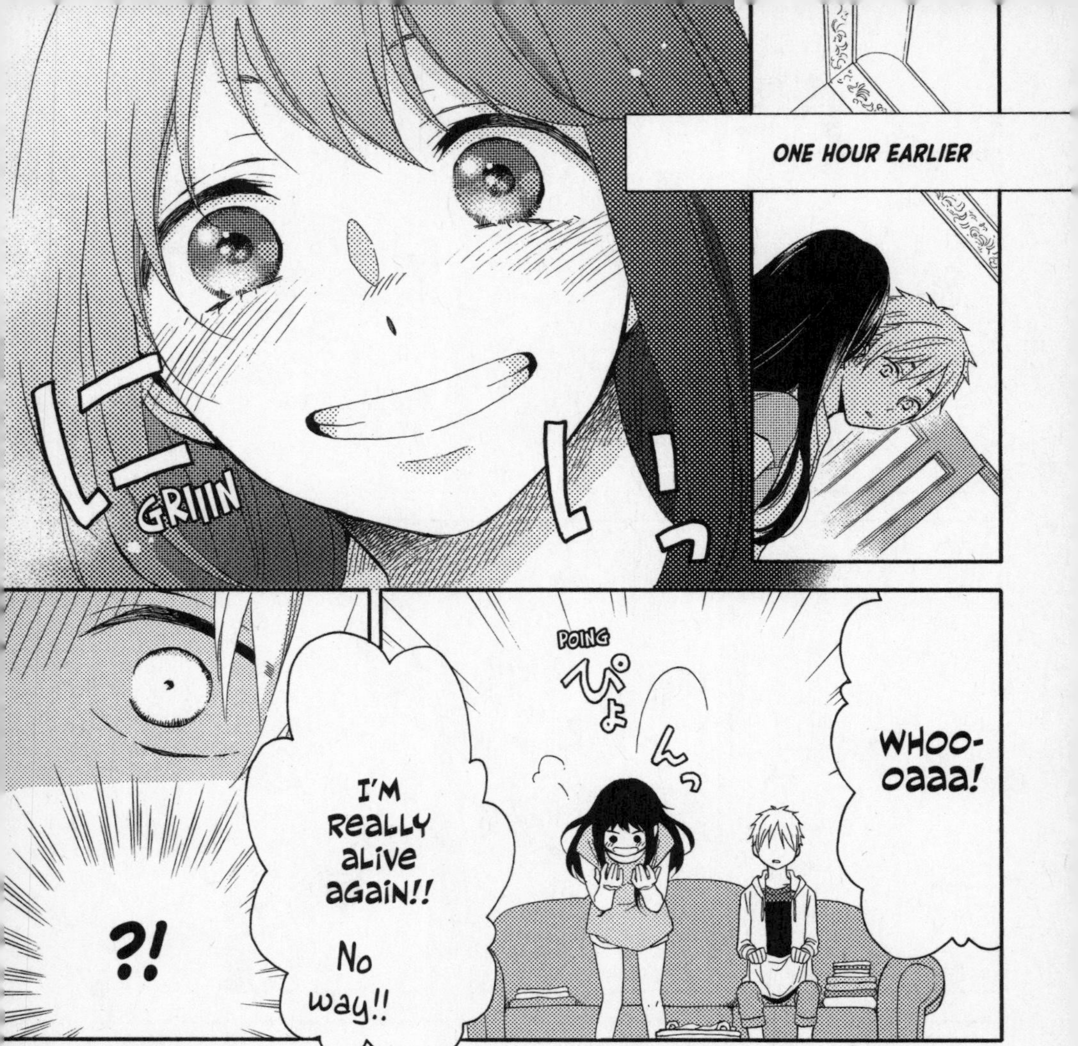
ONE HOUR EARLIER
GRIIIN
WHOO-oaaa!
POING
ぴょんっ
I'M REALLY ALIVE AGAIN!!
No way!!
?!

Wake Up, Sleeping Beauty

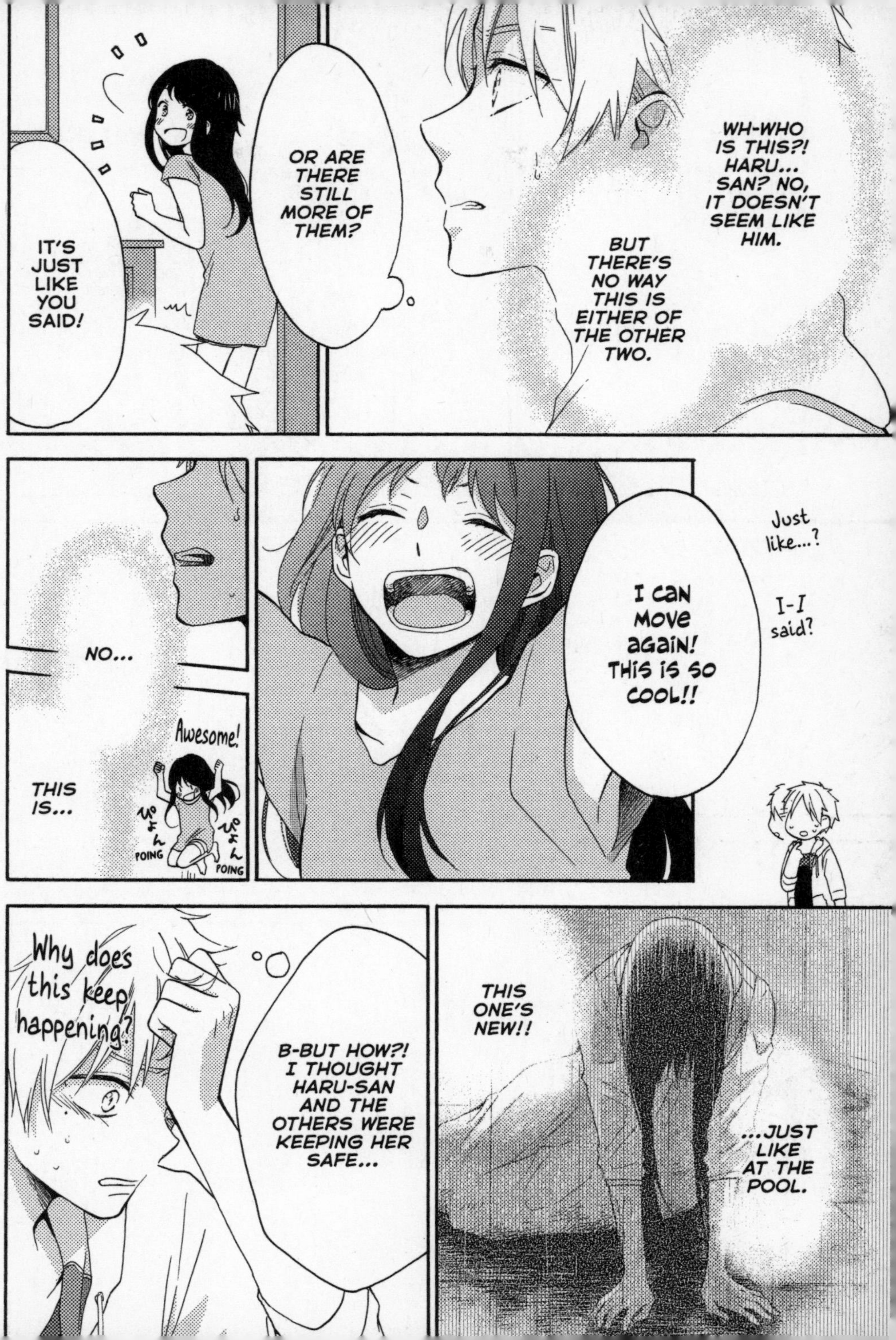
WH-WHO IS THIS?! HARU... SAN? NO, IT DOESN'T SEEM LIKE HIM.
BUT THERE'S NO WAY THIS IS EITHER OF THE OTHER TWO.
OR ARE THERE STILL MORE OF THEM?
IT'S JUST LIKE YOU SAID!
Just like...?
I-I said?
I CAN MOVE AGAIN! THIS IS SO COOL!!
NO...
THIS IS...
Awesome!
ぴょん
POING
ぴょん
POING
THIS ONE'S NEW!!
...JUST LIKE AT THE POOL.
B-BUT HOW?! I THOUGHT HARU-SAN AND THE OTHERS WERE KEEPING HER SAFE...
Why does this keep happening?

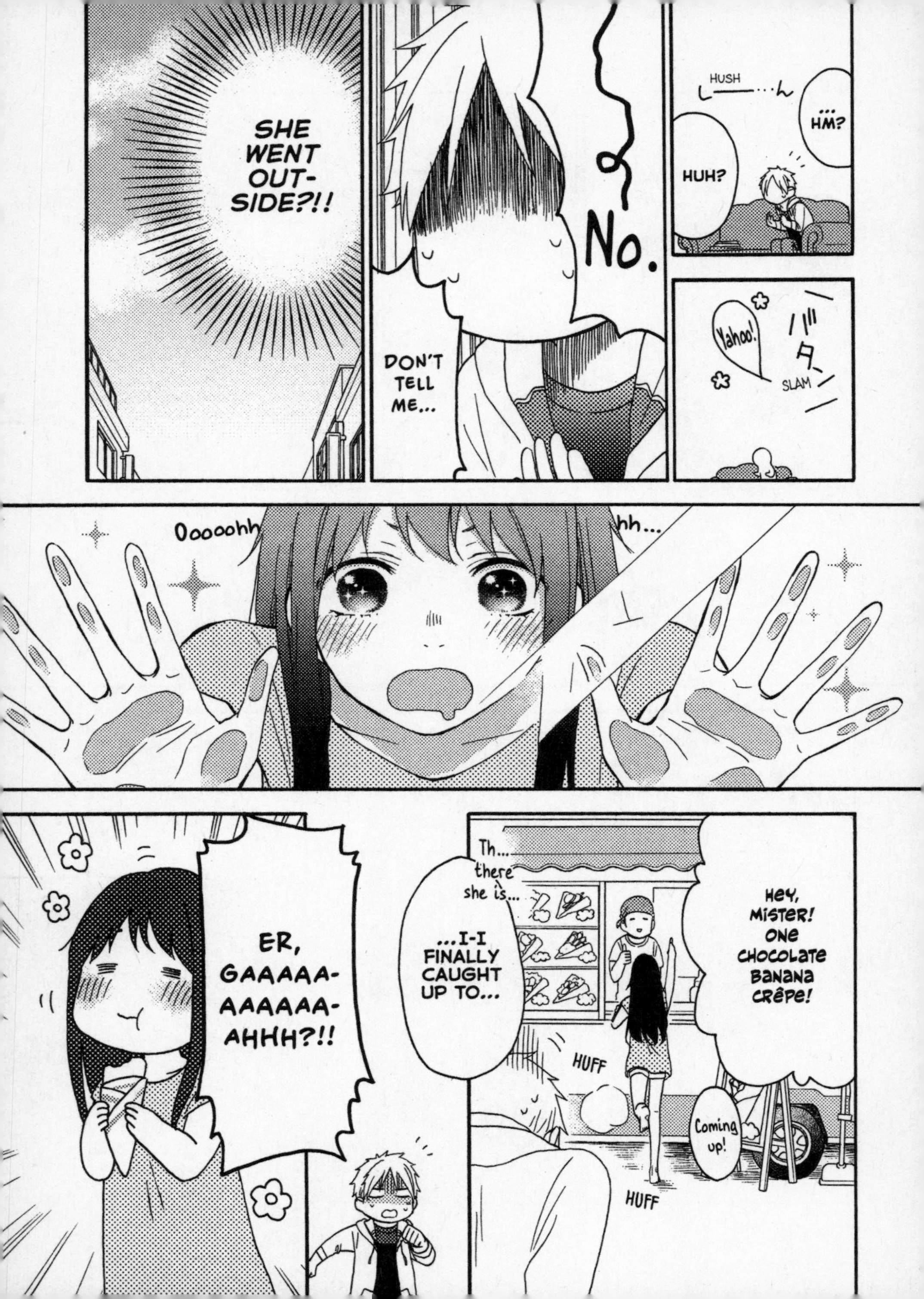
HUSH
...HM?
HUH?
Yahoo!
SLAM
No.
DON'T TELL ME...
SHE WENT OUT-SIDE?!!
Oooooohh hh...
HEY, MISTER! ONE CHOCOLATE BANANA CRÊPE!
Th... there she is...
...I-I FINALLY CAUGHT UP TO...
HUFF
Coming up!
HUFF
ER, GAAAAA-AAAAAA-AHHH?!!

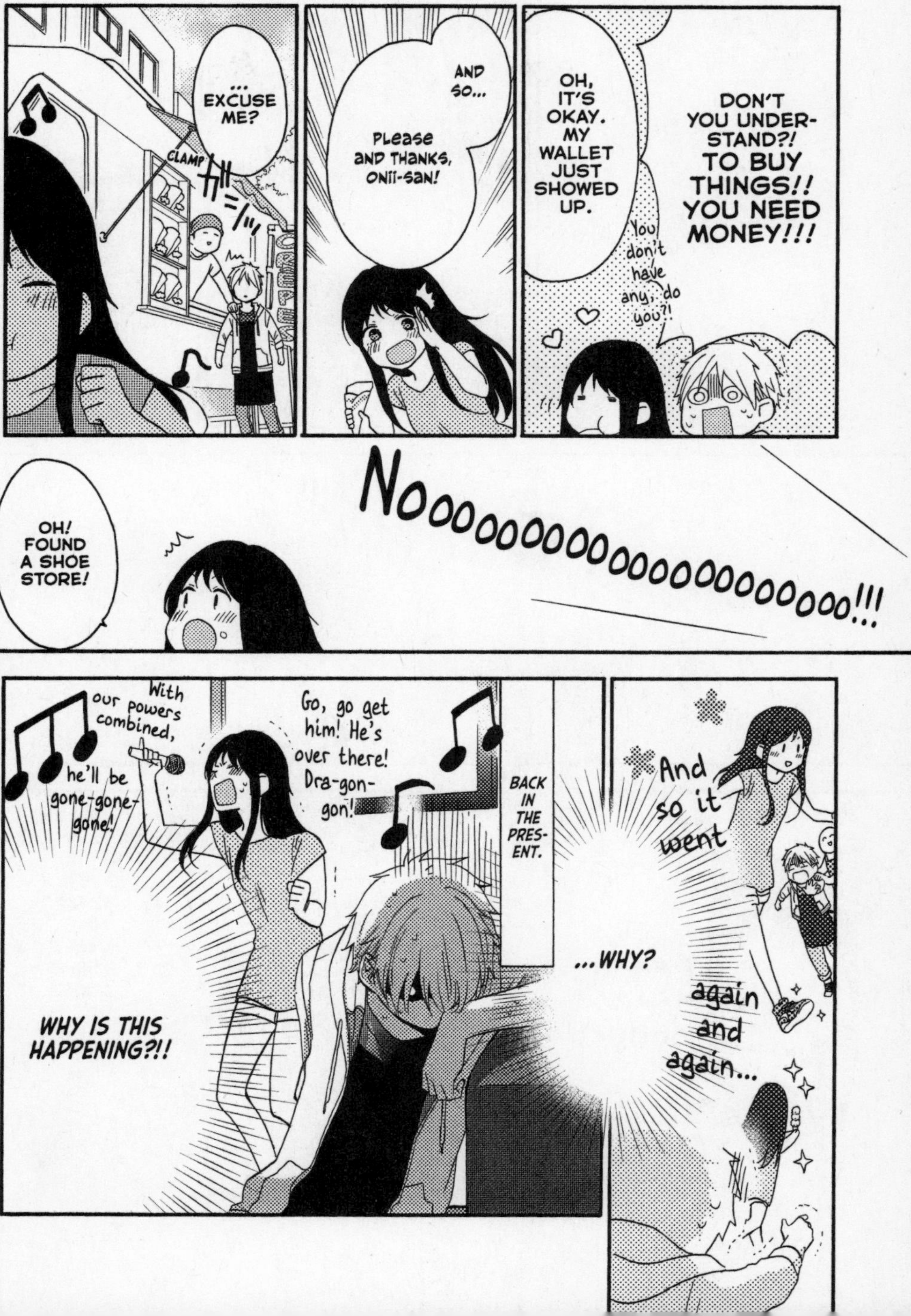
DON'T YOU UNDERSTAND?! TO BUY THINGS!! YOU NEED MONEY!!!
OH, IT'S OKAY. MY WALLET JUST SHOWED UP.
You don't have any, do you?!
AND SO...
Please and thanks, Onii-san!
...EXCUSE ME?
CLAMP
Noooooooooooooooooooooooo!!!
OH! FOUND A SHOE STORE!
And so it went
again and again...
BACK IN THE PRESENT.
...WHY?
Go, go get him! He's over there! Dra-gon-gon!
With our powers combined, he'll be gone-gone-gone!
WHY IS THIS HAPPENING?!!

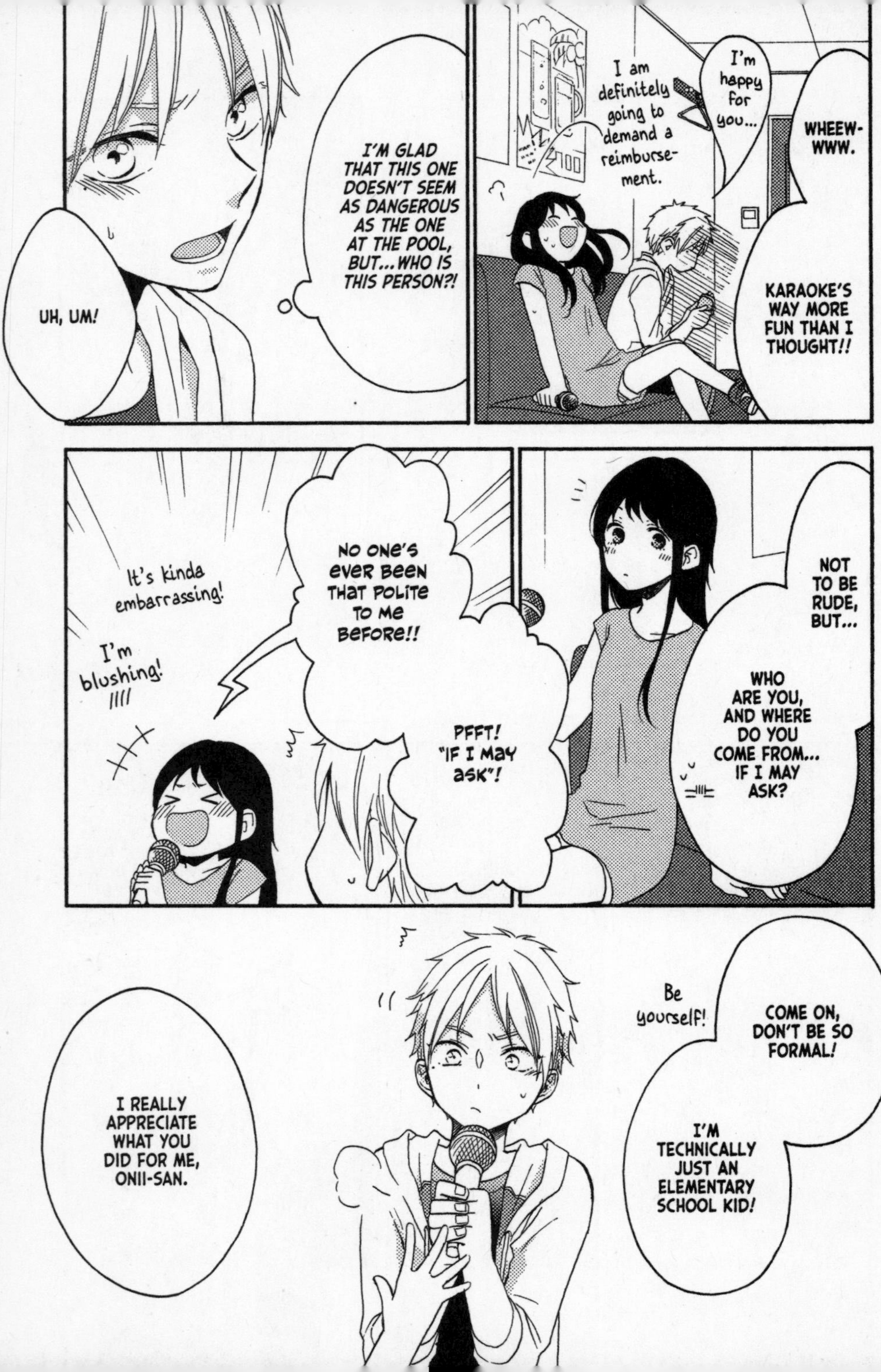

WHEEW-WWW.
KARAOKE'S WAY MORE FUN THAN I THOUGHT!!
I'm happy for you...
I am definitely going to demand a reimburse-ment.
I'M GLAD THAT THIS ONE DOESN'T SEEM AS DANGEROUS AS THE ONE AT THE POOL, BUT...WHO IS THIS PERSON?!
UH, UM!
NOT TO BE RUDE, BUT...
WHO ARE YOU, AND WHERE DO YOU COME FROM... IF I MAY ASK?
PFFT! "IF I MAY ask"!
NO ONE'S ever BEEN THAT POLITE TO ME BEFORE!!
It's kinda embarrassing!
I'm blushing!
COME ON, DON'T BE SO FORMAL!
Be yourself!
I'M TECHNICALLY JUST AN ELEMENTARY SCHOOL KID!
I REALLY APPRECIATE WHAT YOU DID FOR ME, ONII-SAN.

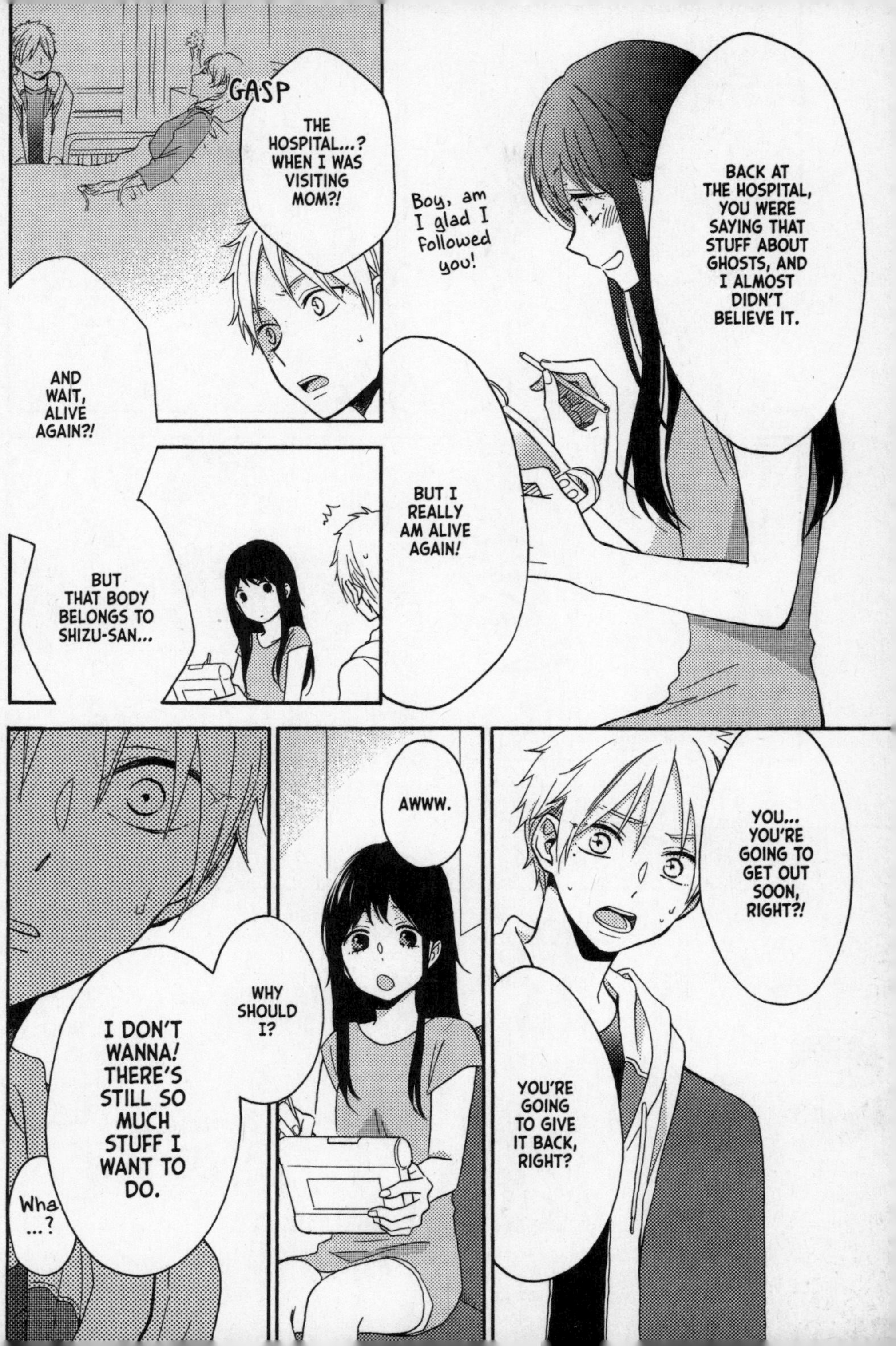
BACK AT THE HOSPITAL, YOU WERE SAYING THAT STUFF ABOUT GHOSTS, AND I ALMOST DIDN'T BELIEVE IT.
Boy, am I glad I followed you!
GASP
THE HOSPITAL...? WHEN I WAS VISITING MOM?!
AND WAIT, ALIVE AGAIN?!
BUT I REALLY AM ALIVE AGAIN!
BUT THAT BODY BELONGS TO SHIZU-SAN...
YOU... YOU'RE GOING TO GET OUT SOON, RIGHT?!
YOU'RE GOING TO GIVE IT BACK, RIGHT?
AWWW.
WHY SHOULD I?
I DON'T WANNA! THERE'S STILL SO MUCH STUFF I WANT TO DO.
Wha ...?

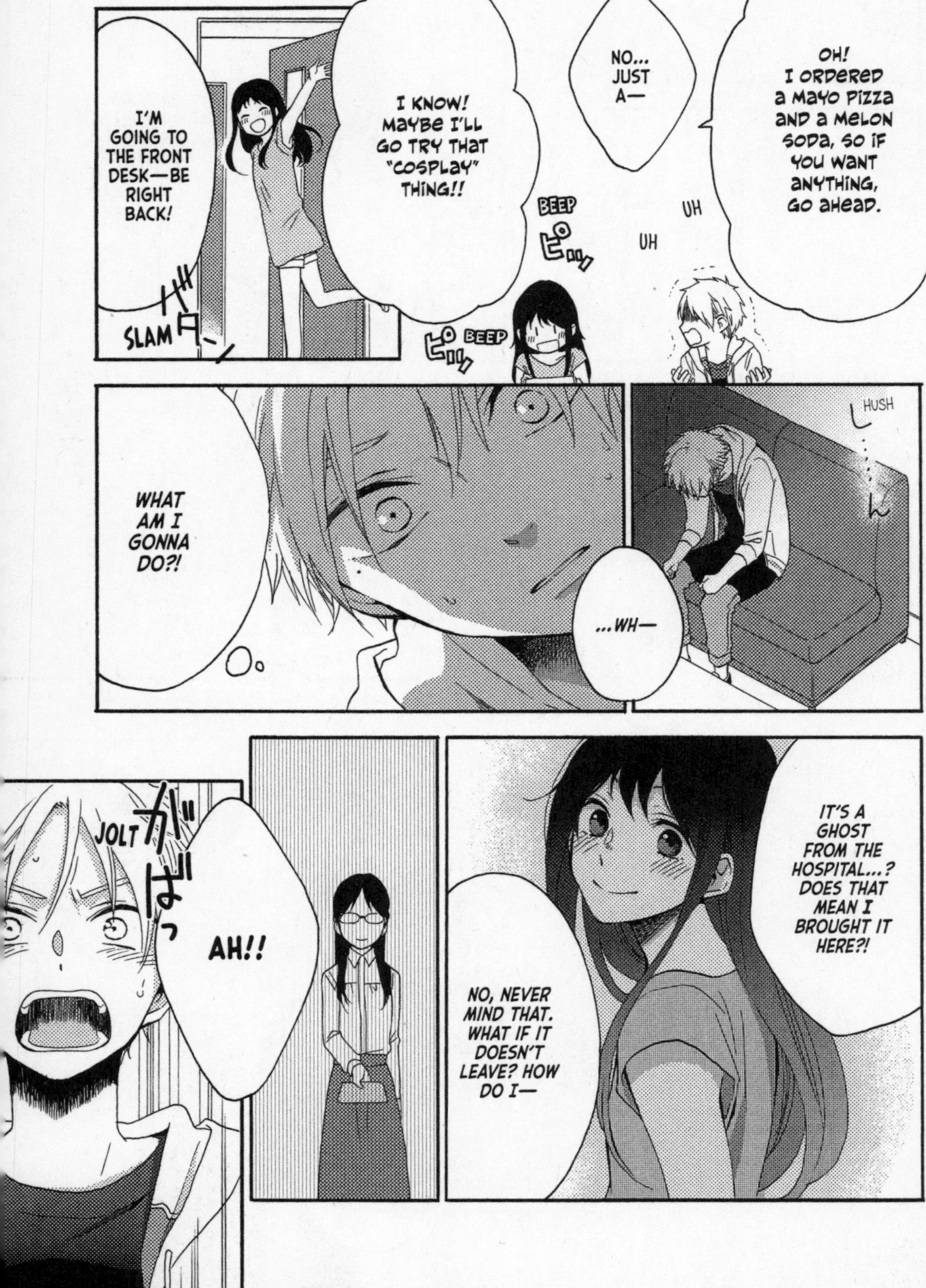
OH! I ORDERED a MAYO PIZZA AND A MELON SODA, SO IF YOU WANT ANYTHING, GO AHEAD.
UH
UH
NO... JUST A—
BEEP
I KNOW! MAYBE I'LL GO TRY THAT "COSPLAY" THING!!
BEEP
I'M GOING TO THE FRONT DESK—BE RIGHT BACK!
SLAM
HUSH
...WH—
WHAT AM I GONNA DO?!
IT'S A GHOST FROM THE HOSPITAL...? DOES THAT MEAN I BROUGHT IT HERE?!
NO, NEVER MIND THAT. WHAT IF IT DOESN'T LEAVE? HOW DO I—
JOLT
AH!!

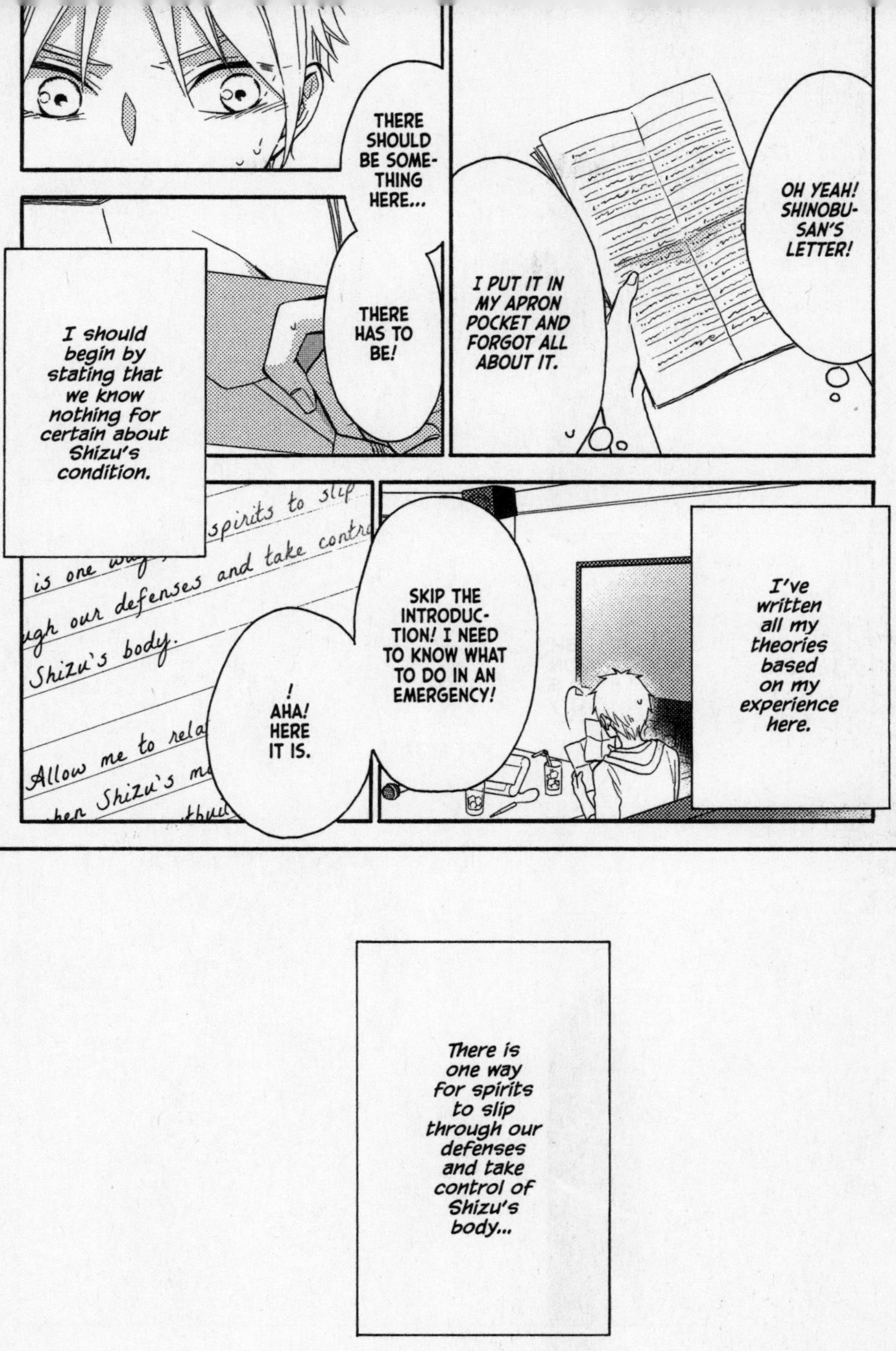
OH YEAH! SHINOBU-SAN'S LETTER!
I PUT IT IN MY APRON POCKET AND FORGOT ALL ABOUT IT.
THERE SHOULD BE SOME-THING HERE...
THERE HAS TO BE!
I should begin by stating that we know nothing for certain about Shizu's condition.
I've written all my theories based on my experience here.
SKIP THE INTRODUC-TION! I NEED TO KNOW WHAT TO DO IN AN EMERGENCY!
! AHA! HERE IT IS.
There is one way for spirits to slip through our defenses and take control of Shizu's body...

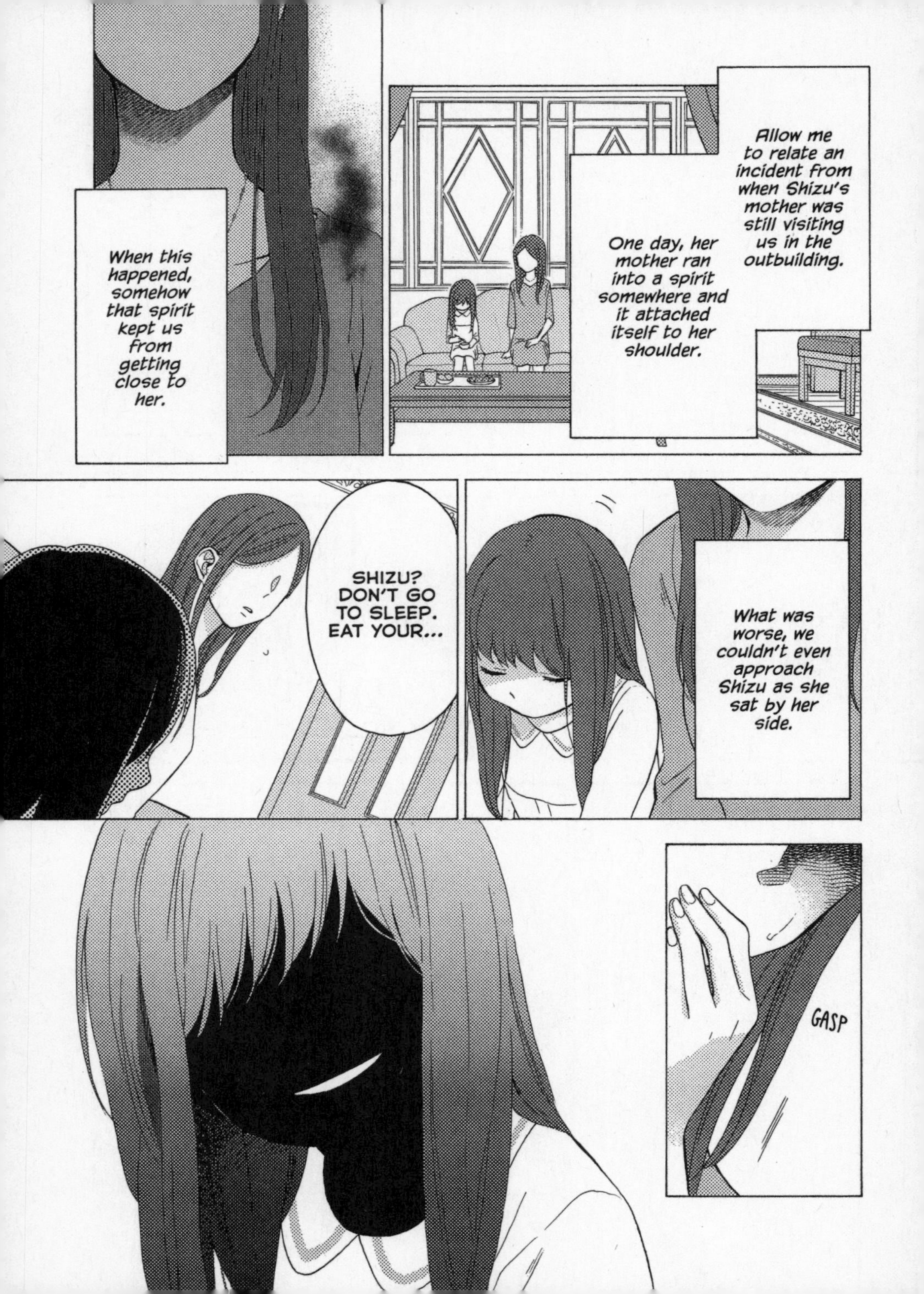
Allow me to relate an incident from when Shizu's mother was still visiting us in the outbuilding.
One day, her mother ran into a spirit somewhere and it attached itself to her shoulder.
When this happened, somehow that spirit kept us from getting close to her.
What was worse, we couldn't even approach Shizu as she sat by her side.
SHIZU? DON'T GO TO SLEEP. EAT YOUR...
GASP

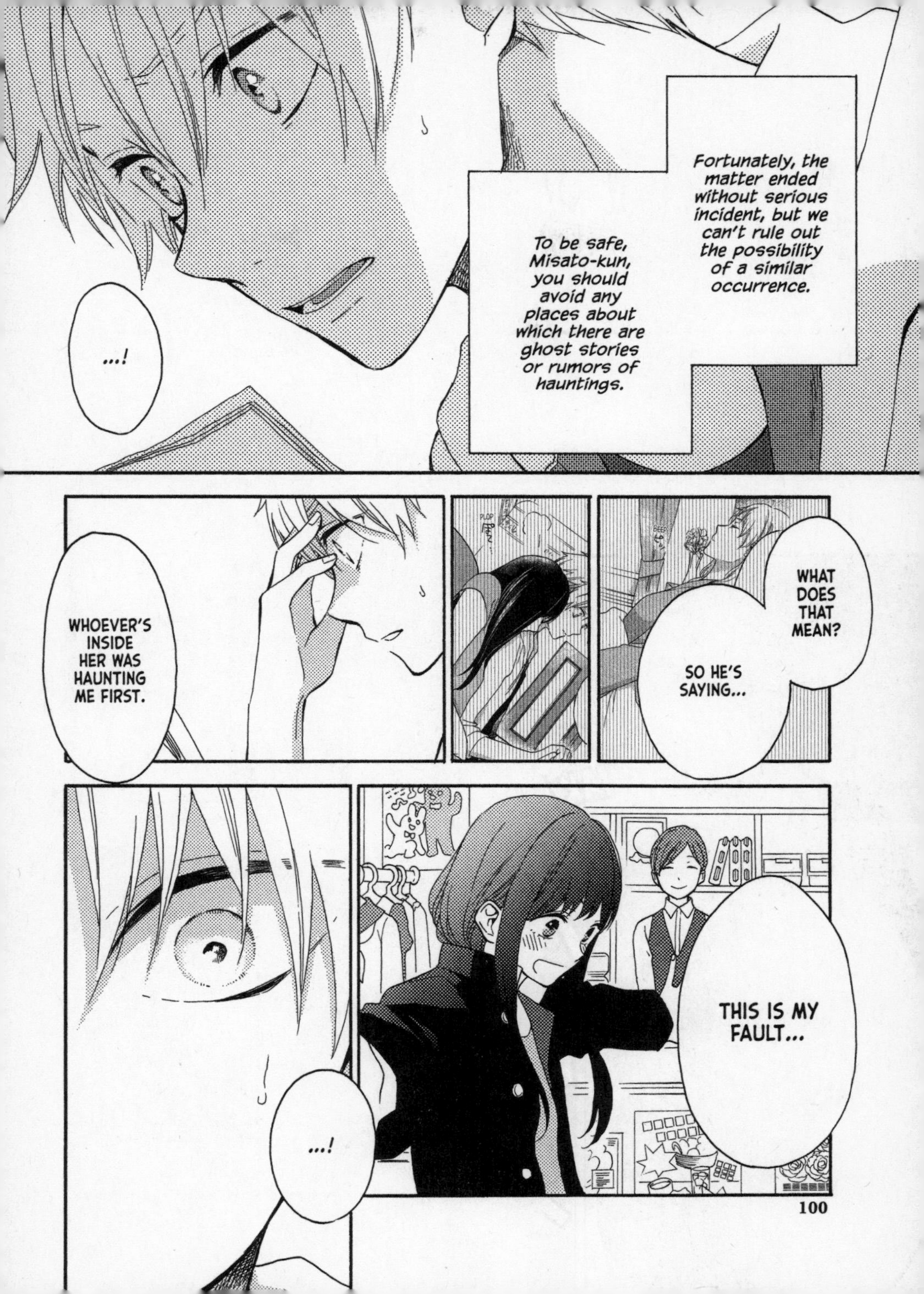
Fortunately, the matter ended without serious incident, but we can't rule out the possibility of a similar occurrence.
To be safe, Misato-kun, you should avoid any places about which there are ghost stories or rumors of hauntings.
...!
BEEP
WHAT DOES THAT MEAN?
SO HE'S SAYING...
PLOP
WHOEVER'S INSIDE HER WAS HAUNTING ME FIRST.
THIS IS MY FAULT...
...!

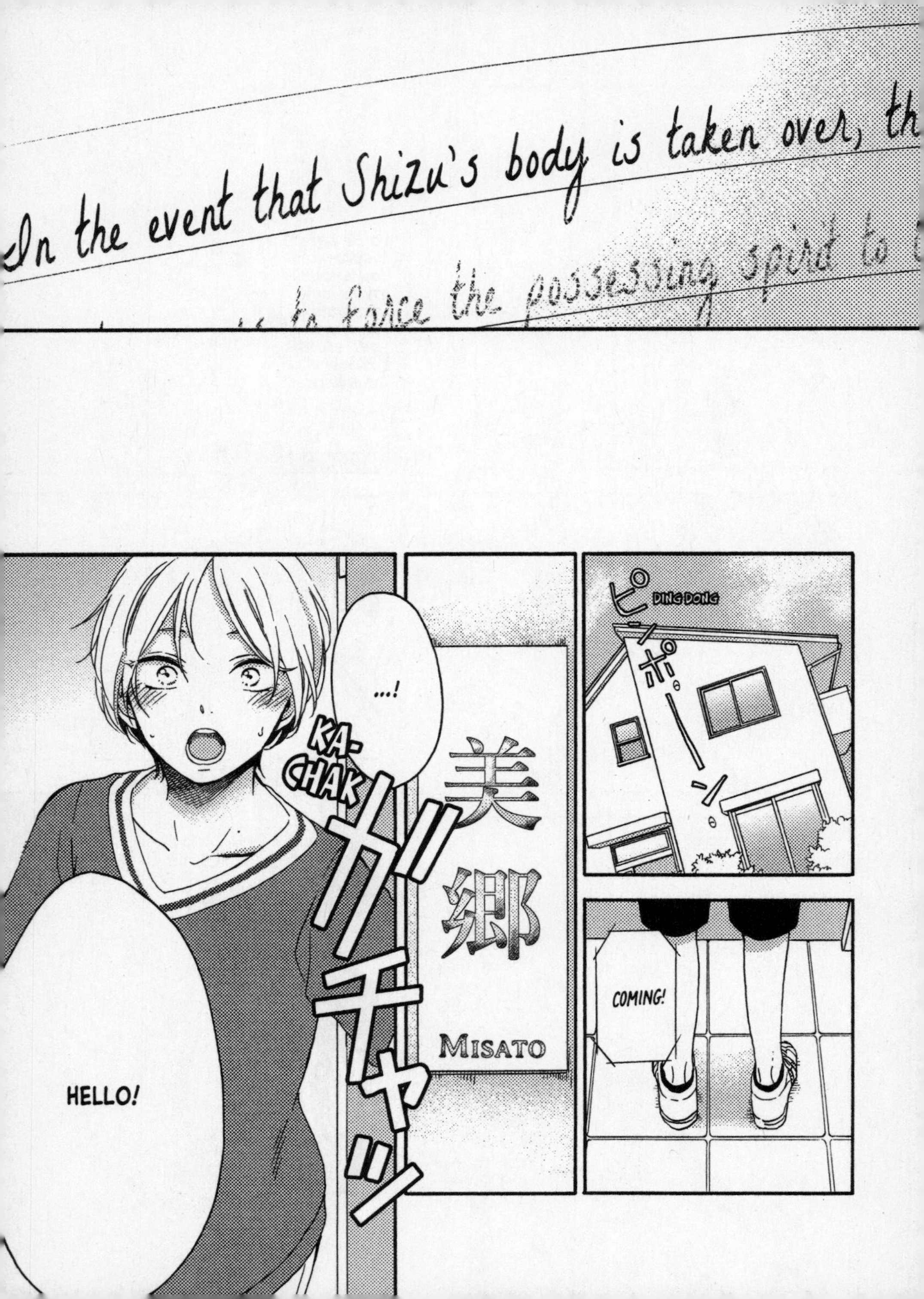

In the event that Shizu's body is taken over, th
to force the possessing spirit to
ピンポーン
DING DONG
COMING!
美郷
MISATO
ガチャッ
KA-CHAK
...!
HELLO!

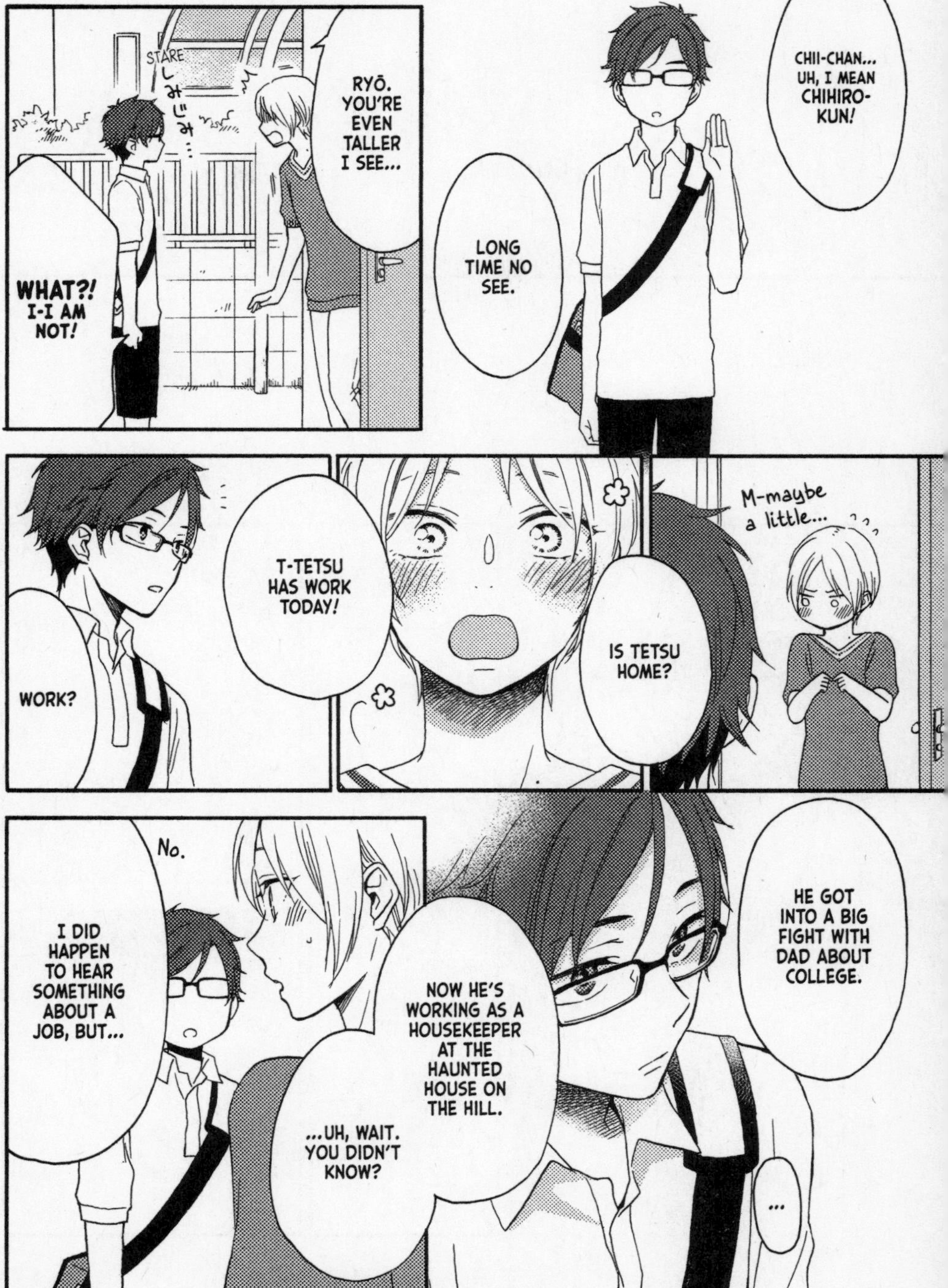
CHII-CHAN... UH, I MEAN CHIHIRO-KUN!
LONG TIME NO SEE.
RYŌ. YOU'RE EVEN TALLER I SEE...
STARE
しみじみ…
WHAT?! I-I AM NOT!
M-maybe a little...
IS TETSU HOME?
T-TETSU HAS WORK TODAY!
WORK?
HE GOT INTO A BIG FIGHT WITH DAD ABOUT COLLEGE.
NOW HE'S WORKING AS A HOUSEKEEPER AT THE HAUNTED HOUSE ON THE HILL.
...
...UH, WAIT. YOU DIDN'T KNOW?
No.
I DID HAPPEN TO HEAR SOMETHING ABOUT A JOB, BUT...

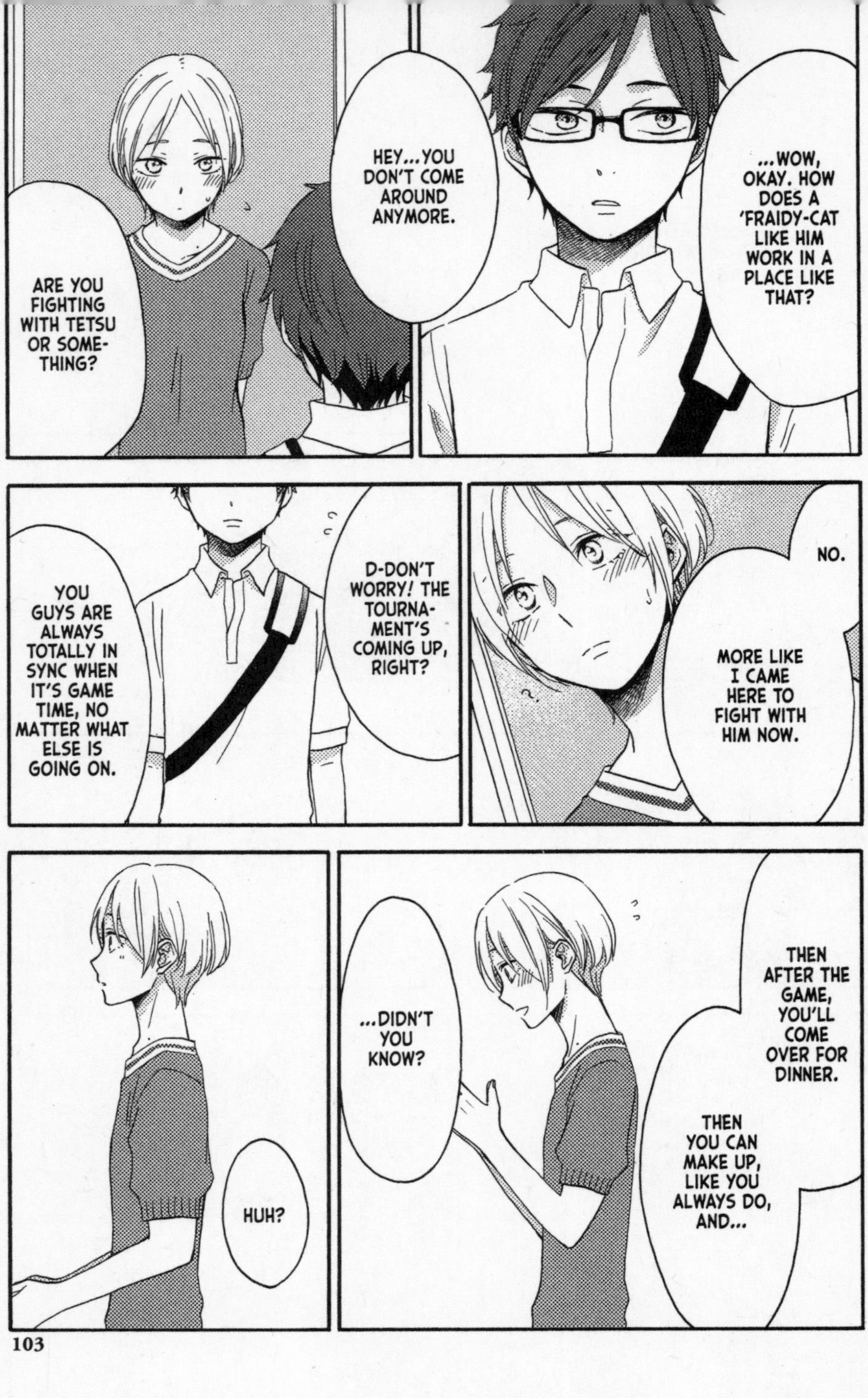
...WOW, OKAY. HOW DOES A 'FRAIDY-CAT LIKE HIM WORK IN A PLACE LIKE THAT?
HEY...YOU DON'T COME AROUND ANYMORE.
ARE YOU FIGHTING WITH TETSU OR SOME-THING?
NO.
MORE LIKE I CAME HERE TO FIGHT WITH HIM NOW.
D-DON'T WORRY! THE TOURNA-MENT'S COMING UP, RIGHT?
YOU GUYS ARE ALWAYS TOTALLY IN SYNC WHEN IT'S GAME TIME, NO MATTER WHAT ELSE IS GOING ON.
THEN AFTER THE GAME, YOU'LL COME OVER FOR DINNER.
THEN YOU CAN MAKE UP, LIKE YOU ALWAYS DO, AND...
...DIDN'T YOU KNOW?
HUH?

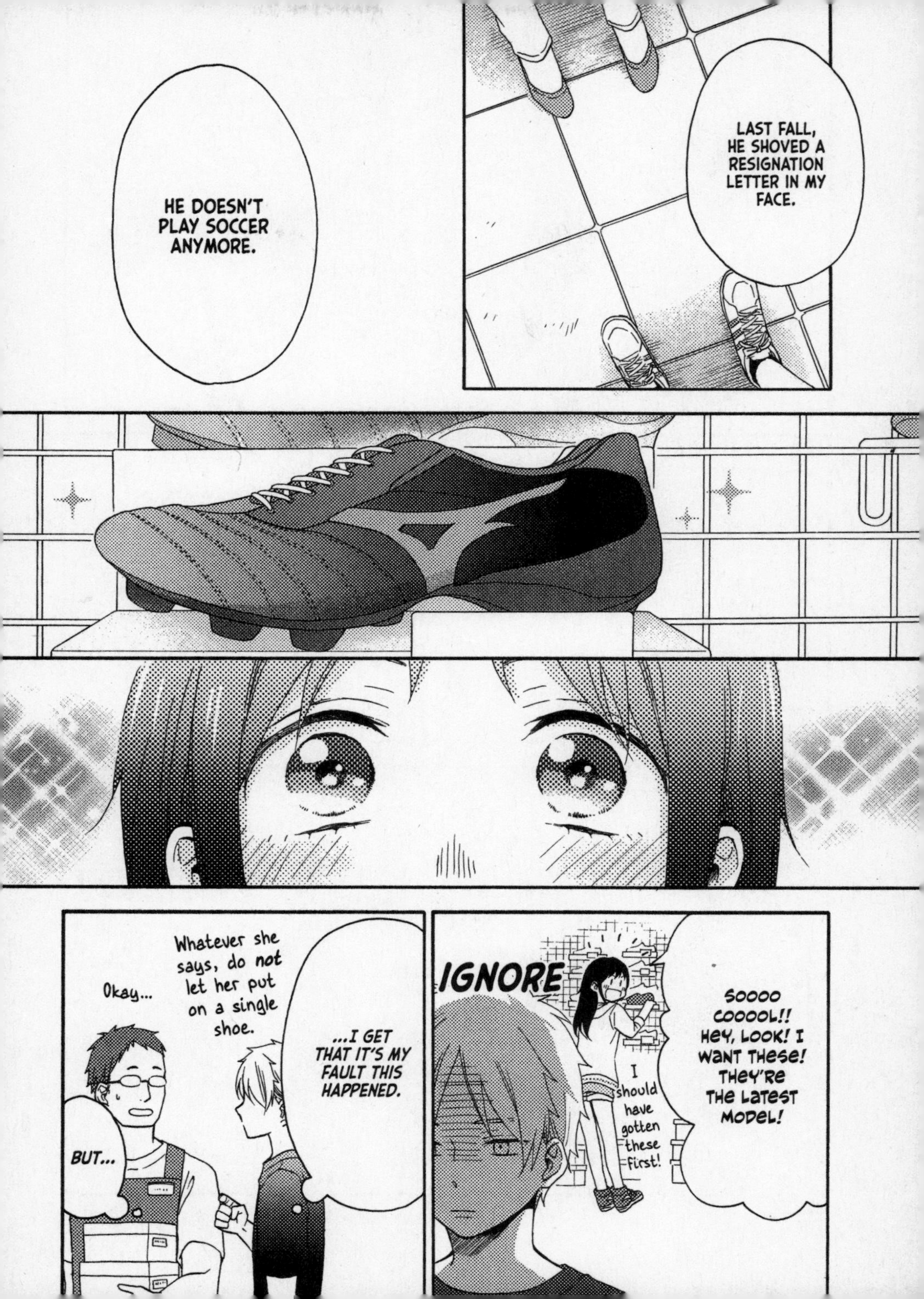
LAST FALL, HE SHOVED A RESIGNATION LETTER IN MY FACE.
HE DOESN'T PLAY SOCCER ANYMORE.
SOOOO COOOOL!! HEY, LOOK! I WANT THESE! THEY'RE THE LATEST MODEL!
IGNORE
I should have gotten these first!
...I GET THAT IT'S MY FAULT THIS HAPPENED.
Whatever she says, do not let her put on a single shoe.
Okay...
BUT...

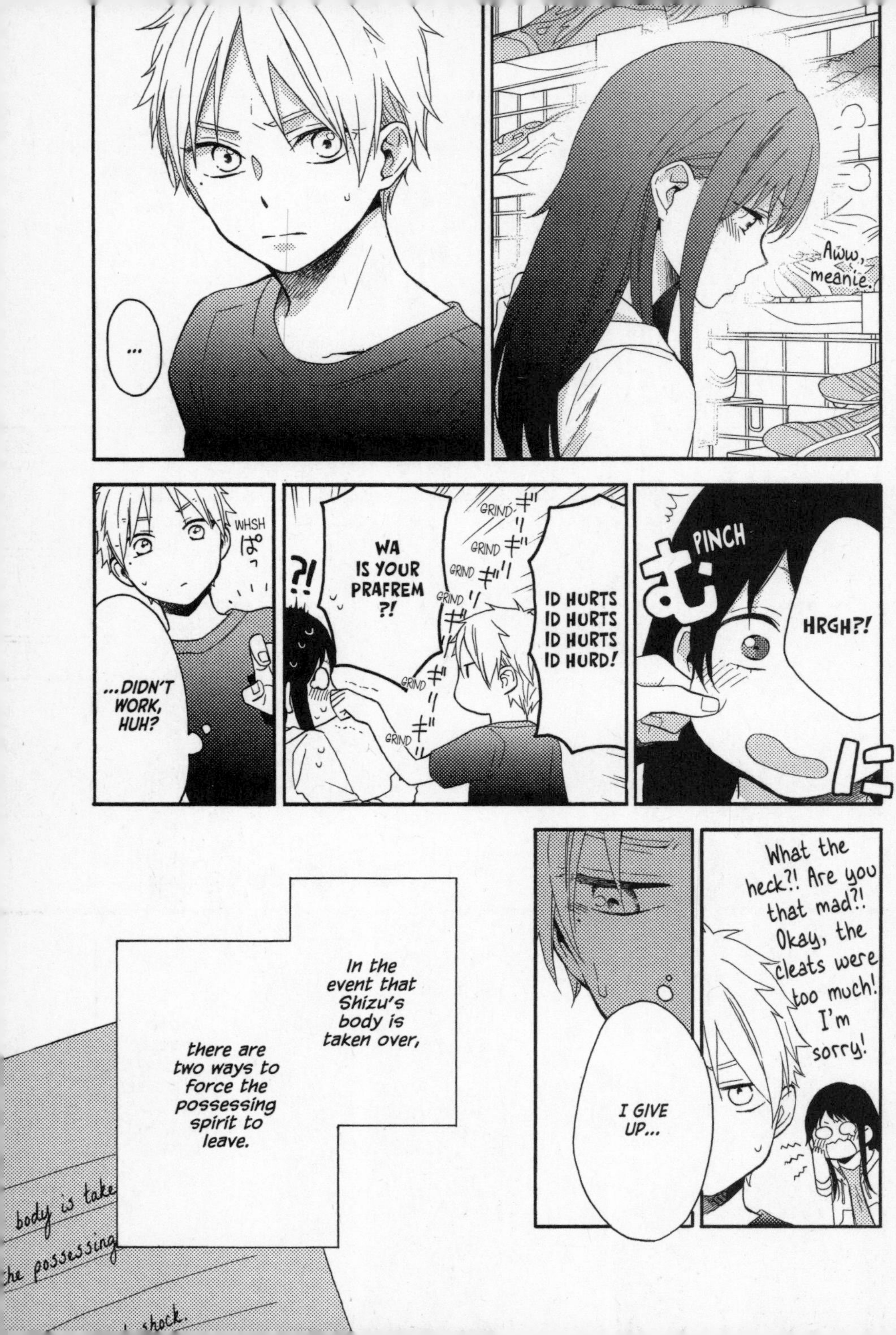
Aww, meanie.
...
PINCH
む
HRGH?!
ID HURTS ID HURTS ID HURTS ID HURD!
GRIND ギリ
GRIND ギリ
GRIND ギリ
GRIND ギリ
GRIND ギリ
GRIND ギリ
WA IS YOUR PRAFREM?!
?!
WHSH ぱっ
...DIDN'T WORK, HUH?
What the heck?! Are you that mad?! Okay, the cleats were too much! I'm sorry!
I GIVE UP...
In the event that Shizu's body is taken over,
there are two ways to force the possessing spirit to leave.

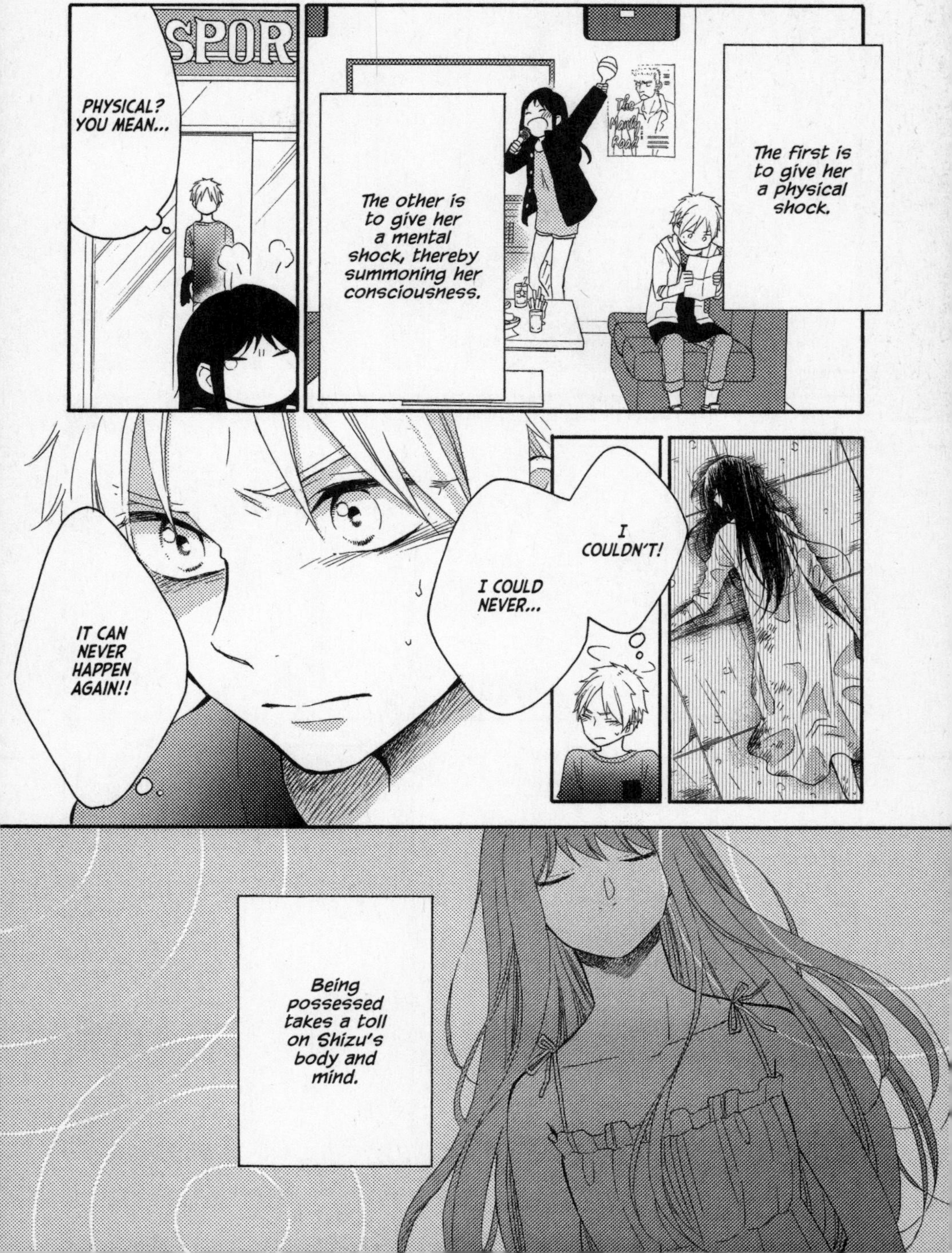
The first is to give her a physical shock.
The Manly Road
The other is to give her a mental shock, thereby summoning her consciousness.
SPOR
PHYSICAL? YOU MEAN...
I COULDN'T!
I COULD NEVER...
IT CAN NEVER HAPPEN AGAIN!!
Being possessed takes a toll on Shizu's body and mind.

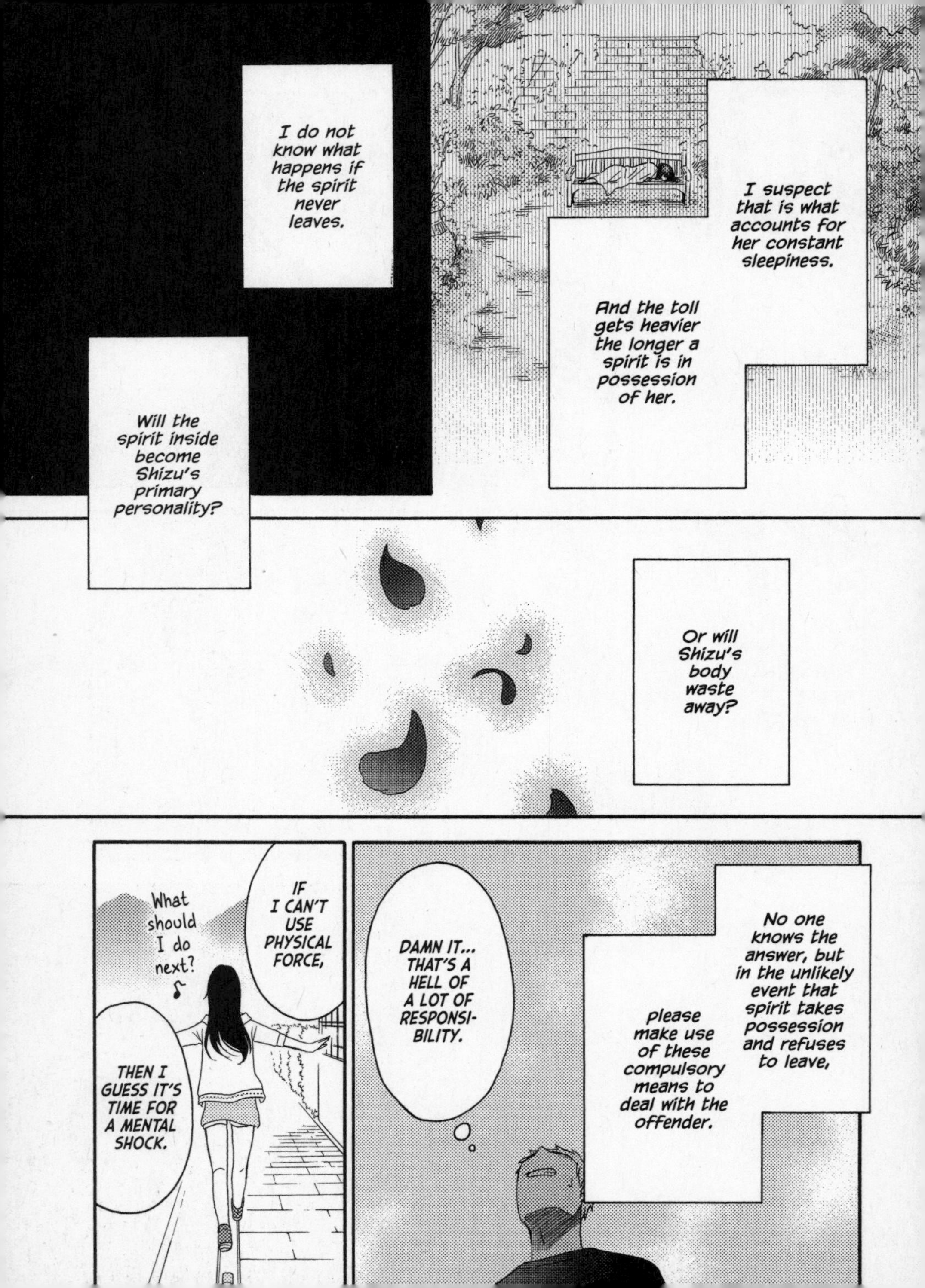
I suspect that is what accounts for her constant sleepiness.
And the toll gets heavier the longer a spirit is in possession of her.
I do not know what happens if the spirit never leaves.
Will the spirit inside become Shizu's primary personality?
Or will Shizu's body waste away?
No one knows the answer, but in the unlikely event that spirit takes possession and refuses to leave,
please make use of these compulsory means to deal with the offender.
DAMN IT... THAT'S A HELL OF A LOT OF RESPONSI-BILITY.
IF I CAN'T USE PHYSICAL FORCE,
What should I do next?
THEN I GUESS IT'S TIME FOR A MENTAL SHOCK.

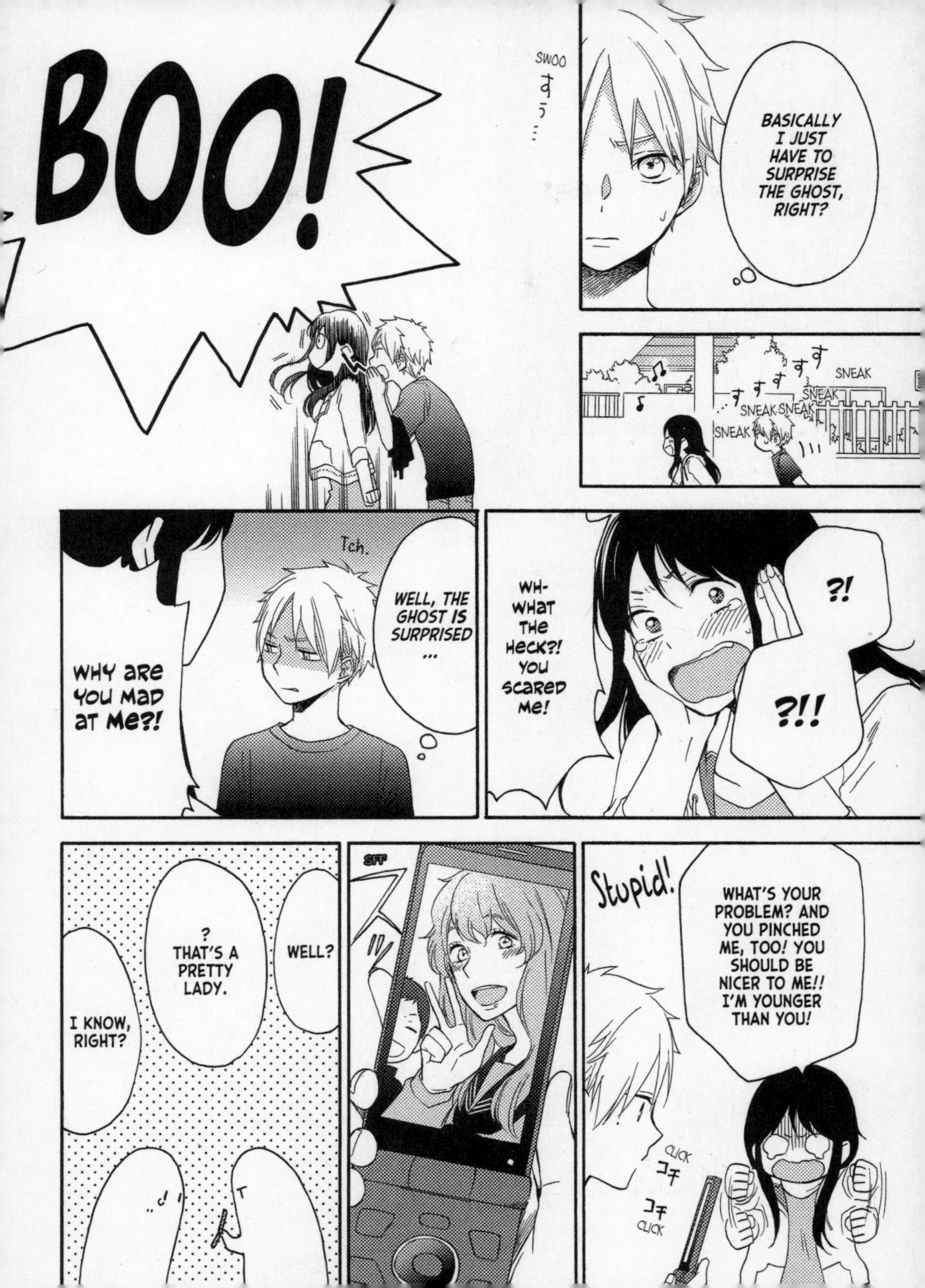

SWOO
すう…
BASICALLY I JUST HAVE TO SURPRISE THE GHOST, RIGHT?
すすすす…
SNEAK SNEAK SNEAK SNEAK SNEAK
BOO!
?!
?!!
WH-WHAT THE HECK?! YOU SCARED ME!
Tch.
WELL, THE GHOST IS SURPRISED...
WHY ARE YOU MAD AT ME?!
Stupid!
WHAT'S YOUR PROBLEM? AND YOU PINCHED ME, TOO! YOU SHOULD BE NICER TO ME!! I'M YOUNGER THAN YOU!
CLICK
コチ
コチ
CLICK
SFF
WELL?
? THAT'S A PRETTY LADY.
I KNOW, RIGHT?

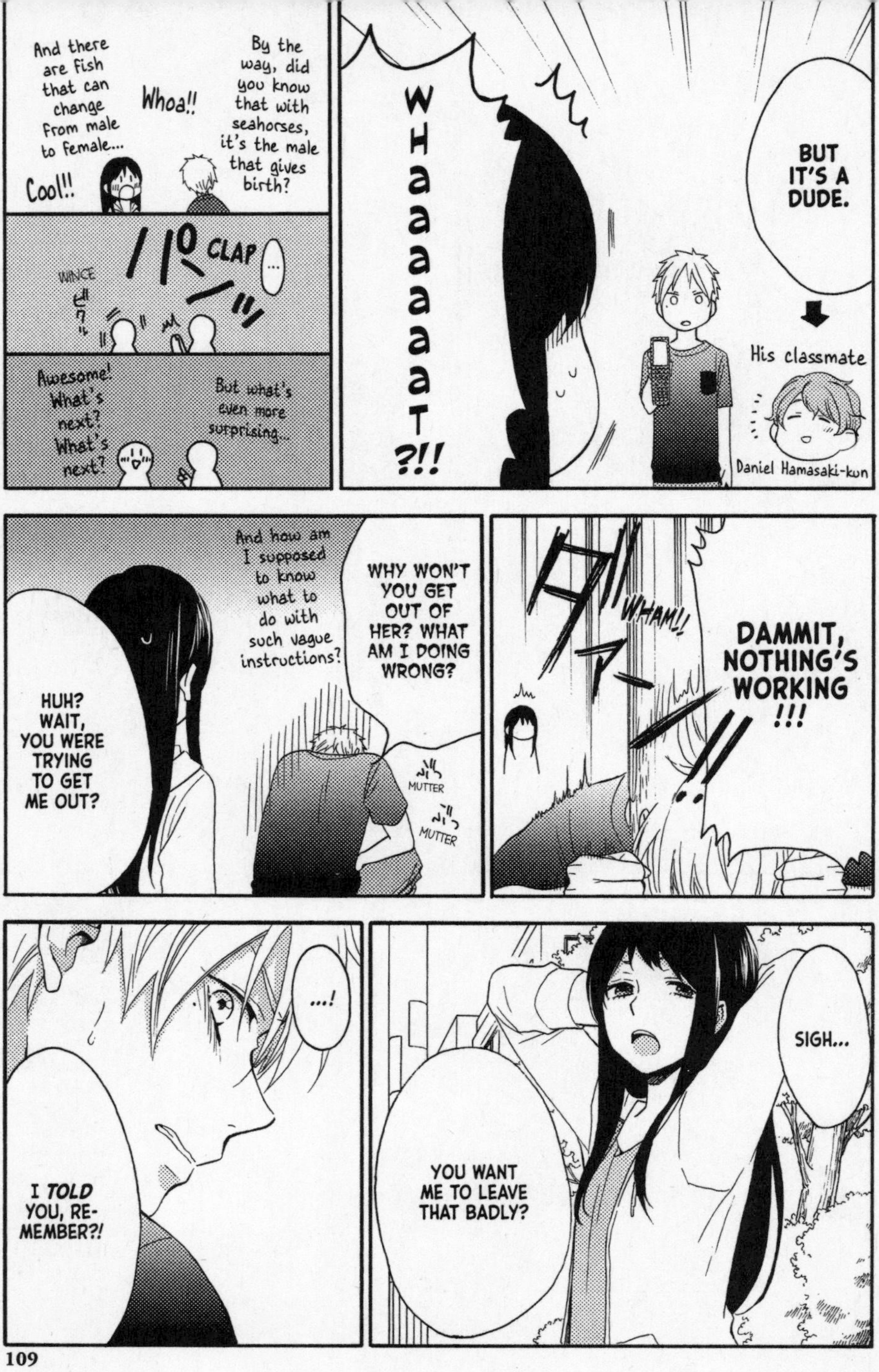

BUT IT'S A DUDE.
His classmate
Daniel Hamasaki-kun
WHaaaaaaT?!!
By the way, did you know that with seahorses, it's the male that gives birth?
Whoa!!
And there are fish that can change from male to female...
Cool!!
...
CLAP
WINCE
But what's even more surprising...
Awesome! What's next? What's next?
DAMMIT, NOTHING'S WORKING!!!
WHAM!!
WHY WON'T YOU GET OUT OF HER? WHAT AM I DOING WRONG?
And how am I supposed to know what to do with such vague instructions?
MUTTER
MUTTER
HUH? WAIT, YOU WERE TRYING TO GET ME OUT?
SIGH...
YOU WANT ME TO LEAVE THAT BADLY?
...!
I *TOLD* YOU, RE-MEMBER?!

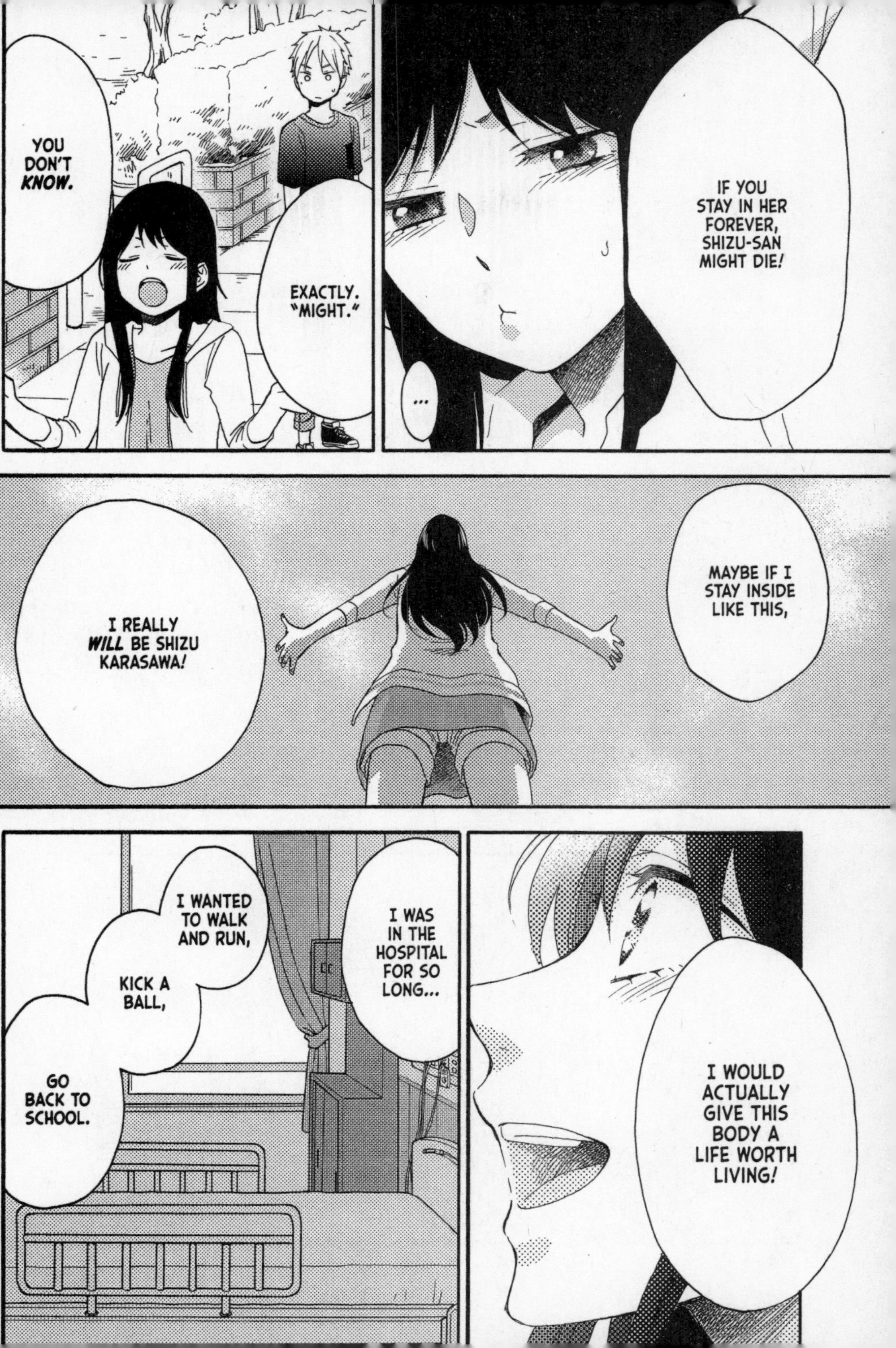
IF YOU STAY IN HER FOREVER, SHIZU-SAN MIGHT DIE!
...
EXACTLY. "MIGHT."
YOU DON'T *KNOW.*
MAYBE IF I STAY INSIDE LIKE THIS,
I REALLY *WILL* BE SHIZU KARASAWA!
I WOULD ACTUALLY GIVE THIS BODY A LIFE WORTH LIVING!
I WAS IN THE HOSPITAL FOR SO LONG...
I WANTED TO WALK AND RUN,
KICK A BALL,
GO BACK TO SCHOOL.

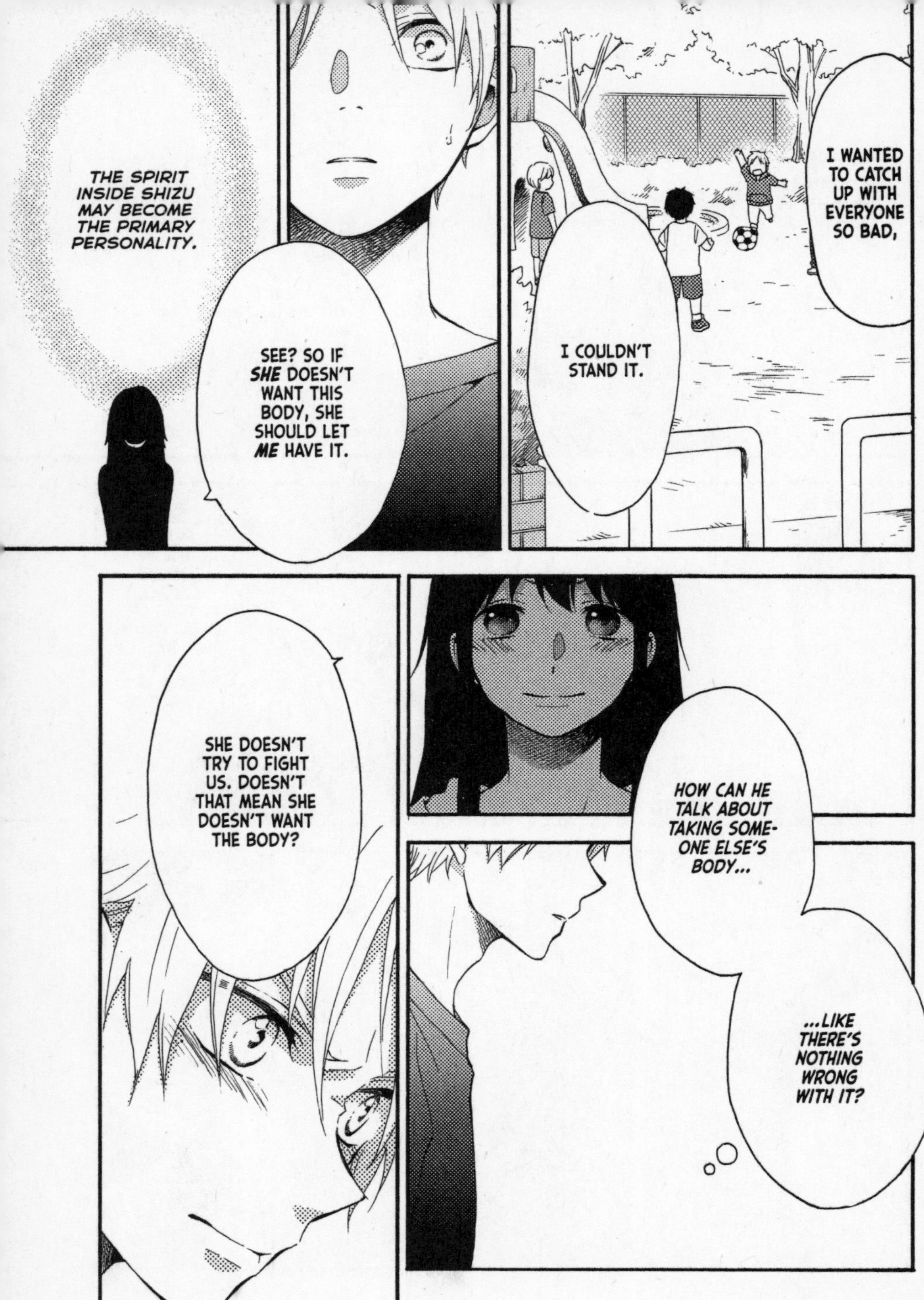
I WANTED TO CATCH UP WITH EVERYONE SO BAD,
I COULDN'T STAND IT.
SEE? SO IF *SHE* DOESN'T WANT THIS BODY, SHE SHOULD LET *ME* HAVE IT.
THE SPIRIT INSIDE SHIZU MAY BECOME THE PRIMARY PERSONALITY.
HOW CAN HE TALK ABOUT TAKING SOME-ONE ELSE'S BODY...
...LIKE THERE'S NOTHING WRONG WITH IT?
SHE DOESN'T TRY TO FIGHT US. DOESN'T THAT MEAN SHE DOESN'T WANT THE BODY?

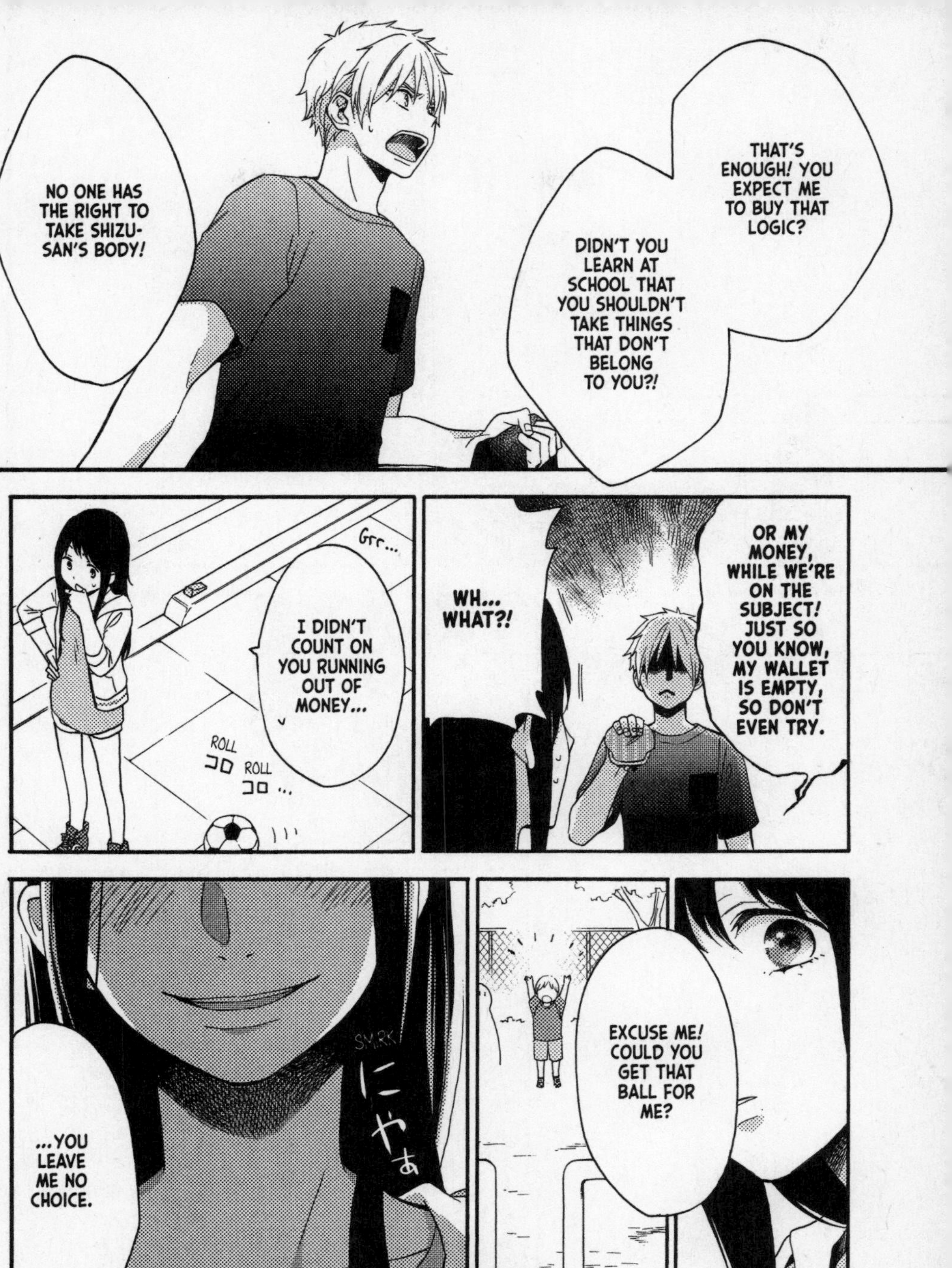

THAT'S ENOUGH! YOU EXPECT ME TO BUY THAT LOGIC?
DIDN'T YOU LEARN AT SCHOOL THAT YOU SHOULDN'T TAKE THINGS THAT DON'T BELONG TO YOU?!
NO ONE HAS THE RIGHT TO TAKE SHIZU-SAN'S BODY!
OR MY MONEY, WHILE WE'RE ON THE SUBJECT! JUST SO YOU KNOW, MY WALLET IS EMPTY, SO DON'T EVEN TRY.
WH... WHAT?!
Grr...
I DIDN'T COUNT ON YOU RUNNING OUT OF MONEY...
ROLL コロ ROLL コロ...
EXCUSE ME! COULD YOU GET THAT BALL FOR ME?
SMRK にやぁ
...YOU LEAVE ME NO CHOICE.

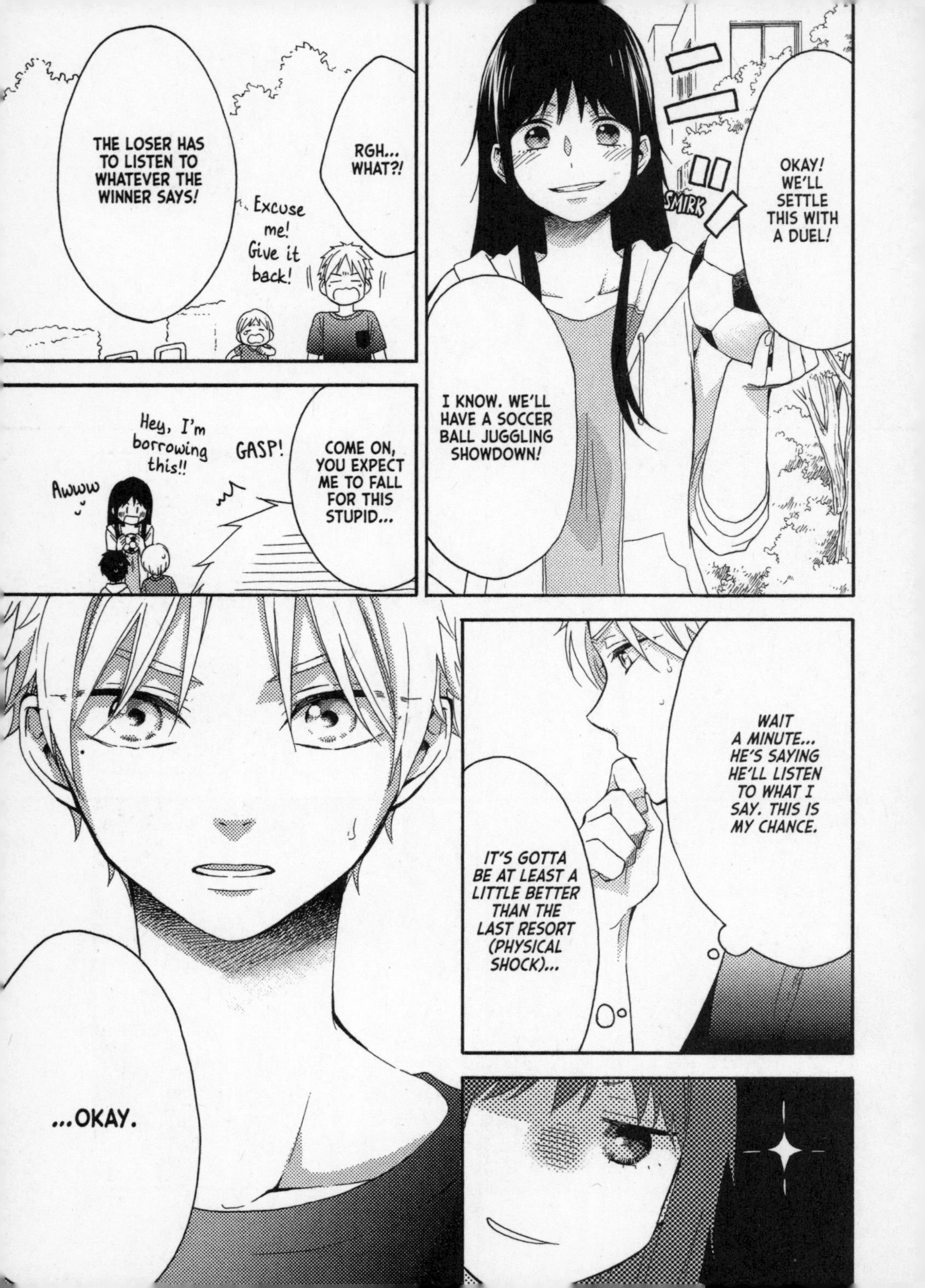

OKAY! WE'LL SETTLE THIS WITH A DUEL!
SMIRK
I KNOW. WE'LL HAVE A SOCCER BALL JUGGLING SHOWDOWN!
RGH... WHAT?!
THE LOSER HAS TO LISTEN TO WHATEVER THE WINNER SAYS!
Excuse me! Give it back!
COME ON, YOU EXPECT ME TO FALL FOR THIS STUPID...
GASP!
Hey, I'm borrowing this!!
Awww
WAIT A MINUTE... HE'S SAYING HE'LL LISTEN TO WHAT I SAY. THIS IS MY CHANCE.
IT'S GOTTA BE AT LEAST A LITTLE BETTER THAN THE LAST RESORT (PHYSICAL SHOCK)...
...OKAY.

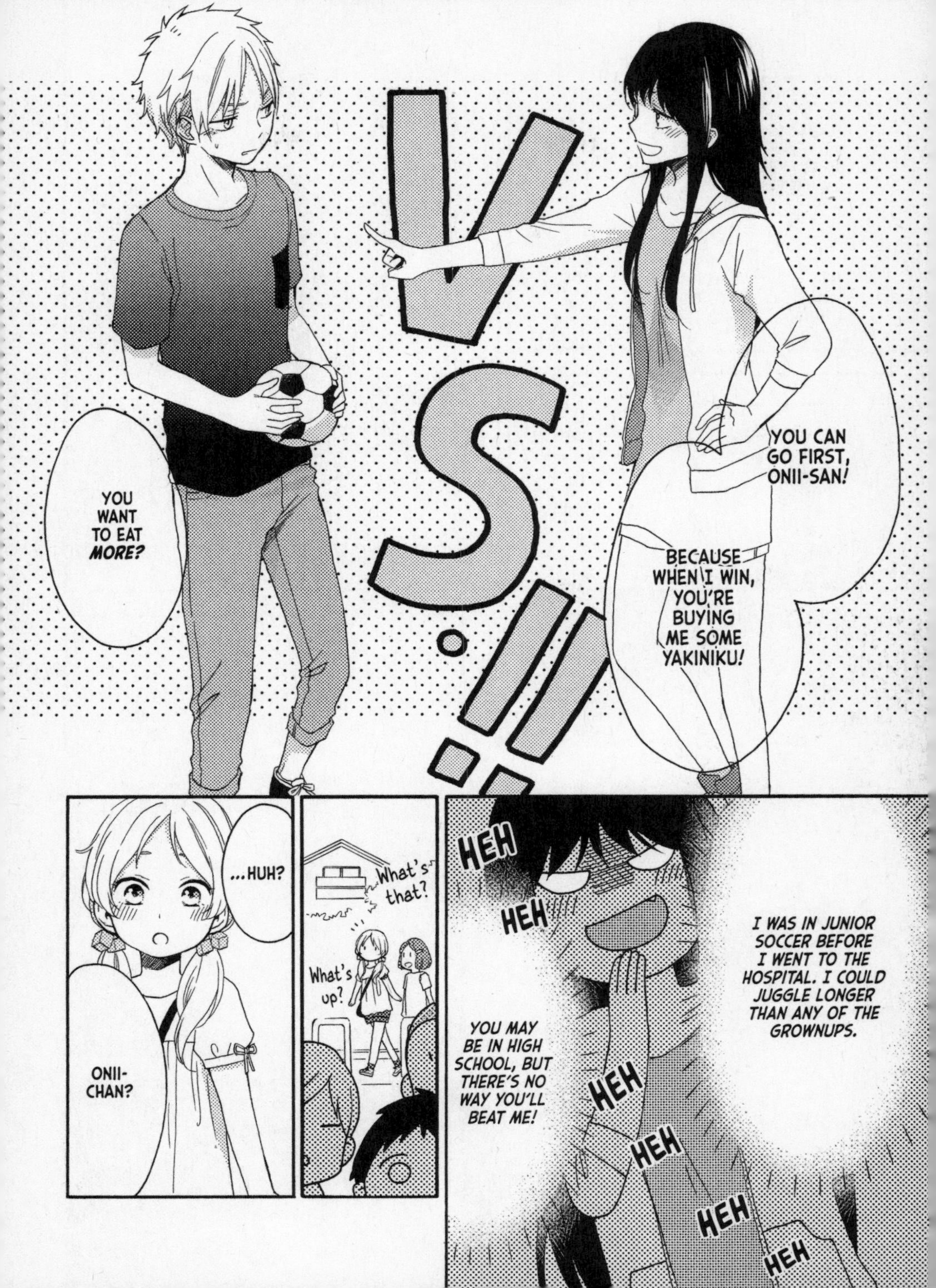
YOU CAN GO FIRST, ONII-SAN!
BECAUSE WHEN I WIN, YOU'RE BUYING ME SOME YAKINIKU!
VS!!
YOU WANT TO EAT MORE?
HEH HEH
I WAS IN JUNIOR SOCCER BEFORE I WENT TO THE HOSPITAL. I COULD JUGGLE LONGER THAN ANY OF THE GROWNUPS.
HEH HEH HEH HEH
YOU MAY BE IN HIGH SCHOOL, BUT THERE'S NO WAY YOU'LL BEAT ME!
What's that?
What's up?
...HUH?
ONII-CHAN?

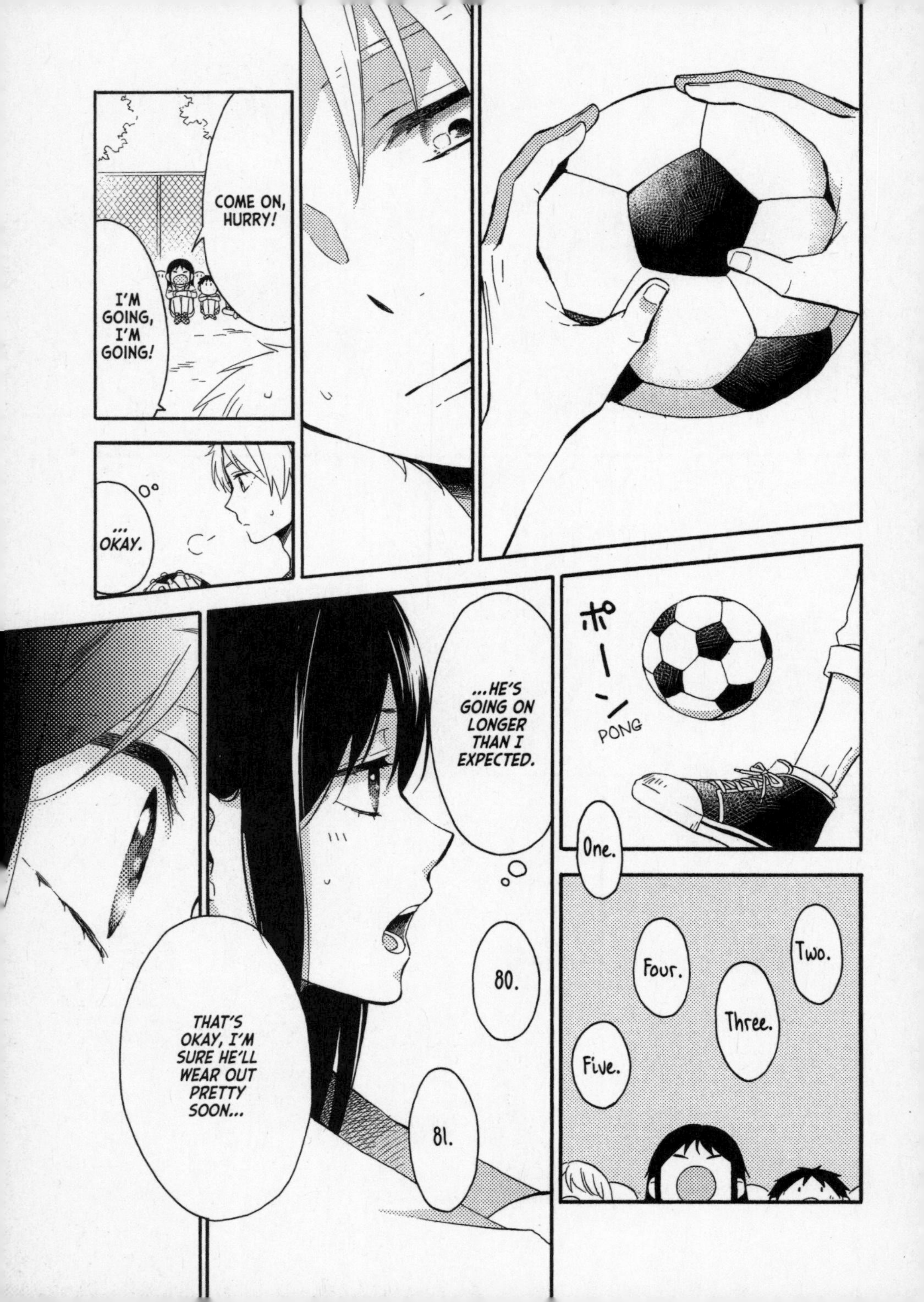
COME ON, HURRY!
I'M GOING, I'M GOING!
...OKAY.
ポーン
PONG
One.
Two.
Three.
Four.
Five.
...HE'S GOING ON LONGER THAN I EXPECTED.
80.
81.
THAT'S OKAY, I'M SURE HE'LL WEAR OUT PRETTY SOON...

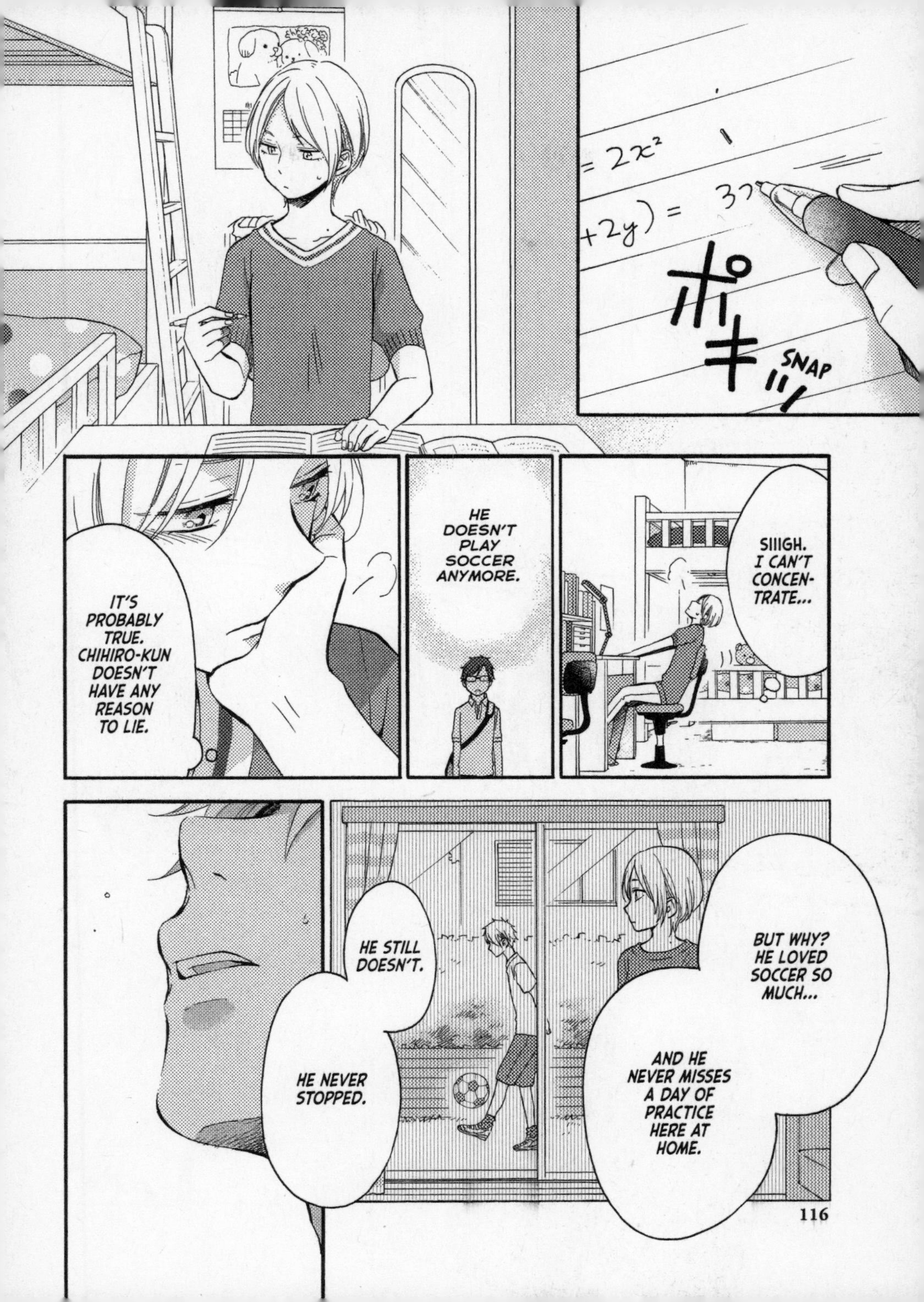
ポキッ
SNAP
SIIIGH. I CAN'T CONCENTRATE...
HE DOESN'T PLAY SOCCER ANYMORE.
IT'S PROBABLY TRUE. CHIHIRO-KUN DOESN'T HAVE ANY REASON TO LIE.
BUT WHY? HE LOVED SOCCER SO MUCH...
AND HE NEVER MISSES A DAY OF PRACTICE HERE AT HOME.
HE STILL DOESN'T.
HE NEVER STOPPED.

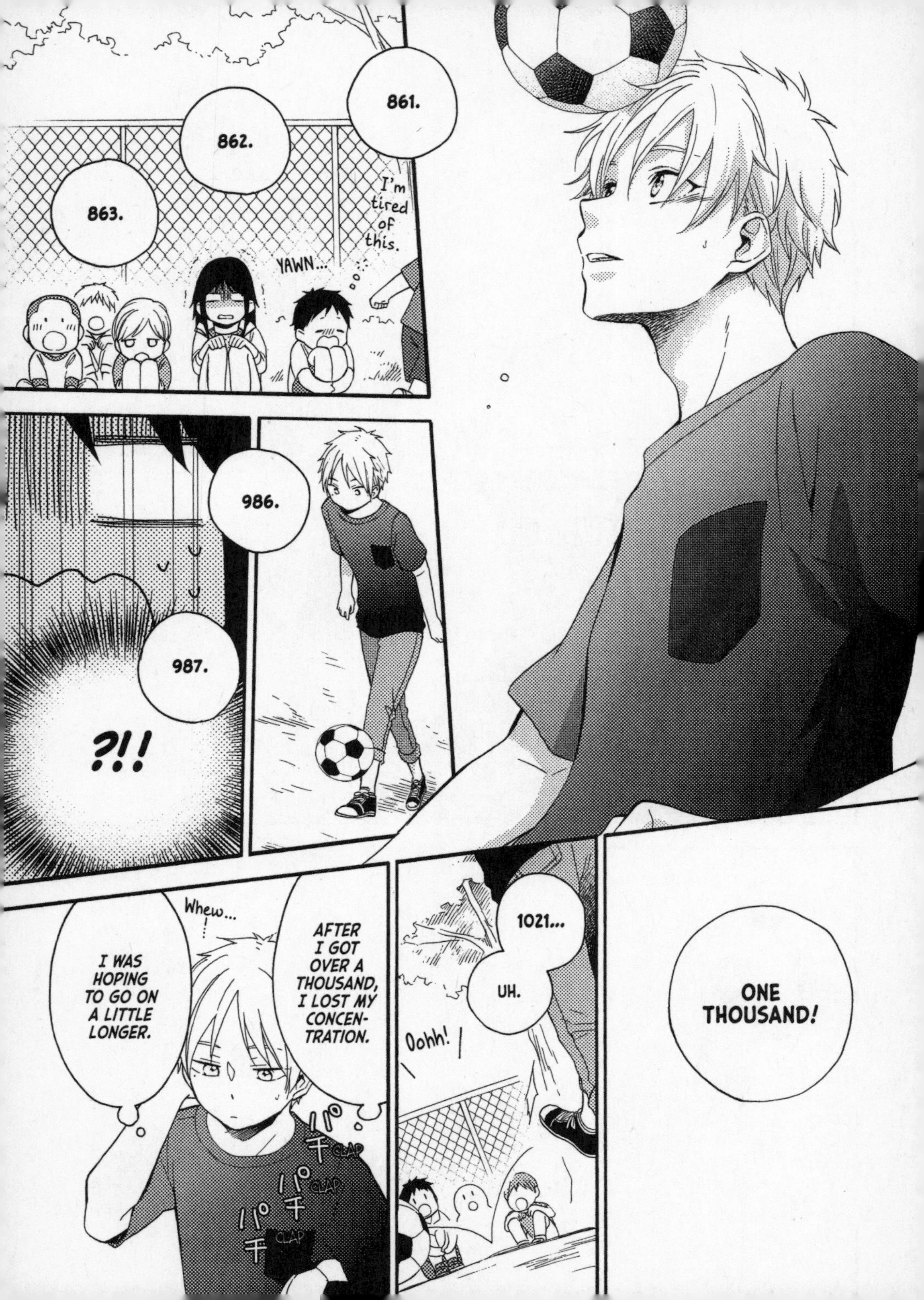
861.
862.
863.
I'm tired of this.
YAWN...
986.
987.
?!!
ONE THOUSAND!
1021...
UH.
Oohh!
Whew...
AFTER I GOT OVER A THOUSAND, I LOST MY CONCENTRATION.
I WAS HOPING TO GO ON A LITTLE LONGER.
パチ CLAP
パチ CLAP
パチ CLAP

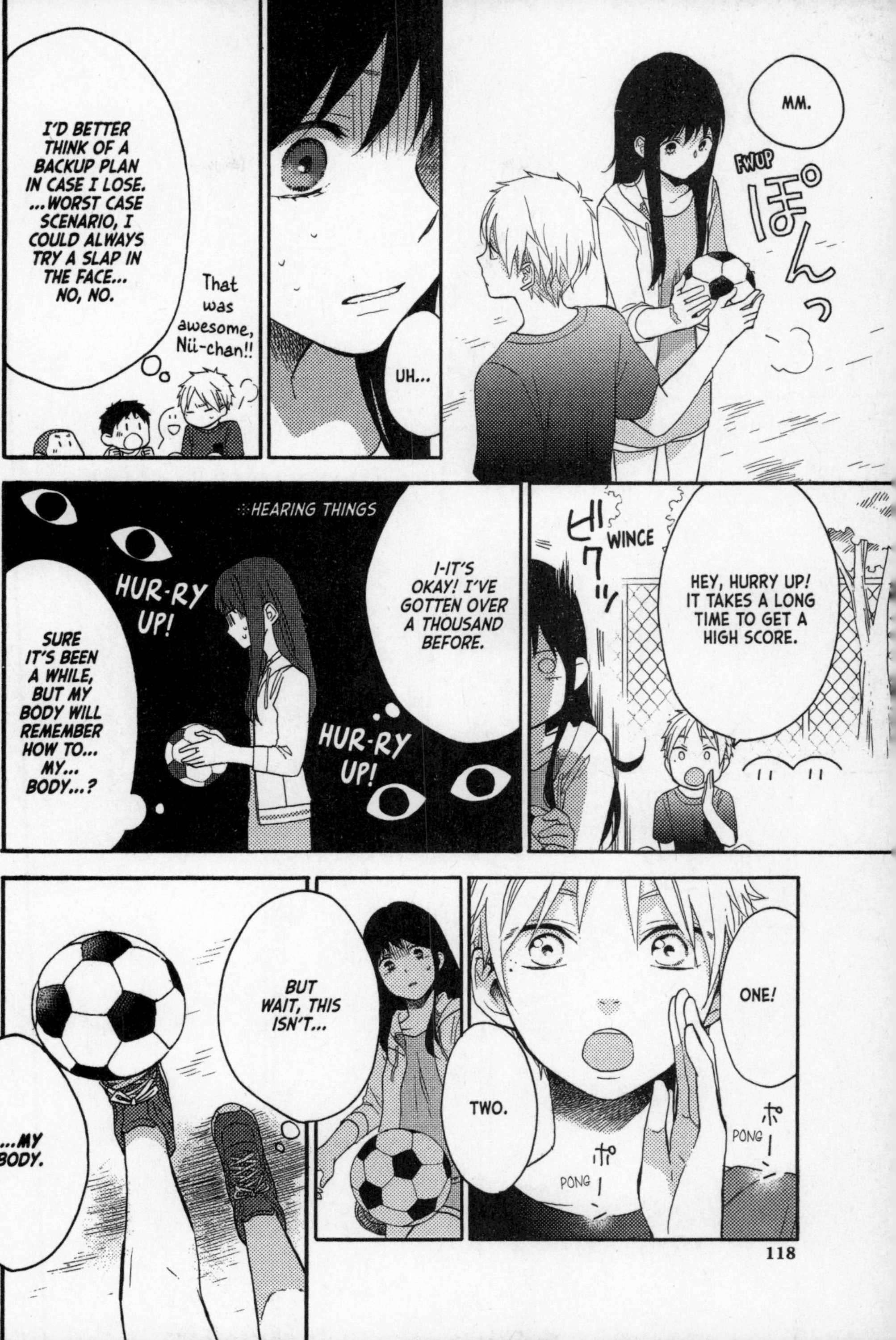
MM.
FWUP
ぽんっ
UH...
I'D BETTER THINK OF A BACKUP PLAN IN CASE I LOSE. ...WORST CASE SCENARIO, I COULD ALWAYS TRY A SLAP IN THE FACE... NO, NO.
That was awesome, Nii-chan!!
ビクッ
WINCE
HEY, HURRY UP! IT TAKES A LONG TIME TO GET A HIGH SCORE.
I-IT'S OKAY! I'VE GOTTEN OVER A THOUSAND BEFORE.
∴HEARING THINGS
HUR-RY UP!
HUR-RY UP!
SURE IT'S BEEN A WHILE, BUT MY BODY WILL REMEMBER HOW TO... MY... BODY...?
ONE!
ポーン
PONG
TWO.
ポン
PONG
BUT WAIT, THIS ISN'T...
...MY BODY.

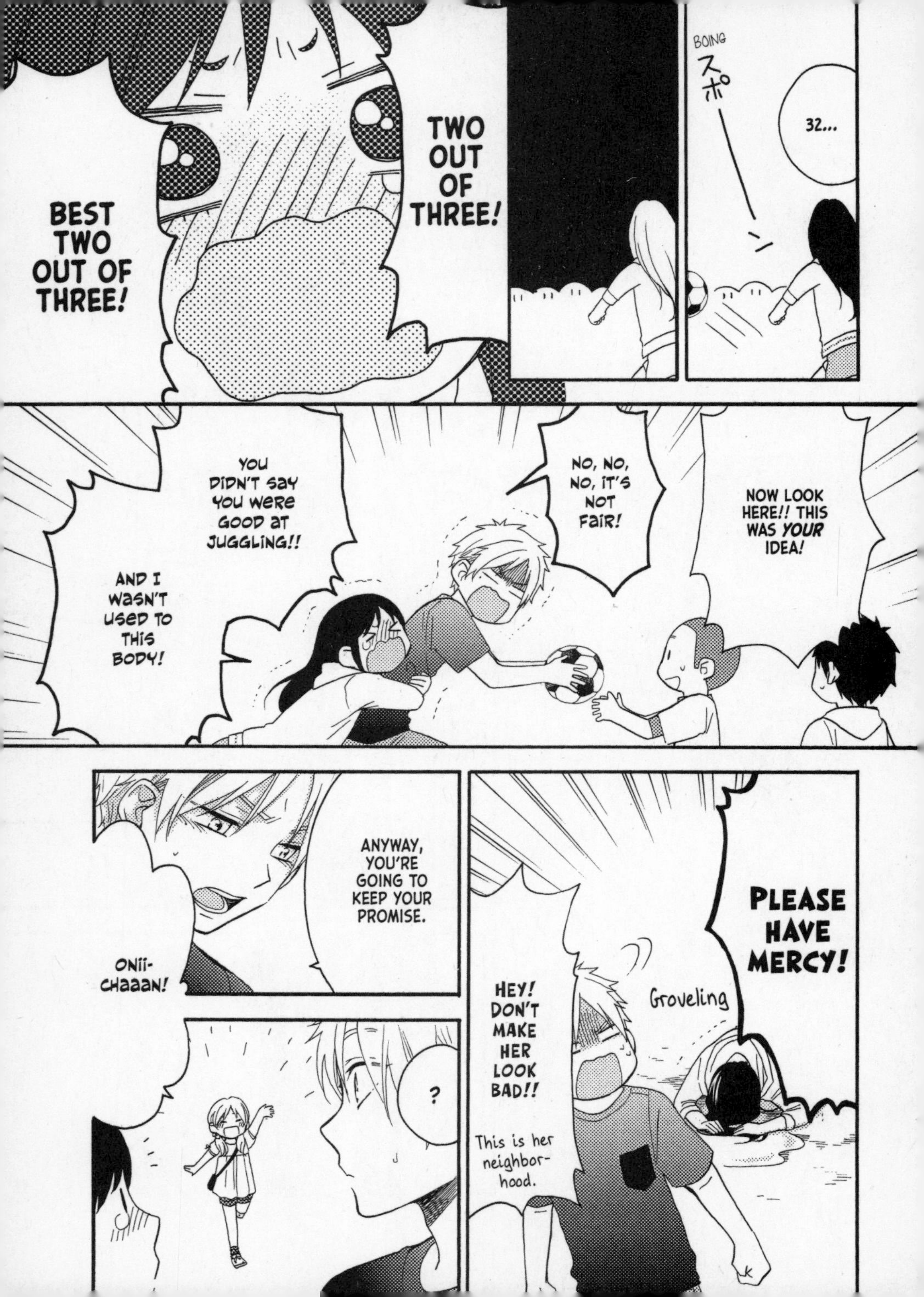
BOING
スポーン
32...
TWO OUT OF THREE!
BEST TWO OUT OF THREE!
NOW LOOK HERE!! THIS WAS YOUR IDEA!
NO, NO, NO, IT'S NOT FAIR!
YOU DIDN'T SAY YOU WERE GOOD AT JUGGLING!!
AND I WASN'T USED TO THIS BODY!
PLEASE HAVE MERCY!
Groveling
HEY! DON'T MAKE HER LOOK BAD!!
This is her neighbor-hood.
ANYWAY, YOU'RE GOING TO KEEP YOUR PROMISE.
ONII-CHAAAN!
?

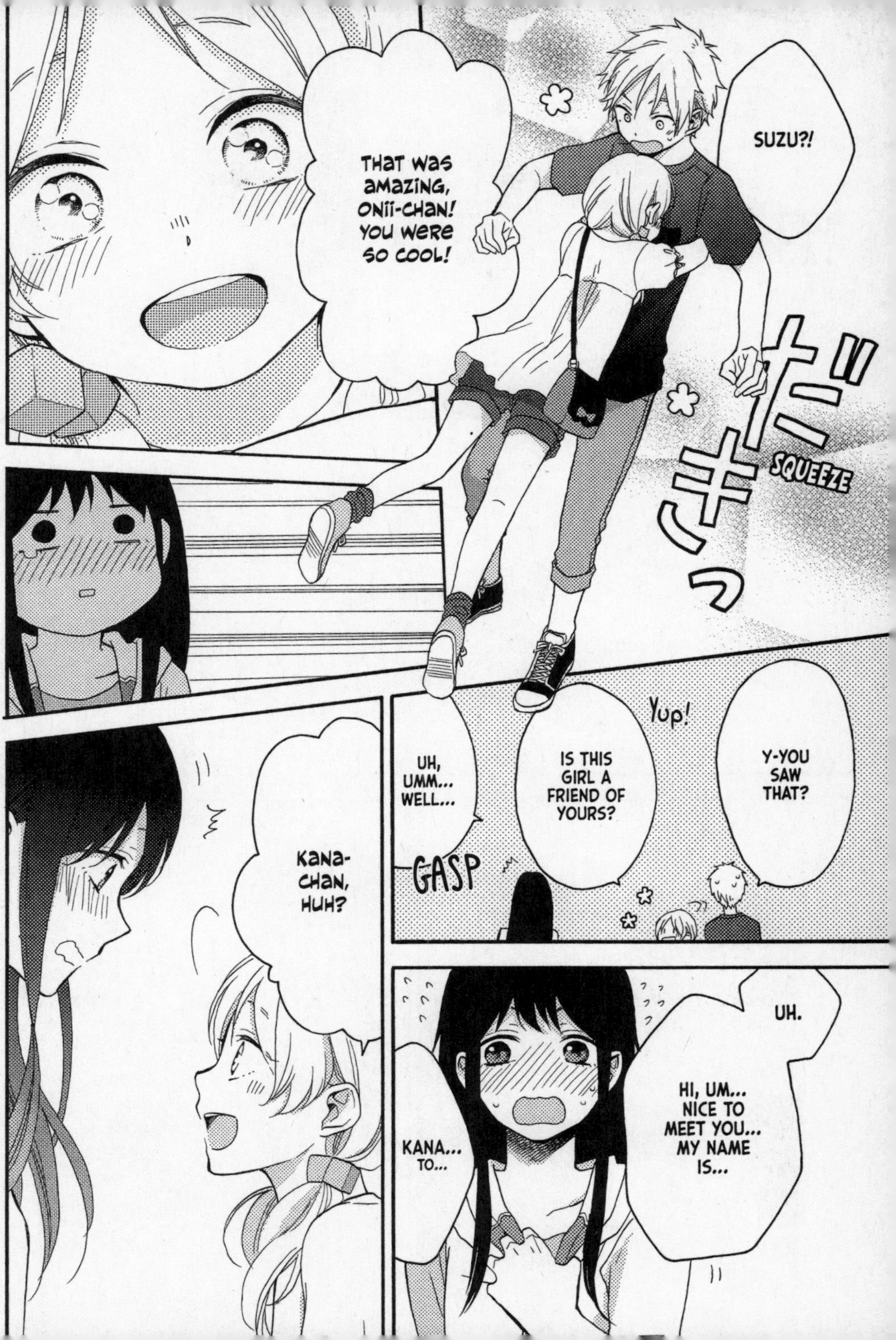
SUZU?!
だきっ
SQUEEZE
That was amazing, Onii-chan! You were so cool!
Y-YOU SAW THAT?
Yup!
IS THIS GIRL A FRIEND OF YOURS?
UH, UMM... WELL...
GASP
UH.
HI, UM... NICE TO MEET YOU... MY NAME IS...
KANA... TO...
Kana-chan, huh?

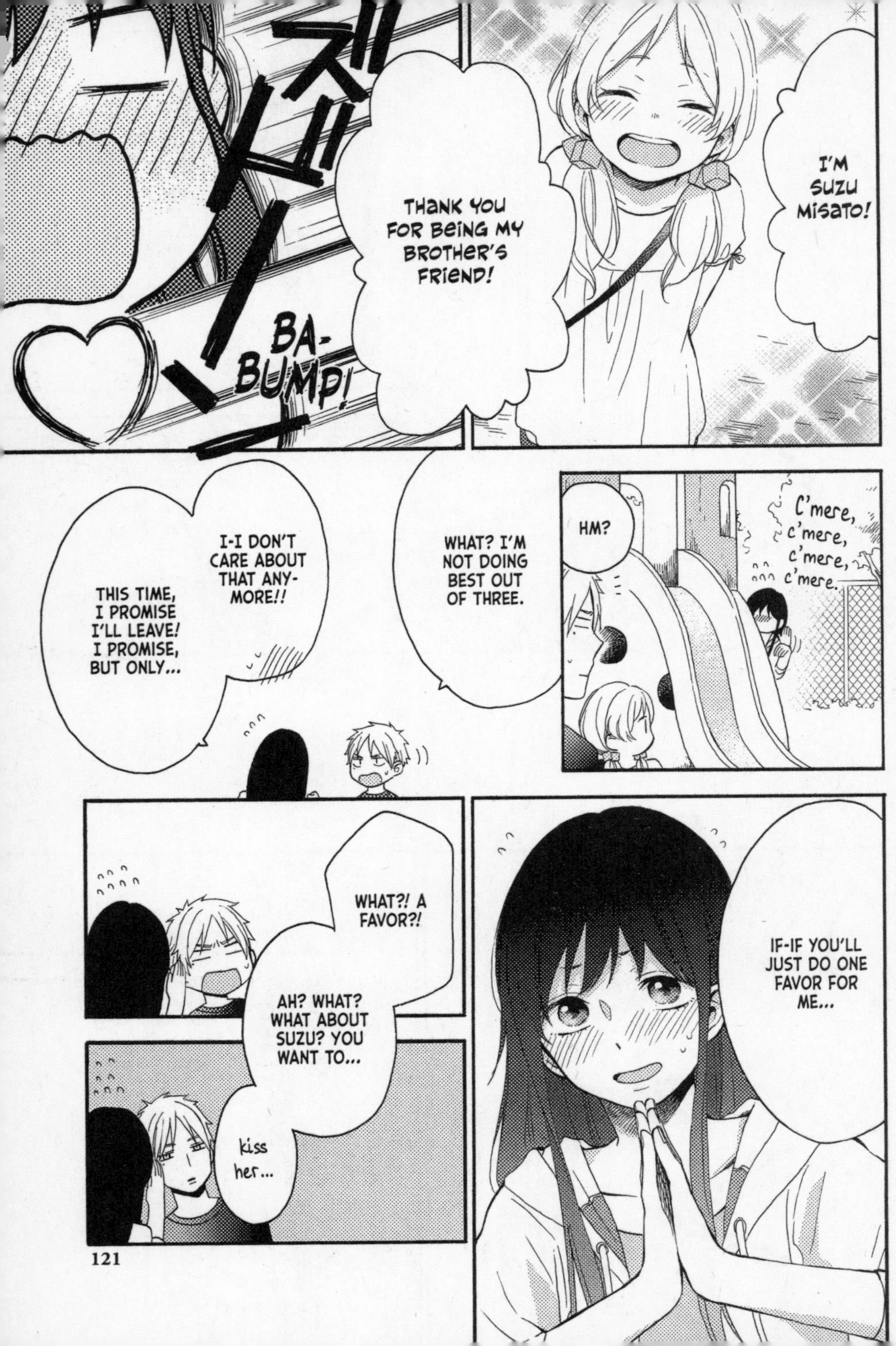
I'M SUZU MISATO!
THANK YOU FOR BEING MY BROTHER'S FRIEND!
BA-BUMP!
C'mere, c'mere, c'mere, c'mere.
HM?
WHAT? I'M NOT DOING BEST OUT OF THREE.
I-I DON'T CARE ABOUT THAT ANYMORE!!
THIS TIME, I PROMISE I'LL LEAVE! I PROMISE, BUT ONLY...
IF-IF YOU'LL JUST DO ONE FAVOR FOR ME...
WHAT?! A FAVOR?!
AH? WHAT? WHAT ABOUT SUZU? YOU WANT TO...
kiss her...

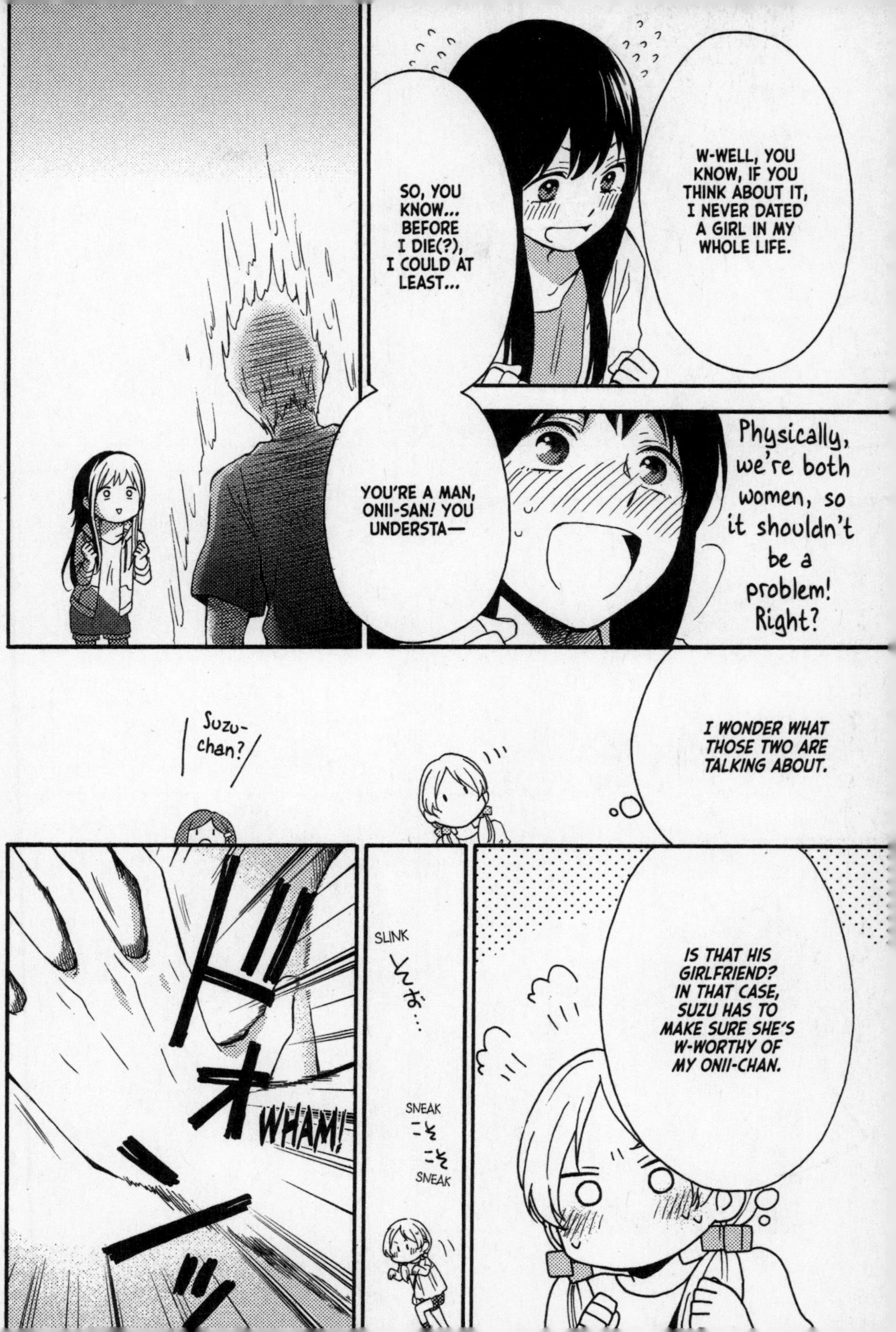
W-WELL, YOU KNOW, IF YOU THINK ABOUT IT, I NEVER DATED A GIRL IN MY WHOLE LIFE.
SO, YOU KNOW... BEFORE I DIE(?), I COULD AT LEAST...
Physically, we're both women, so it shouldn't be a problem! Right?
YOU'RE A MAN, ONII-SAN! YOU UNDERSTA—
I WONDER WHAT THOSE TWO ARE TALKING ABOUT.
Suzu-chan?
IS THAT HIS GIRLFRIEND? IN THAT CASE, SUZU HAS TO MAKE SURE SHE'S W-WORTHY OF MY ONII-CHAN.
SLINK
とぉ…
SNEAK
こそ
こそ
SNEAK
WHAM!

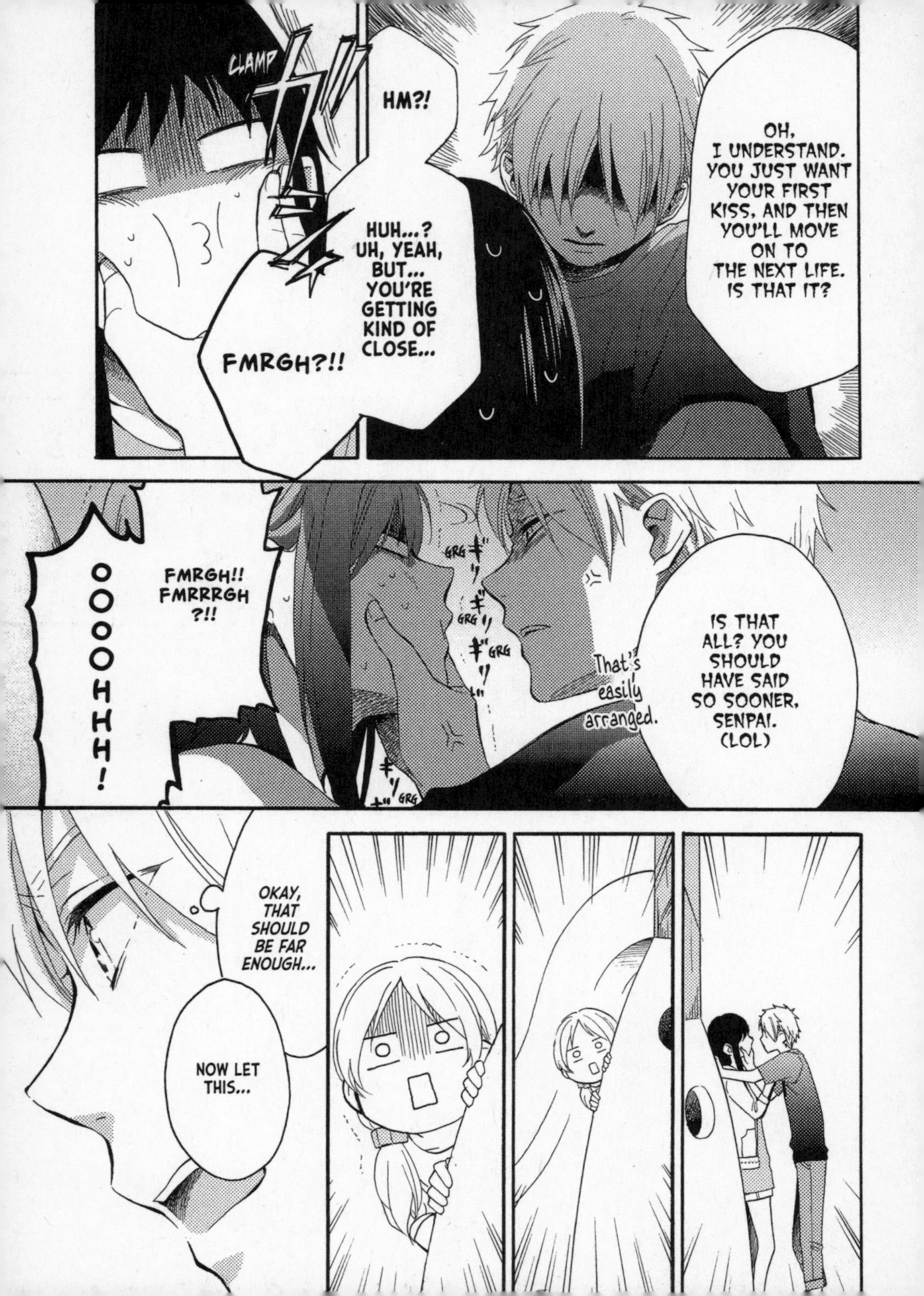
OH, I UNDERSTAND. YOU JUST WANT YOUR FIRST KISS, AND THEN YOU'LL MOVE ON TO THE NEXT LIFE. IS THAT IT?
HM?!
HUH...? UH, YEAH, BUT... YOU'RE GETTING KIND OF CLOSE...
CLAMP
FMRGH?!!
IS THAT ALL? YOU SHOULD HAVE SAID SO SOONER, SENPAI. (LOL)
That's easily arranged.
GRG
GRG
GRG
GRG
FMRGH!! FMRRRGH?!!
OOOOOHHH!
OKAY, THAT SHOULD BE FAR ENOUGH...
NOW LET THIS...

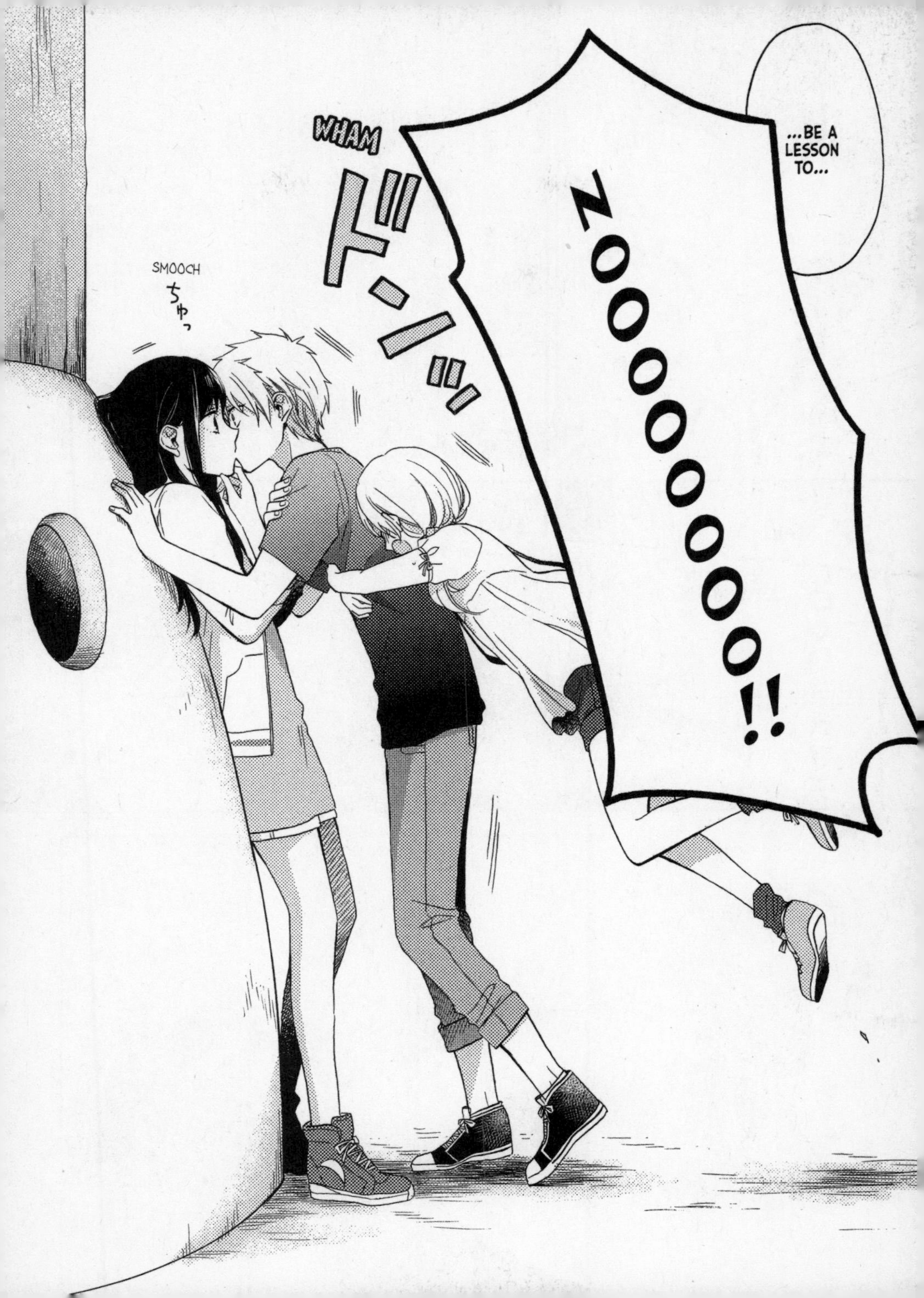
...BE A LESSON TO...
ZOOOOOOOOOO!!
WHAM
ドーンッ
SMOOCH
ちゅっ

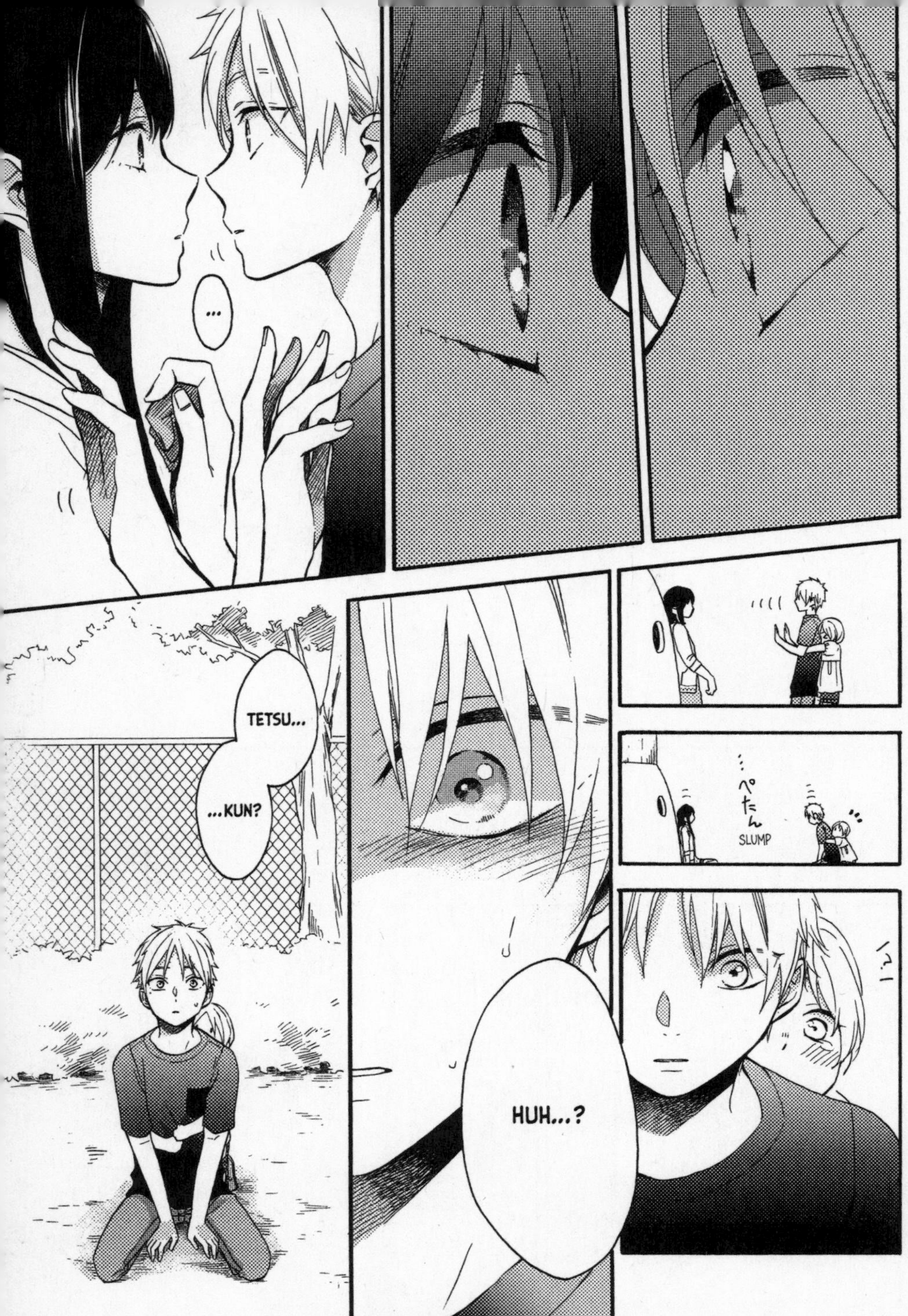
...
ぺたん
SLUMP
!?!
HUH...?
TETSU...
...KUN?

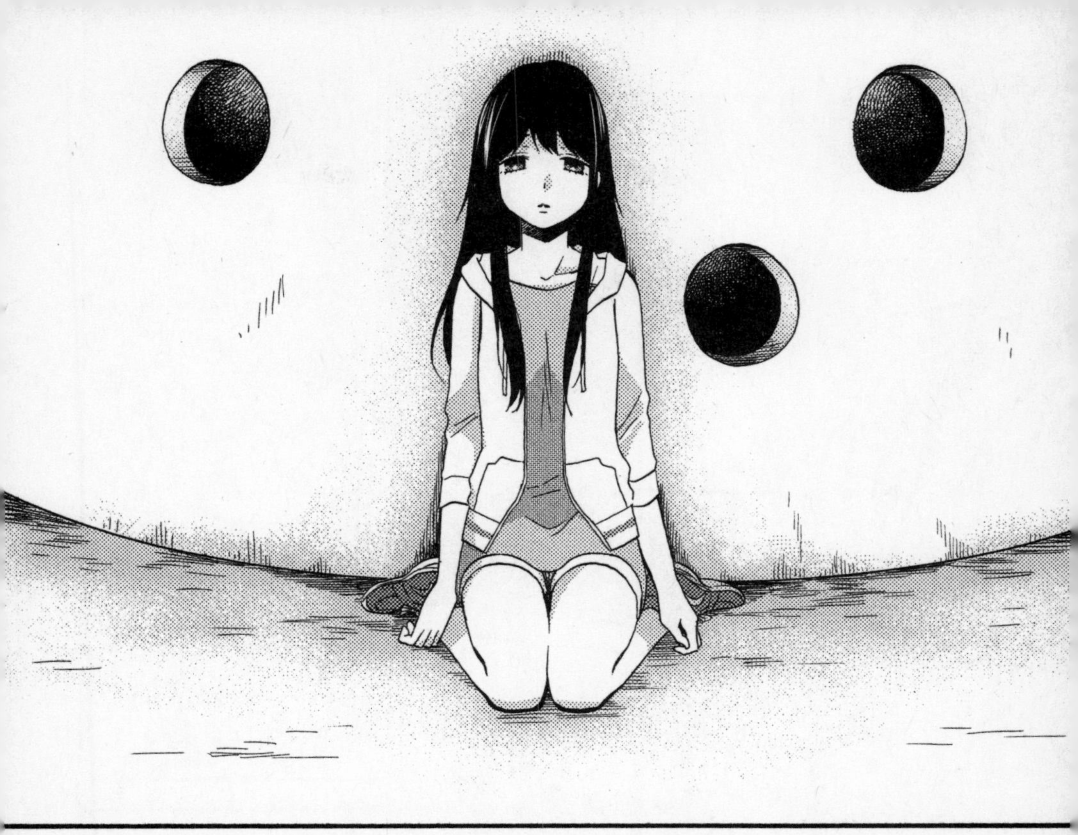

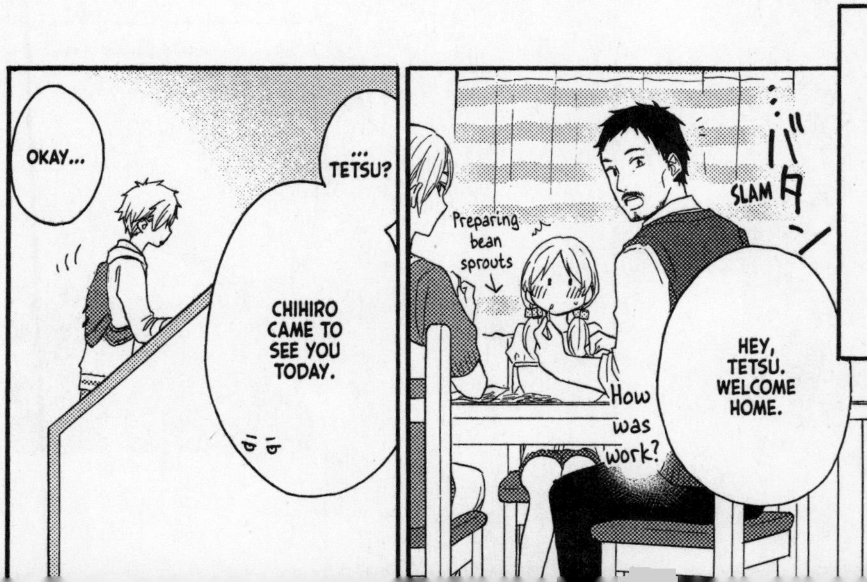
SLAM
HEY, TETSU. WELCOME HOME.
How was work?
Preparing bean sprouts
... TETSU?
CHIHIRO CAME TO SEE YOU TODAY.
OKAY...

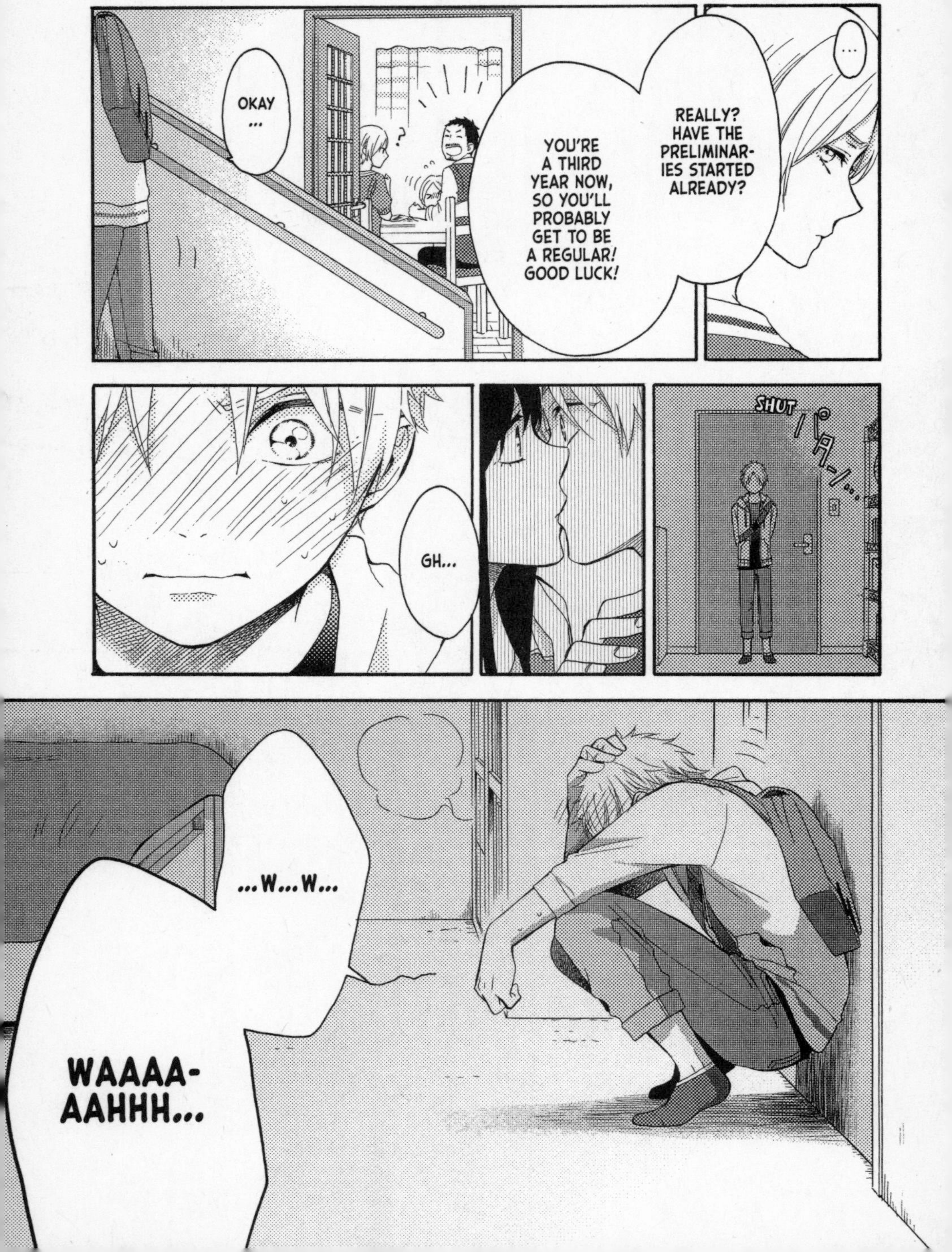
...
REALLY? HAVE THE PRELIMINARIES STARTED ALREADY?
YOU'RE A THIRD YEAR NOW, SO YOU'LL PROBABLY GET TO BE A REGULAR! GOOD LUCK!
OKAY ...
SHUT
パタ―ン…
GH...
...W...W...
WAAAA-AAHHH...

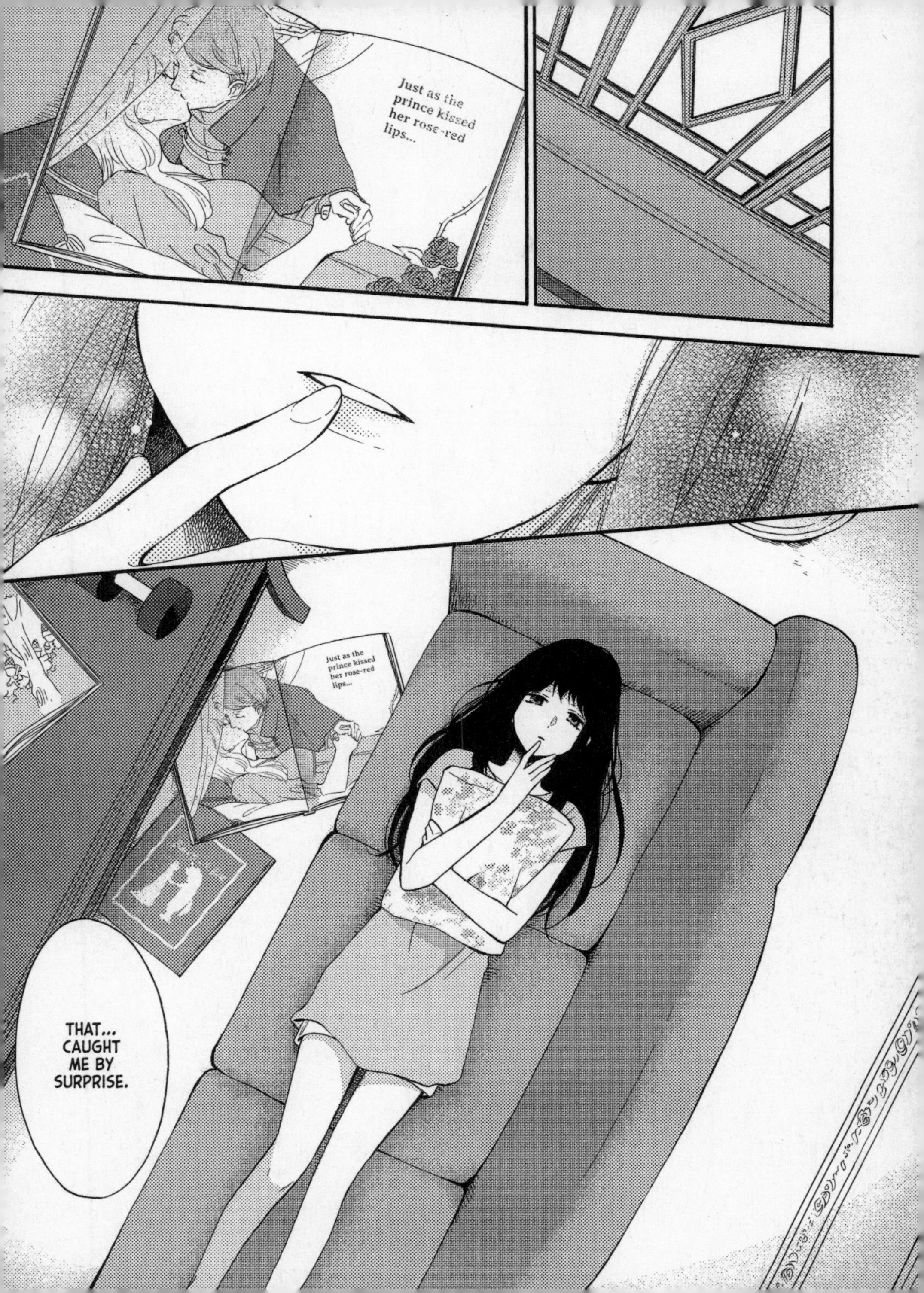
Just as the prince kissed her rose-red lips...
Just as the prince kissed her rose-red lips...
THAT... CAUGHT ME BY SURPRISE.

Chapter 8

A Missing Heart

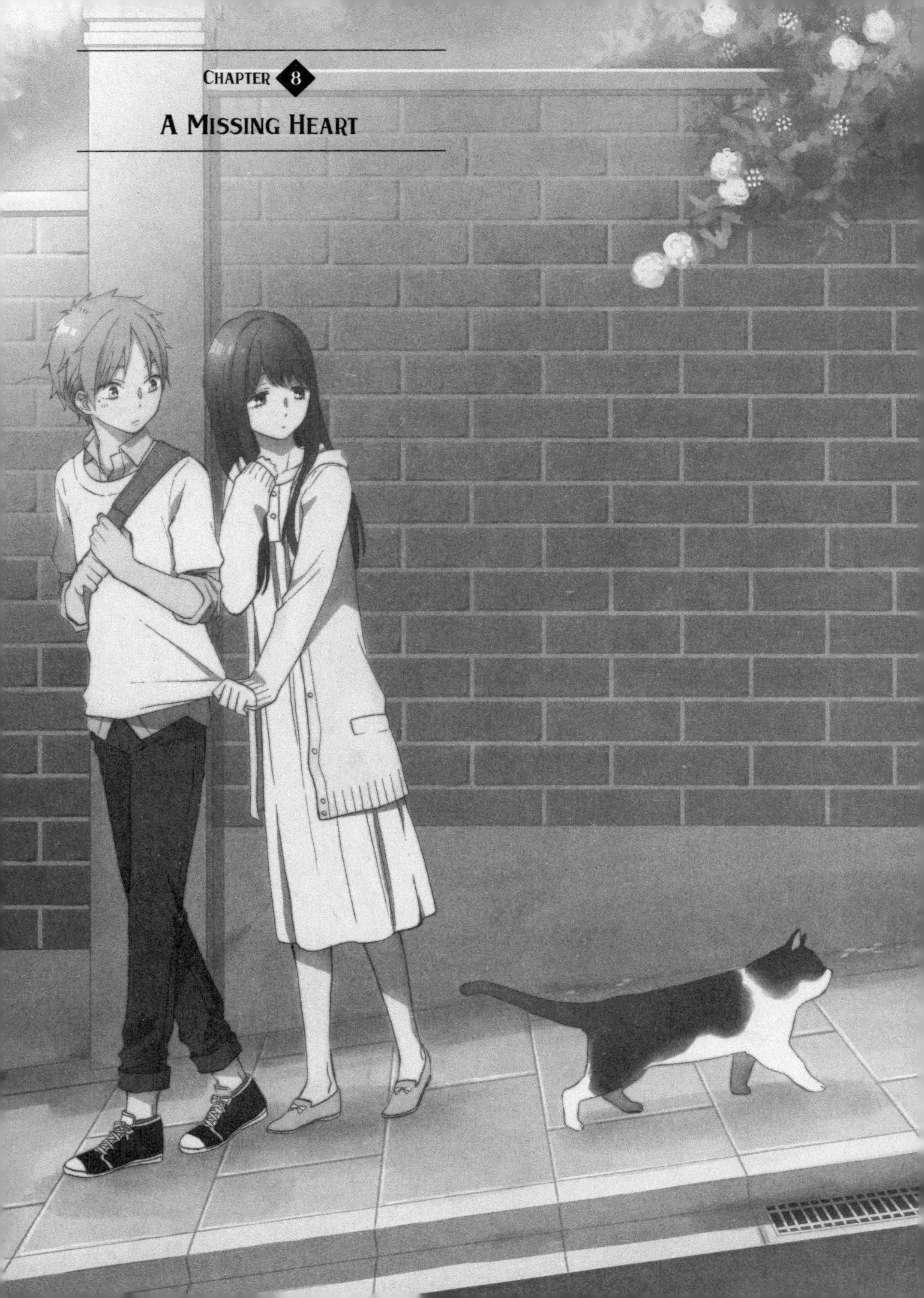

Wake Up,
Sleeping
Beauty

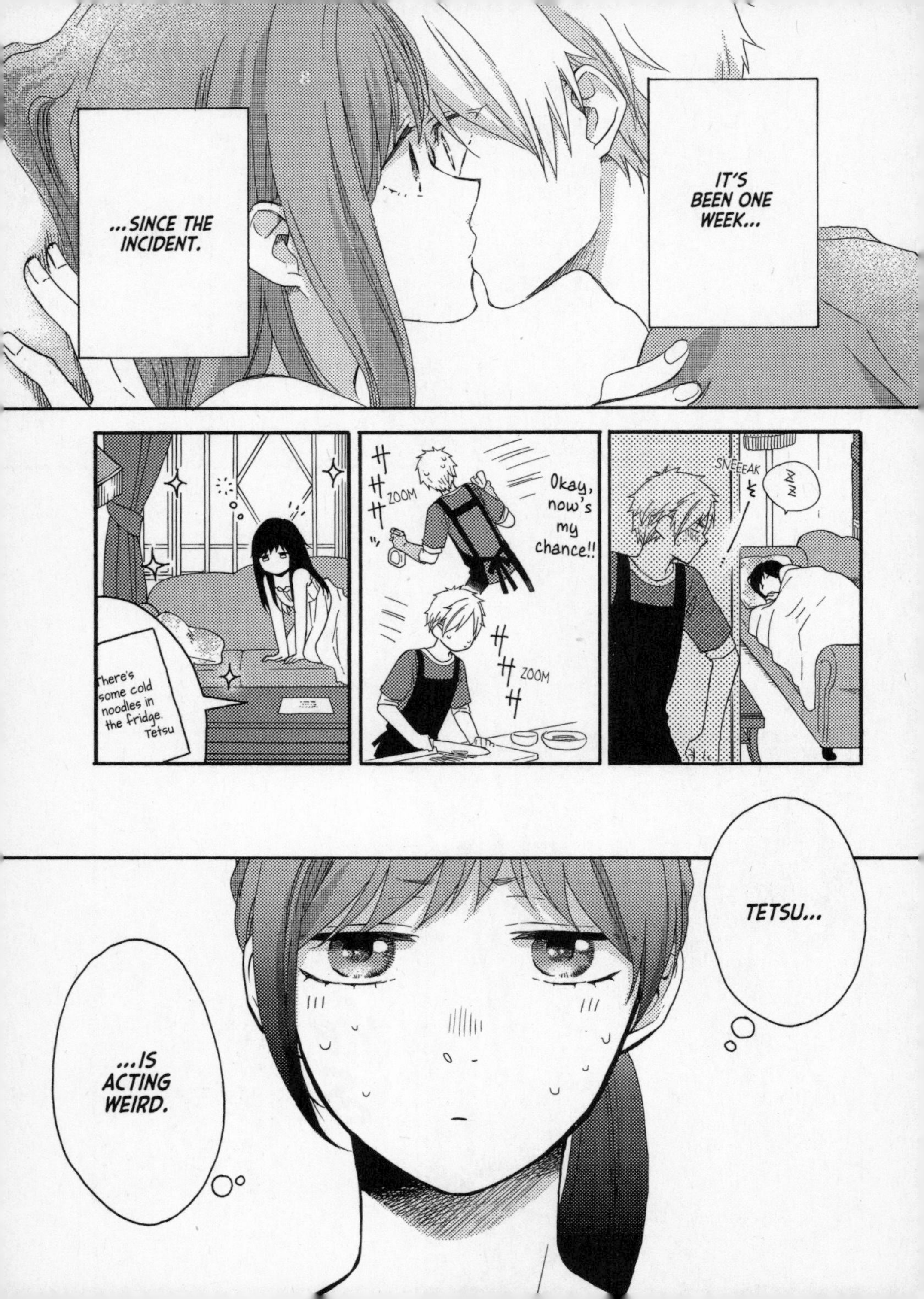
IT'S BEEN ONE WEEK...
...SINCE THE INCIDENT.
SNEEEAK
ZZ
Okay, now's my chance!!
ZOOM
ZOOM
There's some cold noodles in the fridge. Tetsu
TETSU...
...IS ACTING WEIRD.

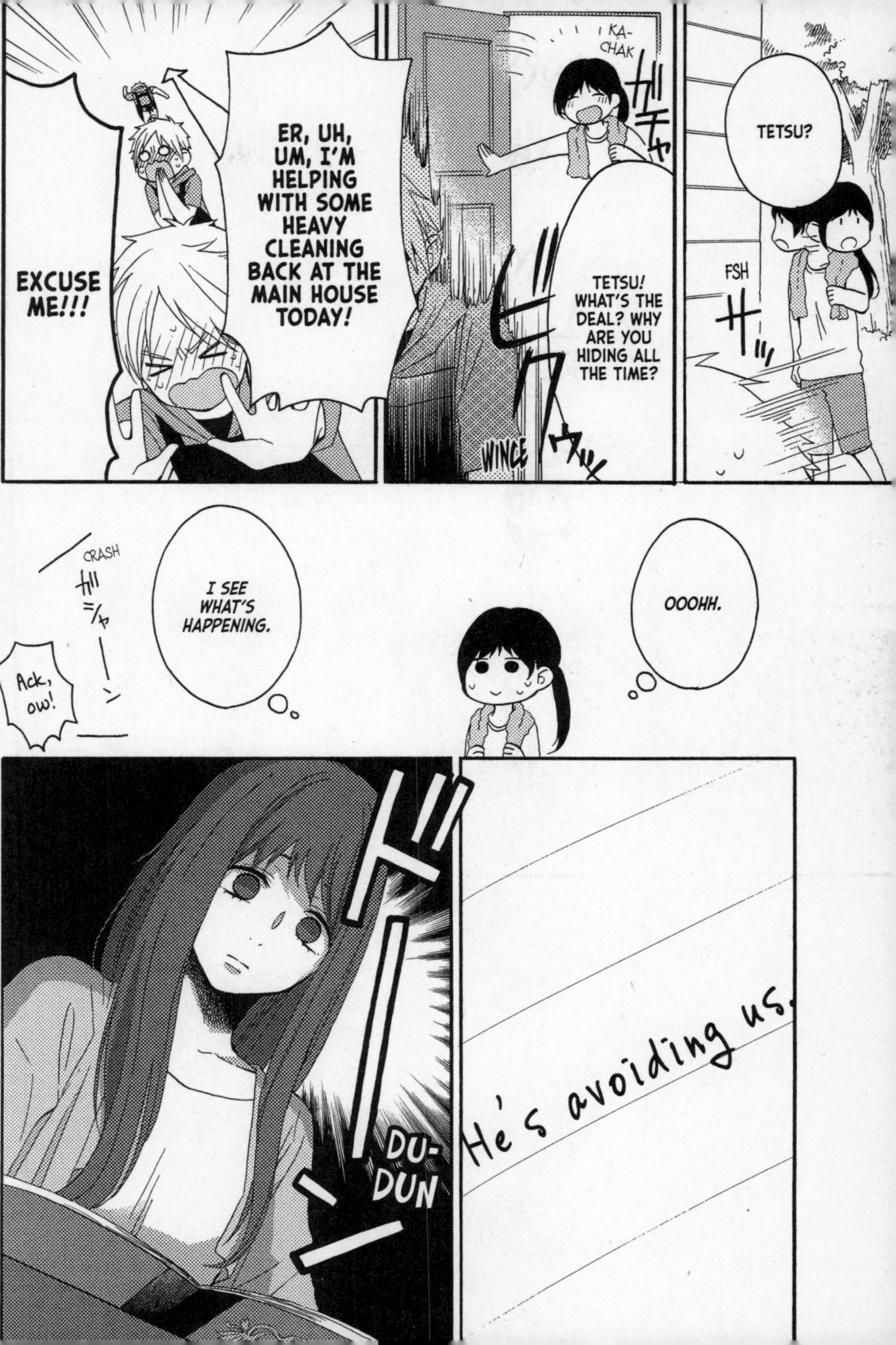
TETSU?
FSH
KA-CHAK
TETSU! WHAT'S THE DEAL? WHY ARE YOU HIDING ALL THE TIME?
WINCE
ER, UH, UM, I'M HELPING WITH SOME HEAVY CLEANING BACK AT THE MAIN HOUSE TODAY!
EXCUSE ME!!!
OOOHH.
I SEE WHAT'S HAPPENING.
CRASH
Ack, ow!
He's avoiding us.
DU-DUN

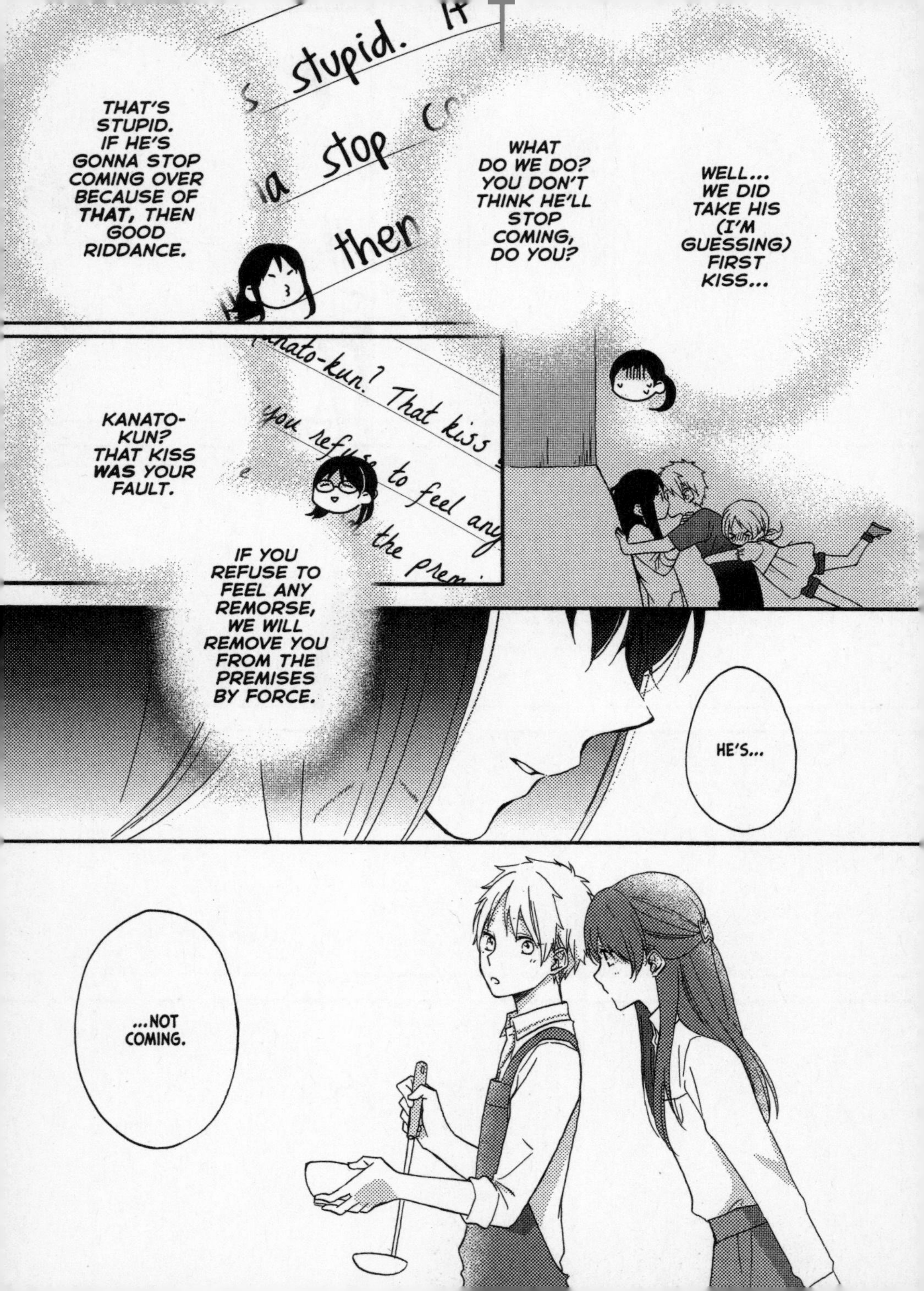

WELL... WE DID TAKE HIS (I'M GUESSING) FIRST KISS...
WHAT DO WE DO? YOU DON'T THINK HE'LL STOP COMING, DO YOU?
THAT'S STUPID. IF HE'S GONNA STOP COMING OVER BECAUSE OF THAT, THEN GOOD RIDDANCE.
KANATO-KUN? THAT KISS WAS YOUR FAULT.
IF YOU REFUSE TO FEEL ANY REMORSE, WE WILL REMOVE YOU FROM THE PREMISES BY FORCE.
HE'S...
...NOT COMING.

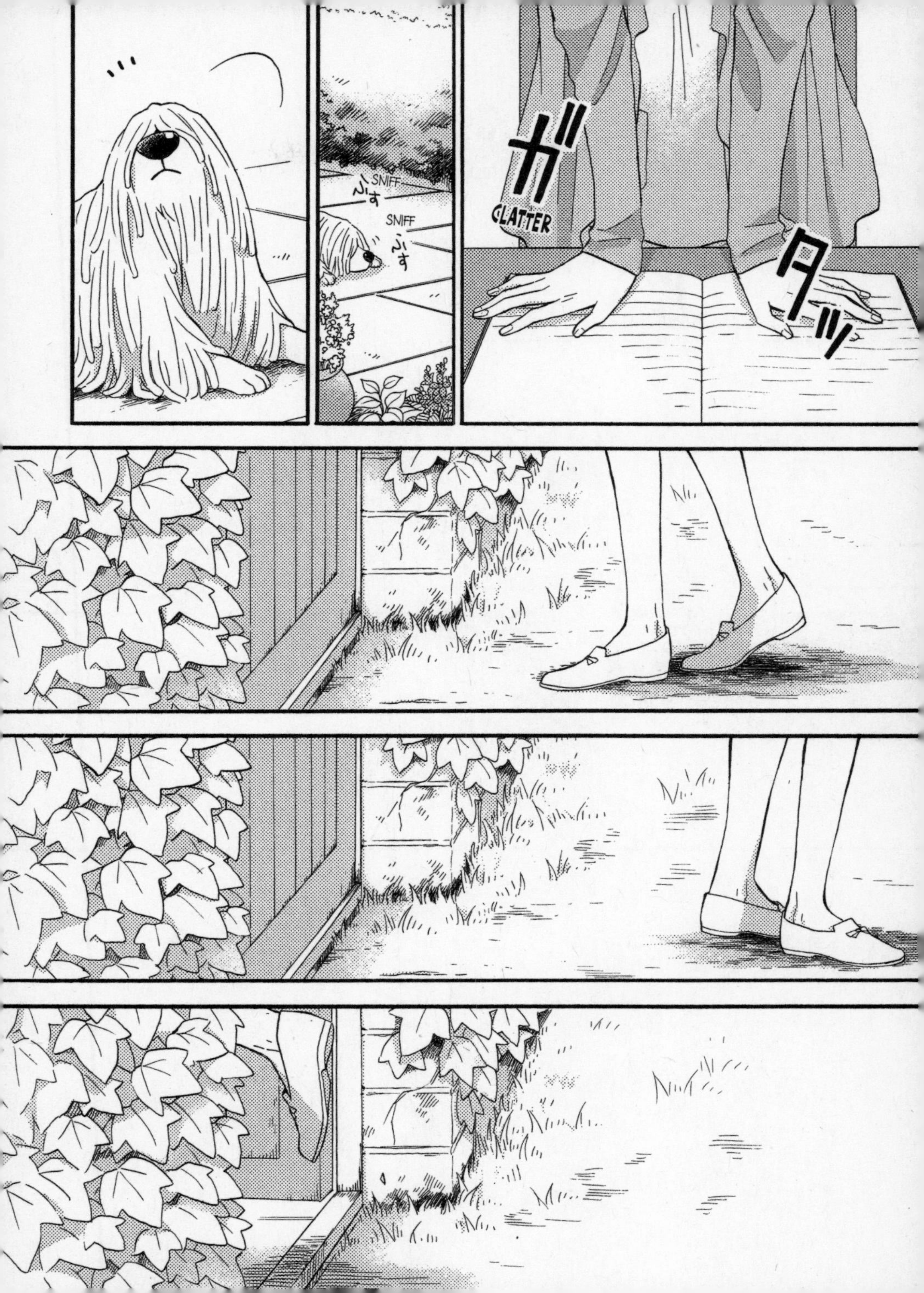
ガ
CLATTER
タッ
SNIFF
ふす
SNIFF
ふす

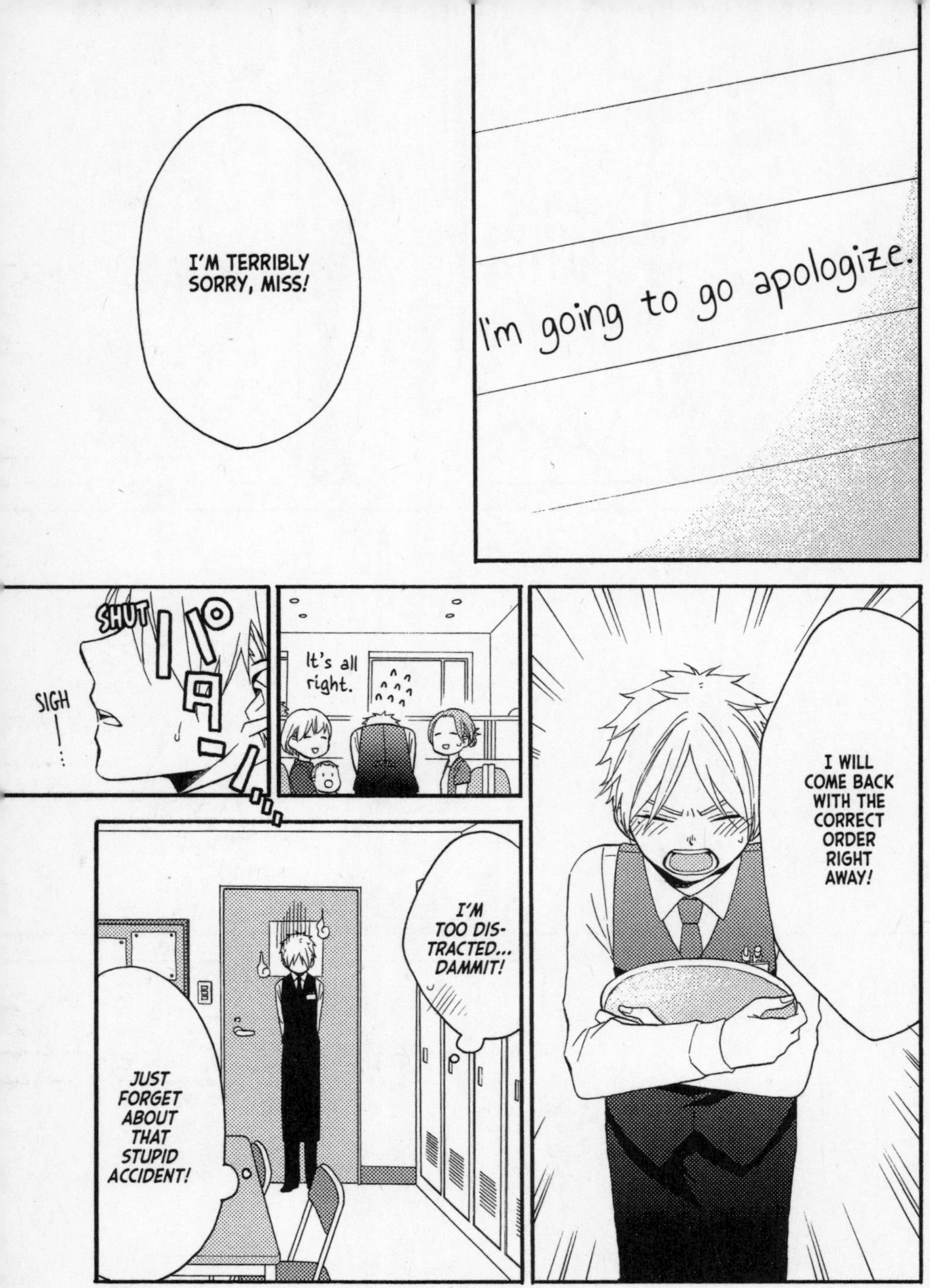
I'm going to go apologize.
I'M TERRIBLY SORRY, MISS!
I WILL COME BACK WITH THE CORRECT ORDER RIGHT AWAY!
It's all right.
SHUT
SIGH...
I'M TOO DIS-TRACTED... DAMMIT!
JUST FORGET ABOUT THAT STUPID ACCIDENT!

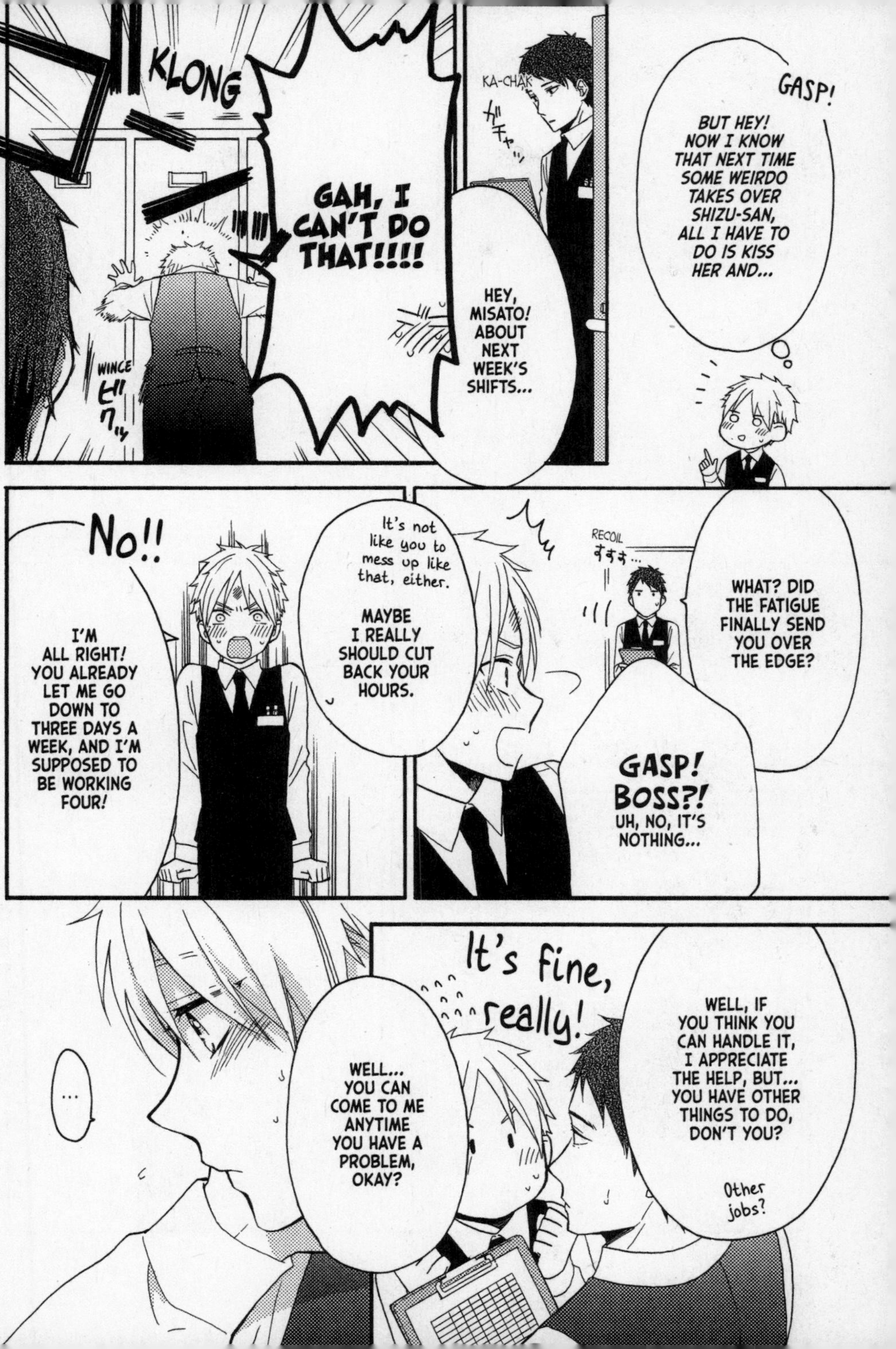
GASP!
BUT HEY! NOW I KNOW THAT NEXT TIME SOME WEIRDO TAKES OVER SHIZU-SAN, ALL I HAVE TO DO IS KISS HER AND...
KLONG
GAH, I CAN'T DO THAT!!!!
WINCE
KA-CHAK
HEY, MISATO! ABOUT NEXT WEEK'S SHIFTS...
RECOIL
すすす…
WHAT? DID THE FATIGUE FINALLY SEND YOU OVER THE EDGE?
GASP! BOSS?! UH, NO, IT'S NOTHING...
It's not like you to mess up like that, either.
MAYBE I REALLY SHOULD CUT BACK YOUR HOURS.
No!!
I'M ALL RIGHT! YOU ALREADY LET ME GO DOWN TO THREE DAYS A WEEK, AND I'M SUPPOSED TO BE WORKING FOUR!
It's fine, really!
WELL, IF YOU THINK YOU CAN HANDLE IT, I APPRECIATE THE HELP, BUT... YOU HAVE OTHER THINGS TO DO, DON'T YOU?
Other jobs?
WELL... YOU CAN COME TO ME ANYTIME YOU HAVE A PROBLEM, OKAY?
...

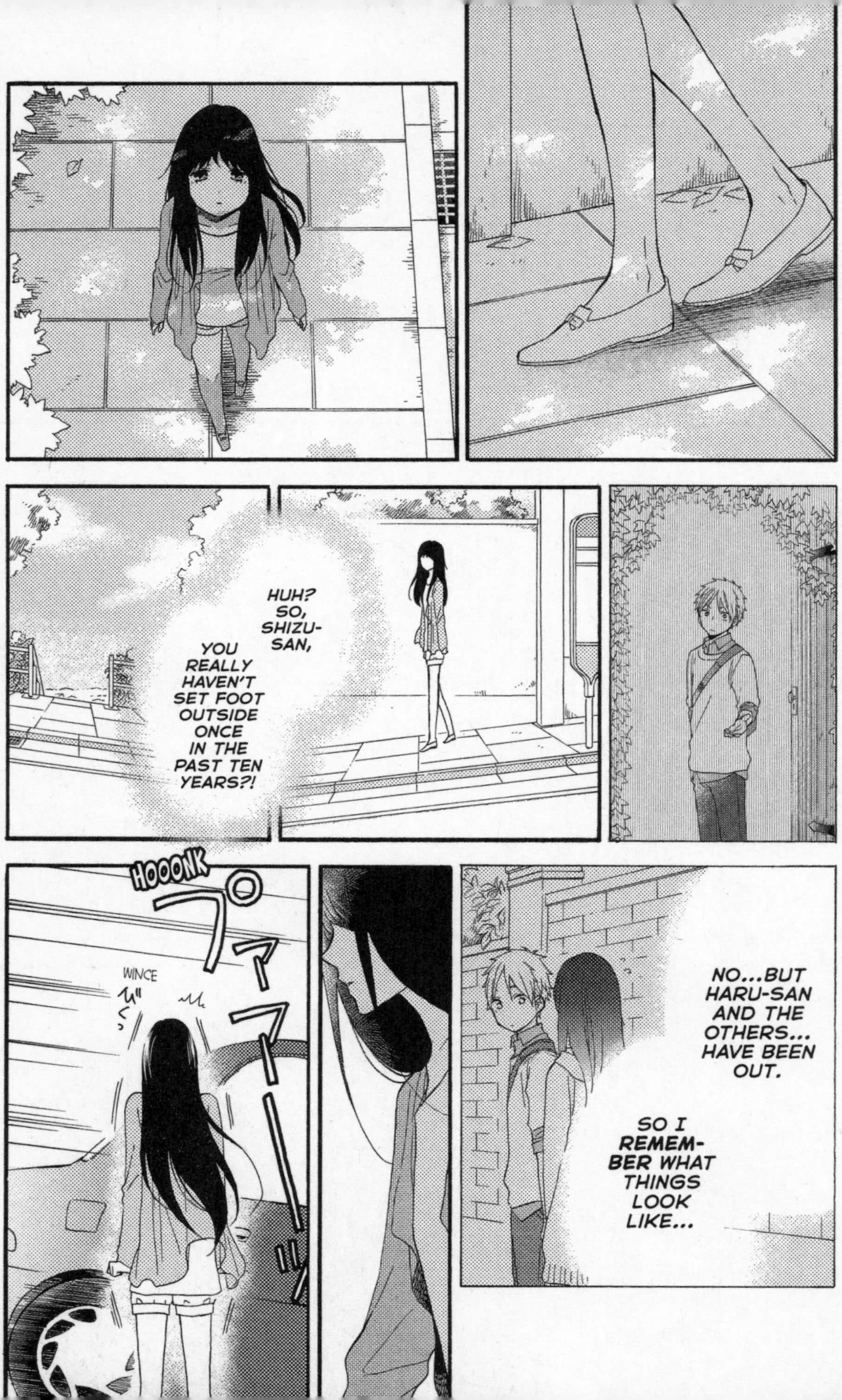
HUH? SO, SHIZU-SAN, YOU REALLY HAVEN'T SET FOOT OUTSIDE ONCE IN THE PAST TEN YEARS?!
NO...BUT HARU-SAN AND THE OTHERS... HAVE BEEN OUT.
SO I REMEMBER WHAT THINGS LOOK LIKE...
HOOONK
プァァーーッ
WINCE
びくっ

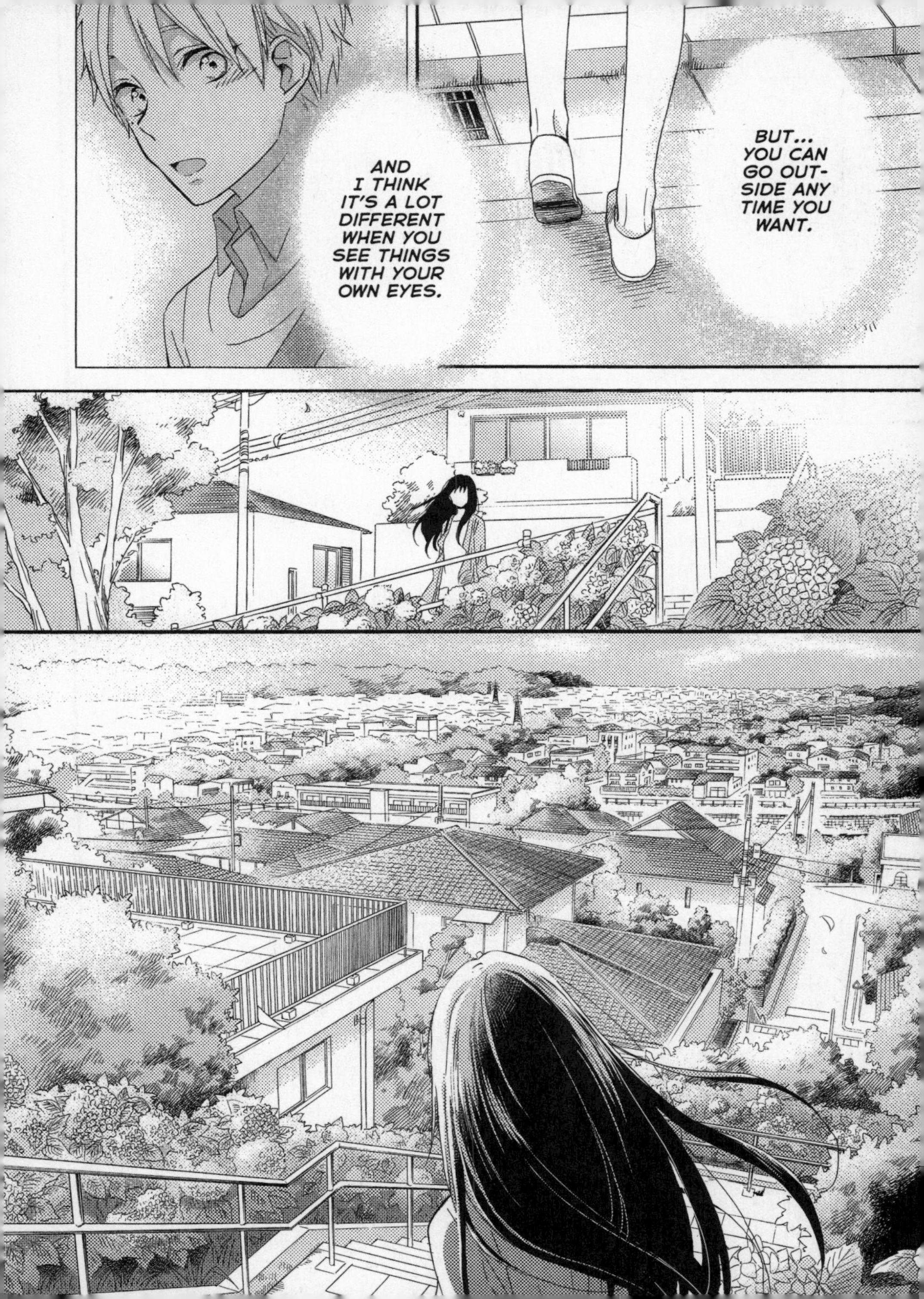
BUT... YOU CAN GO OUT-SIDE ANY TIME YOU WANT.
AND I THINK IT'S A LOT DIFFERENT WHEN YOU SEE THINGS WITH YOUR OWN EYES.

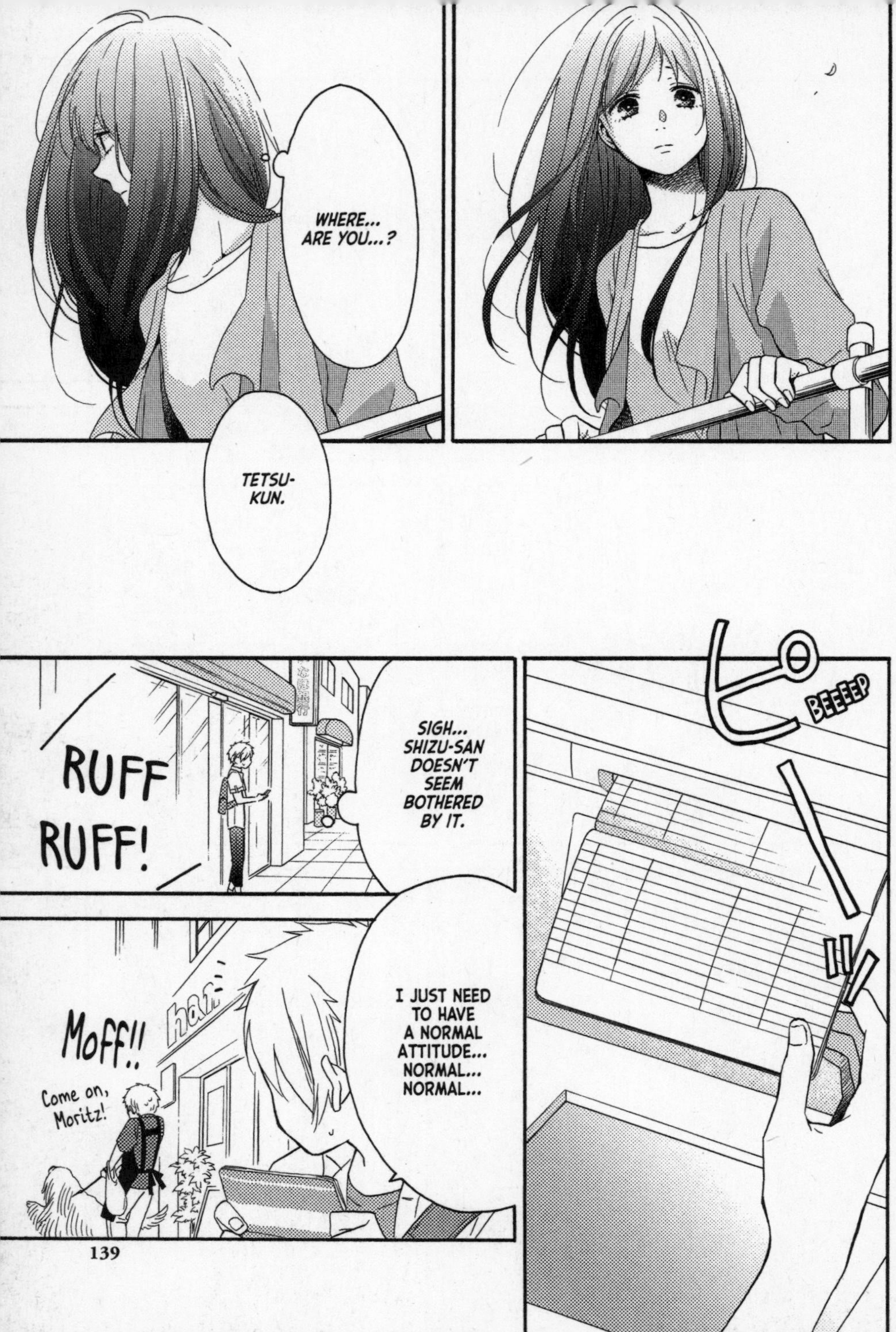
WHERE... ARE YOU...?
TETSU-KUN.
ピー
BEEEP
SIGH... SHIZU-SAN DOESN'T SEEM BOTHERED BY IT.
RUFF RUFF!
I JUST NEED TO HAVE A NORMAL ATTITUDE... NORMAL... NORMAL...
Moff!!
Come on, Moritz!

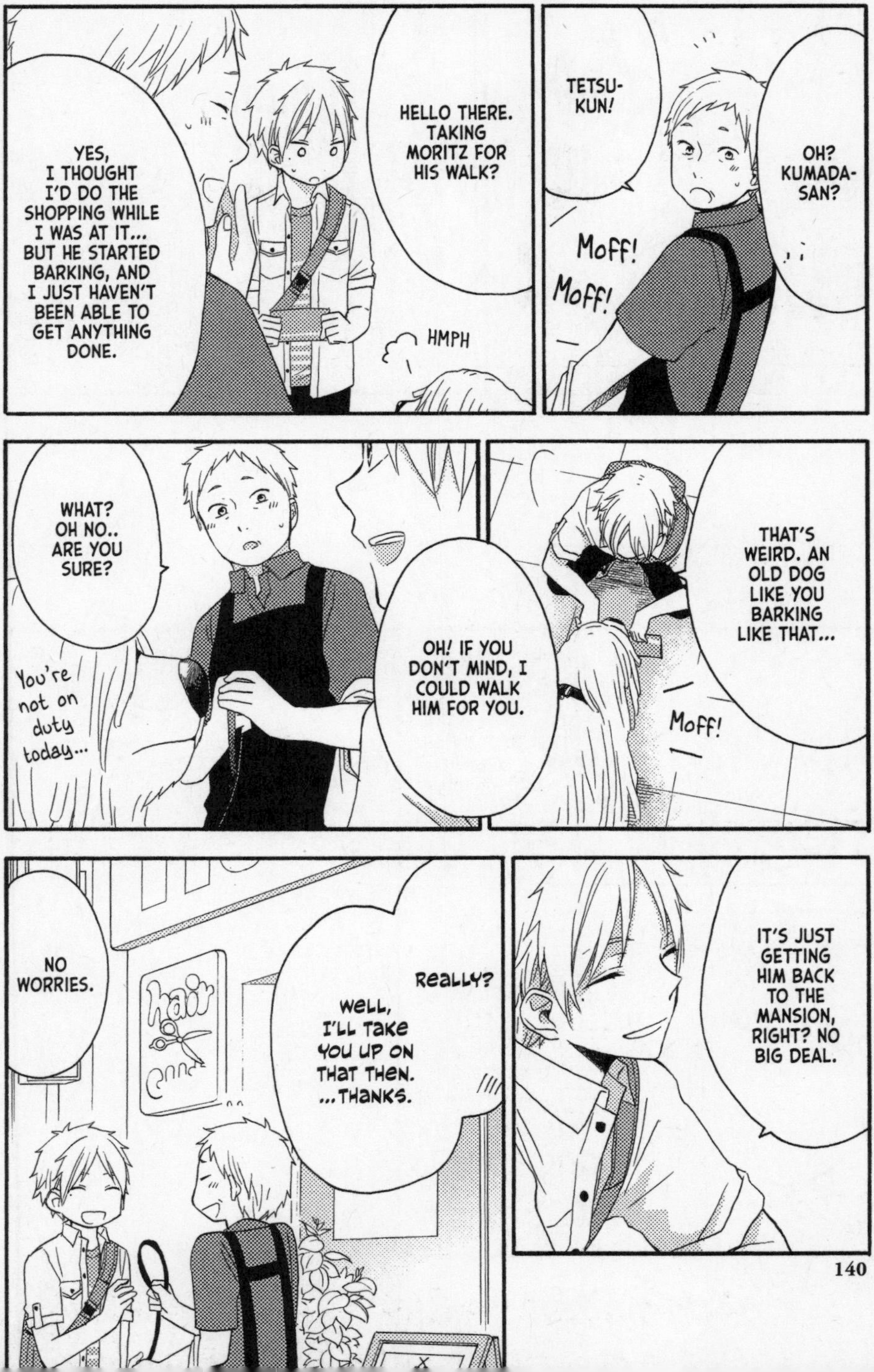
OH? KUMADA-SAN?
TETSU-KUN!
Moff!
Moff!
HELLO THERE. TAKING MORITZ FOR HIS WALK?
HMPH
YES, I THOUGHT I'D DO THE SHOPPING WHILE I WAS AT IT... BUT HE STARTED BARKING, AND I JUST HAVEN'T BEEN ABLE TO GET ANYTHING DONE.
THAT'S WEIRD. AN OLD DOG LIKE YOU BARKING LIKE THAT...
Moff!
OH! IF YOU DON'T MIND, I COULD WALK HIM FOR YOU.
WHAT? OH NO.. ARE YOU SURE?
You're not on duty today...
IT'S JUST GETTING HIM BACK TO THE MANSION, RIGHT? NO BIG DEAL.
Really?
Well, I'll take you up on that then. ...Thanks.
NO WORRIES.

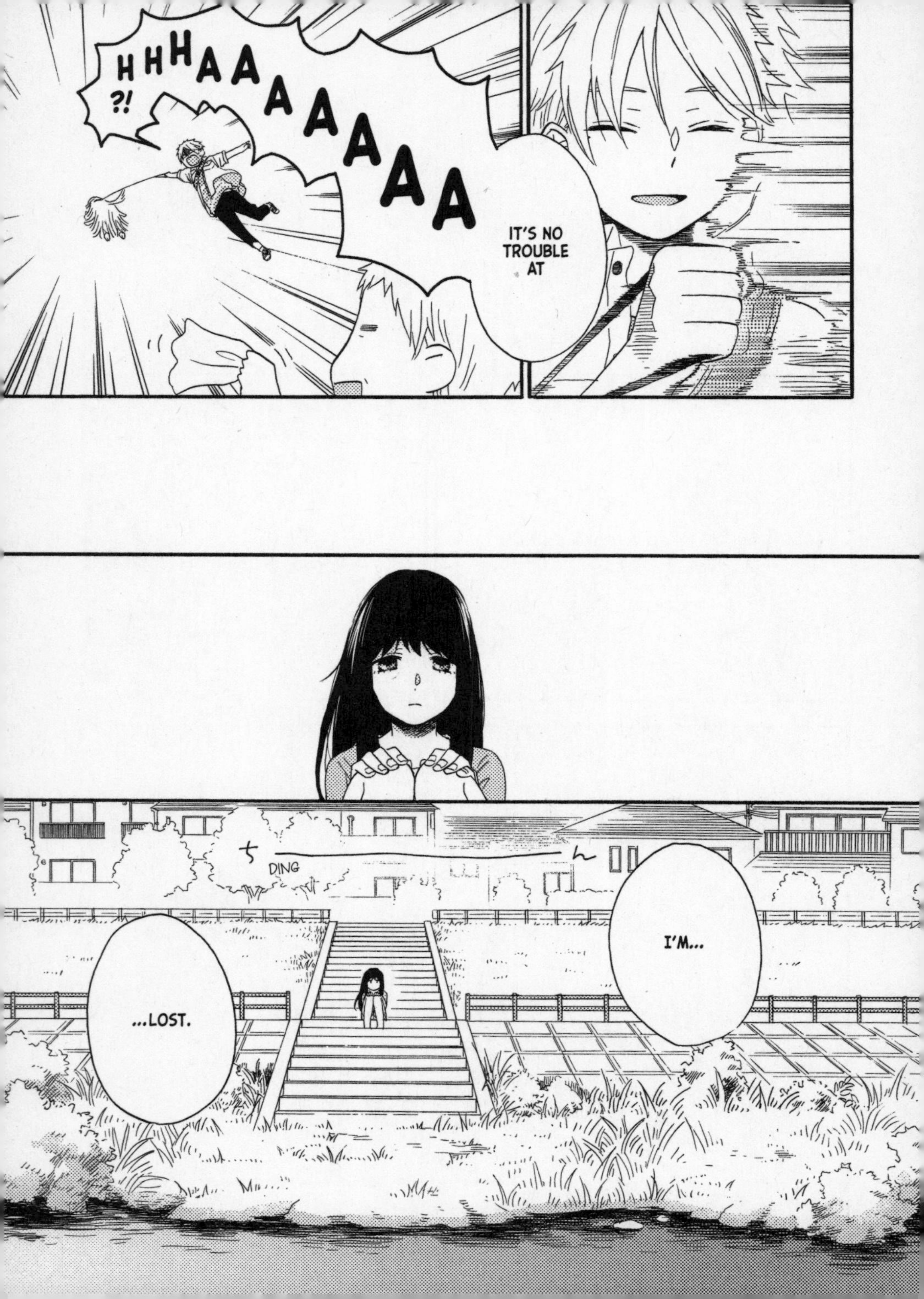
IT'S NO TROUBLE AT
HHHAAAAAAAAA ?!
DING
I'M...
...LOST.

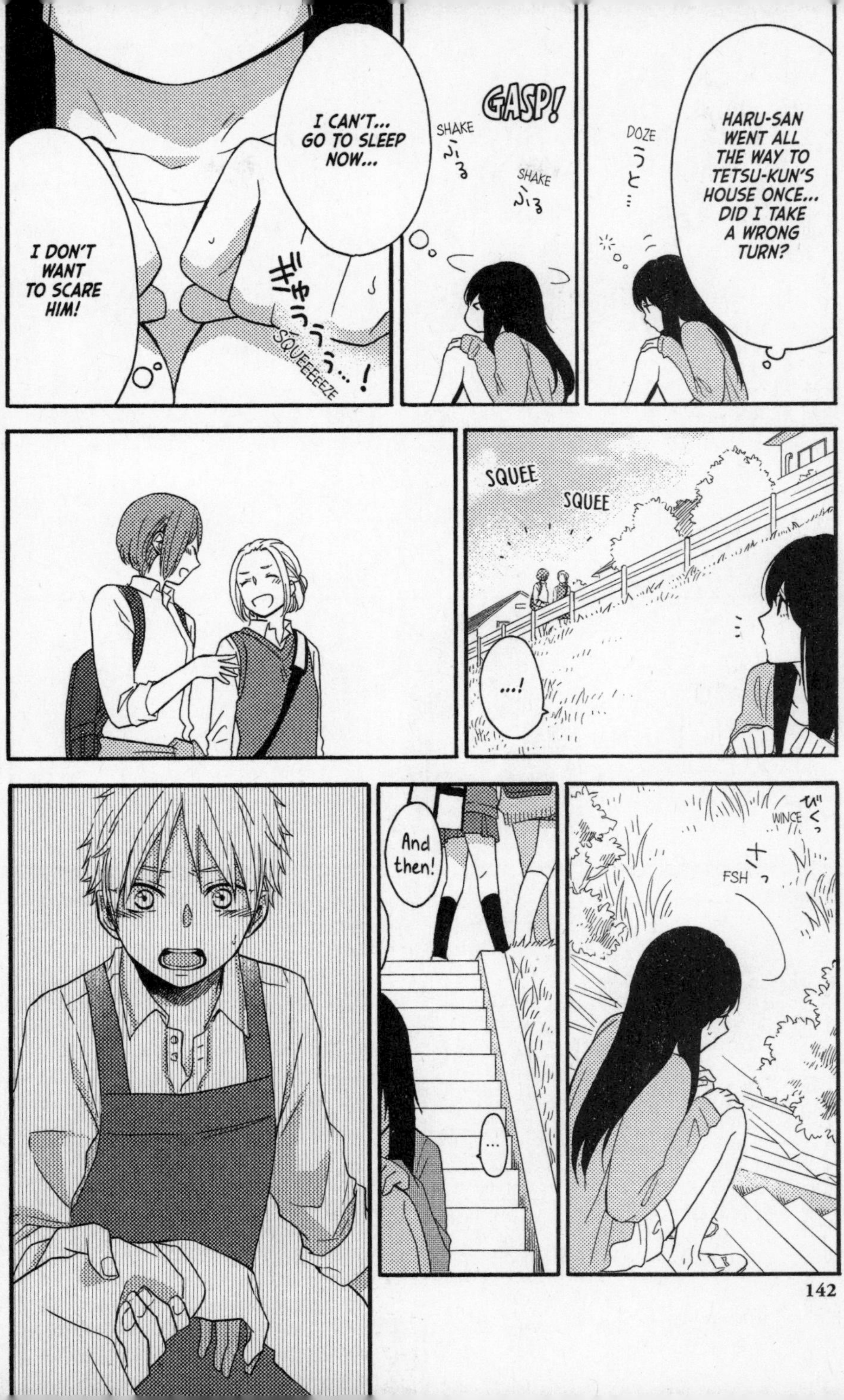
HARU-SAN WENT ALL THE WAY TO TETSU-KUN'S HOUSE ONCE... DID I TAKE A WRONG TURN?
DOZE
GASP!
SHAKE
SHAKE
I CAN'T... GO TO SLEEP NOW...
I DON'T WANT TO SCARE HIM!
SQUEEEEEZE
SQUEE
SQUEE
...!
WINCE
FSH
And then!
...

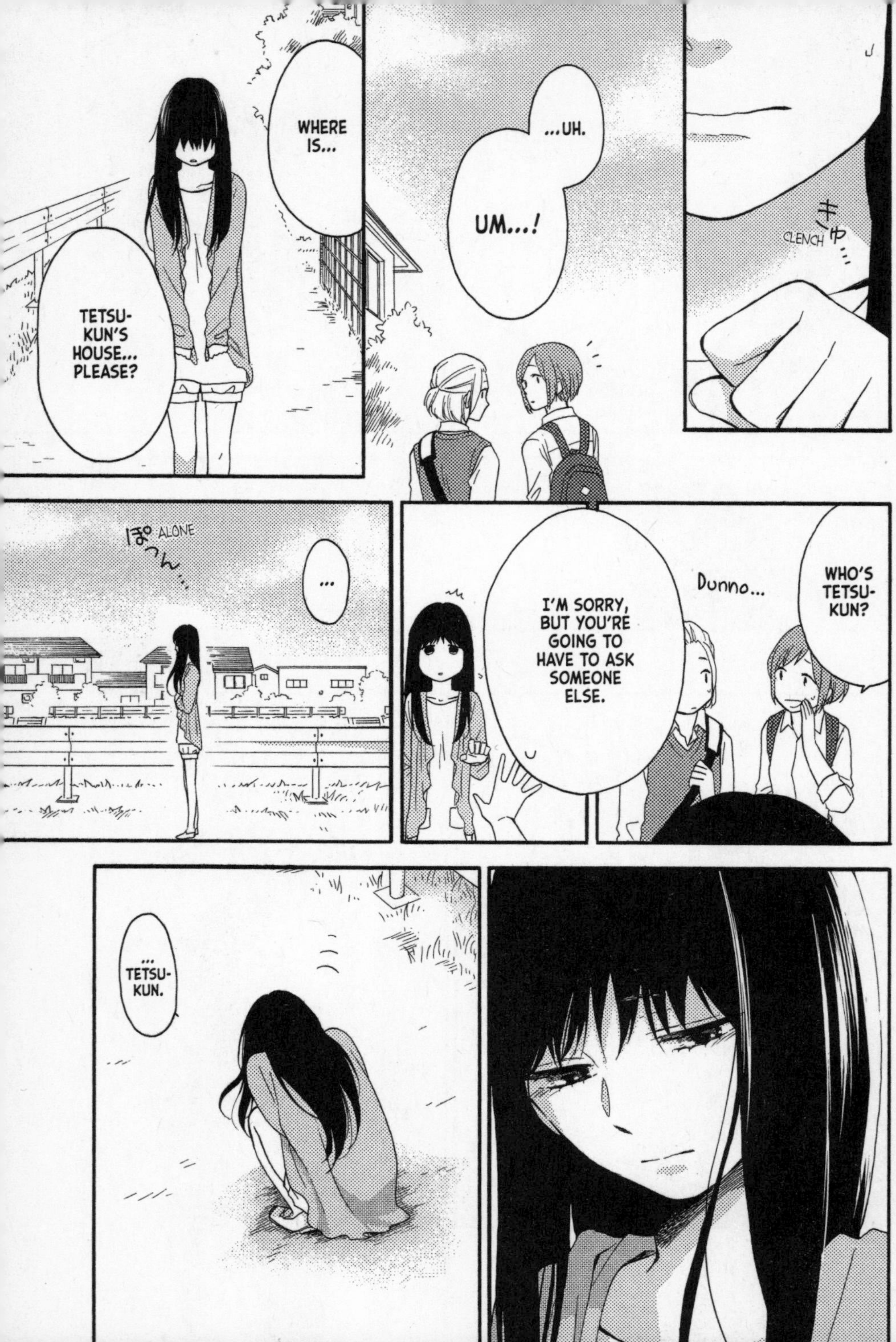
きゅ…
CLENCH
...UH.
UM...!
WHERE IS...
TETSU-KUN'S HOUSE... PLEASE?
WHO'S TETSU-KUN?
Dunno...
I'M SORRY, BUT YOU'RE GOING TO HAVE TO ASK SOMEONE ELSE.
...
ぽつん…
ALONE
...TETSU-KUN.

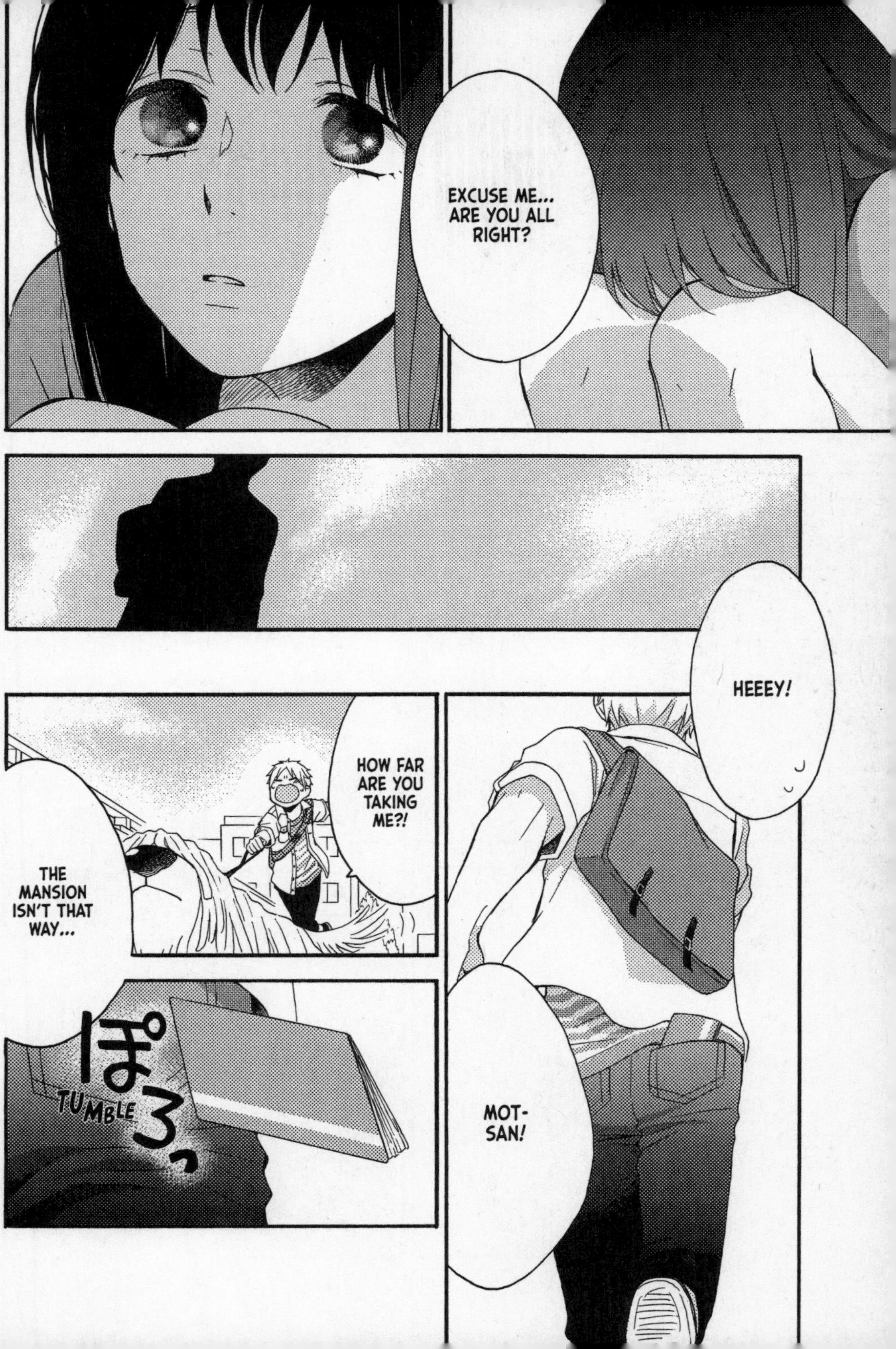
EXCUSE ME... ARE YOU ALL RIGHT?
HEEEY!
MOT-SAN!
HOW FAR ARE YOU TAKING ME?!
THE MANSION ISN'T THAT WAY...
ぽろっ
TUMBLE

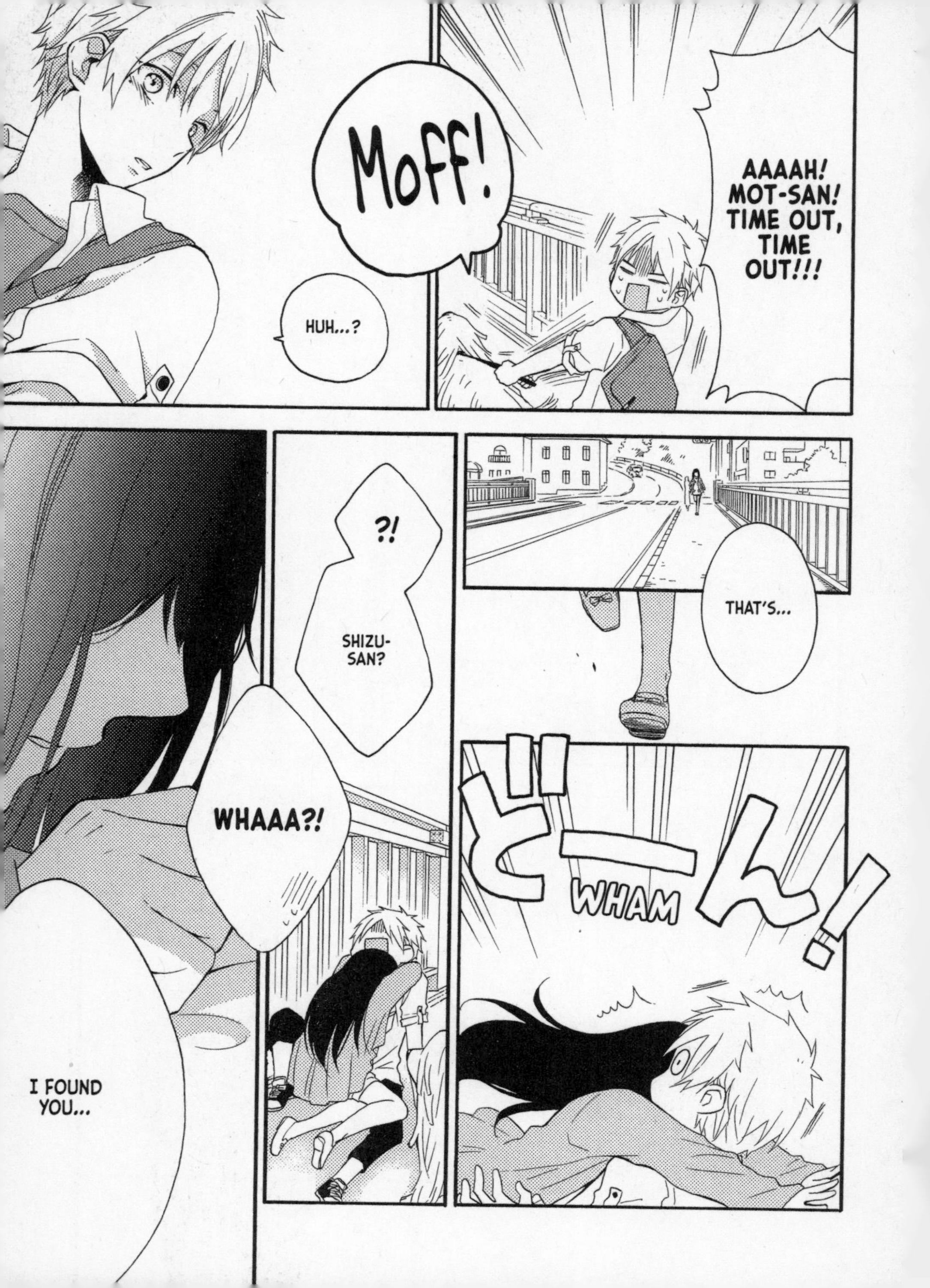
AAAAH! MOT-SAN! TIME OUT, TIME OUT!!!
Moff!
HUH...?
THAT'S...
どーん!
WHAM
?!
SHIZU-SAN?
WHAAA?!
I FOUND YOU...

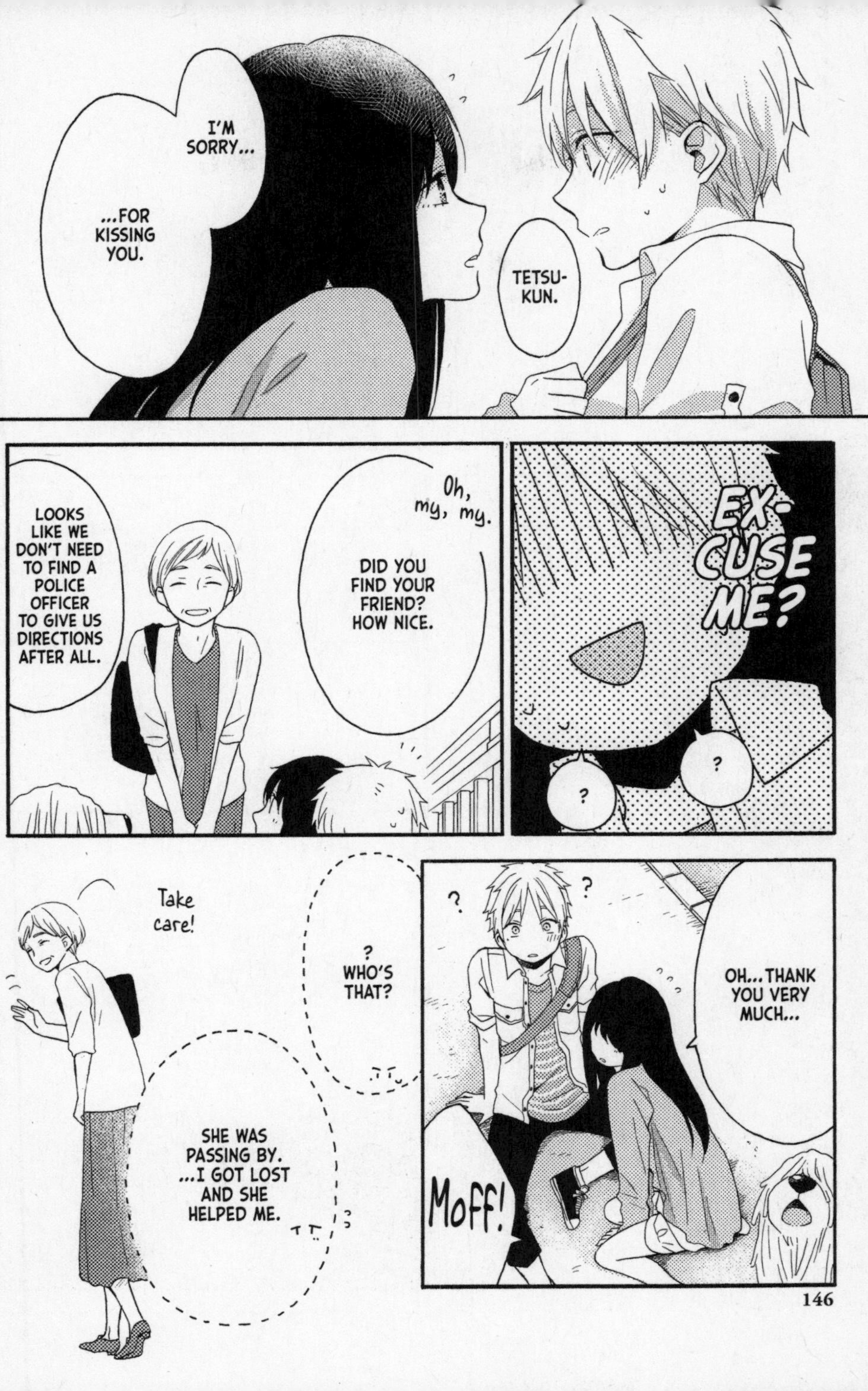
TETSU-KUN.
I'M SORRY...
...FOR KISSING YOU.
EX-CUSE ME?
?
?
Oh, my, my.
DID YOU FIND YOUR FRIEND? HOW NICE.
LOOKS LIKE WE DON'T NEED TO FIND A POLICE OFFICER TO GIVE US DIRECTIONS AFTER ALL.
OH...THANK YOU VERY MUCH...
Moff!
? WHO'S THAT?
Take care!
SHE WAS PASSING BY. ...I GOT LOST AND SHE HELPED ME.

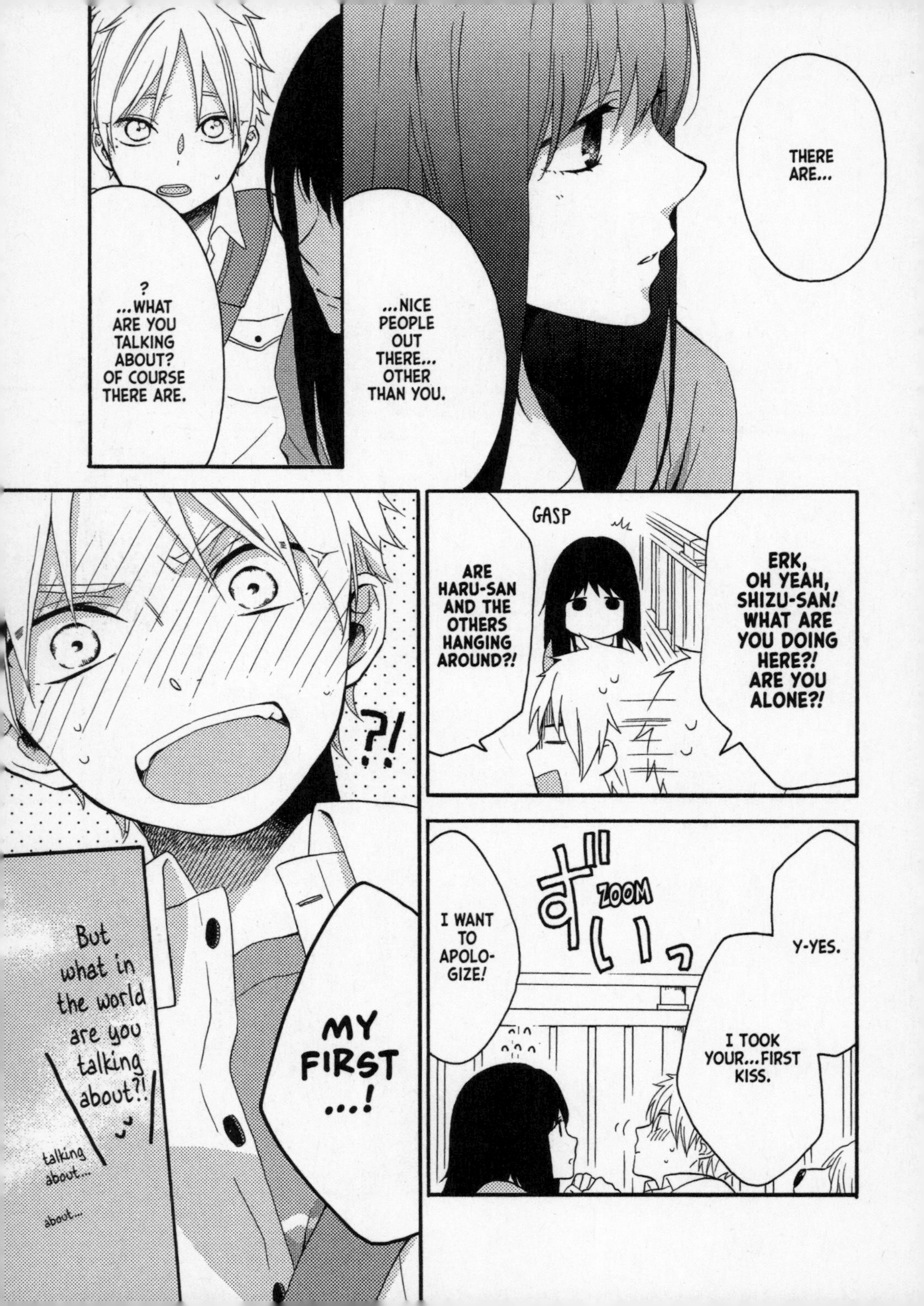
THERE ARE...
...NICE PEOPLE OUT THERE... OTHER THAN YOU.
? ...WHAT ARE YOU TALKING ABOUT? OF COURSE THERE ARE.
ERK, OH YEAH, SHIZU-SAN! WHAT ARE YOU DOING HERE?! ARE YOU ALONE?!
GASP
ARE HARU-SAN AND THE OTHERS HANGING AROUND?!
Y-YES.
I TOOK YOUR...FIRST KISS.
ZOOM
I WANT TO APOLO-GIZE!
?!
MY FIRST ...!
But what in the world are you talking about?!
talking about...
about...

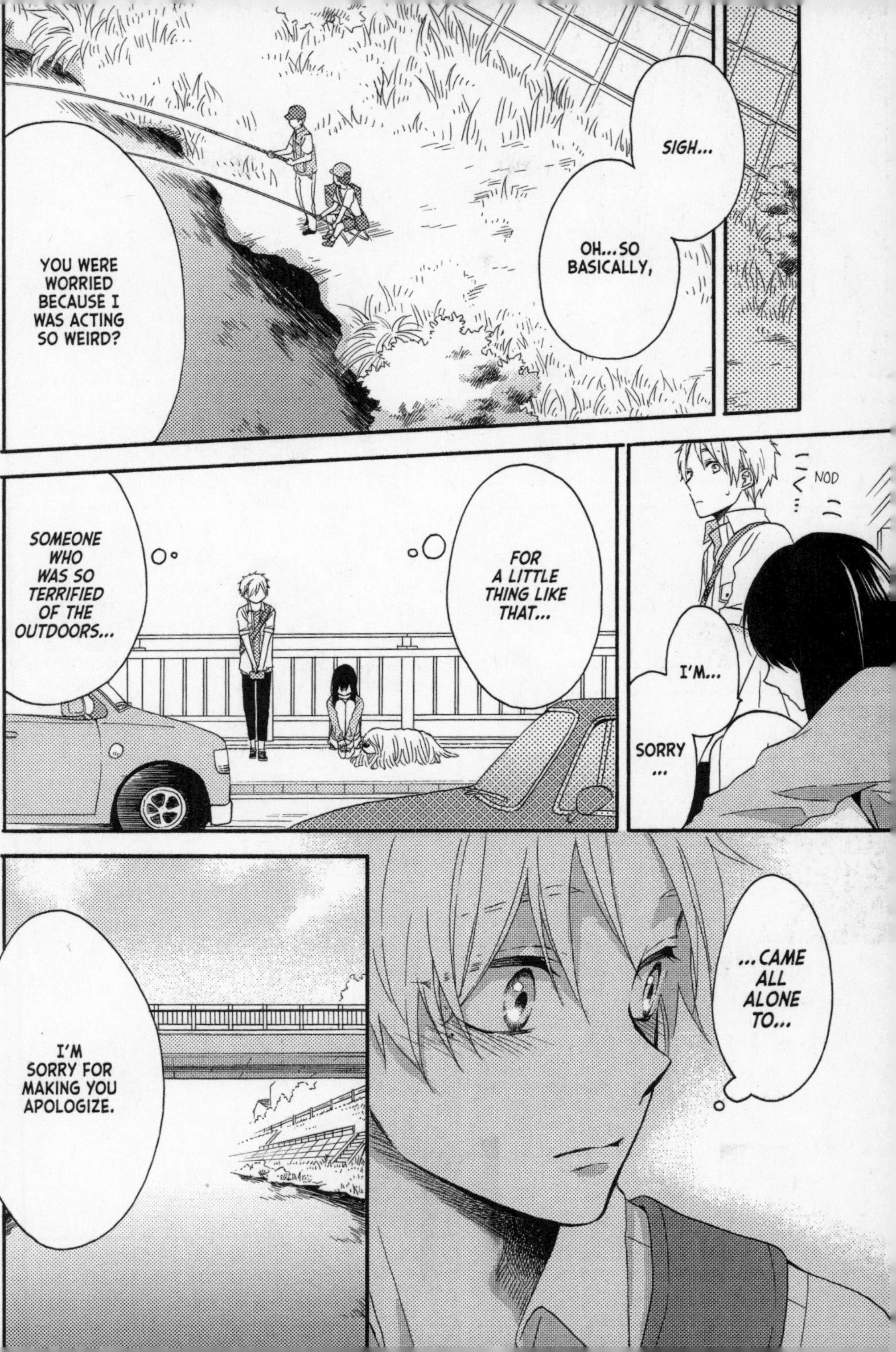
SIGH...
OH...SO BASICALLY,
YOU WERE WORRIED BECAUSE I WAS ACTING SO WEIRD?
NOD
I'M...
SORRY...
FOR A LITTLE THING LIKE THAT...
SOMEONE WHO WAS SO TERRIFIED OF THE OUTDOORS...
...CAME ALL ALONE TO...
I'M SORRY FOR MAKING YOU APOLOGIZE.

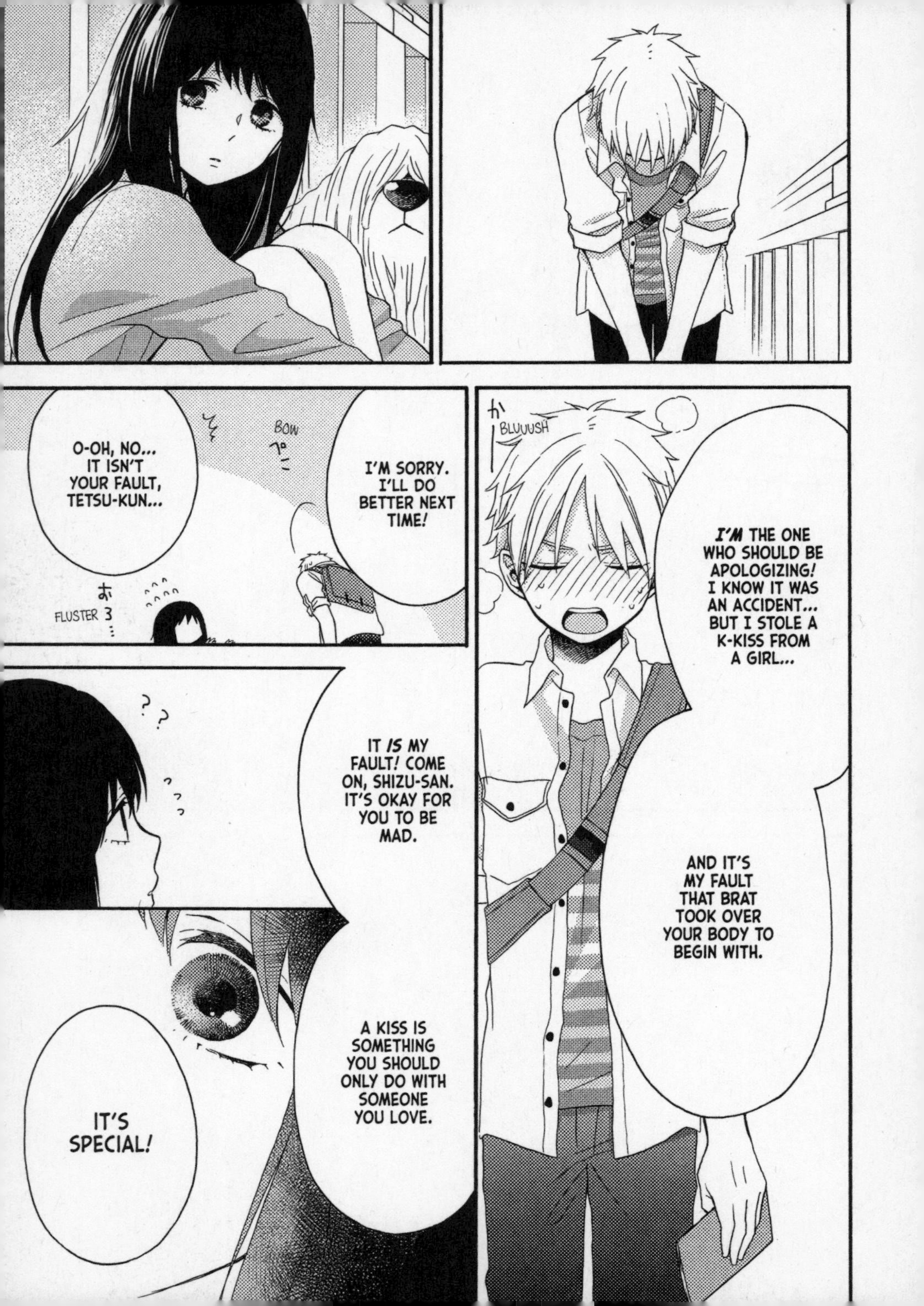
BOW
I'M SORRY. I'LL DO BETTER NEXT TIME!
O-OH, NO... IT ISN'T YOUR FAULT, TETSU-KUN...
FLUSTER
BLUUUSH
I'M THE ONE WHO SHOULD BE APOLOGIZING! I KNOW IT WAS AN ACCIDENT... BUT I STOLE A K-KISS FROM A GIRL...
AND IT'S MY FAULT THAT BRAT TOOK OVER YOUR BODY TO BEGIN WITH.
IT IS MY FAULT! COME ON, SHIZU-SAN. IT'S OKAY FOR YOU TO BE MAD.
A KISS IS SOMETHING YOU SHOULD ONLY DO WITH SOMEONE YOU LOVE.
IT'S SPECIAL!

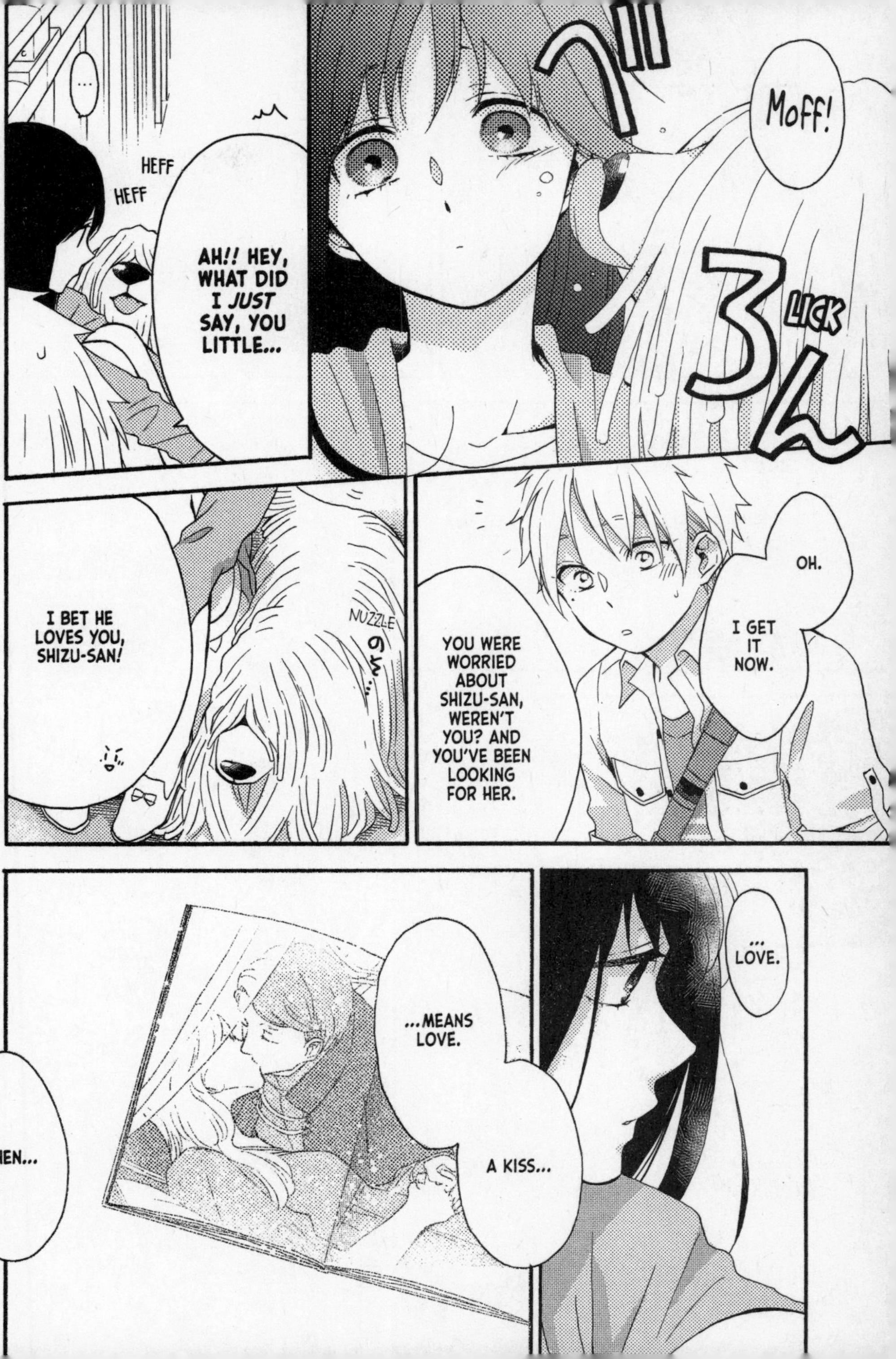
Moff!
LICK
...
HEFF
HEFF
AH!! HEY, WHAT DID I *JUST* SAY, YOU LITTLE...
OH.
I GET IT NOW.
YOU WERE WORRIED ABOUT SHIZU-SAN, WEREN'T YOU? AND YOU'VE BEEN LOOKING FOR HER.
NUZZLE
I BET HE LOVES YOU, SHIZU-SAN!
...LOVE.
...MEANS LOVE.
A KISS...
THEN...

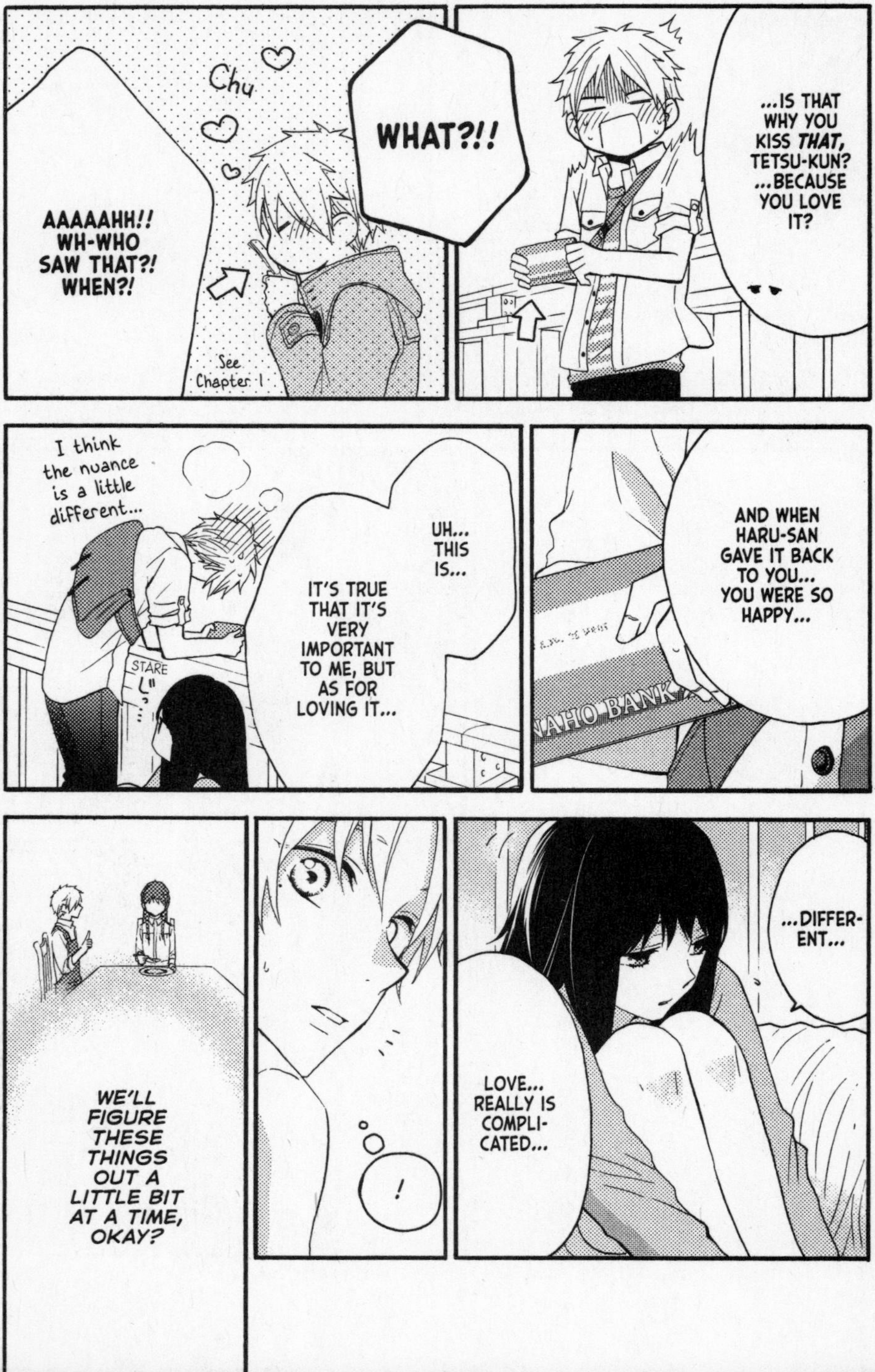

...IS THAT WHY YOU KISS *THAT*, TETSU-KUN? ...BECAUSE YOU LOVE IT?
WHAT?!!
Chu
AAAAAHH!! WH-WHO SAW THAT?! WHEN?!
See Chapter 1
AND WHEN HARU-SAN GAVE IT BACK TO YOU... YOU WERE SO HAPPY...
NAHO BANK
UH... THIS IS...
IT'S TRUE THAT IT'S VERY IMPORTANT TO ME, BUT AS FOR LOVING IT...
STARE
I think the nuance is a little different...
...DIFFER-ENT...
LOVE... REALLY IS COMPLI-CATED...
!
WE'LL FIGURE THESE THINGS OUT A LITTLE BIT AT A TIME, OKAY?

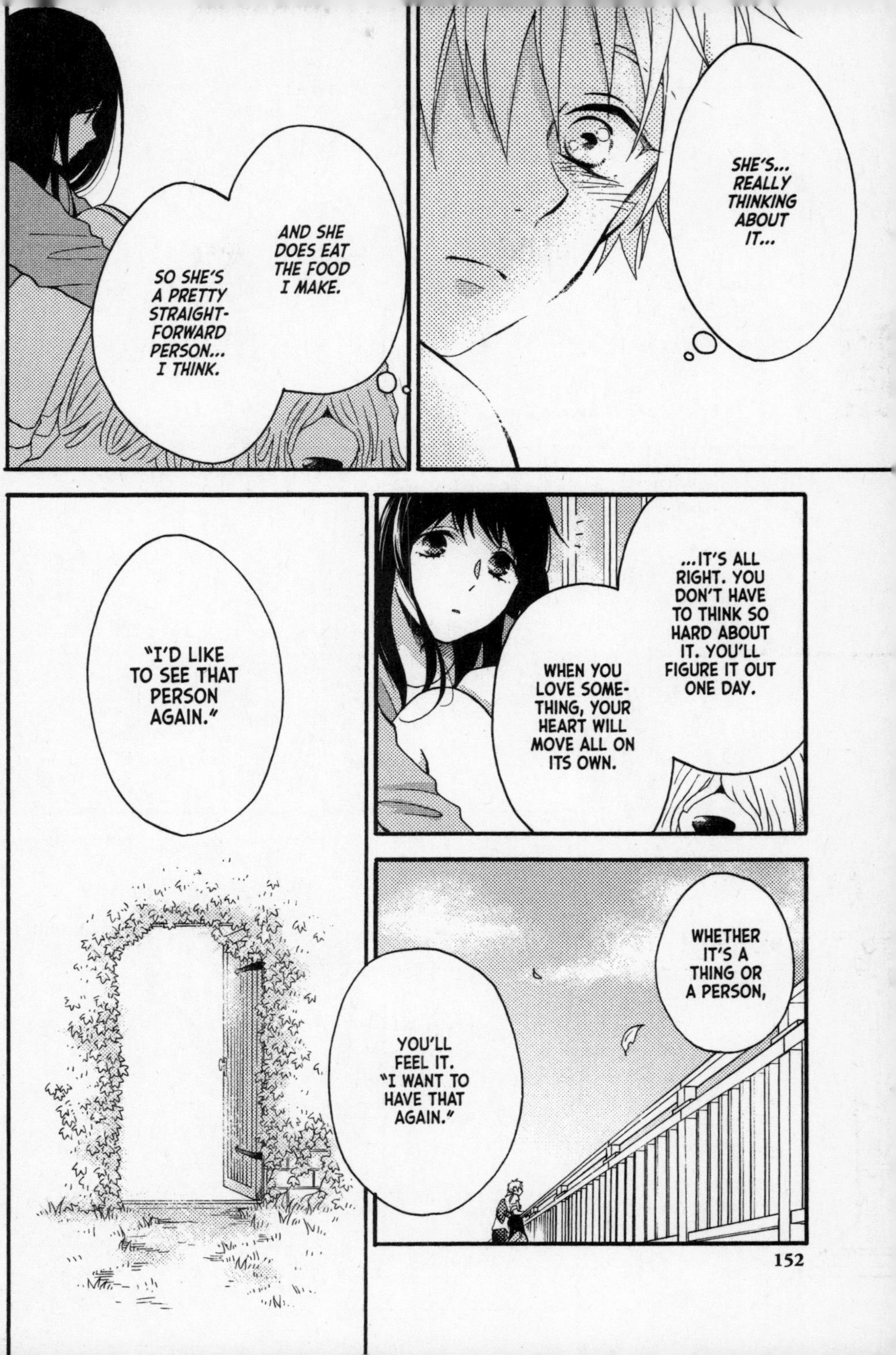
SHE'S... REALLY THINKING ABOUT IT...
AND SHE DOES EAT THE FOOD I MAKE.
SO SHE'S A PRETTY STRAIGHT-FORWARD PERSON... I THINK.
...IT'S ALL RIGHT. YOU DON'T HAVE TO THINK SO HARD ABOUT IT. YOU'LL FIGURE IT OUT ONE DAY.
WHEN YOU LOVE SOME-THING, YOUR HEART WILL MOVE ALL ON ITS OWN.
WHETHER IT'S A THING OR A PERSON,
YOU'LL FEEL IT. "I WANT TO HAVE THAT AGAIN."
"I'D LIKE TO SEE THAT PERSON AGAIN."

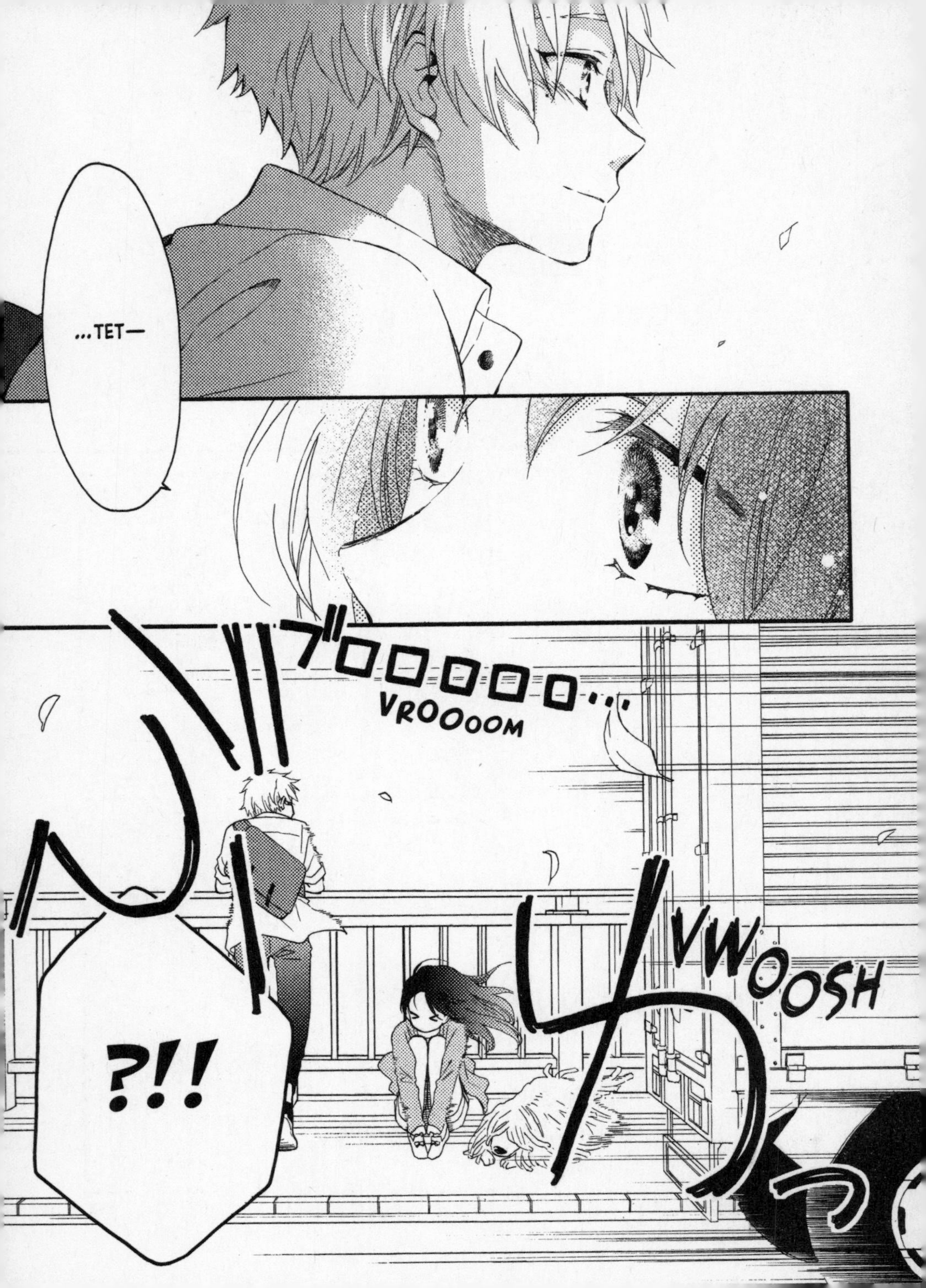
...TET—
ブロロロロロ…
VROOOOM
VWOOSH
?!!

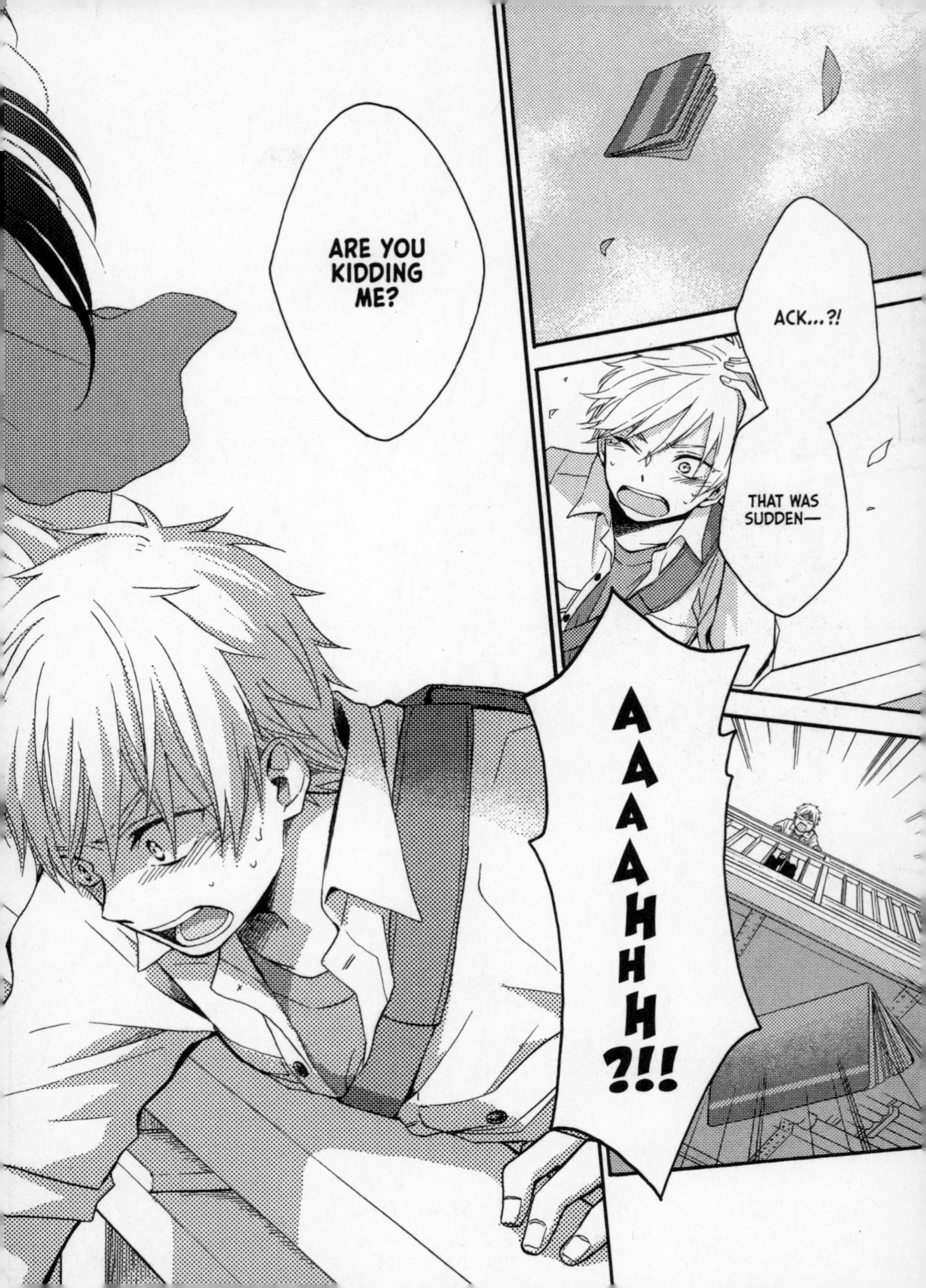
ACK...?!
THAT WAS SUDDEN—
AAAAHHH?!!
ARE YOU KIDDING ME?

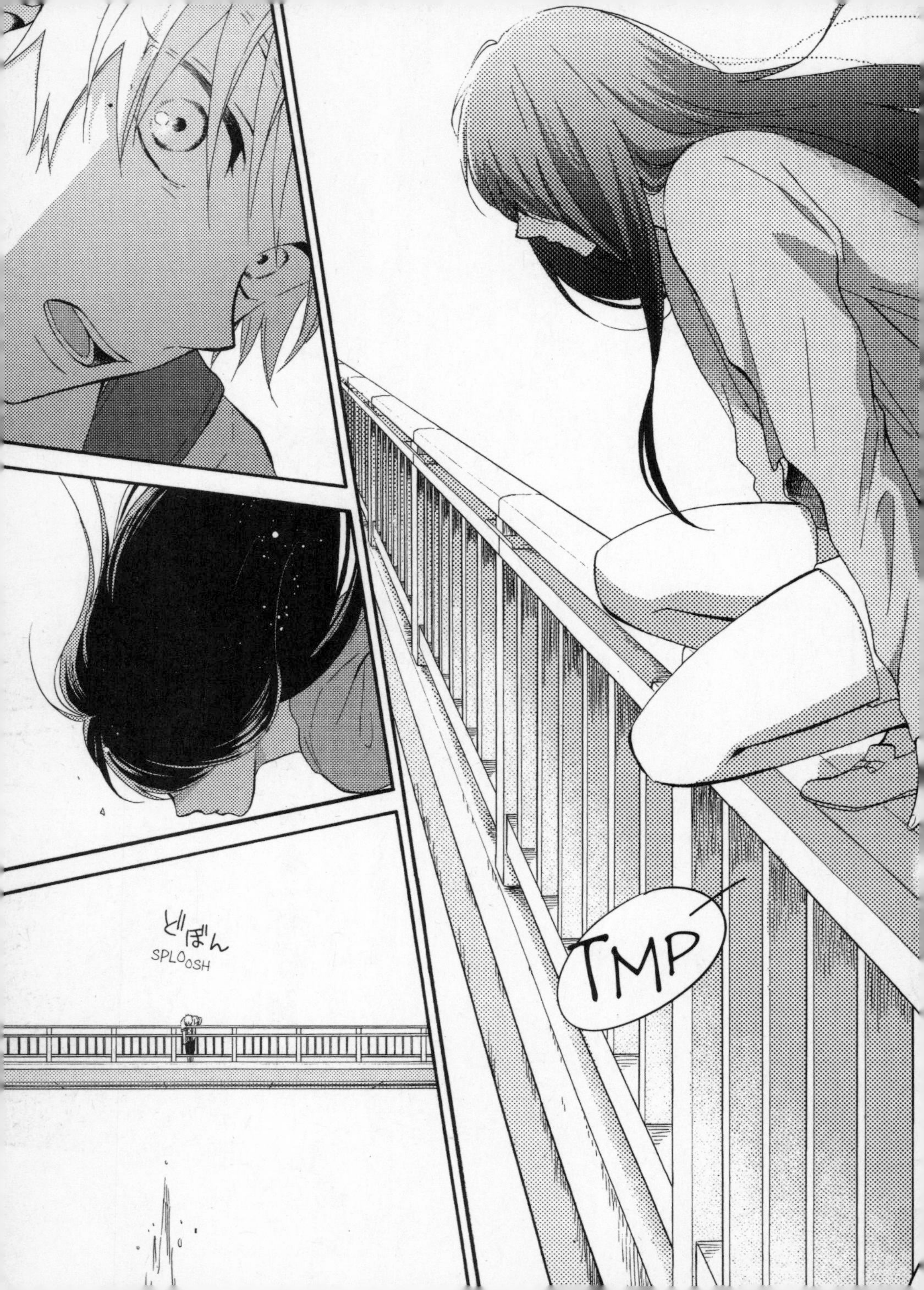
TMP
どぼん
SPLOOSH

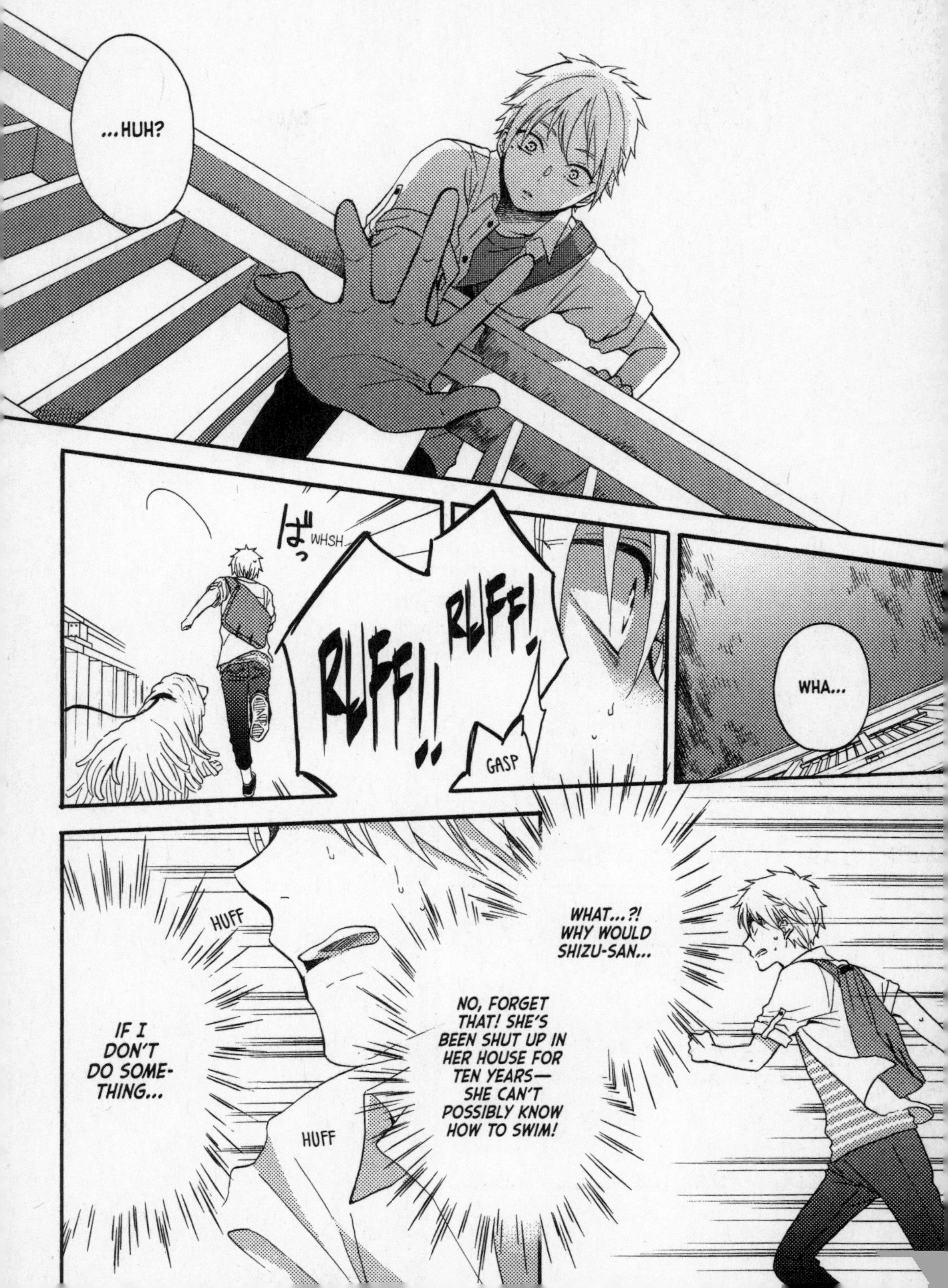
...HUH?
WHA...
GASP
RUFF!
RUFF!!
ばっ WHSH
WHAT...?! WHY WOULD SHIZU-SAN...
NO, FORGET THAT! SHE'S BEEN SHUT UP IN HER HOUSE FOR TEN YEARS—SHE CAN'T POSSIBLY KNOW HOW TO SWIM!
HUFF
IF I DON'T DO SOME-THING...
HUFF

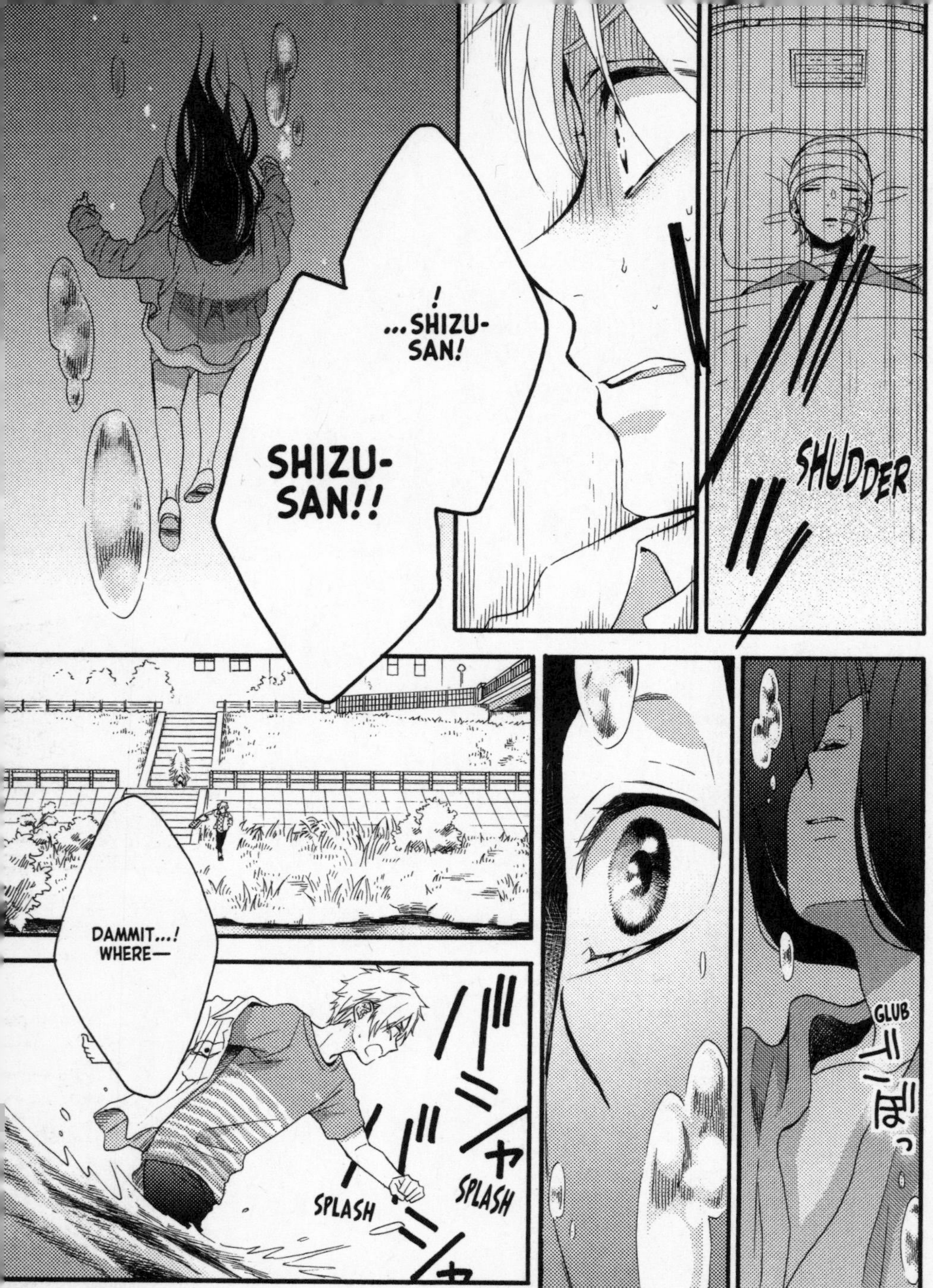
SHUDDER
! ...SHIZU-SAN!
SHIZU-SAN!!
GLUB
DAMMIT...! WHERE—
SPLASH
SPLASH

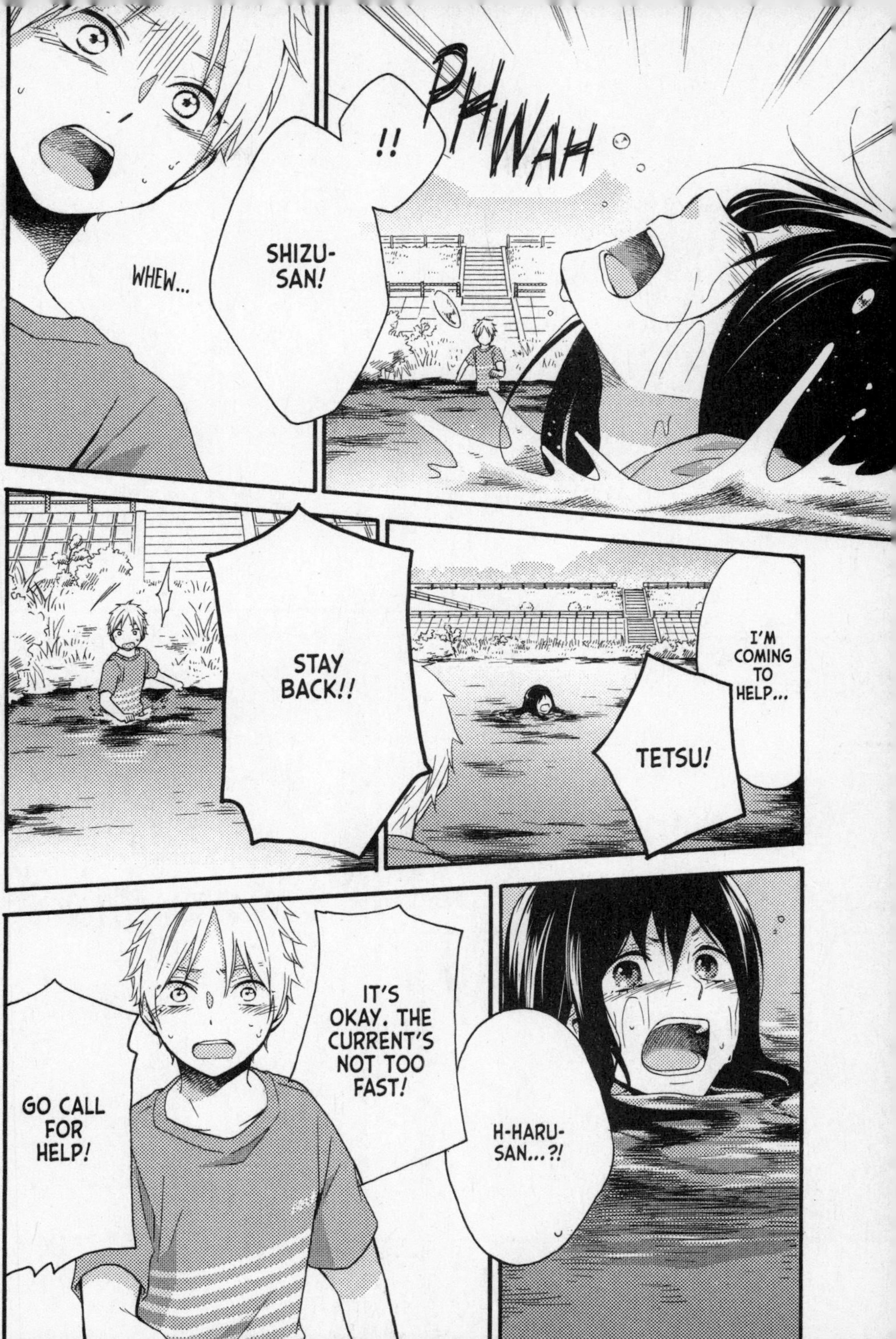
PHWAH
!!
SHIZU-SAN!
WHEW...
I'M COMING TO HELP...
TETSU!
STAY BACK!!
H-HARU-SAN...?!
IT'S OKAY. THE CURRENT'S NOT TOO FAST!
GO CALL FOR HELP!

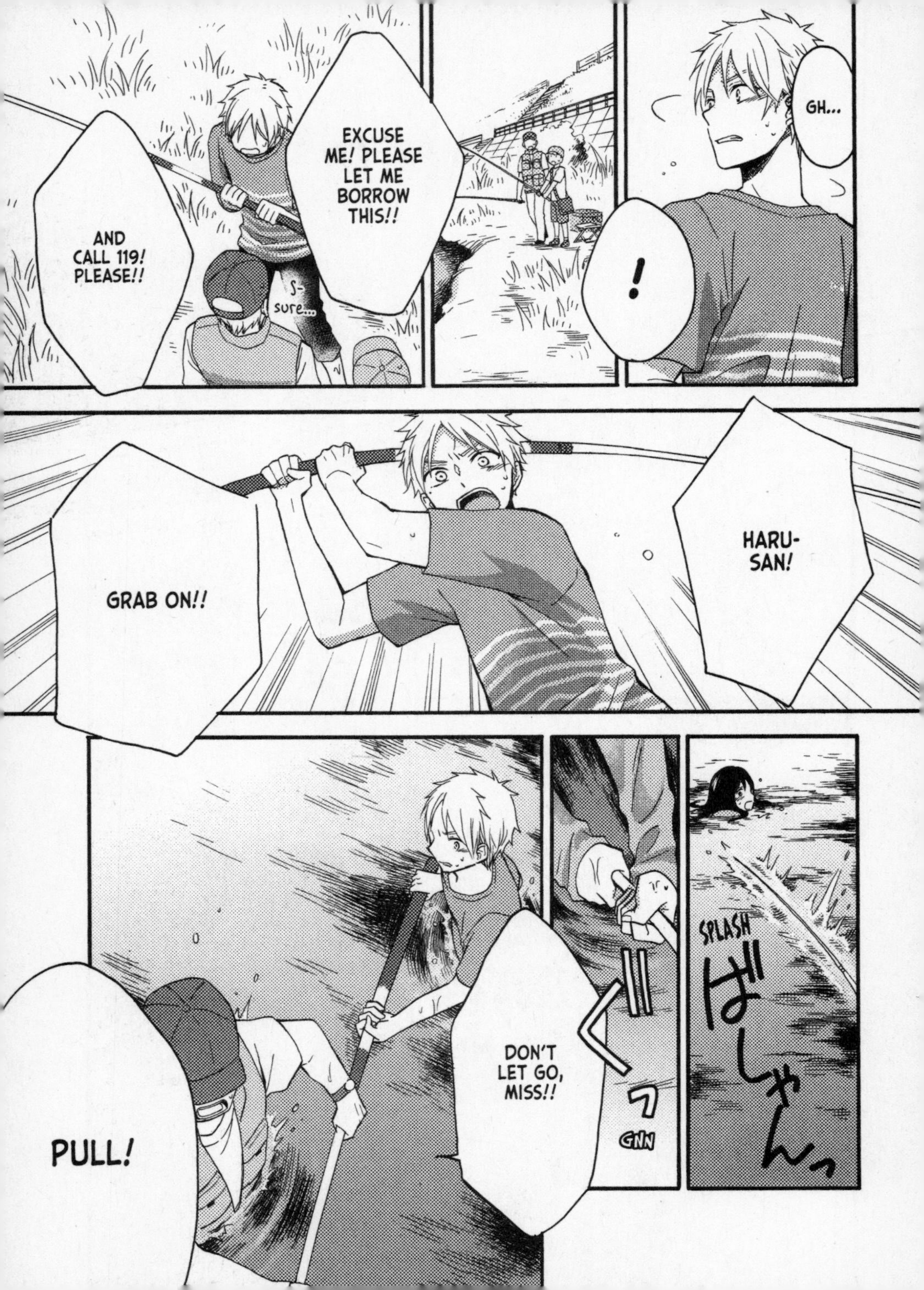
GH...
!
EXCUSE ME! PLEASE LET ME BORROW THIS!!
AND CALL 119! PLEASE!!
S- sure...
HARU-SAN!
GRAB ON!!
SPLASH
ばしゃんっ
GNN
ぐっ
DON'T LET GO, MISS!!
PULL!

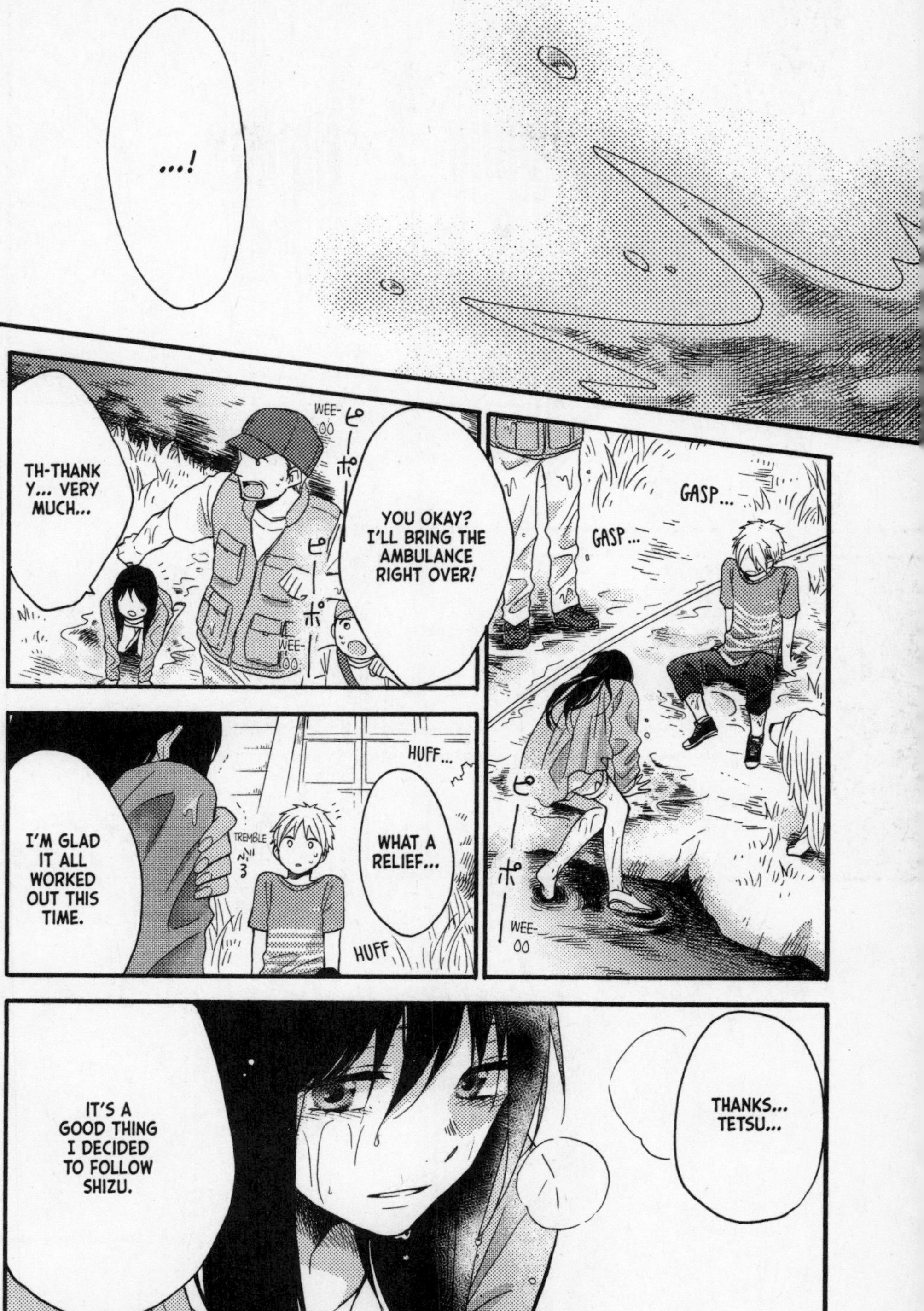
...!
GASP...
GASP...
WEE-OO
WEE-OO
YOU OKAY? I'LL BRING THE AMBULANCE RIGHT OVER!
WEE-OO
TH-THANK Y... VERY MUCH...
HUFF...
WHAT A RELIEF...
TREMBLE
HUFF
I'M GLAD IT ALL WORKED OUT THIS TIME.
THANKS... TETSU...
IT'S A GOOD THING I DECIDED TO FOLLOW SHIZU.

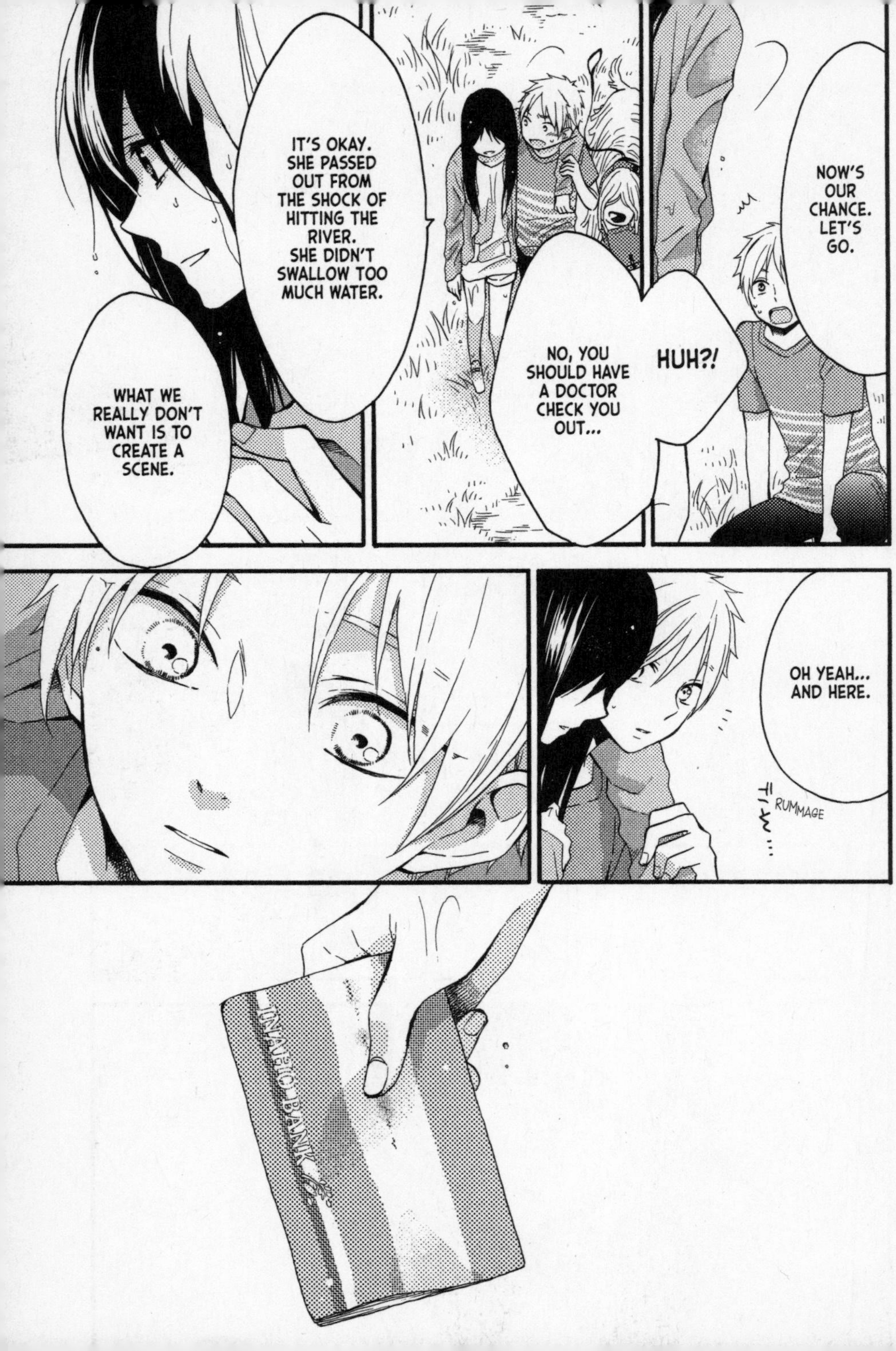
NOW'S OUR CHANCE. LET'S GO.
HUH?!
NO, YOU SHOULD HAVE A DOCTOR CHECK YOU OUT...
IT'S OKAY. SHE PASSED OUT FROM THE SHOCK OF HITTING THE RIVER. SHE DIDN'T SWALLOW TOO MUCH WATER.
WHAT WE REALLY DON'T WANT IS TO CREATE A SCENE.
OH YEAH... AND HERE.
RUMMAGE

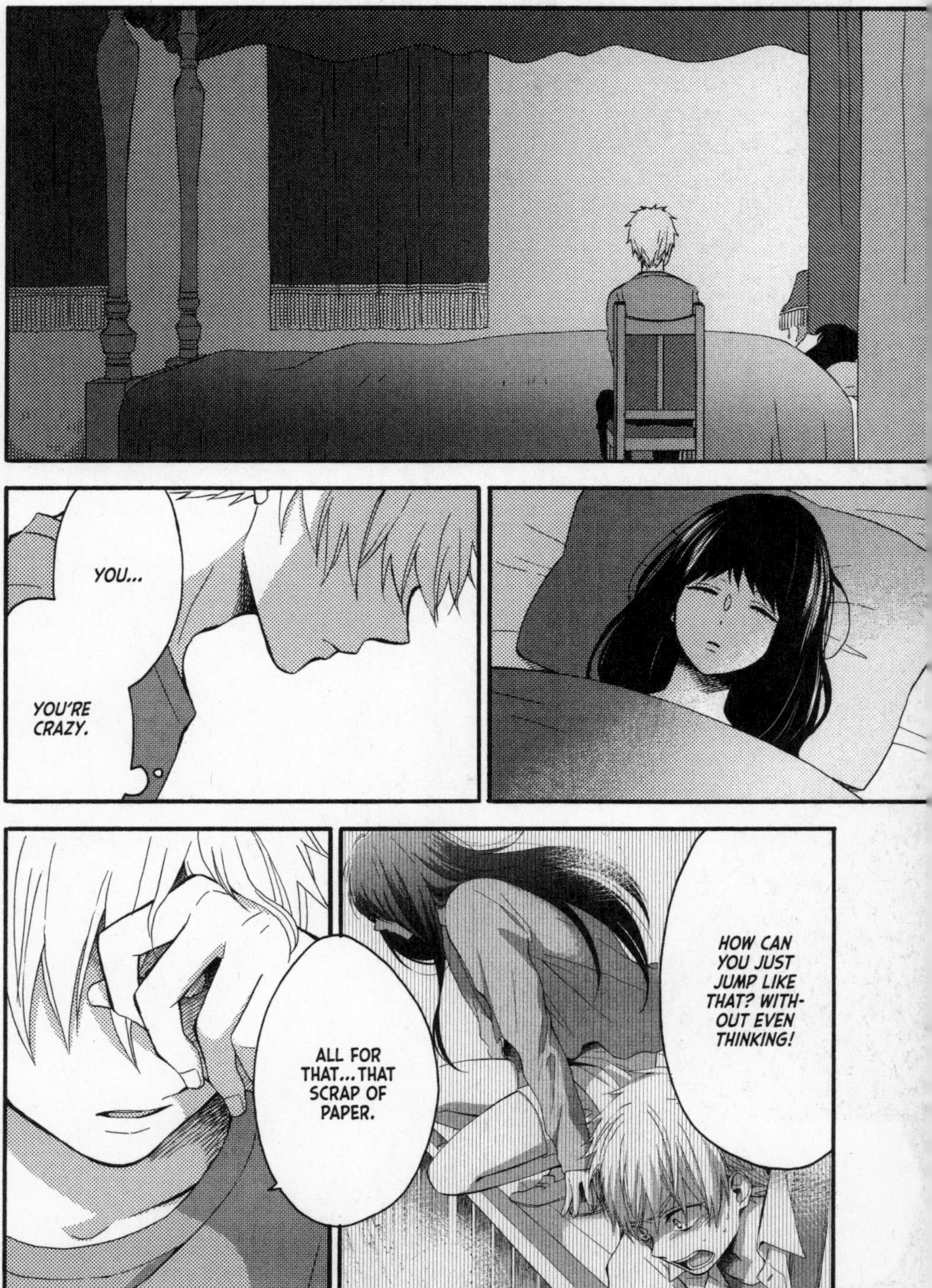
YOU...
YOU'RE CRAZY.
HOW CAN YOU JUST JUMP LIKE THAT? WITH-OUT EVEN THINKING!
ALL FOR THAT...THAT SCRAP OF PAPER.

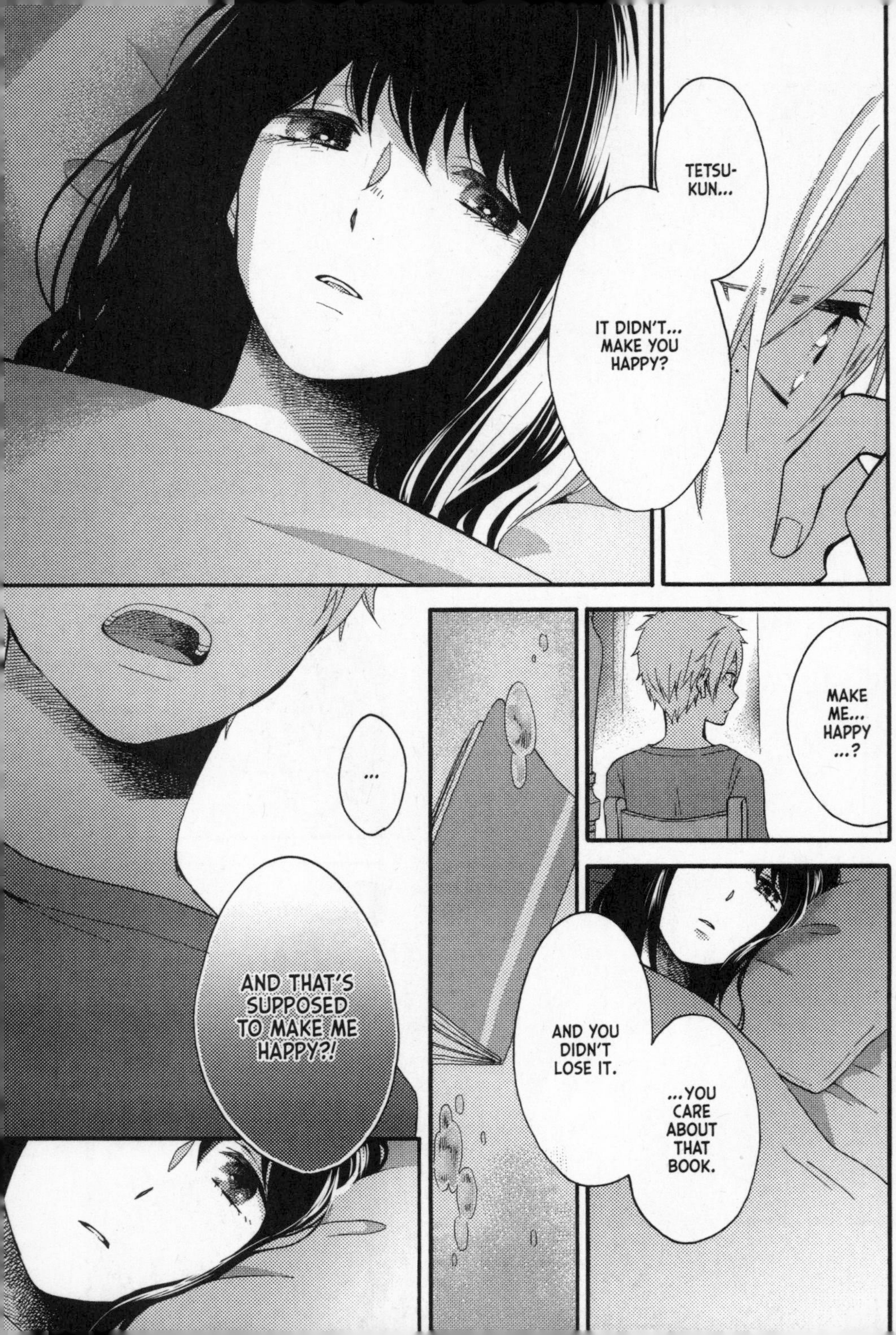
TETSU-KUN...
IT DIDN'T... MAKE YOU HAPPY?
MAKE ME... HAPPY ...?
AND YOU DIDN'T LOSE IT.
...YOU CARE ABOUT THAT BOOK.
...
AND THAT'S SUPPOSED TO MAKE ME HAPPY?!

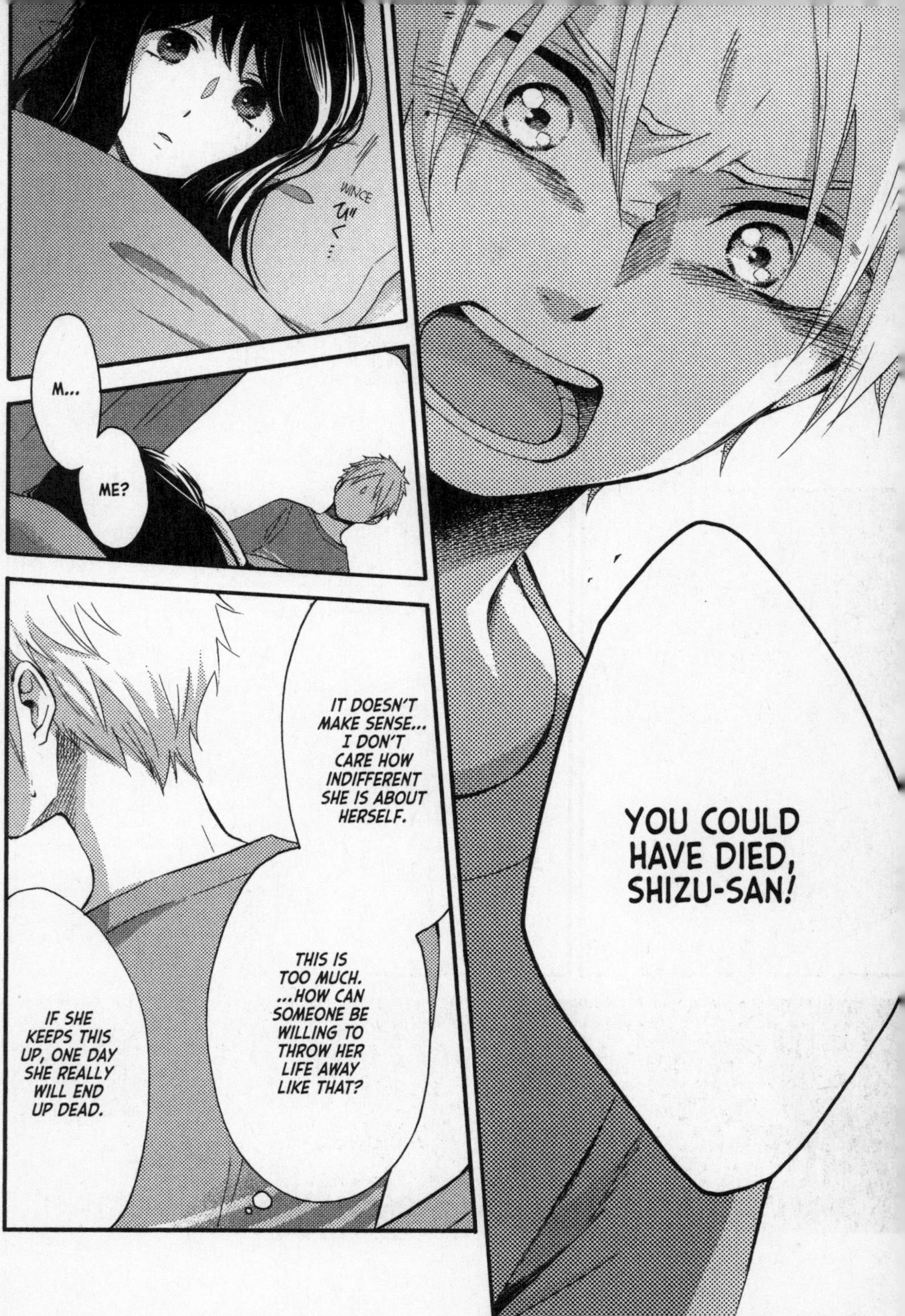
YOU COULD HAVE DIED, SHIZU-SAN!
WINCE
M...
ME?
IT DOESN'T MAKE SENSE... I DON'T CARE HOW INDIFFERENT SHE IS ABOUT HERSELF.
THIS IS TOO MUCH. ...HOW CAN SOMEONE BE WILLING TO THROW HER LIFE AWAY LIKE THAT?
IF SHE KEEPS THIS UP, ONE DAY SHE REALLY WILL END UP DEAD.

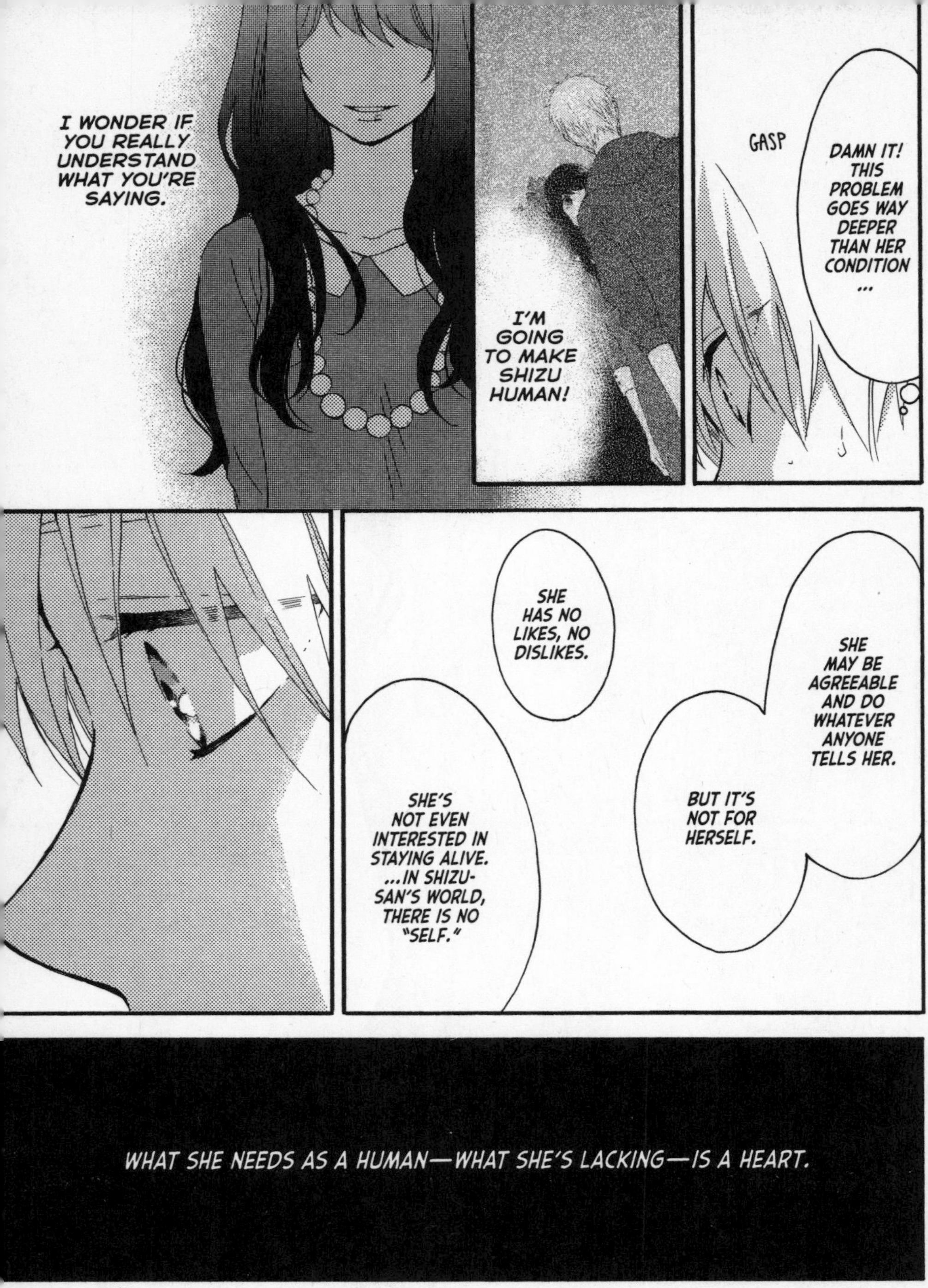
GASP
DAMN IT! THIS PROBLEM GOES WAY DEEPER THAN HER CONDITION ...
I'M GOING TO MAKE SHIZU HUMAN!
I WONDER IF YOU REALLY UNDERSTAND WHAT YOU'RE SAYING.
SHE HAS NO LIKES, NO DISLIKES.
SHE MAY BE AGREEABLE AND DO WHATEVER ANYONE TELLS HER.
BUT IT'S NOT FOR HERSELF.
SHE'S NOT EVEN INTERESTED IN STAYING ALIVE. ...IN SHIZU-SAN'S WORLD, THERE IS NO "SELF."
WHAT SHE NEEDS AS A HUMAN—WHAT SHE'S LACKING—IS A HEART.

I'M... SORRY.

IT'S OKAY... I'M SORRY I YELLED AT YOU.

BUT PLEASE DON'T DO ANYTHING THAT DANGEROUS EVER AGAIN.

...I WON'T.

MOFF...

SEE? MOT-SAN'S WORRIED ABOUT YOU, TOO.

166

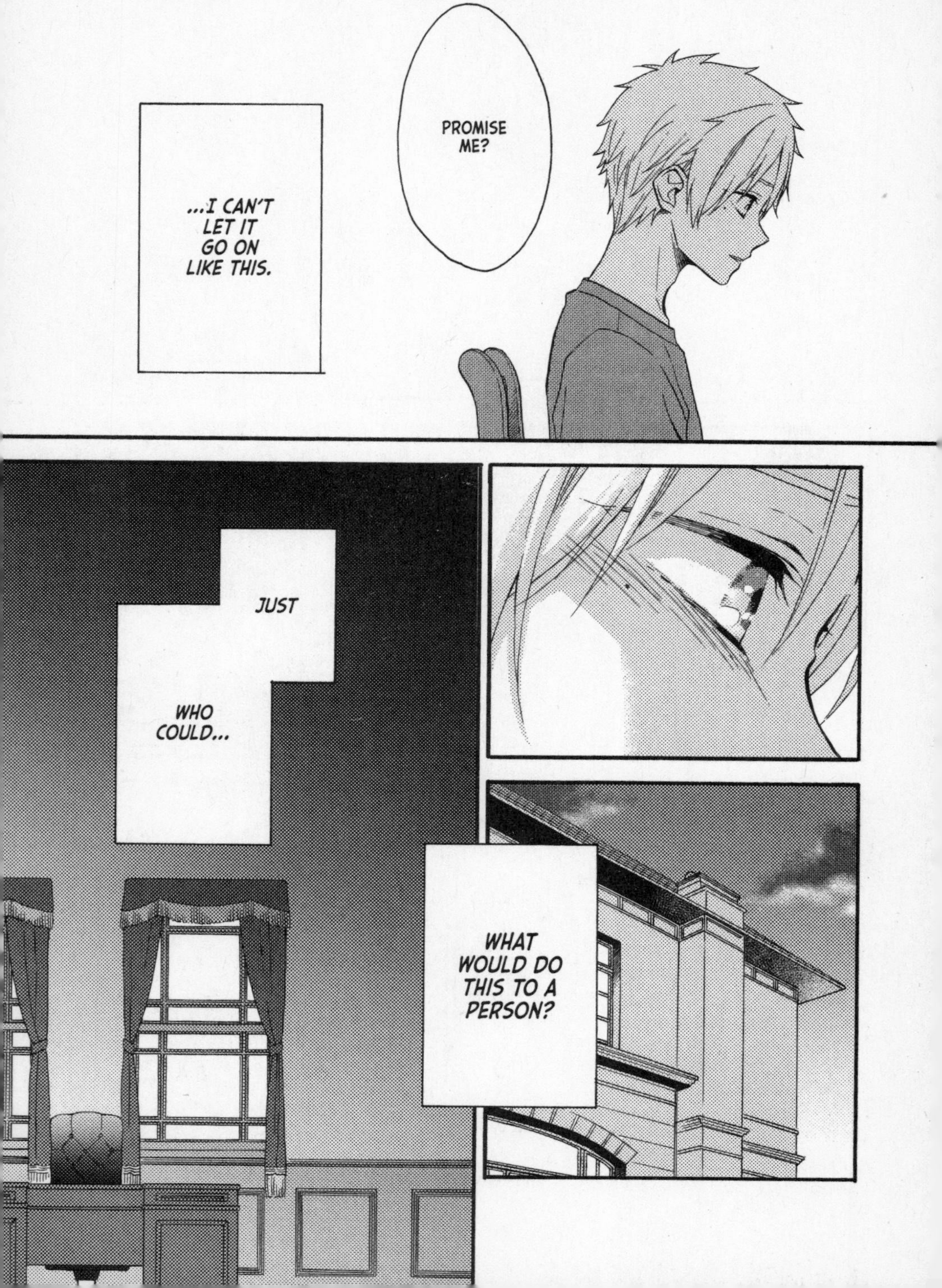
PROMISE ME?
...I CAN'T LET IT GO ON LIKE THIS.
WHAT WOULD DO THIS TO A PERSON?
JUST WHO COULD...

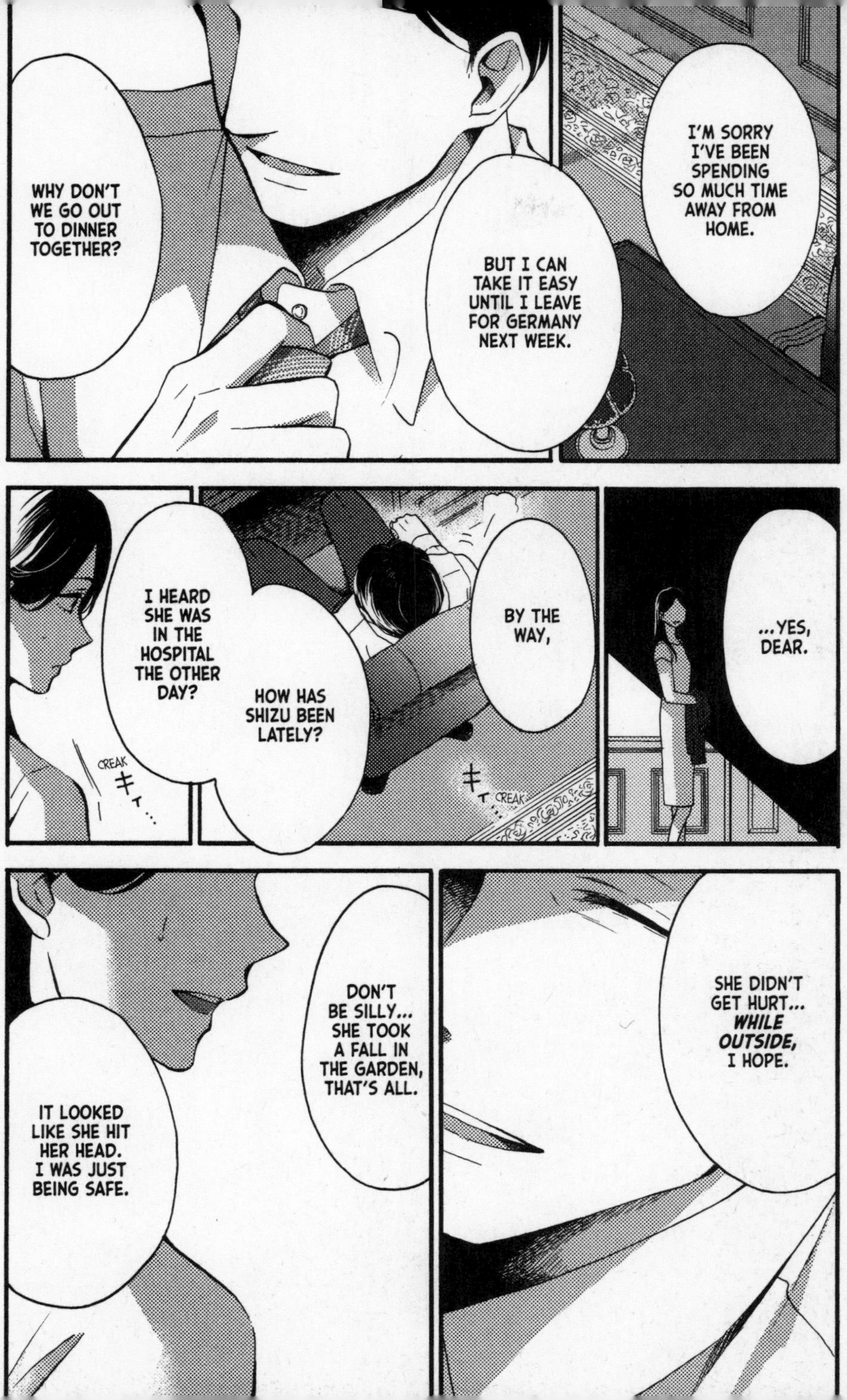
I'M SORRY I'VE BEEN SPENDING SO MUCH TIME AWAY FROM HOME.
BUT I CAN TAKE IT EASY UNTIL I LEAVE FOR GERMANY NEXT WEEK.
WHY DON'T WE GO OUT TO DINNER TOGETHER?
...YES, DEAR.
BY THE WAY,
HOW HAS SHIZU BEEN LATELY?
CREAK
I HEARD SHE WAS IN THE HOSPITAL THE OTHER DAY?
CREAK
SHE DIDN'T GET HURT... ***WHILE OUTSIDE,*** I HOPE.
DON'T BE SILLY... SHE TOOK A FALL IN THE GARDEN, THAT'S ALL.
IT LOOKED LIKE SHE HIT HER HEAD. I WAS JUST BEING SAFE.

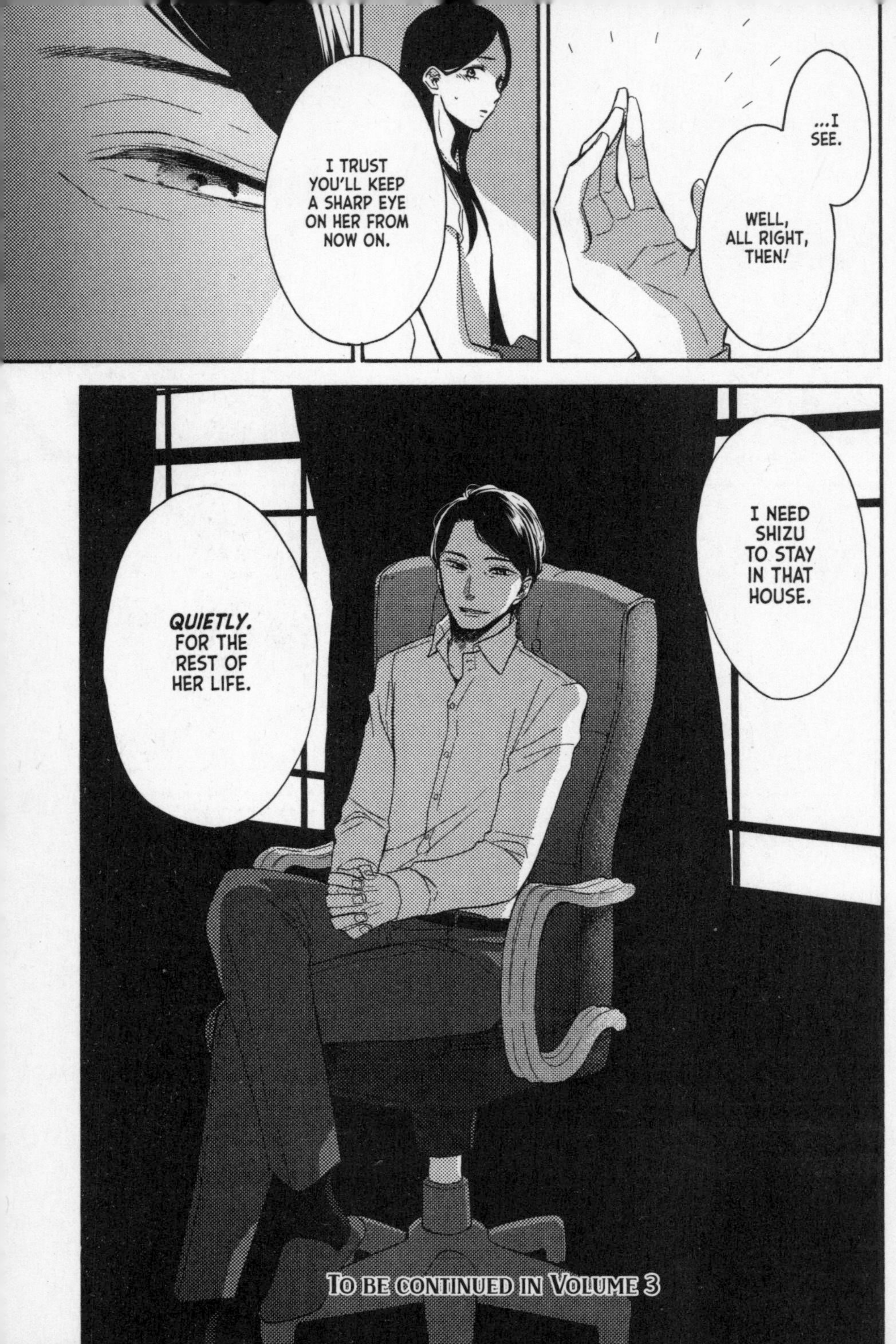
...I SEE.
WELL, ALL RIGHT, THEN!
I TRUST YOU'LL KEEP A SHARP EYE ON HER FROM NOW ON.
I NEED SHIZU TO STAY IN THAT HOUSE.
QUIETLY. FOR THE REST OF HER LIFE.
To be continued in Volume 3

Wake Up, Sleeping Beauty [Extra 2]

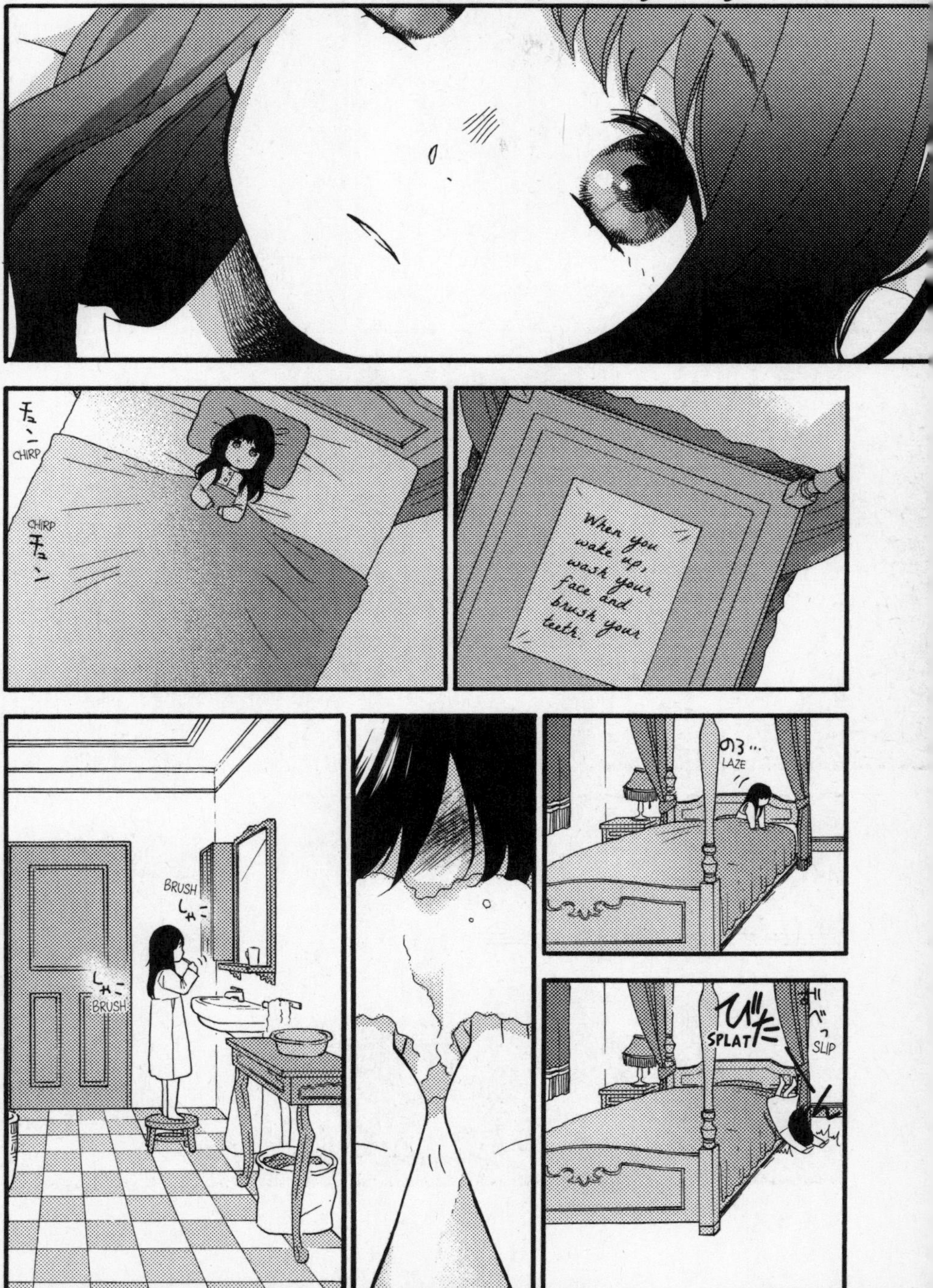
When you wake up, wash your face and brush your teeth.
CHIRP
CHIRP
LAZE
SPLAT
SLIP
BRUSH
BRUSH

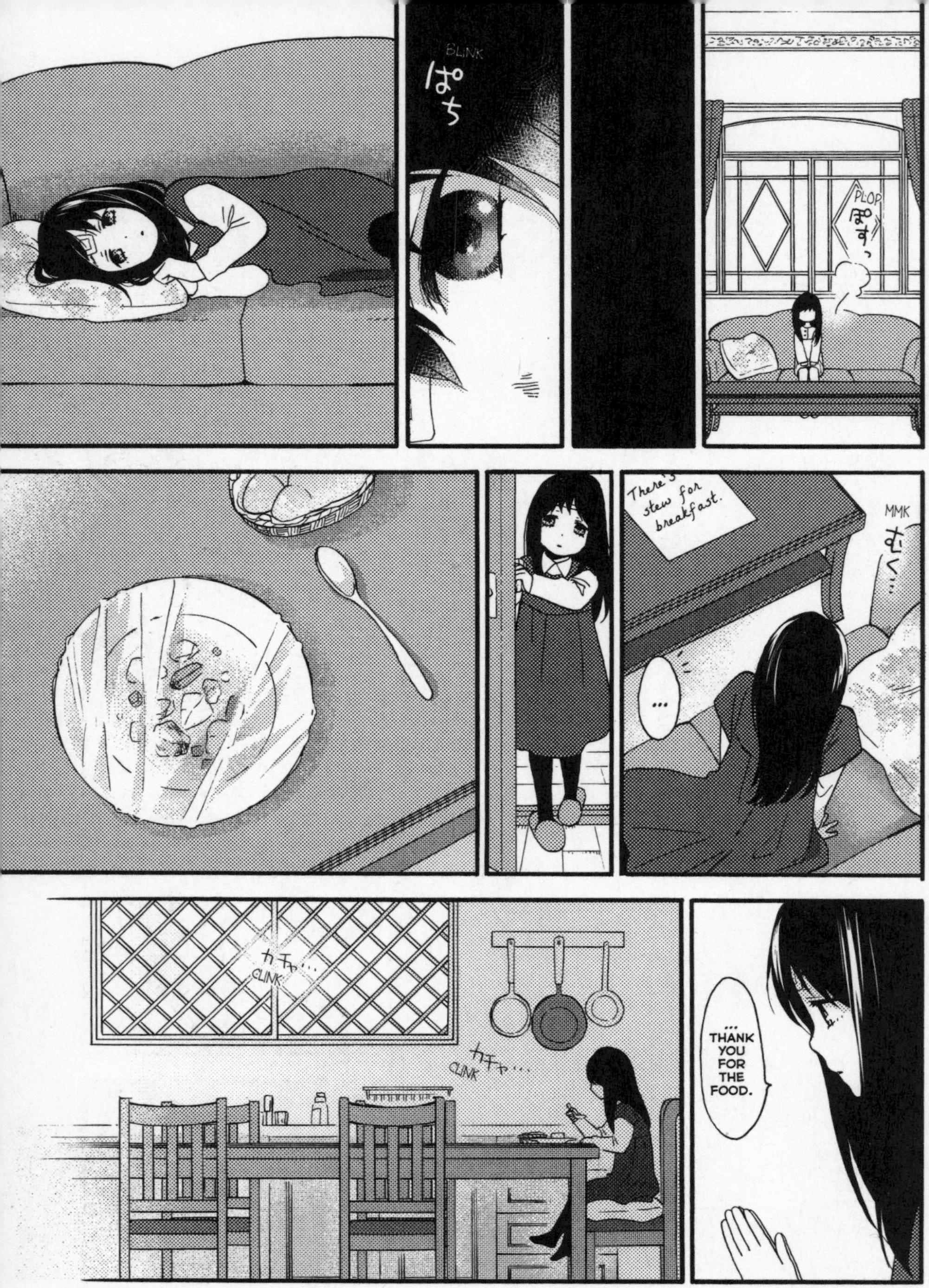
PLOP
ぽすっ
BLINK
ぱち
There's stew for breakfast.
MMK
むく…
…
…THANK YOU FOR THE FOOD.
カチャ…
CLINK
カチャ…
CLINK

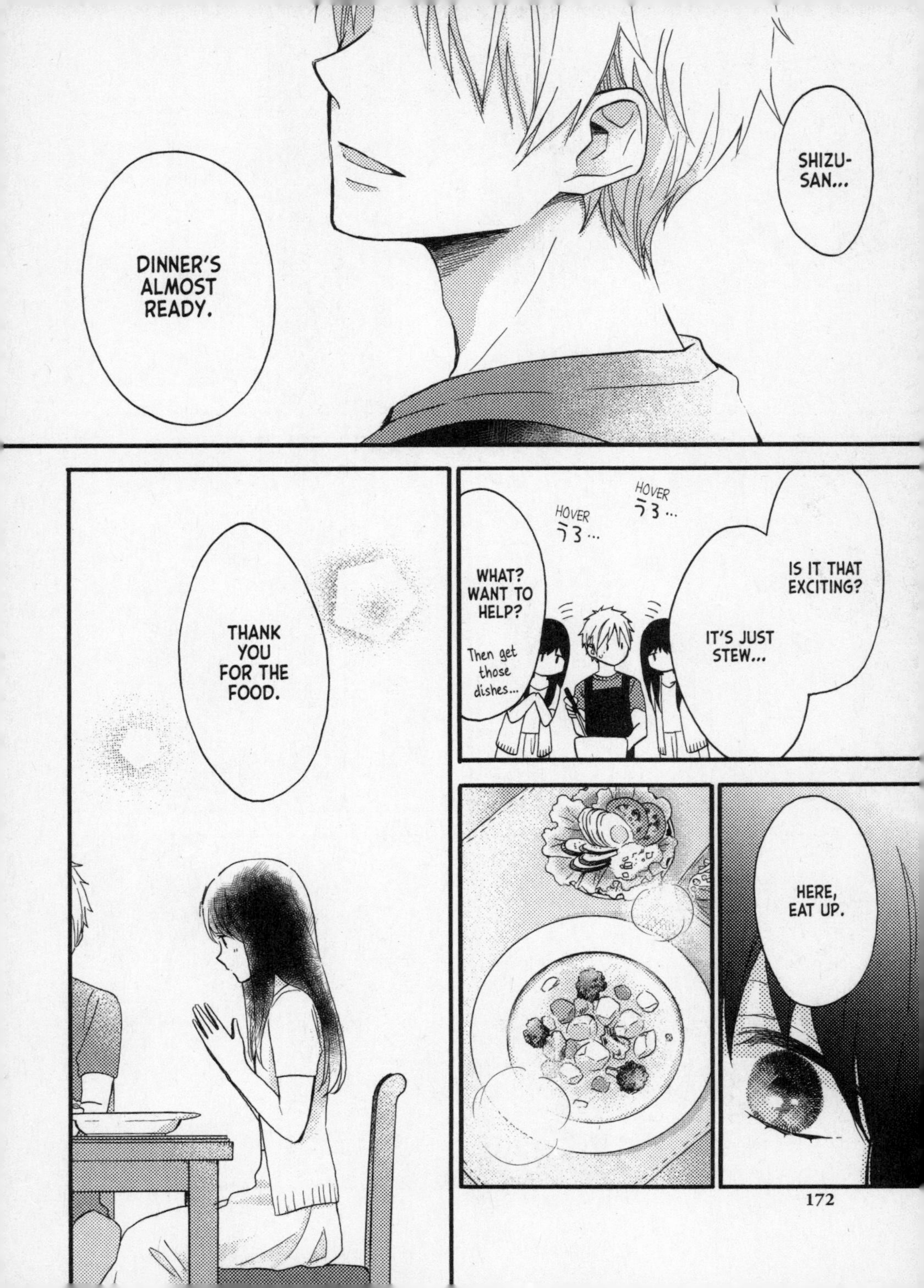
SHIZU-SAN...
DINNER'S ALMOST READY.
IS IT THAT EXCITING?
IT'S JUST STEW...
HOVER うろ...
HOVER うろ...
WHAT? WANT TO HELP?
Then get those dishes...
HERE, EAT UP.
THANK YOU FOR THE FOOD.

Wake Up,
Sleeping
Beauty

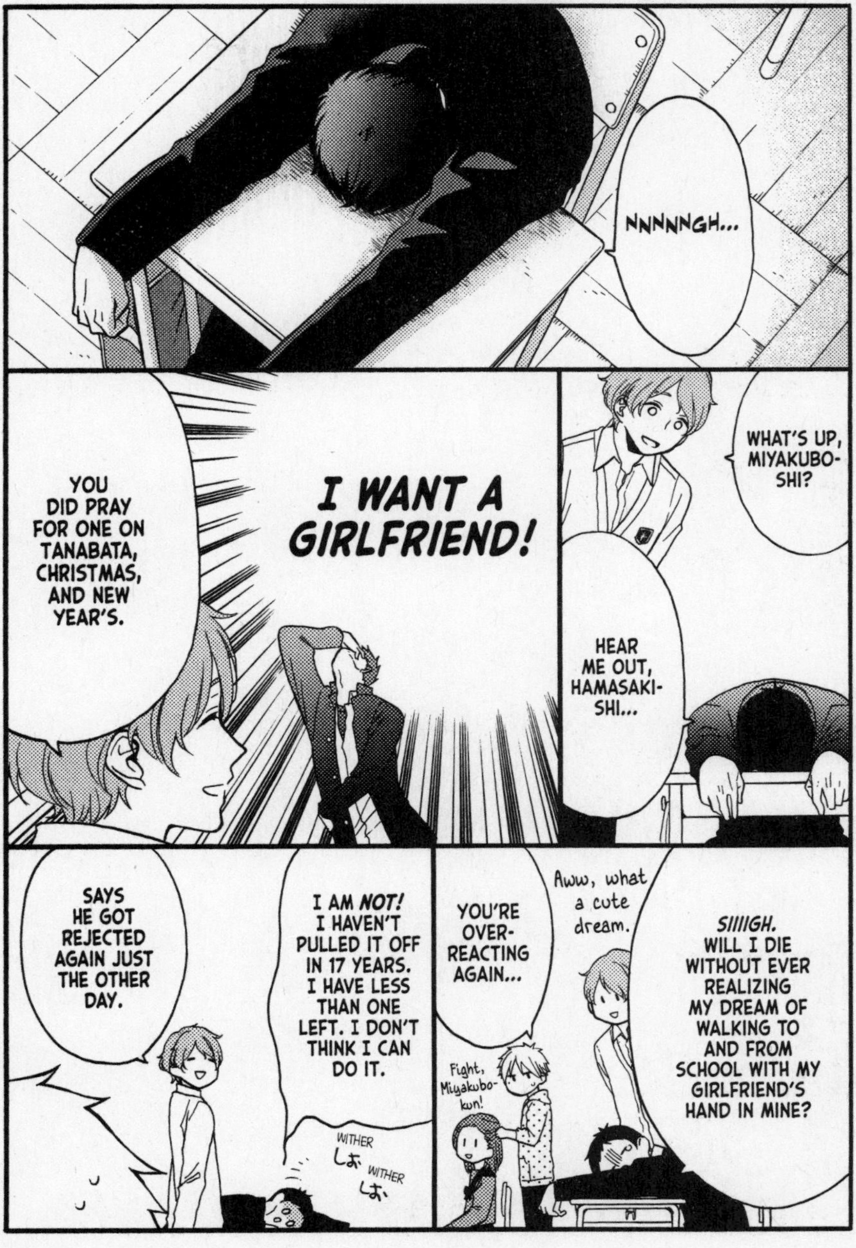
NNNNNGH...
WHAT'S UP, MIYAKUBO-SHI?
HEAR ME OUT, HAMASAKI-SHI...
I WANT A GIRLFRIEND!
YOU DID PRAY FOR ONE ON TANABATA, CHRISTMAS, AND NEW YEAR'S.
SIIIGH. WILL I DIE WITHOUT EVER REALIZING MY DREAM OF WALKING TO AND FROM SCHOOL WITH MY GIRLFRIEND'S HAND IN MINE?
Aww, what a cute dream.
YOU'RE OVER-REACTING AGAIN...
Fight, Miyakubo-kun!
I AM *NOT!* I HAVEN'T PULLED IT OFF IN 17 YEARS. I HAVE LESS THAN ONE LEFT. I DON'T THINK I CAN DO IT.
SAYS HE GOT REJECTED AGAIN JUST THE OTHER DAY.
WITHER しお
WITHER しお

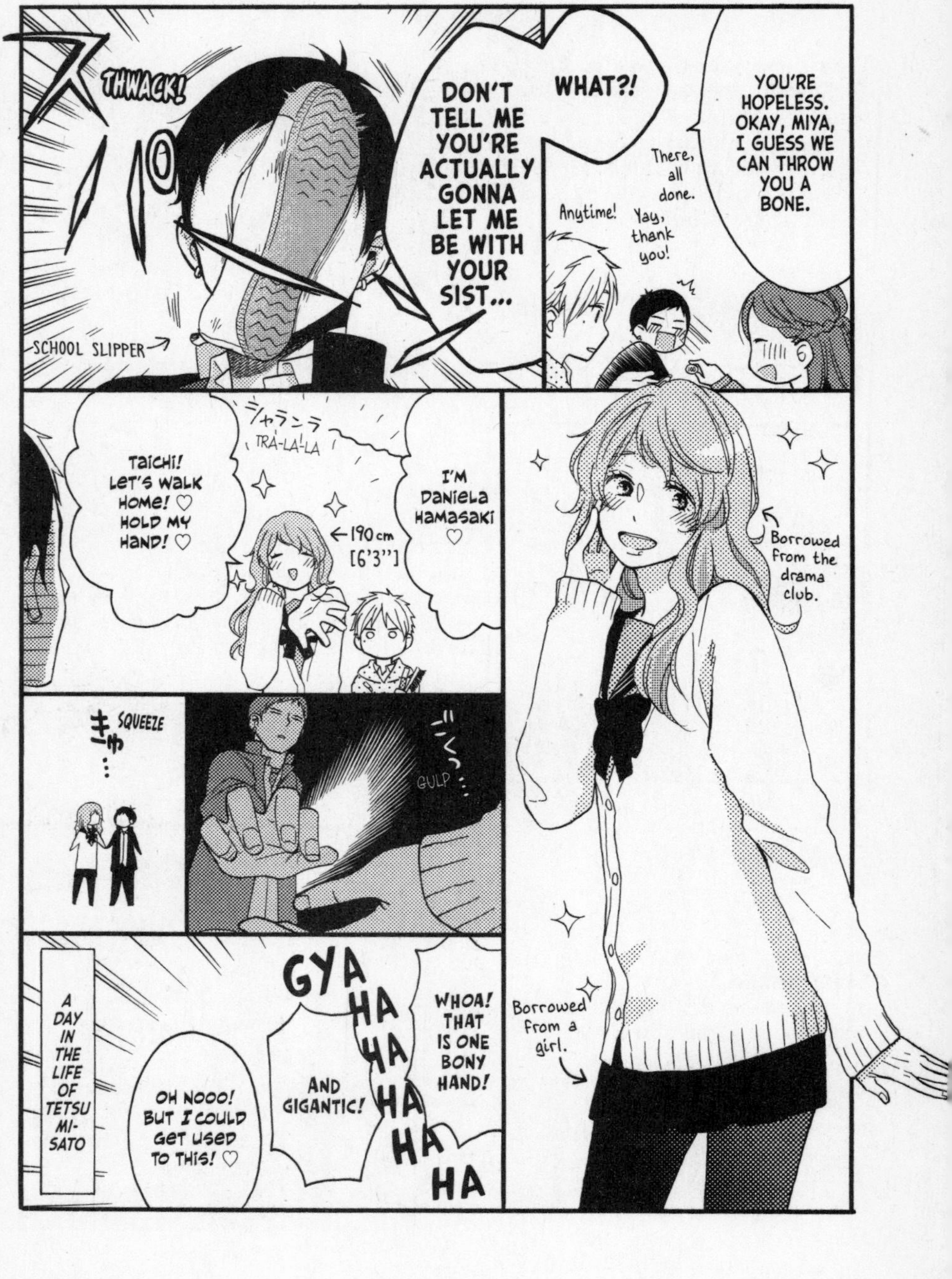
YOU'RE HOPELESS. OKAY, MIYA, I GUESS WE CAN THROW YOU A BONE.
There, all done.
Yay, thank you!
Anytime!
WHAT?!
DON'T TELL ME YOU'RE ACTUALLY GONNA LET ME BE WITH YOUR SIST...
THWACK!
SCHOOL SLIPPER
Borrowed from the drama club.
Borrowed from a girl.
I'M Daniela Hamasaki ♡
シャランラ TRA-LA-LA
← 190 cm [6'3"]
Taichi! Let's walk home! ♡ Hold my hand! ♡
GULP
きゅ SQUEEZE
WHOA! THAT IS ONE BONY HAND!
GYA HA HA HA HA HA HA
AND GIGANTIC!
OH NOOO! BUT I COULD GET USED TO THIS! ♡
A DAY IN THE LIFE OF TETSU MI-SATO

Translation Notes

Don't drink until you're 21!, page 36
Technically, the Japanese text admonished readers not to drink until they are 20, which is the age of majority, and legal drinking age, in Japan. Incidentally, this is also part of why the girls at the meetup checked to make sure Tetsu was older than 20.

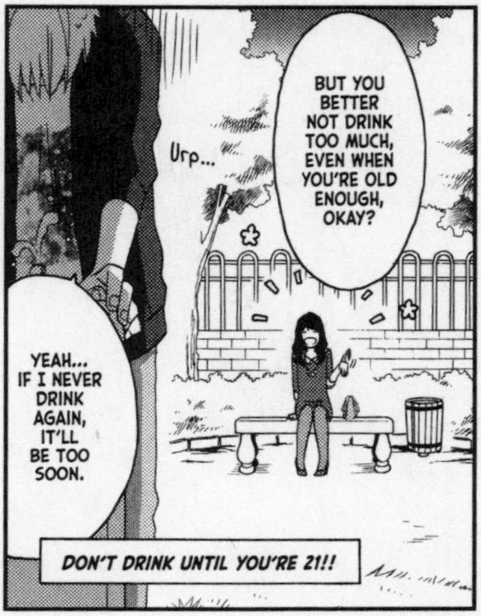
BUT YOU BETTER NOT DRINK TOO MUCH, EVEN WHEN YOU'RE OLD ENOUGH, OKAY?
Urp...
YEAH... IF I NEVER DRINK AGAIN, IT'LL BE TOO SOON.
DON'T DRINK UNTIL YOU'RE 21!!

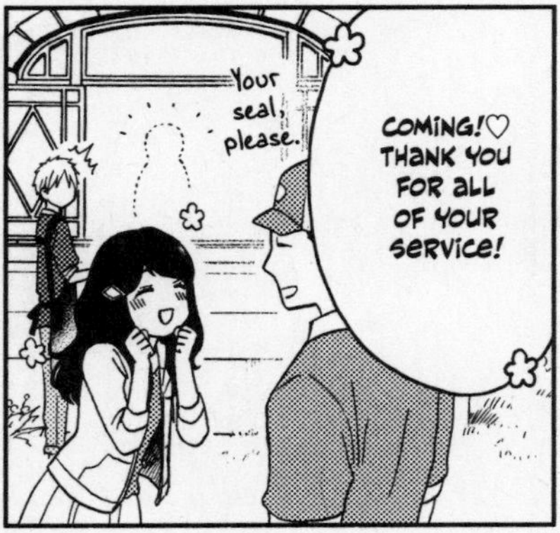
COMING!♡ THANK YOU FOR ALL OF YOUR SERVICE!
Your seal, please.

Your seal, please, page 52
In Japan, it is common practice to use an *inkan*, or signature seal, to stamp one's name on official documents, package delivery forms, etc., in lieu of signing one's name.

Shōgi, page 59
Shōgi, the Generals' Game, is a strategy board game, similar to chess.

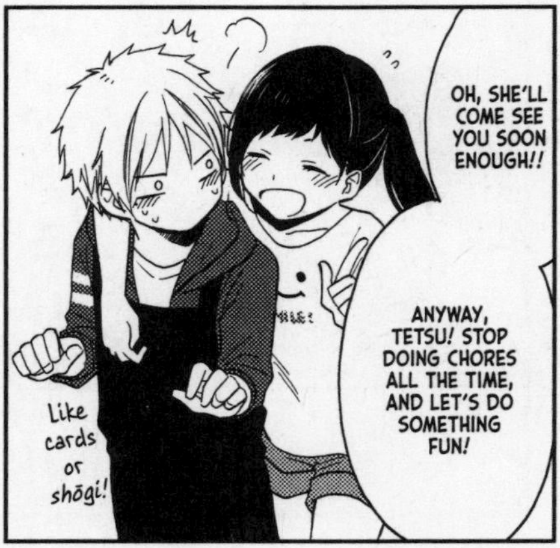
OH, SHE'LL COME SEE YOU SOON ENOUGH!!
ANYWAY, TETSU! STOP DOING CHORES ALL THE TIME, AND LET'S DO SOMETHING FUN!
Like cards or shōgi!

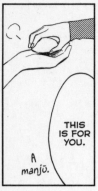

THIS IS FOR YOU.
A manjū.

***Manjū*, page 61**
A manjū is a Japanese confection with a dough outside and filled with something sweet, kind of like a jelly donut. The filling is usually anko red bean paste, but can be any kind of sweet filling.

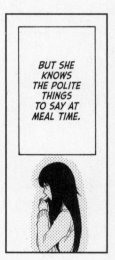

BUT SHE KNOWS THE POLITE THINGS TO SAY AT MEAL TIME.

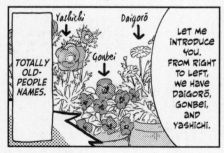

The polite things to say, page 78
In Japan, it is customary at meal times to express gratitude before and after a meal. Before a meal, the polite thing to say is *itadakimasu*, which means "I humbly partake," and is more loosely translated to "thanks for the food," or even, "let's eat." The idea is to express appreciation to the provider of the meal. After a meal, the polite thing to say is *gochisō-sama*, which can translate roughly to "I have been fed."

LET ME INTRODUCE YOU. FROM RIGHT TO LEFT, WE HAVE DAIGORŌ, GONBEI, AND YASHICHI.
Daigorō
Gonbei
Yashichi
TOTALLY OLD-PEOPLE NAMES.

Totally old-people names, page 88
Being an older gentleman, Shinobu has given his plants older names as well. The names Daigorō, Gonbei, and Yashichi have fallen out of common use in modern Japan, but can all be found in the long-running historical drama, *Mito Kōmon*, which aired from 1969 to 2011. The series was inspired by Tokugawa Mitsukuni, also known as Mito Kōmon, who lived from 1628 to 1701.

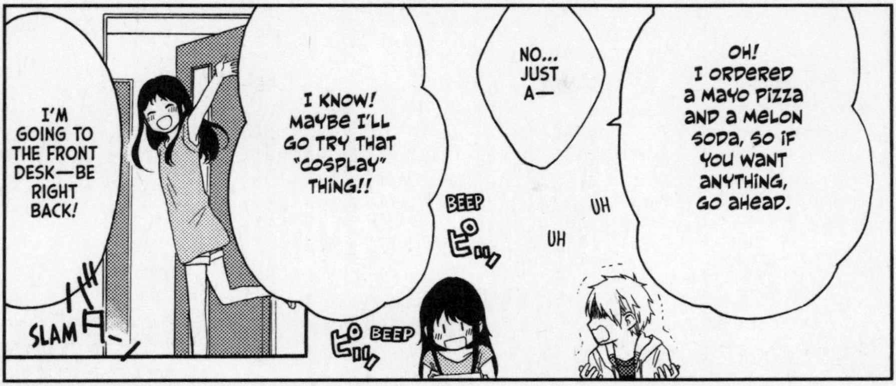
OH! I ORDERED A MAYO PIZZA AND A MELON SODA, SO IF YOU WANT ANYTHING, GO AHEAD.
UH
UH
NO... JUST A—
BEEP
BEEP
I KNOW! MAYBE I'LL GO TRY THAT "COSPLAY" THING!!
I'M GOING TO THE FRONT DESK—BE RIGHT BACK!
SLAM

That "cosplay" thing, page 97

If manga is to be believed, karaoke is one of the most popular hang-out activities for Japanese teens. In Japan, in addition to being able to rent out private rooms, many establishments offer party snacks, props, and even costumes to wear during performances.

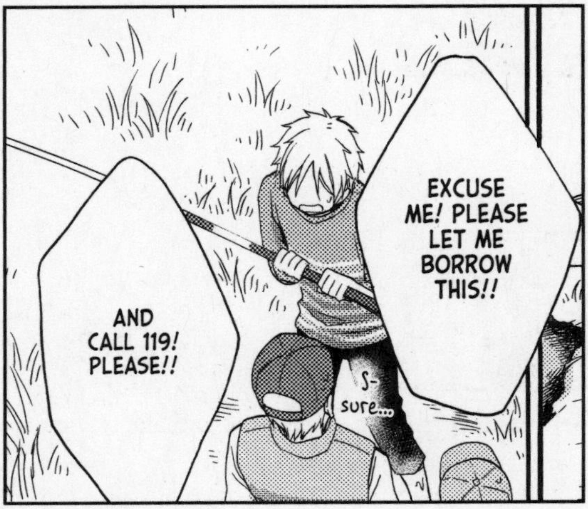
EXCUSE ME! PLEASE LET ME BORROW THIS!!
S-sure...
AND CALL 119! PLEASE!!

Call 119, page 159

In Japan, there are two emergency phone numbers—for police, you would dial 110, and for a fire or ambulance, you would dial 119.

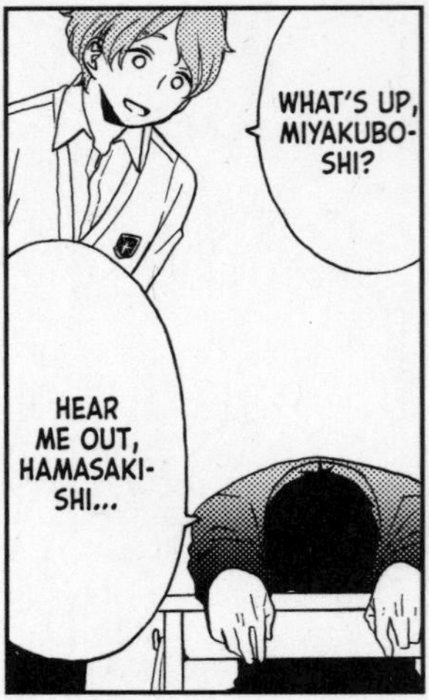
WHAT'S UP, MIYAKUBO-SHI?
HEAR ME OUT, HAMASAKI-SHI...

Miyakubo-shi, page 174
The suffix *-shi* is a term of respect roughly equivalent to Mr., as it is mainly applied to men. It was also generally used only in writing, but in recent years, it has come to be used in anime and manga as an "otaku" way to address people.

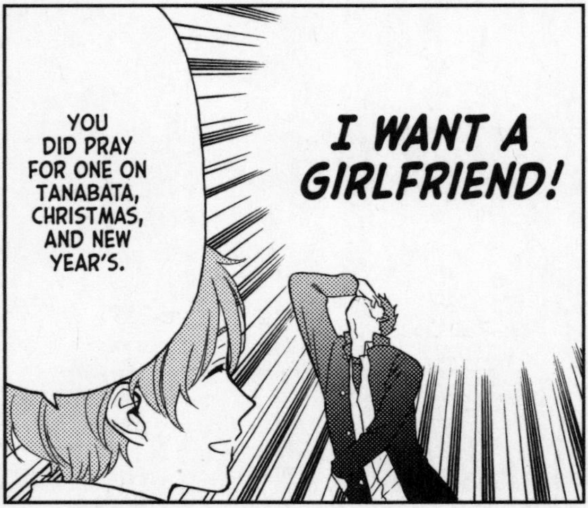
I WANT A GIRLFRIEND!
YOU DID PRAY FOR ONE ON TANABATA, CHRISTMAS, AND NEW YEAR'S.

Tanabata, page 174
Also known the Star Festival, Tanabata is a holiday on July 7 that celebrates the annual reunion of Orihime and Hikoboshi, two deities whose love so distracted them from their duties that the Milky Way was put between them to keep them apart every other day of the year. It is customary to make wishes on this holiday.

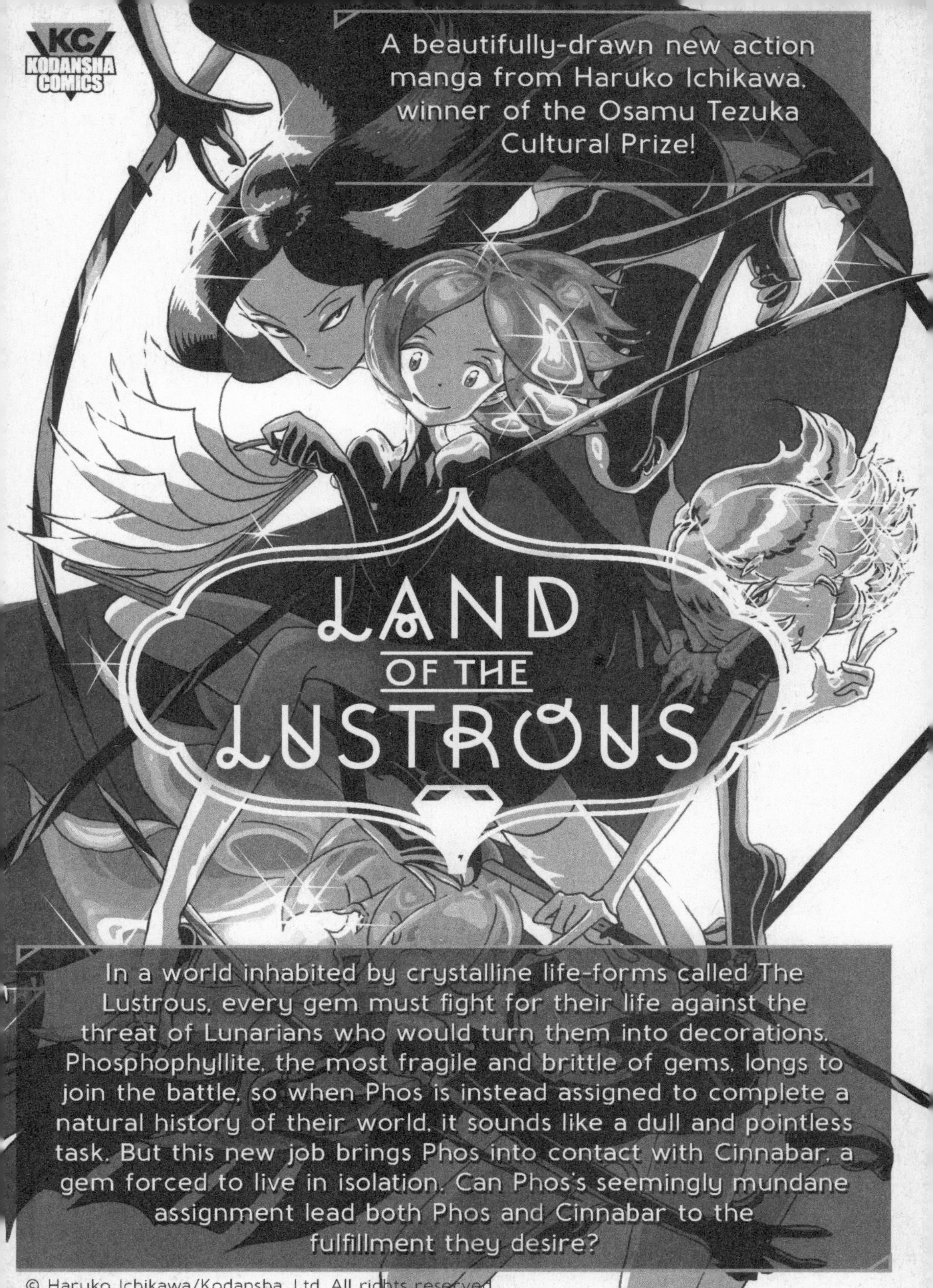
KC KODANSHA COMICS
A beautifully-drawn new action manga from Haruko Ichikawa, winner of the Osamu Tezuka Cultural Prize!
LAND OF THE LUSTROUS
In a world inhabited by crystalline life-forms called The Lustrous, every gem must fight for their life against the threat of Lunarians who would turn them into decorations. Phosphophyllite, the most fragile and brittle of gems, longs to join the battle, so when Phos is instead assigned to complete a natural history of their world, it sounds like a dull and pointless task. But this new job brings Phos into contact with Cinnabar, a gem forced to live in isolation. Can Phos's seemingly mundane assignment lead both Phos and Cinnabar to the fulfillment they desire?

A Kodansha Comics Trade Paperback Original.

Published in the United States by Kodansha Comics,
an imprint of Kodansha USA Publishing, LLC, New York.

Publication rights for this English edition arranged through Kodansha Ltd., Tokyo.

First published in Japan in 2015 by Kodansha Ltd., Tokyo,
as *Ohayou, Ibarahime* volume 2.

Cover Design: Tomohiro Kusume (arcoinc)

ISBN 978-1-63236-588-0

Printed in the United States of America.

www.kodanshacomics.com

9 8 7 6 5 4 3 2 1

Translation: Alethea and Athena Nibley
Lettering: Lys Blakeslee
Editing: Haruko Hashimoto
Kodansha Comics Edition Cover Design: Phil Balsman

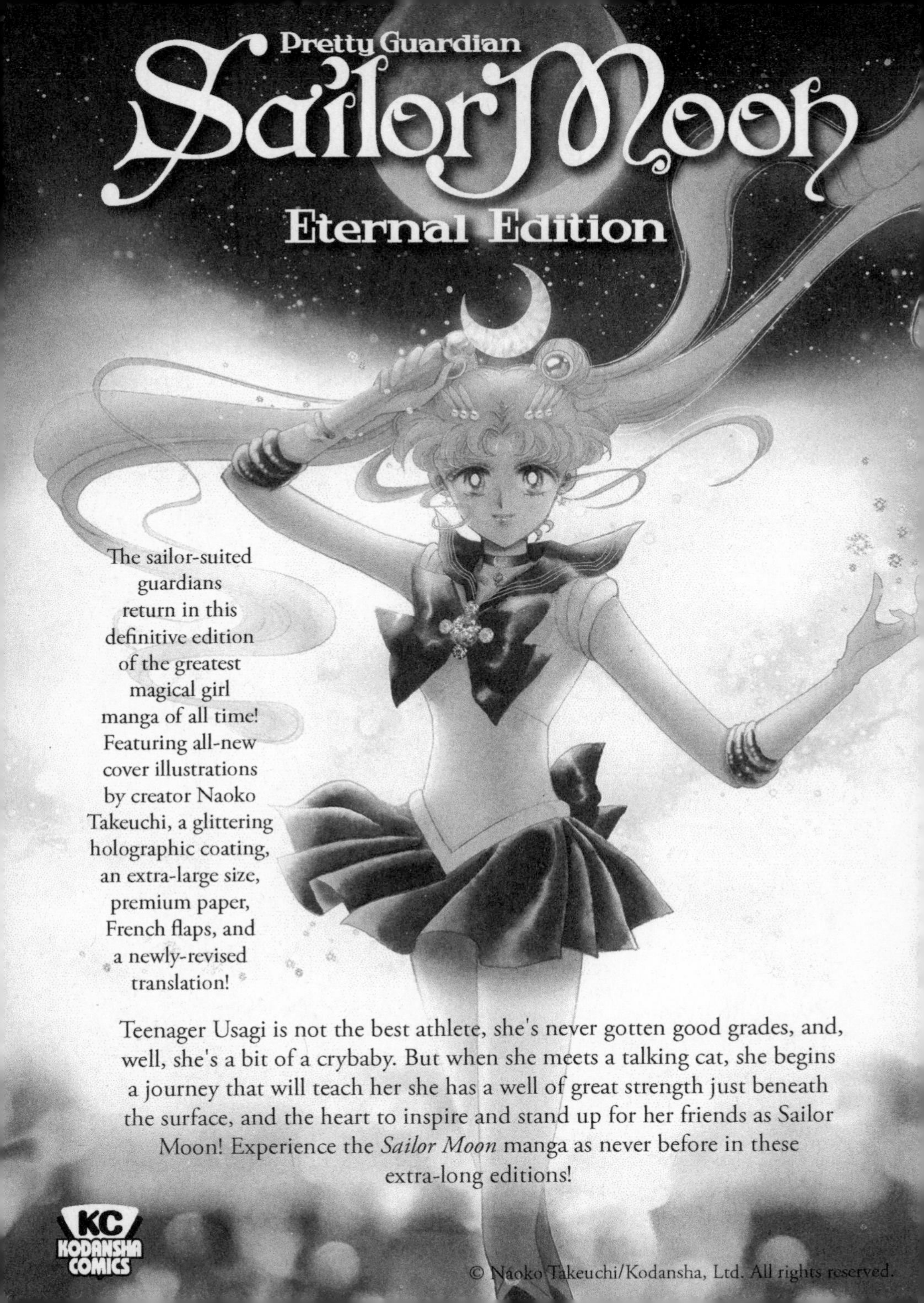
Pretty Guardian
Sailor Moon
Eternal Edition
The sailor-suited guardians return in this definitive edition of the greatest magical girl manga of all time! Featuring all-new cover illustrations by creator Naoko Takeuchi, a glittering holographic coating, an extra-large size, premium paper, French flaps, and a newly-revised translation!
Teenager Usagi is not the best athlete, she's never gotten good grades, and, well, she's a bit of a crybaby. But when she meets a talking cat, she begins a journey that will teach her she has a well of great strength just beneath the surface, and the heart to inspire and stand up for her friends as Sailor Moon! Experience the *Sailor Moon* manga as never before in these extra-long editions!
KC KODANSHA COMICS
© Naoko Takeuchi/Kodansha, Ltd. All rights reserved.